Latin American Vanguards

The Art of Contentious Encounters

VICKY UNRUH

UNIVERSITY OF CALIFORNIA PRESS

Berkeley / Los Angeles / London

University of California Press
Berkeley and Los Angeles, California

University of California Press, Ltd.
London, England

© 1994 by
The Regents of the University of California

Library of Congress Cataloging-in-Publication Data

Unruh, Vicky.
    Latin American vanguards : the art of contentious encounters /
Vicky Unruh.
      p. cm. — (Latin American literature and culture ; 11)
    Includes bibliographical references and index.
    ISBN 0-520-08561-2. — ISBN 0-520-08794-1 (pbk.)
    1. Latin American literature—20th century—History and
criticism.   2. Literature, Experimental—Latin America—History and
criticism.   3. Avant-garde (Aesthetics)—Latin America.   4. Latin
America—Intellectual life—20th century.   I. Series: Latin American
literature and culture (Berkeley, Calif.) ; 11.
    PQ7081.U45   1995
    860.9'98—dc20
                                     93-42216
                                         CIP

Printed in the United States of America

The paper used in this publication meets the minimum requirements
of American National Standard for Information Sciences—Permanence
of Paper for Printed Library Materials, ANSI Z39.48-1984.

For David,
and for Jennifer and Rachel

Contents

Acknowledgments

The story of a book encompasses numerous individuals and institutions. My work on Latin America's literary vanguards began with a 1984 doctoral dissertation on the connections between literary aesthetics and cultural nationalism in the vanguard movement in Peru. The unanswered questions emerging from that project took me on a very different course that has culminated with this book. Initial research was supported by a postdoctoral resident fellowship at the Center for Twentieth Century Studies, University of Wisconsin–Milwaukee, in 1985–86, made possible by release time from the Department of Spanish and Portuguese. At the center, I was privileged to participate in a remarkable faculty seminar, "Rewriting Modernism," eminently enriched by the intellectual guidance of center director Kathleen Woodward and seminar organizer Andreas Huyssen and by the participation of other fellows. Subsequent support came from the Graduate School of the University of Wisconsin–Milwaukee and the General Research Fund of the University of Kansas, and the presentation of project material at professional conferences was supported by the Center for Latin America at the University of Wisconsin–Milwaukee and the Graduate School and Center of Latin American Studies at the University of Kansas. I was also assisted by the staff of the Benson Latin American Collection of the University of Texas at Austin, in particular, Ann Hartness, and, in very early stages, of the Sala de Investigaciones Bibliográficas of the Biblioteca Nacional del Perú. The Spencer Research Library at the University of Kansas provided a study during the final revisions.

I am profoundly indebted to each and every one of my colleagues in the Department of Spanish and Portuguese at the University of Kansas for creating, under the superb leadership of Robert Spires and, more recently, Roberta Johnson, a singularly warm and vital atmosphere of collegial support and intellectual exchange that enabled me to complete this book. I have also been favored with the challenging dialogue provided by many graduate students, particularly those in my seminars on the vanguards. As the project moved toward completion, the interest and encouragement of Roberto González Echevarría were fundamental, as was the enduring conversation with fellow *vanguardista* Merlin H. Forster, an exchange begun in Texas days. Eileen McWilliam, editor at the University of California Press, provided perceptive and learned guidance for the review process, and Erika Büky and Sheila Berg provided careful and intelligent editing for transforming the manuscript into a book. Gustavo Pérez Firmat, as a reader for the University of California Press, provided insightful and substantive suggestions, as did two other, anonymous, readers. John Brushwood, Andrew Debicki, Klaus Müller-Bergh, Robert Spires, and George Woodyard gave me thoughtful feedback on project proposals or on versions of individual chapters or chapter sections.

I am also grateful to the numerous people who at various stages provided me with materials or contacts, suggested material I might examine, or raised or answered questions vital for the book's progress: Raquel Aguilú de Murphy, Severino Albuquerque, Danny Anderson, Leslie Bary, William R. Blue, John Brushwood, Lilly Caballero de Cueto, Alonso Cueto, Michael Doudoroff, Merlin Forster, Regina Harrison, Mark Hernández, David Jackson, Elizabeth Jackson, Roberta Johnson, Elizabeth Kuznesof, Ramón Layera, Linda Ledford-Miller, Naomi Lindstrom, Javier Mariátegui Chiappe, Nieves Martínez de Olcoz, Margo Milleret, Klaus Müller-Bergh, Julio Ortega, Charles Perrone, Daniel Reedy, Judith Richards, Enylton de Sá Rego, Jorge Schwartz, Janet Sharistanian, Amelia Simpson, Raymond Souza, Charles Stansifer, David Unruh, Emilio Vásquez, Jon Vincent, David Wise, and George Yúdice. Superb technical assistance was provided by Victoria Hays, Pam LeRow, Paula Malone, and Lynn Porter of the University of Kansas and by my patient daughter, Jennifer Unruh, my navigator in the transition from Nota Bene to WordPerfect. Above all, I have been favored by the support of a family that keeps the intensity of my professional life in balance. This includes my extended parental network—Virginia and Dell Hymes, Norma Wolff, and Til and Victor Unruh—and, above all, my best friend, David Unruh, and our wise daughters, Jennifer and Rachel.

Some material in this book appeared in earlier forms. The chapter 1 section on the *Chinfonía burguesa* is a revised version of "The *Chinfonía burguesa:* A Linguistic Manifesto of Nicaragua's Avant-Garde," published in *Latin American Theatre Review* 20.2 (Spring 1987): 37–48, and is reprinted with permission. The chapter 2 section on *La educación sentimental* is a revised version of "Art's 'Disorderly Humanity' in Torres Bodet's *La educación sentimental,*" *Revista Canadiense de Estudios Hispánicos* 17.1 (Fall 1992): 123–36, and is reprinted with permission. The chapter 4 section on *A morta* is a revised version of "A Theatre of Autopsy: Oswald de Andrade's *A morta* (The Dead Woman)," published in *One Hundred Years of Invention: Oswald de Andrade and the Modern Tradition in Latin American Literature,* ed. K. David Jackson (Austin: Dept. of Spanish and Portuguese/Abaporu Press, 1992, 31–40), and is reprinted with permission. The chapter 4 section on *En la luna* is a revised version of "Language and Performance in Vicente Huidobro's *En la luna,*" published in *Romance Quarterly* 36.2 (May 1989): 203–12 by the University Press of Kentucky, and is reprinted with permission. The chapter 5 section on *Cuculcán* is a revised version of "Double Talk: Asturias's America in *Cuculcán,*" published previously in *Hispania,* the journal of the American Association of Teachers of Spanish and Portuguese, 75.3 (September 1992): 527–33.

Abbreviations

For frequently cited works, I have used the following abbreviations. Unless otherwise indicated, all translations from Spanish and Portuguese are my own. When citing published translations, I provide two separate page sources: the first for the Spanish or Portuguese original and the second for the translated version.

I. WORKS AND COLLECTIONS

50A   *50 años del movimiento de vanguardia de Nicaragua,* ed. Pablo Antonio Cuadra (Managua: El Pez y la Serpiente, 1979).

BMP   Giovanni Pontiero, ed., *An Anthology of Brazilian Modernist Poetry* (Oxford: Pergamon, 1969).

GMT   Gilberto Mendonça Teles, *Vanguarda européia e modernismo brasileiro* (Petrópolis, Brazil: Vozes, 1976).

HV   Hugo Verani, *Las vanguardias literarias en Hispanoamérica: Manifiestos, proclamas y otros escritos* (Rome: Bulzoni, 1986).

INPA   Alberto Hidalgo, Vicente Huidobro, and Jorge Luis Borges, *Indice de la nueva poesía americana* (Buenos Aires: El Inca, 1926).

LHA   Luis Hernández Aquino, *Nuestra aventura literaria: Los ismos en la poesía puertorriqueña, 1913–1948* (San Juan: Ediciones de la Torre, University of Puerto Rico, 1966).

MPP   Nelson Osorio, *Manifiestos, proclamas y polémicas de la vanguardia literaria hispanoamericana* (Caracas: Ayacucho, 1988).

OC   *Obras completas.* Used with volume and page number for several authors.

OP   Nicolás Guillén, *Obra poética, 1920–1972* (Havana: Arte y Literatura, 1974).

OPC   Pablo Antonio Cuadra, *Obra poética completa* (San José, Costa Rica: Libro Libre, 1983).

PC   Mário de Andrade, *Poesias completas* (São Paulo: Livraria Martins, 1980).

2. TRANSLATIONS

EAG   E. A. Goodland translation of *Macunaíma* by Mário de Andrade.

EW   Eliot Weinberger translation of *Altazor* by Vicente Huidobro.

HW   Helene Weyl translation of *La deshumanización del arte* by José Ortega y Gasset.

JT   Jack Tomlin translation of *Paulicéia desvairada* by Mário de Andrade, including "As enfibraturas do Ipiranga."

KDJ   Kenneth D. Jackson and Albert Bork translation of *Serafim Ponte Grande* by Oswald de Andrade.

KS   Katherine Silver translation of *La casa de cartón* by Martín Adán.

LB   Leslie Bary translation of the "Manifesto antropófago" by Oswald de Andrade.

RM   Robert Márquez and David Arthur McMurray translations in *Man-Making Words: Selected Poems of Nicolás Guillén.*

RN   Ralph Niebuhr and Albert Bork translation of *Memórias sentimentais de João Miramar* by Oswald de Andrade.

RS   Rebecca Seiferle translation of *Trilce* by César Vallejo.

SMSR Stella M. de Sá Rego translation of the "Manifesto da poesia Pau-Brasil" by Oswald de Andrade.

Introduction

Contentious Encounters in Life and Art

In Julio Cortázar's novel *Rayuela* (1963), a canonical work in Latin America's new narrative, the protagonist Horacio Oliveira concocts numerous games as paths to the existential insight and metaphysical unity he pursues. Two singular pastimes are linguistic. Horacio and his friends exhume obscure words from the "cemetery," their pet name for the Royal Academy's dictionary of the Spanish language. He and his lover, La Maga, communicate secretly in *glíglico* (or Gliglish), a language of her creation, and the novel's "Expendable Chapters" include samples of this enigmatic idiom. In a similar vein, the 1970 dramatic experiment *La orgástula* by Chile's Jorge Díaz presents two characters totally bound in gauze who communicate with an invented language conforming to the morphology and syntax of Spanish but otherwise unintelligible.

The linguistic strategies, antiacademic spirit, and implicit social critique of Horacio Oliveira's cemetery game have their roots in the literary vanguard movements that emerged throughout Latin America in the 1920s and early 1930s. The hermetic neologisms typical of *La orgástula* and Cortázar's *glíglico* had made their Latin American literary debut in the word games of early vanguardist poets and, more specifically, in the verbal acrobatics of Vicente Huidobro's master poetic work *Altazor* and the rhetorical posturings of the politically manipulative marionettes in his 1934 play *En la luna*. In fact, vanguardist antecedents of Latin America's contemporary literary innovations are numerous. The confrontations between high art and popular or mass culture

I

that emerge in novels by Manuel Puig or Luis Rafael Sánchez or in Marco Antonio de la Parra's postmodernist dramatic exercises are anticipated by Roberto Arlt's novels and plays of the late 1920s and early 1930s and by Oswald de Andrade's 1920s collage narratives. Literary encounters between modernity and the autochthonous undertaken in Alejo Carpentier's *Los pasos perdidos* (1953), in 1950s and 1960s indigenist prose fiction experiments by José María Arguedas, Elena Garro, and Rosario Castellanos, and in Mario Vargas Llosa's 1987 novel *El hablador* were initiated several decades earlier in Mário de Andrade's *Macunaíma* (1928), Miguel Angel Asturias's *Leyendas de Guatemala* (1930), and Carpentier's own early prose fiction and experimental performance pieces. The assaults on narrative subjectivity offered by such works as Juan Rulfo's *Pedro Páramo* (1955), Carlos Fuentes's *La muerte de Artemio Cruz* and *Aura* (both from 1962), Guillermo Cabrera Infante's *Tres tristes tigres* (1967), Osman Lins's *Avalovara* (1973), or Luisa Valenzuela's *Cambio de armas* (1982) are foreshadowed by Martín Adán's 1928 prose experiment *La casa de cartón*. Carlos Oquendo de Amat's typographically unconventional *5 metros de poemas* (1927), printed on a single unfolding sheet, anticipates Octavio Paz's *Blanco* (1967). And the metatheatrical challenges to traditional spectator roles associated with contemporary playwrights such as José Triana, Emilio Carballido, Griselda Gambaro, and Díaz, among others, had already been undertaken in experimental theatrical exercises written in the late 1920s and the 1930s by Xavier Villaurrutia, Huidobro, Oswald de Andrade, and Arlt.

Recent scholarship has affirmed the historical importance of Latin America's interwar vanguard movements for the outstanding achievements of contemporary Latin American literature. But my brief exercise in parallelisms and antecedents in and of itself provides a limited and even distorted view of these movements. This is because Latin America's early twentieth-century vanguards may best be understood not in terms of selected canonical works or individual authors' careers but rather as a multifaceted cultural activity, manifested in a variety of creative endeavors and events and seeking to challenge and redefine the nature and purpose of art. André Breton himself characterized Parisian surrealism as a form of activity, and theorists and investigators such as Peter Bürger, Renato Poggioli, Matei Calinescu, Rosalind Krauss, Marjorie Perloff, and James Clifford have also approached the international pre– and post–World War I avant-gardes—the "historical" avant-gardes, in Bürger's terms—as a type of activity that encompasses a

broad range of phenomena: artistic experiments in many genres, polemics, manifestos, and public events and performances.

Between the late teens and the mid-1930s, vanguardist activity
emerged throughout Latin America.[1] This activity included several possible forms: the emergence of small groups of writers committed to
innovation; the affirmation by groups or individuals of aesthetic or cultural positions often designated by a particular "ism" or more broadly
as *arte nuevo* (new art) or *vanguardismo;* the dissemination of these
positions through written manifestos or public manifestations; engagement by some groups in debates and polemics with others; experimentation in multiple literary and artistic genres and across generic boundaries; the publication of often ephemeral little magazines as outlets for
both artistic experiments and cultural debates; the organization of
study groups or seminars; and serious investigations by these study
groups or by individual writers into language, folklore, and cultural history. These activities were unquestionably stimulated in part by the European avant-gardes of the pre– and post–World War I era, with key
figures such as Vicente Huidobro, Jorge Luis Borges, Alejo Carpentier,
Oswald de Andrade, César Vallejo, Evaristo Ribera Chevremont, and
Miguel Angel Asturias serving as transcontinental links. But Latin
American vanguardism grew out of and responded to the continent's
own cultural concerns. Out of these multiple activities, there emerged
a serious critical inquiry into ways of thinking about art and culture in
Latin America. On the broadest level, the five chapters in this study
examine the substance of that inquiry. Specifically, I analyze manifestos
and creative texts from all genres to discern the changing ideas that
these pose about the interaction between art and experience; about the
purpose of literary activity and the changing roles of artists; about new
roles for audiences and readers; and about connections between new
aesthetic ideas and long-standing concerns about Latin America's cultural and linguistic identity.

The Context and Character of the Vanguards

My approach to Latin American vanguardism as a form
of activity rather than simply a collection of experimental texts exhibiting certain common features underscores the fact that vanguardists
themselves often conceptualized art and intellectual life as action or

doing. The pervasive activist spirit that characterized much of this literary work was consonant with the historical context in which the vanguards emerged. Nelson Osorio, one of the more context-sensitive analysts of these movements, has called attention to the antioligarchic spirit of the era (*MPP* xxvi), an observation supported by the historical record. The years from the late teens through the early 1930s constituted an epoch of contentious encounters manifesting the changing alliances that accompany shifting economic, social, and political conditions. Latin American nations experienced the impact of World War I era economic changes, of political hopes generated by the Russian revolution and international workers' movements, and of the pervasive postwar disillusionment with European culture epitomized in Oswald Spengler's *The Decline of the West* (1918–22). Although specific situations varied from one country to another, certain features characterized continental life as a whole.[2]

Economically, the period was shaped by the consolidation of the export-import growth model (Skidmore and Smith) and the "neocolonialist pact" (Halperin Donghi). The years of the literary vanguards were marked by an intensification of rapid growth grounded in region-specific dependence on one or two major exports and a consequent interlocking of Latin American economies with world markets and financial institutions. These developments were accompanied by a gradual shift in hegemony from Europe to the United States with regard to Latin America's economic—and often political—affairs. Economic expansion and demographic change stimulated the growth of major cities, including Bogotá, Havana, Lima, Mexico City, Montevideo, Santiago, São Paulo, and, most dramatically, Buenos Aires. Many of these also provided the sites of the limited industrial growth associated with consumer goods production and with the creation of infrastructures necessary to sustain export-import economies. This metropolitan growth exacerbated imbalances and tensions between urban and rural sectors. Large portions of rural populations continued to function at a subsistence level, on the margins of mainstream national economic life, and were vulnerable to the economic highs and lows produced by single-export economies controlled by outside investors.

Political changes shaped by these demographic conditions included the growth of a more politically aware and active middle class and the development of significant workers' movements. In Argentina and Brazil and, to a lesser degree, in Chile and Peru, European immigration contributed to working-class growth, whereas in Mexico and Caribbean countries, Indians, mestizos, and slave descendants continued to be used as sources of cheap labor. Between the mid-teens and the late 1920s, workers' groups in Argentina, Brazil, Chile, Cuba, Peru, Mexico, Uruguay, and Ecuador, and to varying degrees in other countries as well, organized demonstrations or general strikes, activities that usually met with repressive official responses. In the Andean region, particularly in Ecuador and Peru, periodic indigenous rebellions intensified the ambience of class and cultural confrontation. Antiforeign reaction in cities like Buenos Aires or São Paulo with large immigrant populations produced additional tensions as well. And in Mexico, the intersection of urban-based pressures for liberal reform with a broadly based agrarian revolt produced the continent's most consequential contentious encounter of the epoch, the Mexican Revolution.

During this primarily reformist period of Latin American history, the middle class, from which many vanguardist writers emerged, experienced conflicting pulls. Its interaction with traditional oligarchies seeking to shore up their own power broadened political participation (far more in some countries than in others) and led to growth in the number and influence of political parties, franchise extensions (though notably not yet to women), and government-sponsored educational and social reforms.[3] Activist pressure for change, though often harshly punished by a politically engaged military, intensified even under the authoritarian regimes of Gerardo Machado in Cuba, Juan Vicente Gómez in Venezuela, and Manuel Estrada Cabrera in Guatemala and the eleven-year reformist dictatorship of Augusto B. Leguía in Peru. This more politicized middle class at times directed its attention to social inequities. More radical developments included the formation of Latin America's first socialist and Communist parties (though some were not officially recognized until years later) and the emergence of the continent's first important Marxist thinker, the Peruvian José Carlos Mariátegui, who was also an active promoter of Peruvian vanguardist activity and a knowledgeable analyst of the international literary vanguards. Historians regard the continental university reform movement as a major component of the middle class's political awakening. This activity took shape in Córdoba, Argentina, in 1918, and national and international student gatherings followed in Mexico, Chile, Panama, Peru, Brazil, Cuba, Uruguay, Colombia, and Puerto Rico. In addition, Peru's Víctor Raúl Haya de la Torre, founder of the nascent APRA (Alianza Popular Revolucionaria Americana) movement, traveled widely throughout the continent and abroad, and he and his followers often reinforced the political and intellectual contacts initiated at the university reform congresses. This network is documented in numerous vanguardist periodicals, through intellectual and political debates, and in editorial expressions of support extended from social activists in one country to those in another.

According to Osorio, the university reform movement went beyond immediate pedagogic concerns to seek "a new conception of culture and teaching in line with popular interests, national needs, and social transformation" (*MPP* xxvi). For Osorio, moreover, this movement provides a direct link between the antioligarchic spirit of the political and economic context and the work of the literary vanguards. But while not disagreeing about the "common character" of aesthetic and political calls for change, I would caution against seeking too literal links between political confrontations and class struggles played out on Latin America's streets in the late teens and 1920s and the contentious encounters with audiences, readers, and one another provoked by literary vanguardists through confrontational manifestos, experimental creative texts, and engaging performance events.

Since the early nineteenth century, international vanguardism had always embodied tensions and correlations between the cultural and the political. Matei Calinescu has carefully traced points of historical intersection and divergence between the two in the European concept of the avant-gardes.[4] In Latin America, as Gloria Videla has observed, the lines between a political vanguard and an artistic one can rarely be sharply drawn.[5] But neither do political and aesthetic activism of the period, while often intertwined, neatly mirror one another. Certainly many vanguardist artists and groups were at one time or another willfully engaged in the contentious encounters of politics as well as art. Cuba's Grupo Minorista, for example, whose members included the founders of the vanguardist journal *Revista de Avance* (1927–30), supported a broad program of social and political change in Cuba, protested U.S. involvement in Cuban, Mexican, and Nicaraguan affairs, and actively opposed the repressive measures of Gerardo Machado. As a student activist, Miguel Angel Asturias worked against Guatemala's dictator Estrada Cabrera and participated in popular education reform. In their later vanguardist years, Chilean Vicente Huidobro and Brazilian Oswald de Andrade both joined the Communist party. Peru's principal vanguardist journal *Amauta* was closed for six months by the Leguía regime for its prolabor positions, and police briefly detained the journal's editor, Mariátegui, who was also, as I have noted, the Marxist founder of Peruvian socialism. Puerto Rico's *atalayistas,* in particular, the poet Clemente Soto Vélez, supported the incipient Puerto Rican nationalism and separatism being disseminated by Pedro Albizu Campos. Mexico's *estridentistas* called for their country's intellectuals to emulate the spirit of revolt embodied in the Mexican Revolution, and some members of Mexico's Contemporáneos group had, prior to its formation, supported educational reforms undertaken by José Vasconcelos. The *vanguardistas'* political activism was dominated by but not limited to progressive or leftist causes, moreover. Some Nicaraguan vanguardists, for example, supported Augusto Sandino's resistance to U.S. intervention in Central America and the reactionary nationalism of the first Anastasio Somoza as well. Leaders of Brazil's Verde-Amarelo group, who as artists endorsed a mystical kind of ultranationalism, later organized Brazil's fascistic Integralist party.

But the contentious encounters I explore in the chapters that follow unfold in the realm of culture and art. The "common character" of political and cultural activism is to be found neither exclusively in the concrete political acts of vanguardist writers (some were aggressively apolitical) nor in the explicit social content of their artistic experiments. Some avant-garde creative texts do actually incorporate obvious critiques of specific social conditions. But, in general, vanguardist aesthetic activism is profoundly different in kind from the literary realist's exposé. For Peter Bürger in *Theory of the Avant-Garde,* the most radical feature of the European historical avant-gardes was the assault on the role of art as an institution in bourgeois society. Within these movements, he argues, "the social subsystem that is art enters the stage of self-criticism" (22). Bürger uses *institution* here to indicate not only a "productive and distributive apparatus" for art but also the "ideas about art that prevail at a given time and that determine the reception of works" (22). In Latin American vanguardism, one rarely finds the absolute anti-art stance normally associated with European Dada. Institutionalizing literary traditions was a relatively recent phenomenon in Latin American cultural life, and, in some cases, the vanguardist movements themselves became enmeshed with the construction of national literatures or canons.[6] But Latin American vanguardists were profoundly concerned with ideas about art prevailing in their own times and, even when taking ostensibly apolitical stands, seriously examined art's possible roles within the problematic social and cultural contexts surrounding its production. As they cast a critical eye on the value of their own artistic activities, they often imagined art as an integral part of an activist intellectual life. Aesthetic activism was manifested in the needling presence of vanguardist artists on the cultural scene, in engaging communicative modes (manifestos, broadsides, literary polemics, confrontational literary surveys, or public performance events), or in difficult literary experiments demanding new reader reactions.

(Re)Reading Vanguardist Activity

Because I approach vanguardism as a form of activity rather than as an assemblage of individually outstanding texts, in this work I often examine the implicit dialogues that emerge between critical and creative endeavors, between manifestos or similar documents and creative texts. Although I do present close readings of numerous literary texts, the underlying premise is that a brief manifesto or a literary survey appearing in a short-lived vanguardist periodical may constitute as significant a factor in the dialogue of artistic and cultural ideas as a critically acclaimed creative work. My own approach has unquestionably been shaped by other recent scholarship. Once Latin American vanguardism was recognized as a significant component of the continent's literary history, investigators undertook individual studies of specific countries, groups, magazines, or major figures. Early studies also focused primarily on poetry. Although important work of this kind continues, the last ten years have witnessed a more comprehensive reassessment that has recognized the multifaceted quality of vanguardist activity and has generally pursued two lines of inquiry.

The first investigative line has sought a historical and bibliographical reconstruction of the period on a continental basis, yielding four major anthologies of vanguardist materials as well as a book-length bibliography. These include Hugo Verani's *Las vanguardias literarias en Hispanoamérica: Manifiestos, proclamas y otros escritos* (1986); Nelson Osorio's *Manifiestos, proclamas y polémicas de la vanguardia literaria hispanoamericana* (1988); volume two (*Documentos*) of Gloria Videla's *Direcciones del vanguardismo hispanoamericano* (1990); Jorge Schwartz's *Las vanguardias latinoamericanas: Textos programáticos y críticos* (1991); and *Vanguardism in Latin American Literature: An Annotated Bibliographical Guide,* compiled by Merlin H. Forster and K. David Jackson (1990). The last two of these include Brazil in their broad scope. The titles of the anthologies underscore the eclectic substance of materials resistant to tidy classification; thus we have "other writings," "documents," or "programmatic texts." The Forster-Jackson bibliography manifests the same resistance to neat categories, as primary sources from the vanguardist period include journals, creative works, and the elusive "other materials." These problems in classification reinforce the idea of vanguardism as a form of activity rather than an assemblage of canonical authors or works. In their very constitution, these collections also suggest that, to arrive at meaningful understandings of the vanguard period in Latin America, one must go beyond specific individual works, writers, or even genres.

The same premise emerges in a second line of inquiry in recent vanguardist scholarship, the search for comprehensive characterizations of the vanguards in Latin America as related to but distinct from the European avant-gardes. This second investigative line has produced article-length studies seeking to define more broadly what Latin American vanguardism was actually like or about and to map out what kinds of approaches are appropriate for arriving at such definitions. Forster's 1975 piece, "Latin American *Vanguardismo:* Chronology and Terminology," constituted a fundamental step in this direction, and his "Toward a Synthesis of Latin American Vanguardism" (1990), introducing the Forster-Jackson bibliography, expands this line of inquiry. Other fundamental pieces of this type include Osorio's "Para una caracterización histórica del vanguardismo literario hispanoamericano" (1981; reworked in the introduction to his manifesto anthology); Haroldo de Campos's "Da razão antropofágica: A Europa sob o signo da devoração" (1981); Klaus Müller-Bergh's "El hombre y la técnica: Contribución al conocimiento de corrientes vanguardistas hispanoamericanas" (1982; second version 1987); Saúl Yurkievich's "Los avatares de la vanguardia" (1982); Jorge Schwartz's "La vanguardia en América Latina: Una estética comparada" (1983) and the introduction to his 1991 anthology; the introductory study to Hugo Verani's anthology of vanguardist materials (1986); and the introduction to Gloria Videla's *Direcciones del vanguardismo hispanoamericano* (1990).[7]

Much of this material shares certain premises that also underlie my own work: (1) that Latin American vanguardism was a continental development and should therefore be examined comparatively; (2) that the vanguards provoked significant changes in prose fiction and drama as well as poetry and, in fact, frequently challenged generic divisions;

(3) that manifestos and manifesto-style texts constituted a primary out-
let for vanguardist critical and creative expression; and (4) that Latin
American vanguardism as a whole was simultaneously international and
autochthonous in its orientation, as artists interacted with European
avant-garde currents in keeping with their own cultural exigencies. In
this vein, and unlike national or genre studies, my own work, based on
close readings of critical and creative texts from all genres and from
Spanish America and Brazil, seeks to establish the common ground
among the sometimes quite diverse continental movements and activities in the ideas that they pose about art and culture in Latin America.
In keeping with the definition of vanguardism as a form of activity,
four of the five chapters also examine the complex interaction between
manifestos or critical articles, affirming certain artistic positions, and the
experimental creative works that both reinforce and undermine these
positions. The selection criteria for particular works and critical documents examined also reflect the definition of vanguardism as a cultural
activity. Thus my objective is neither to establish a vanguardist canon
nor to focus on outstanding individual writers per se, although I do
examine the work of many major figures pertinent to the artistic and
cultural issues addressed. Instead, I tap the broad and eclectic range of
materials through which the vanguards' complex and often contradictory dialogue of ideas was carried out. These chapters do not undertake
a historical survey of vanguardist activity in Latin America, a project
already carried out in some of the work described above. Finally, although I address the Latin American vanguards as a historically and
culturally specific development, I also identify, when appropriate, interaction at the level of ideas with the international avant-gardes. Although this work constitutes neither a national nor a genre study, it is
worth noting that important recent work of this kind has also addressed
vanguardism as a form of cultural activity. Two of these studies in particular have had an impact on my own approach. Francine Masiello's
book on the vanguards in Argentina, *Lenguaje e ideología: Las escuelas
argentinas de vanguardia* (1986), employs a multigenre approach and
examines the role of manifestos in constructing a particular critical climate for the production of creative works. Although it includes both
Spain and Spanish America, Gustavo Pérez Firmat's groundbreaking
study of the Hispanic vanguard novel, *Idle Fictions* (1982), addresses
the interaction between prose fiction works and their contemporary
critical reception.

Regional Differences through Common Ground

The premise that Latin American vanguardism was a continental phenomenon provides my point of departure in the chapters that follow. Vanguardist activity actually encompassed a variety of national or regional movements that manifested site-specific peculiarities. But, as Forster has argued, Latin American vanguardists also knew that they were participating in a "common enterprise" (*Vanguardism in Latin American Literature* 8). In fact, even the most casual examination of little magazines and vanguardist documents reveals this awareness, documented through a continental network of magazine and creative work exchanges. Even very ephemeral little magazines participated in this exchange, which was also reinforced by the Costa Rica–based *Repertorio Americano,* a continentally circulated periodical that disseminated vanguardist currents.

But in exploring through these chapters the common ground of multiple literary vanguard movements, I do not dismiss national differences. Bringing together around specific topics materials from several countries invariably points back to singular contexts from which individual works emerge. A very brief review of those national contexts underscores the plurality of Latin America's vanguards.[8] Avant-garde literary activity was most extensive in Argentina, Brazil, Cuba, Mexico, Peru, and, if one considers the impact of major figures rather than groups, Chile. Less extensive but significant activity also developed in Ecuador, Nicaragua, Puerto Rico, Uruguay, and Venezuela.

Centered in Buenos Aires during the reformist presidencies of Hipólito Yrigoyen and Marcelo T. de Alvear, Argentine vanguardism presented an assortment of artistic and political postures that reflected the polemical atmosphere of a rapidly changing city marked by conflictive cultural and social diversity. Argentine vanguardist writers were highly active and visible, produced literary works in all genres, and participated in journals, publishing houses, and provocative public performances. In contrast to other countries, here the lines between aestheticist and political conceptions of art were more sharply drawn. Literary history typically classifies artistic innovation around the two major groups, Florida and Boedo. The more aestheticist Florida published the vanguardist periodical *Prisma* (1921–22), a broadside, *Proa* (1922–23; 1924–26), and the widely distributed *Martín Fierro* (1924–27). Its literary production included the *ultraísmo* poetry of Jorge Luis Borges and Oliverio Girondo, prose fiction by Eduardo Mallea and Eduardo González Lanuza, and the work of many other writers as well. Although women infrequently participated actively or visibly in vanguardist activities, Florida included the poet and prose fiction writer Norah Lange, who was married to Girondo. Members of the leftist Boedo group favored socially engaged art, published *Claridad* (modeled in spirit after Henri Barbusse's Parisian Clarté group), established a publishing house of the same name, and wrote poetry and prose fiction. Roberto Mariani's prose fiction is perhaps the best known of Boedo's offerings. Members also organized the enduring Teatro del Pueblo, which transformed Argentine theatrical production. But, as Christopher Towne Leland has pointed out, the lines between the two groups often blur, as in the figure of novelist and playwright Roberto Arlt, admired by both but allied with neither. It is also difficult to ascribe a consistent literary style to either group. Although Argentine vanguardists, particularly the Florida group, generally eschewed programmatic cultural nationalism, certain events manifested autochthonist tensions and concerns. These included intense discussions over *Martín Fierro*'s name (drawn from the title of the nineteenth-century gauchesque poetry classic), attacks on Florida by Boedo for the former's Parisian (rather than national) orientation, and Florida's adulation of Ricardo Güiraldes's 1926 novel *Don Segundo Sombra,* which transformed the vanished gaucho into national myth.[9]

Although the term *modernismo* designates the renovation of Brazilian literature from the early 1920s through the mid-1940s, the radically innovative activities of the 1920s paralleled Spanish American vanguardism. This period of Brazil's Old Republic (1889–1930) was marked by nascent (though not enormously successful) struggles against entrenched regional oligarchies, emergent middle-class pressures for governmental reform, attention to national self-definition coinciding with the 1922 independence centennial celebrations, and the preeminence of São Paulo among the country's autonomously developing individual states. This city also provided the center for vanguardist activity, although important manifestations also evolved in Rio de Janeiro and in Belo Horizonte and Cataguazes in Minas Gerais. São Paulo's Semana de Arte Moderna (Week of Modern Art) in February 1922, a multifield artistic celebration, coincided with centennial celebrations, a link that forecast the movement's strong inclination toward cultural nationalism. Characterized by its multidisciplinary nature, Brazilian vanguardist activity produced two subsequently canonized major figures: Mário de Andrade, poet, novelist, musicologist, folklorist, and literary critic, and Oswald de Andrade, manifesto writer, poet, novelist, dramatist, and cultural theorist. Other important writers included poets Manuel Bandeira, Raul Bopp, Ronald de Carvalho, and Carlos Drummond de Andrade, among others. Principal journals included *Klaxon* (São Paulo, 1922–23), *Terra Roxa e Outras Terras* (São Paulo, 1926), *Festa* (Rio de Janeiro, 1927–28), *A Revista* (Belo Horizonte, 1925–26), *Verde* (Cataguazes, Minas Gerais, 1927–28; 1929), and, the most important in its impact, the *Revista de Antropofagia* (São Paulo, 1928–29). Three women contributed notably to early Brazilian vanguardist production: cubist painter Anita Malfatti, who participated in the Week of Modern Art, painter Tarsila do Amaral, Oswald de Andrade's second wife, who made major contributions to the Antropofagia group's cultural critique, and poet Cecília Meireles, briefly associated with the magazine *Festa*. As in Peru, Cuba, and Nicaragua, Brazilian vanguardist activity was often strongly marked by local autochthonist concerns and, in many creative works, a broader Americanist cast.[10]

Chilean vanguardism emerged during a tense and haltingly reformist period, as workers and a growing middle class pressured traditional oligarchies for greater participation in public life. Underscoring the pitfalls inherent in characterizing Latin American vanguardism solely in national terms, Chile produced two outstanding figures whose forums for innovative activity were often more international and continental than national or local. Vicente Huidobro—poet, novelist, dramatist, and manifesto and film script writer—is widely regarded as both the precursor and the founder of Latin American vanguardism. An active participant in Parisian avant-gardes, he also published the journal *Creación* in Madrid from 1921 to 1924. Huidobro's antimimetic literary creed *creacionismo* extolled the virtues of autonomous art. But Huidobro's aesthetic and political activism sometimes overlapped, not only through his 1934 play *En la luna* satirizing Chilean political events of the 1920s but also with his own 1925 incursion into Chilean politics. Through his ephemeral journal *Acción*, he employed a vanguardist style to advocate programs for national reform. In the 1920s and early 1930s, Huidobro's compatriot, Pablo Neruda, one of the twentieth century's outstanding poets, produced verse with many surrealist features. Like Huidobro's *Creación*, Neruda's principal journal, *Caballo Verde para la Poesía*, was published in Madrid (1935–36). But Neruda was also involved during the 1920s, often in a highly contentious mode, with other vanguardist writers and periodicals in Chile. Writers more active in local activities included poets Juan Emar and Juan Marín as well as Pablo de Rokha and Rosamel del Valle, both of whom produced both poetry and prose fiction. Although María Luisa Bombal's prose fiction was first published toward the end of the vanguardist period, her work was strongly marked by her contacts with avant-garde activities in Paris, Chile, and Buenos Aires. Chile's in-country vanguardist periodicals included the politically contentious *Claridad* (1920–24) from Santiago and *Antena* (1922), *Elipse* (1922), and *Nguillatún* (1924) from Valparaíso. A nativist agenda characterized *Nguillatún* as well as the activities of Santiago's *runrunista* poets who emerged between 1927 and 1934, whereas the "Rosa Náutica" manifesto (1922), published in *Antena,* displayed more affinities toward futurism and Spanish *ultraísmo.*[11]

As a U.S. protectorate during the century's first three decades, Cuba experienced a tightening of U.S. involvement in its economic and political life and increasingly corrupt national governments. The seeds of the country's vanguardist activity, centered in Havana, were sown in the collective reaction of student activists, middle-class political reformers, and labor leaders against the repressive measures of President Alberto Zayas and the Gerardo Machado dictatorship that followed. Formed in 1923, the Grupo Minorista published a 1927 manifesto dedicating itself to multifaceted intellectual work, social reform, and aesthetic innovation. Several signers of this document—Alejo Carpentier, Martí Casanovas, Francisco Ichaso, Jorge Mañach, and Juan Marinello—also founded the influential and relatively long-lived *Revista de Avance* (1927–30), a major nucleus both for artistic innovation and Cuban cultural life. Conceiving social and aesthetic activism as components of the same intellectual enterprise, the *Revista de Avance* provided a dynamic forum for national, Latin American, and European writers, promoted modern developments in visual arts, celebrated the legacy of the Cuban nationalist and poet José Martí, and carried on an exchange with Latin America's other major vanguardist journals. The magazine also reflected the strong concerns for national self-definition and interest in autochthonous cultural forms characteristic of Cuban intellectual activity as a whole during this period, as in its publication of sections from Jorge Mañach's classic inquiry into Cuban identity, *Indagación del choteo,* or Juan Marinello's "El poeta José Martí" and "Sobre la inquietud cubana."[12] Cuban vanguardist literary production, both within and outside of the *Revista de Avance* sphere, included Alejo Carpentier's early prose fiction, poetry, and dramatic experiments, Nicolás Guillén's Afro-Cuban poetry, Mariano Brull's *jitanjáfora* linguistic experiments in verse, poetry by Manuel Navarro Luna, and the 1930s *"gaseiforme"* novels of Enrique Labrador Ruiz.[13]

Mexican vanguardism developed in the early 1920s in the interim between the revolution's most activist phase and the more radical efforts initiated by Lázaro Cárdenas in the mid-1930s to fulfill the revolutionary promise. Although undertaking significant rural educational reform under José Vasconcelos's direction, the short-lived 1920s presidencies sought to neutralize genuine labor or leftist dissent. Mexican vanguardism emerged in two principal groups: the *estridentistas,* more active from the beginning through the middle of the decade, and the Contemporáneos, identified ex post facto with the name of their journal published from 1928 through 1931. Although both groups operated primarily in Mexico City, the *estridentistas* were also active in Xalapa. Often regarded as the more politicized of the two gatherings, the *estridentistas* saw their cultural project as an extension of the revolution's activist spirit. Their short-lived magazines included the broadside *Actual* (Mexico City, 1921–22), *Irradiador* (Mexico City, 1923), and *Horizonte* (Xalapa, 1926–27). Members included the poets Manuel Maples Arce, Germán List Arzubide, and Luis Quintanilla, the prose fiction writers Salvador Gallardo, Xavier Icaza, and Arqueles Vela, and the artist Ramón Alva de la Canal whose woodcuts illustrated several *estridentista* publications. Other group work included multidisciplinary performance events organized by the ephemeral Teatro del Murciélago. The *estridentistas* saw themselves as a cosmopolitan movement, as in Arqueles Vela's short novel *El café de nadie* documenting the group's activities in the ambience of the modern city café. They also expressed internationalist political affinities, as in Maples Arce's long poem "Urbe" with the subtitle "Bolshevik Super-Poem in 5 Cantos" and dedicated to Mexico's workers. At the same time, they promoted explicitly autochthonous work such as Icaza's prose fiction and Alva de la Canal's woodcuts.

Although their principal journals *Ulíses* (1927–28) and *Contemporáneos* (1928–31) did not appear until later in the decade, several of the precocious young writers involved in these projects began their associations early in the 1920s. Although they are considered to have been less political than the *estridentistas,* some attended the International Student Congress held in Mexico City in 1921, participated in José Vasconcelos's far-reaching reform activities through the Ministry of

Public Education, and contributed to the interdisciplinary and socially oriented magazine *El Maestro* (1921–23). Several also participated in *La Falange: Revista de Cultura Latina* (1922–23), edited by the future Contemporáneos leader Jaime Torres Bodet, which advocated strengthening Hispanic Latinist traditions against the incursion of North American culture. The group's widely distributed principal journal *Contemporáneos,* edited mainly by Bernardo Ortíz de Montellano, provided an intellectual and literary forum of superior quality. The journal's literary offerings included poetry, prose fiction, and plays. With the participation of additional group members, Celestino Gorostiza, Xavier Villaurrutia, and Salvador Novo also organized the experimental Teatro Ulíses. This gathering and the more enduring Teatro Orientación in which some group members also collaborated constituted founding events in the development of modern Mexican drama. Antonieta Rivas Mercado, a Mexico City cultural activist and aspiring writer who also participated in Vasconcelos's nationalist presidential campaign, provided creative and financial support for the Contemporáneos' theatrical endeavors. Other participants in the group included Jorge Cuesta, José Gorostiza, and Carlos Pellicer. Contemporáneos literary production included poetry, prose fiction, drama, travel chronicles, and literary criticism, and Novo, Torres Bodet, and Villaurrutia produced significant work in multiple genres. Although deeply concerned about Mexican and Latin American cultural life, most Contemporáneos participants came to avoid the kind of polemical cultural nationalism that characterized much Mexican intellectual life of their time.[14]

Peru's literary vanguards coincided historically with the eleven-year reformist dictatorship of Augusto B. Leguía. Leguía sought alliances between capital and labor and initiated cursory social and educational reforms while seeking to eradicate the significant dissent by labor movements and student radicals that had emerged in the century's first two decades. Literary vanguardism in Lima evolved around José Carlos Mariátegui's *Amauta* (1926–30). Designed in part to maintain the kind of open intellectual and political exchange being stifled by the Leguía government, this journal was comparable in its eclecticism and breadth to Cuba's *Revista de Avance* and, like the Cuban journal, conceptualized art within a broader context of cultural work. In contrast to Leguía's plans to assimilate Peru's large Indian population into mainstream Peruvian culture, *Amauta* affirmed the intrinsic value of indigenous culture and art forms. Numerous *provincianos* brought to the city by student reform activities participated in Lima's vanguards, and Peru also produced the most lasting regional vanguardist magazine, Puno's *Boletín Titikaka* (1926–30), dedicated, like its Lima counterpart, to an indigenist agenda.

Numerous other short-lived vanguardist magazines appeared in Lima, Arequipa, and Cuzco during the 1920s. Although he eschewed active involvement with local vanguardist activities and frequently criticized such efforts, César Vallejo, Peru's major vanguardist poet, co-edited with Juan Larrea in Paris the short-lived vanguardist periodical *Favorables Paris Poema* (1926). Ironically, many of his compatriots regarded Vallejo's poetry as the prime example of the autochthonist vanguardism that they espoused and he ostensibly rejected. Other notable writers included symbolist José María Eguren, regarded as the key predecessor of Peruvian vanguardist poetry; poet Alberto Hidalgo, transplanted to Buenos Aires, where he founded his own literary creed *simplismo;* surrealist poets César Moro and Emilio Adolfo Westphalen; Carlos Oquendo de Amat and Alejandro Peralta, both of whom wrote avant-garde poetry with indigenist themes and motifs; poet and prose fiction writer Martín Adán; and Gamaliel Churata, author of surrealist-indigenist prose. In keeping with the vanguards' redefinitions of art, however, it is fitting that Peru's principal resident vanguardist figure should be Mariátegui, not a creative writer but a cultural activist and literary critic. Also notable is the presence of women in Peru's vanguardist activities, including the poet and political activist Magda Portal, a cofounder of several little magazines, and María Wiesse, a film critic for *Amauta*.[15]

Although less extensive and enduring than movements in Argentina, Brazil, Chile, Cuba, and Peru, significant vanguardist activity or debates also developed in Ecuador, Nicaragua, Puerto Rico, Uruguay, and Venezuela. Ecuador in the 1920s was marked by intense liberal-conservative struggles, mounting pressures for progressive political change and social reforms, student activism prompted by a broadening class base in university attendance, and a brief dictatorship (1927–30). According to Humberto Robles, such events intertwined Ecuadorean vanguardist inquiries and experiments with prevailing cultural politics and polemics. Short-lived periodicals included *Síngulus* (1921), *Proteo* (1922), and *Motocicleta* (1924) (all from Guayaquil). Important literary experiments included Hugo Mayo's poetry and Pablo Palacio's prose fiction and brief dramatic experiments, and avant-garde techniques shaped the early poetry of Jorge Carrera Andrade, one of the country's leading twentieth-century poets. Still, vanguardist activity in Ecuador may perhaps best be characterized as a sustained debate about the pertinence of the new international artistic currents to the country's cultural situation. Robles has argued that polarized positions between classical and socially committed concepts of art allowed for little middle ground and that, by the decade's end, socially oriented art had become the norm. Social, Americanist, or indigenist concerns often marked the thinking of those who did support the idea of an avant-garde or undertook vanguardist experiments.[16]

Its late development notwithstanding, Nicaraguan vanguardist activity constituted a major event in the country's cultural life and the only sustained group effort of its kind in Central America. During the late 1920s and early 1930s, Nicaraguan conservatives and liberals struggled for power. Seeking an alternative site for the Panama Canal, the United States had intervened in the country's economic and political affairs for two decades, and Augusto Sandino emerged as a progressive symbol of national autonomy and resistance to U.S. involvement. Nicaraguan vanguardists, whose political allegiances ultimately spanned the spectrum, also opposed U.S. military involvement in their region. Although contact with U.S. poets was important for their creative endeavors, they also worked for their country's linguistic and cultural autonomy. The Nicaraguan Anti-Academy, a group of young poets from Granada, including Pablo Antonio Cuadra, Joaquín Pasos, Octavio Rocha, and José Coronel Urtecho, undertook this cultural project in 1931–32. Regular pages in Granada's daily *El Correo, vanguardia* and *rincón de vanguardia*, constituted the group's periodical. Its inaugural manifesto sought the cultural renovation of Nicaragua through dissemination of international avant-garde trends and the development of national art forms in every field. Like the associates of *Amauta* in Lima and *Revista de Avance* in Havana, the Anti-Academy resembled an activist study group. Its activities included debates and polemics, public performance events, and the collection of Nicaraguan folklore and popular linguistic, poetic, and musical forms to be incorporated in experimental works. Literary production included mainly poetry, some experimental prose, literary commentary, and performance pieces. The short-lived group's work profoundly influenced Nicaraguan artistic life for years to come, and Cuadra became one of the country's major contemporary writers and intellectuals.[17]

The "status" issue, that is, Puerto Rico's anomalous colonial relationship with the United States, has shaped the island's political and cultural life throughout the twentieth century. During the 1920s, political positions on this issue were being redrawn, paving the way in the early 1930s for renewed advocacy of autonomy or independence and for sustained manifestations of nationalism in politics and intellectual life. Puerto Rican vanguardist activity, which spanned these years, was marked by a comparable intensification of autochthonist concerns. This innovating activity included a rapid succession of "isms" undertaken by a relatively small groups of poets: *diepalismo* (1921–22), *euforismo* (1923–24), *noísmo* (1925–28), the Grupo Meñique (1930–31), and *atalayismo* (1929–35), probably the most enduring through its long-term impact on Puerto Rican poetry. Periodicals included the ephemeral *Faro* (1926), *Vórtice* (1926), and *Hostos* (1929) and the more broadly conceived *Indice* (1929–31). Major literary figures included poets Evaristo Ribera Chevremont, Puerto Rico's bridge with the European avant-gardes, José I. de Diego Padró, Luis Palés Matos, Vicente Palés Matos, Luis Hernández Aquino, Graciany Miranda Archilla, and Clemente Soto Vélez. As a whole, Puerto Rico's vanguardist activity was characterized by the predominance of poetry and linguistic experiment, by an Americanist continental orientation, by a gradually emerging focus on national and Antillean cultural motifs, and by the island's first literary affirmations of West African language and culture as significant cultural presences.[18]

Uruguay in the early decades of the twentieth century provided, by one account, "the happiest example of political democratization and social modernization in Latin America" (Halperin Donghi 326). Notwithstanding a sometimes marked division between Montevideo prosperity and the persistently *latifundista*-dominated countryside, the popular reformist president José Batlle y Ordóñez sought to reconcile urban-rural differences. This era was marked, according to Tulio Halperin Donghi, by an openness to change and an optimistic sense of national identity (323–26). In a comparable spirit, Uruguayan vanguardist activity of the 1920s was, as Gloria Videla has shown with regard to one of its principal journals, *La Pluma* (1927–31), both eclectic—open to a range of international and Latin American influences—and often nativist in its concerns.[19] Experimental literary production was primarily poetic and included *ultraísta*, nativist poetry by Pedro Leandro Ipuche and Fernán Silva Valdés, the Americanist verse of Carlos Sabat Ercasty, *afronegrista* poetry by Ildefonso Pereda Valdés, *ultraísta* experiments by Nicolás Fusco Sansone, and eclectically vanguardist compositions by Alfredo Mario Ferreiro, creator of the 1927 collection *El hombre que se comió un autobús: Poemas con olor a nafta*

(The Man Who Ate a Bus: Poems with the Odor of Naphtha). Felisberto Hernández contributed significant experimental prose fiction. Montevideo journals disseminating new artistic trends included *Los Nuevos* (1919–20), *Pégaso* (1918–24), *La Cruz del Sur* (1924–31), and *Cartel* (1929–31). But *La Pluma*, edited by Alberto Zum Felde and later by Carlos Sabat Ercasty, was perhaps the most comparable to other major Latin American vanguardist journals in its synthesis of international trends with continental connections and local concerns.

The dictatorship of Juan Vicente Gómez shaped Venezuelan political life in the 1920s and, through the growing dissent that it generated, marked the country's cultural life as well. Although group vanguardist activity in the country was relatively late developing and short-lived, according to Osorio, an ambience of student and intellectual resistance culminating in 1928 generated new thinking about art and culture with long-term consequences. The two significant periodicals were *Elite* (1925–28), disseminating information about international and regional avant-garde currents, and the single issue of *válvula* (1928) that included the manifesto "somos." The participation of young Venezuelan intellectuals and artists in the vanguardist network is also documented in comments on Venezuelan writers and political events in other journals throughout the continent. Innovative literary production included poetry by Antonio Arráiz, Luis Barrios Cruz (whose work presents autochthonous motifs), and José Antonio Ramos Sucre, as well as experimental prose fiction by Julio Garmendia and Arturo Uslar Pietri.[20] Recent scholarship also suggests that the novels and intellectual life of Teresa de la Parra might usefully be reexamined in their complex interaction with vanguardist discourse.[21]

Vanguardist activities in other countries were either extremely brief, limited to a single work or writer, or too late in their emergence to be considered within the historical and artistic parameters normally defining these movements in Latin America. But a few others should be mentioned. In the Dominican Republic, the early *postumista* manifesto (1921) signed by Andrés Avelino and poetry by Domingo Moreno Jimenes anticipated autochthonous and Americanist concerns that emerged later in both Cuba and Puerto Rico. Critics have hesitated to characterize either the Colombian journal *Los Nuevos* (1925) or the group of poets that published it as vanguardists, but León de Greiff (through linguistic and musical experiments) and Luis Vidales wrote vanguardist poetry. Although no notable vanguardist activity developed in Guatemala itself, Miguel Angel Asturias's early prose fiction and dramatic experiments and Luis Cardoza y Aragón's poetry constitute major contributions to the movements. Both also participated in Parisian and Latin American vanguardist networks.

A Rehumanization of Art

Regional differences notwithstanding, the common ground of these vanguardist activities throughout Latin America provides the focus for the chapters that follow. As detailed below, each of these presents its own thesis and conclusions. But the pieces are also connected by a concept that is useful for characterizing Latin American vanguardism as a whole: its drive toward a "rehumanization" of art. This phrase, of course, invokes and recasts the title of José Ortega y Gasset's landmark 1925 essay, *La deshumanización del arte* (The Dehumanization of Art). It also brings into focus three fundamental ideas about the vanguards in Latin America that weave through my own five chapters. The first of these is my contention, in keeping with Bürger's *Theory of the Avant-Garde,* that the vanguard movements, notwithstanding their promotion of artistic strategies that Ortega characterized as "dehumanized," sought an active reengagement between art and experience. In his descriptive essay, which was often misread as prescriptive, Ortega characterized modern art as a whole (not only the vanguards) as "dehumanized." This word was intended to highlight modern art's distancing and antimimetic quality, or its "will to style," that is, the propensity to stylize or "derealize" its human content or living forms (67; HW 25). In the modern mode, Ortega observed, an object of art is artistic only to the degree that it is not real. Whereas the average person, he asserted, prefers art that most resembles ordinary life, in modern art, a "preoccupation with the human content of the work is in principle incompatible with aesthetic enjoyment" (53; HW 9–10). To make his point, Ortega constructed the now cliché example of the windowpane through which we view a garden. While mimetic or realist art encourages the recipient to focus on the garden or the human content, modern art, in Ortega's view, turns perception toward the pane and the transparency inherent in a work of art.

In its focus on modern art's distancing strategies that shift perceptual modes, Ortega's concept of dehumanization is not unlike the early Russian formalist idea of defamiliarization (*ostranenie* in Victor Shklovsky's

1917 essay, "Art as Technique") or Bertolt Brecht's alienation, or *Ver-fremdungseffekt*. In their emphasis on the change in reader or spectator habits of perception provoked by art that displays its own fabricated substance, all of these concepts are comparable on the simply formal level to what Bürger denominates in *Theory of the Avant-Garde* the "nonorganic" work of art. Here again Bürger is talking about the kind of art that calls attention to its constituent parts and resists the receiver's attempts to naturalize it or perceive it as a comfortably organic whole. But Bürger—and here Brecht may be considered his predecessor—examines the estranging or distancing quality of vanguardist art and comes to conclusions about its effects quite different from those we find in *The Dehumanization of Art*. This is because for Bürger the distancing effects of nonorganic art constitute far more than a matter of technique.

In the historical avant-gardes, Bürger argues, "shocking the recipient becomes the dominant principle of artistic intent" (18), a principle he situates within vanguardist activity as a whole. During the historical avant-gardes, he affirms, art entered a stage of self-criticism as artists questioned the category *art* and its claims to autonomy from nonart or life. Vanguardist activity, Bürger argues, involved far more than challenging the notion of a work of art and sought rather "the liquidation of art as an activity that is split off from the praxis of life" (56). In this view, then, it is precisely through the "dehumanization" that alters perceptions by calling attention to the Orteguian windowpane that the avant-gardes forced artistic recipients to think about the idea of art itself and its relationship to life. If we filter Ortega's metaphor through Bürger's view, we can argue that the vanguards challenged artistic recipients, notwithstanding the daunting optical gymnastics required, to focus on the interaction of the windowpane and the garden, a reflexive engagement of art with life. Thus the very distancing quality in modern art that Ortega called dehumanization turns the public toward, not away from, lived experience.

I have already argued that Latin American vanguardism conceived art and intellectual endeavors in activist terms. Extending Bürger's view, I would also argue more specifically that the drive toward engagement—intellectual, social, or metaphysical—was a defining feature of the international vanguard movements and that this was particularly true in Latin America. Artists employed antimimetic strategies, among a range of vanguardist activities, precisely in order to turn art toward experience in more provocative ways. By "engagement" I do not mean concrete, politically motivated encounters, although, as I have already noted, many vanguardists did turn at particular moments to openly political causes. I use the term more comprehensively to designate various kinds of involvement or immersion, including confrontational engagement by artistic works or events with readers or spectators; critical or intellectual engagement through their work by artists with their immediate surroundings; or a desired metaphysical engagement with existence or the cosmos by artists seeking transrational plenitude. In Latin America, moreover, vanguardist activity, as I have shown for individual countries, was quite often critically engaged with what was regarded as specifically Latin American experience.

In this vein, the concept of a "rehumanization" of art alludes on a second level to a contemporary response within the Latin American vanguard movements to Ortega's essay, an averse reaction more to the word *dehumanization* itself than to the specific points raised in the piece. This negative response to a word or to what was perceived as the spirit behind it in no way minimized Ortega's contribution to the emergence of vanguardist activity in Latin America. Along with the transcontinental connections established by Latin American writers in direct contact with French or Spanish peninsular movements, Ortega's widely distributed *Revista de Occidente* was a primary source of information about the latest developments in modern art. This debt was frequently acknowledged, and Ortega's 1916 and 1929 visits to Latin America fostered enduring intellectual contacts. Nonetheless, there was a fairly widespread reaction in Latin America's vanguard movements to what was perceived, accurately or not, as the gist of Ortega's widely disseminated essay. Art, it was argued in countless manifestos and critical writings, even in its most modern forms, had everything to do with experience, and the words *human* and *humanized* became veritable buzzwords in Latin American vanguardist discourse. This did not always constitute a direct response to Ortega but sometimes simply expressed a particular artistic orientation or tone. But it is significant, for example, that even Vicente Huidobro, Latin America's most ardent advocate of autonomous art, who in his 1916 "Arte poética" urged poets to create their own roses rather than celebrate nature's, spoke of art's humanizing effects. Thus he argued that art should "humanize things" (*OC* 1: 680) and explained in the 1925 "Manifiesto de manifiestos" (published in the same year as Ortega's essay) that poets must have a certain dose of "singular humanity" with which to imbue their work (*OC* 1: 670). César Vallejo, whose poetry is often lauded for its human qualities even when it sabotages reader comprehension, defined "human" art as that which made contact in some way with its creator's lived experience and urged artists to seek a "human timbre" in their work (*MPP* 242). The poet Carlos Drummond de Andrade, in the manifesto launching Brazil's *A Revista* in 1925, included in his plan for action the resolution to "humanize Brazil" and suggested that this would be accomplished by artists ready to "collide with real life" (GMT 338).

Although they did not necessarily delve as deeply as Ortega into the theoretical problems he had posed, other writers were clearly reacting specifically to his essay. In a 1927 piece for the Puerto Rican periodical *Vórtice,* for example, the poet Evaristo Ribera Chevremont argued passionately for a vitalist and engaged conception of artistic activity and suggested that modern art could best be characterized by substituting the prefix *des-* (as in *deshumanización*) with the prefix *super-*. The new art, he argued, "does not become dehumanized but instead becomes humanized just as it penetrates the soul of humanity and nature" ("Trozos" 2). In his observations on surrealism, Alejo Carpentier explained that those using the term "dehumanization" (he did not mention Ortega by name) were accurately describing a modern turn away from sentimental, domestic intrigues. But he then went on to argue against characterizing the vanguards, surrealism in particular, as aloof or skeptical and to affirm that his was an era of passionate faith in the value of intellectual and artistic pursuits (HV 145–49). Martí Casanovas of Cuba's *Revista de Avance* and Magda Portal writing for Peru's *Amauta* both invoked humanized art with more explicitly sociopolitical tones. Casanovas attributed dehumanization to the bourgeois spirit and rejected artistic speculations of a merely formal quality because they lacked "human value" or "social transcendence." The best art of all periods, including the modern, he affirmed, responded to the "richness of its human content" ("Arte nuevo" 119). Portal argued in 1927, two years after the appearance of Ortega's essay, that while some new artists had failed to see a connection between innovation and social engagement, the more recent Latin American vanguardists had emerged in a milieu marked by the "humanization of art," conscious of a "double mission in aesthetics and in life" (*MPP* 208).

The two supporters of vanguardist activity who responded most directly to Ortega and revealed a careful reading of his central points were Jaime Torres Bodet of Mexico's Contemporáneos group and Mariátegui, editor of Peru's *Amauta* and one of Latin America's most discerning commentators on both Latin American and European vanguardism. In a 1928 piece appropriately entitled "La deshumanización del arte," Torres Bodet, who was then developing antimimetic strategies in his own prose fiction, challenged Ortega's assessment that modern art sought to "triumph over the human" (*Contemporáneos* 127). Art, he explained, should always make contact in some way with the "disorderly humanity" that Ortega believed modernity had exiled from the work of art. In fact, Torres Bodet argued, art, however modern, required by definition a "struggle" with the "human matter" that it sought to stylize (*Contemporáneos* 123–27). Torres Bodet further underscored his position in an essay on the new poetry affirming that "reality itself" would always supply the stimulus for a true work of art (*Contemporáneos* 29). In one of his most important essays, "Arte, revolución y decadencia," Mariátegui suggested that Ortega's essay, though on target with many points, was also responsible for fostering within the Hispanic world a misunderstanding about the nature of modern art. The concept of dehumanization, Mariátegui argued, responded primarily to modern art's detached spirit (decadent, he called it) but failed to recognize its simultaneously engaging and even revolutionary qualities. In other writings, Mariátegui advocated for artists a synthesis of technical innovation and critical engagement with the world. Although he recognized the critical power of what he called "formal conquests," that is, of the vanguards' "dehumanized" strategies in Ortega's terms, he also argued that art's paradoxical relationship to life should be one of engaged autonomy.

A New World orientation permeated the work of both of these writers and of many of their contemporaries addressing the question of Latin American art's human substance. Torres Bodet spelled it out. "*The Dehumanization of Art*," he wrote, "is a European book, with European facts, written for Europeans. This circumstance . . . is a danger for the youth of America who have yet to venture to dream of an art of their own, free of sentimental heritages and biological servitude" (*Contemporáneos* 125). Mariátegui, too, while frequently criticizing his generation's utopian Americanism and guarded about what new creations might spring forth from his continent's soil, shared many of his contemporaries' attraction to Spengler's New World idealism and peppered his own assessment of postwar European culture with Spenglerian metaphors: a decadent civilization of "decrepitude" was facing its "twilight" and its "sunset." Thus the concept of a "rehumanization" of art alludes on a third level to the problem of Latin America's culturally specific relationship to the currents of modernity embodied in the literary vanguards. I address this issue most directly in the third and fifth chapters, but the problem shapes the entire study. On the broadest level, my work is founded on the rather evident premise, to which I have already alluded in describing regional developments, that Latin American vanguardism, notwithstanding the interaction with European currents, unfolded within its own cultural contexts and that the life experience with which it openly engaged was often peculiarly its own. More specifically, some Latin American writers claimed vanguardism itself as a fundamentally Latin American phenomenon. As I explore in the chapters on Americanism and language, this move was actually quite different in kind from, even counter to, the broader claim that Latin American innovative art was more "humanized" than the European. Instead, Latin American vanguardist activity sometimes constructed images comparable to what Ortega would call dehumanization, or to similar ideas of estrangement or nonorganicity, not as mere aesthetic strategies or effects but as phenomena peculiar to Latin America's lived, historical experience.

To recapitulate, then, the concept of a "rehumanization" of art points to three broad ideas that underlie these five chapters: (1) that Latin America's vanguards sought a reengagement between art and experience; (2) that Latin American writers often sought to reshape and redefine, with various purposes in mind, what Ortega had identified as the dehumanized quality of modern art; and (3) that Latin American vanguardist activity sometimes recast vanguardism itself, in particular, the defamiliarizing features encompassed in Ortega's word *dehumanized,* as peculiarly Latin American phenomena. Framed by these ideas, each chapter addresses the more specific artistic and cultural problems investigated by Latin American vanguardists. In the first chapter, "Constructing an Audience, Concrete and Illusory: Manifestos for Performing and Performance Manifestos," I analyze numerous manifestos as well as creative works by Mário de Andrade, Xavier Icaza, Joaquín Pasos and José Coronel Urtecho, and Alejo Carpentier. Here I show first how vanguardist manifestos employ specific rhetorical strategies to act out a given aesthetic position as the dramatic confrontation of a dynamic speaker with two audiences, one participatory and one adversarial. In a comparable mode, the four generically hybrid manifesto-style performance texts examined here display the type of art that they espouse, portray art as a "doing" process that incorporates its recipient into the doing, and dramatize the desired spectator's participation in an encounter of conflicting artistic positions within a context of cultural affirmation.

Chapter 2, "Outward Turns of the Vagabond Eye/I: The Vanguards' Portraits of the Artist," examines, in addition to vanguardist manifestos and some poetry, prose fiction texts by Roberto Arlt, Jaime Torres Bodet, Martín Adán, and Oswald de Andrade. Here I demonstrate that, interacting with prevalent poetic images of the artist and drawing on modernity's technological and activist motifs, the manifestos recast the aestheticist tradition of lyric subjectivity and cosmic detachment into an artist figure of movement and action, still introspective but also marked by the dynamic images of the times. Intensifying these tensions, prose fiction portraits of the artist construct an urban-vagabond artistic persona. Marked by an elusive interior consistency, this artist's lyric inheritance—verbal virtuosity and a sharp inner eye—is often turned outward toward critical interaction with both literary tradition and a concrete world.

The third chapter, " 'Surely from his lips a cockatoo will fly': The Vanguards' Stories of the New World," turns to problems of cultural specificity raised both in the manifestos and in creative texts by Mário de Andrade, Miguel Angel Asturias, Gamaliel Churata, Luis Cardoza y Aragón, and Alejo Carpentier. Manifestos with an Americanist orientation generally perpetuate romantic, organicist myths of America through images of an integrated, telluric body-continent, rooted to ancestral origins, a body for which the new American artist will provide a voice. On the surface, prose and poetic creative texts reinforce these images. But, playing with vanguardist motifs of originality, discovery, and totalizing quests, these works also undermine organicist New World myths and pose an America of the "radically disparate" (Bürger 63), in which vanguardism's dislocations and nonorganicity are recast as peculiar to Latin American experience.

Chapter 4, "On the Interstices of Art and Life: Theatrical Workouts in Critical Perception," returns in a more theoretical vein and through plays by Roberto Arlt, Xavier Villaurrutia, Vicente Huidobro, and Oswald de Andrade to the artistic recipient. The vanguards' attention to the interaction between art and experience is often manifested in an antimimetic impulse and a focus on the process of representation. Theater's palpable connections with that process offered singular opportunities for vanguardist inquiries. Through sometimes highly abstract dramatic texts, writers exploited the stresses in theatrical expression between Artaudian antimimetic yearnings for immediacy and presence (as identified by Derrida), on the one hand, and the stage's "testament to what separates," on the other (Herbert Blau, *The Eye of Prey* 183), to explore theoretically the boundaries between art and life. Focusing on theatrical fantasies of personal or social transformation, the works examined tamper with performative conventions. In the process, they expose spectator complicity in the performance and reconstruct the act of watching a play as a strenuous exercise in critical perception, designed, if not to transform worlds, to challenge the ways that we see them.

Chapter 5, "From Early Words to the Vernacular Inflection: Vanguard Tales of Linguistic Encounter," readdresses the vanguardist focus on the autochthonous but with more specific attention to language and linguistic identity. Here I draw on manifestos and a wide range of poetic, prose, and dramatic works with language themes. As with the Americanist stories, the vanguards' focus on language becomes intertwined in Latin America with issues of cultural critique. On one level, the movement's linguistic thematics intersect with ongoing historical debates about the oral and the written. In addition, inventive and recuperative linguistic ventures, incorporating fabricated, "primary" languages or autochthonous linguistic artifacts into self-consciously modern texts, are embedded in seemingly contradictory stories. On the one hand, artists seek their expressive power in the utopian notion of a linguistically pure, original space. On the other, they undermine this idea with a culturally affirmative poetics of linguistic impurity and estrangement, underscoring the foreignness of all language and the critical power of cultural translations.

Although the five chapters address major artistic and cultural problems posed by the vanguards in Latin America, this study does not pretend to present an all-encompassing or conclusive assessment of the movement. Other issues touched on here might well provide the focus for future work by the growing community of *vanguardista* investigators, for example, the complex and problematic relationship of women writers and intellectuals to primarily male-dominated vanguardist activities or the often contradictory vanguardist approach to popular or mass culture.[22] Within the scope of the topics they do address, however, these chapters reveal the serious, intellectually rigorous, and sometimes theoretically dense nature of vanguardist activity in Latin America. The writers who participated in these movements asked themselves difficult questions about what art should be like and how artists should be spending their time in rapidly changing modern milieus, about how to make forceful contact of consequence with readers and spectators, about the unstable quality and elusive interior consistency of an artistically defined self, and about the pertinence of radical artistic experimentation to long-standing cultural and linguistic identity problems shaping Latin American life. Readers will find that their polemical, exploratory, contentious, and qualified answers point directly to many of the artistic, linguistic, and cultural questions that continue to mark literary and theoretical discourses in these, our own times.

I.

Constructing an Audience, Concrete and Illusory

Manifestos for Performing and Performance Manifestos

It is necessary . . . to undertake the conquest of the public, seizing its attention by means of artistic coups.
　　　　—"Ligera exposición y proclama de la Anti-Academia Nicaragüense"

Comrade reader: A great pleasure and a great honor to discover you.
　　　　—"Apresentação," *Terra Roxa e Outras Terras*

At this moment, we are witnessing the spectacle of ourselves.
　　　　—Manuel Maples Arce, *Actual—No. 1— Hoja de Vanguardia*

On a summer evening in 1931, a group of aspiring young Nicaraguan artists executed a curious recital for a Granada audience. Dressed as a clown and carrying a ladder, a nail, a hammer, and a rope, Luis Downing recited "El arenque," his translation of Charles Cross's "Le Hareng Saur." Simultaneously, Pablo Antonio Cuadra donned boxing gloves and, according to Jorge Arellano's account, declaimed his own poem "Stadium," punctuating his performance with punches in the air. Octavio Rocha, made up as a crocodile, recited selections from the Cuban poet Nicolás Guillén's *Sóngoro cosongo* (1931). The evening culminated with a dramatic recital by Joaquín Pasos of an early version of the *Chinfonía burguesa,* a performative, multivoiced poetic composition that was later transformed into a play. Pasos's recitation was accompanied by an offstage orchestration of drums, cymbals, whistles, and shots (Arellano, "El movimiento," 32–33).

Through this event, the Anti-Academia Nicaragüense (Nicaraguan Anti-Academy) sought to confront a live audience with a palpable manifestation of the varieties of art the group had advocated in its detailed first manifesto published in Granada in April of that year. Although the Anti-Academy was one of the later vanguardist groups to emerge in Latin America, its activities were still reminiscent in spirit of the audience-assaulting, performative phase of the early European historical avant-gardes. An integral part of that movement's carnivalesque legend, this phase included the most notorious early futurist parades and *serate*, confrontational and occasionally riot-producing evening demonstrations, the dadaist "Africa Nights" in Zurich's Cabaret Voltaire, and the public-provoking manifestations of later Berlin dadaists and early Parisian surrealists. The radical playfulness of these manifestations thinly disguised a serious sense of purpose. These events constituted a fundamental component of the vanguards' exploration of artistic media and the social processes that shape them, as well as the impulse to create new audiences for a new art.[1]

There is a fundamental connection between the oral public manifestation and the written manifesto that usually provided the self-defining cornerstone of vanguardist activity. Both the manifesto and the manifestation assume a polemical stance on a new kind of art; both dramatize the conflict with aesthetic tradition and societal expectations posed by that art; and both seek to resituate the artistic recipient in the eye of the creative storm. Because of the specific cultural environments in which Latin American vanguardism unfolded, audience-engaging evenings such as the Nicaraguan Anti-Academy's multimedia production were somewhat less frequent than the futurists' ribald evenings or Dada's public-provoking events. But the written manifesto was a predilect genre for Latin American vanguardists. In addition, some writers also produced a hybrid of manifestation and manifesto in a singular kind of text I call a performance manifesto. Combining elements of poetry, music, drama, oratory, and sometimes dance, these multigeneric texts constitute scripts for a public performance and build on the intrinsic theatricality of the manifesto itself. Such performance manifestos include Brazilian writer Mário de Andrade's "As enfibraturas do Ipiranga" (1922), Mexican Xavier Icaza's *Magnavox 1926* (1926), the *Chinfonía burguesa* (1931–1936) by the Nicaraguans Joaquín Pasos and José Coronel Urtecho, and *El milagro de Anaquillé* (1927) by the Cuban Alejo Carpentier. The manifesto quality of these multigeneric creative works becomes most evident if we examine first the performative qualities of the vanguardist manifesto itself.

Palpable Public Display: Manifestations and Manifestos

From the late teens into the early 1930s, written manifestos that directly confronted an implicit audience with particular aesthetic and cultural positions proliferated in Latin America as widely as the ephemeral groups and little magazines that produced and published them. But because until recently research on Latin America's avantgardes had often focused more on authors and works than on vanguardism as an activity, it is difficult to determine the extent to which self-designated vanguardist groups and individuals engaged in actual public manifestations. But, in addition to the Nicaraguan Anti-Academy's evening of lyric theater, a few other such activities have been documented. The legendary 1922 Semana de Arte Moderna that officially launched the São Paulo phase of Brazilian *modernismo* included three evenings of audacious multigeneric, multimedia presentations that were confrontational in their novelty: lectures on *modernismo* and contemporary art by Graça Aranha and Ronald de Carvalho; poetry and prose readings by Mário and Oswald de Andrade, Manuel Bandeira, Ribeiro Couto, Plínio Salgado, and Guilherme de Almeida; exhibitions of cubist paintings by Anita Malfatti and sculptures by Vítor Brécheret; and a piano recital of music by Heitor Villa-Lobos. Mexico's *estridentistas* gradually took over the Europa café in Mexico City. This establishment, which the group renamed "El café de nadie" (Nobody's Café) and which provided the title and setting for Arqueles Vela's 1926 *estridentista* novel, was the site of polemics, recitations, and the concoction of group endeavors. In April 1924, for example, the group organized a public exhibition including prose and poetry readings, paintings by various artists, a display of Germán Cueto's "masks" of the group's principal members, and an exhibition of cubist sculpture (Schneider, *El estridentismo* 85–86). Also, in 1924, the *estridentista* Luis Quintanilla along with Carlos González and Francisco Domínguez organized the short-lived Teatro del Murciélago, a multidisciplinary project conceived to develop Mexican cultural life in literature, plastic arts, music, and theater. In September, the theater group presented a performative evening at the Teatro Olympia in a multimedia synthesis of folkloric music, dance, and dramatizations designed to promote the idea of a national art as well as to suggest a comprehensive concept of a total performative event (Schneider, *El estridentismo* 107–8).

In a similar spirit, during the mid-1920s members of Buenos Aires's Florida group produced the *Revista Oral,* the brainchild of the transplanted Peruvian *simplista* poet Alberto Hidalgo. Staged at the Royal Keller Café, each of the review's sixteen "issues," by Christopher Towne Leland's account, included readings or recitations of poetry, polemics, and literary satires, or even public trials of favorite artistic targets such as Argentine poet Leopoldo Lugones (Leland 35). Peru's principal regional vanguardist gathering, the *indigenista* Grupo Orkopata of Puno that met regularly between 1925 and 1930, periodically counterbalanced its serious seminar-style exchanges on art, literature, folklore, and history with more boisterous and bohemian *Pascanas nocturnas* (Nocturnal Interludes). On these occasions, group members reportedly dressed up as Indians, drank *chicha,* chewed coca leaves, and interspersed experimental poetry and prose readings with songs in Quechua and Aymara (Tamayo Herrera 265).[2] In 1929, Puerto Rico's *atalayistas,* who held regular secret meetings at San Juan's Ateneo puertorriqueño, sought to shock the public with long hair, unusual attire, and new names (such as "Mistagogo en Ayunas" and "Archimpámpano de Zintar"). In July 1930, the group held a public soirée at the Ateneo with guitar music, poetry readings, and a provocative lecture entitled "Cristo debió tener un hijo" (Christ Should Have Had a Son) (LHA 99–105).

More enduring than these extravagant events were the numerous manifestos published in Latin America primarily during the 1920s. These texts served several functions. A few, in particular those produced by the most prolific of Latin America's manifesto writers, Vicente Huidobro, laid out in detail the aesthetic ideas of a particular individual. More commonly, manifestos were published by groups or individuals representing them to announce the creation of a new "ism" or aesthetic orientation, the constitution of a new artistic gathering, or the publication of a new little magazine. Thus manifestos, proclamations, or polemical pieces with a manifesto style or tone appeared in Argentina, Brazil, Chile, Cuba, the Dominican Republic, Ecuador, Mexico, Nicaragua, Peru, Puerto Rico, Uruguay, and Venezuela.

If one examines these confrontational documents closely, the recasting of vanguardist manifestos into more explicitly performative texts such as Mário de Andrade's "As enfibraturas do Ipiranga" or Pasos and Coronel Urtecho's *Chinfonía burguesa* seems like an obvious move. The aesthetic details of a particular program advocated by a written manifesto—radical metaphors, disruptive syntax, typographical experiments, free verse, culturally specific art—were often less critical for what these documents communicated than were the expository structures and rhetorical strategies with which these programs were laid out. The prototypical manifesto possessed a highly dramatic structure, and its confrontational discourse put into play conflicting views of art and culture by employing rhetorical strategies with a potentially theatrical effect. In *The Futurist Moment,* the title for which is drawn from Renato Poggioli's characterization of vanguardism's futuristic phase (Poggioli 68–74), Marjorie Perloff notes the theatrical quality of the futurist manifestos. Indeed, the futurists, Perloff and others have insisted, provided the model for subsequent vanguardist manifestos. While suggesting that he wrote mediocre and derivative poetry and prose, Perloff notes that Marinetti was a brilliant conceptual artist who employed public performances and written manifestos to "transform politics into a kind of *lyric theater*" (84; my emphasis). In "The Work of Art in the Age of Mechanical Reproduction," Walter Benjamin noted a similar quality in the vanguards' advocacy of an art of palpable public engagement that eventually unfolded into the Fascist aestheticizing of politics and the Communist politicizing of art (242), two sides of the same audience-engaging coin. It is true, as Nelson Osorio has pointed out, that Latin American writers and critics of the period frequently kept their distance from Marinetti himself (*MPP* 29),[3] and Latin American manifesto writers of the 1920s drew on varied models, including early Huidobro manifestos, the writings of peninsular Spanish *ultraísmo,* and, eventually, Parisian Dada and even surrealist activities. But the "futurist moment," as Poggioli demonstrates, is a characteristic that belongs to all of the avant-gardes (68), and, to some extent, this is also true of futurism's rhetorical strategies. Thus many Latin American manifestos possess the striking theatrical tone and display specific dramatic qualities observed by Perloff in the futurist documents.

Specifically, Perloff notes a we-you communicative framework in Marinetti's manifestos, a scheme in which a communal "we" of the artists addresses the collective "you" of the mass audience (87), a group that most manifestos simultaneously provoke and court. I believe that Perloff's observation may be expanded, however, for in many Latin

American manifestos there is actually a more complex we-you-they scheme, a triadic relationship that is fundamental for defining the artistic confrontation that the manifesto embodies. The manifesto's speaking voice frequently assumes the first person, an "I" or a "we" identified with a specific aesthetic or ideological position. But this speaker is actually inclined to address two audiences, one more directly than the other. An explicit audience, the "you" openly addressed, is courted in openly engaging tones. The manifesto's speaker seeks this audience's support for whatever cultural or aesthetic program is being proposed and casts this "you" as an ally in the struggle against the other, more implicit audience that provides a target for the document's attack. This second audience is rarely addressed directly, but the vehemence with which the manifesto's speakers characterize this absent "they" betrays an unconfessed hope that this audience, too, is listening and will be moved. This absent but (it is hoped) eavesdropping audience is held accountable for everything the manifesto challenges: the "fossilized" past, artistic conventions, and outmoded cultural institutions. Thus the manifesto dramatizes a sharply drawn opposition between a new aesthetic program and the implicit, third-person audience whose views it assaults. This communicative scheme is not unlike that adopted by a political candidate who addresses an absent but deliberately unnamed opponent: "There are those who would do things differently." At the same time, the manifesto's explicit recipient, the "you" it openly addresses, is cast in a position analogous to that of the spectator to an almost Manichaean dramatic conflict and is emphatically directed to take sides.

A closer analysis of the Latin American manifestos' communicative structure reveals how essential this scheme is for constructing a concrete identity and artistic position. In her study of Argentina's vanguards, Francine Masiello has insightfully observed that manifestos for different groups constructed diverse images of an artistic self and the foundation for pacts among writers often based on an oppositional stance (70–78). But I am concerned more specifically here with examining the concrete strategies employed in manifestos throughout Latin America for imagining particular kinds of relationships between an artistic group and its varied audiences. Most speaking voices in these documents use specific rhetorical moves to create a sense of collectivity, a single identity constituted through many. Often this is accomplished simply with various forms of the grammatical first-person plural, "nosotros," "nós," "nuestro," and so on. In other cases, as in the first *estridentismo* manifesto "Actual," a singular, first-person speaker occasionally slips into the plural but, more important, offers a concluding list of supporters, a "Directory of the Vanguard." This common strategy is employed to legitimize a single speaker through the support of a concrete collectivity. In other cases, as in Alberto Hidalgo's manifesto poem "La nueva poesía," the speaker slides back and forth between a series of "Yo soi" (I am) affirmations and references to groups with whom this "I" identifies, for example, "the men of this Century of War and Valor" (*MPP* 49). Even Vicente Huidobro, known for an aggressive overuse of the grammatical first person in constructing his individual literary creed, broadens his speaking position in the landmark "Non serviam" manifesto by incorporating his fellow poets into "we" statements and makes similar references in the "Arte poética" of *creacionismo:* "Only for us do all things exist under the sun" (*OC* 1: 255). Manifesto-style editorials in both *Martín Fierro* and *Klaxon* create a sense of group identity by substituting the journal's name for the personal pronoun and combining this name with a singular verb, for example, "Klaxon is Klaxist" or, more explicitly, "Klaxon has a collective soul" (GMT 295).

Much of what the manifesto's first-person voice actually says serves simply to affirm the speakers' own sense of being and identity: "We are to be!" in the "Gesto" manifesto of *noísmo* (LHA 245); "We are we" and "We are Green" in Brazil's *Verde* magazine (GMT 350); "We shall be! We shall be!" in the second manifesto of *euforismo* (LHA 232); or the simple, affirmative "Somos" ("We Are") title for a manifesto appearing in *válvula* of Caracas (*MPP* 277). *Martín Fierro* makes explicit this affirmation-of-being process: *"Martín Fierro* feels the indispensable need to define itself" (*MPP* 134). The concrete definitions that follow identify the speakers closely with the advocated new art or "new sensibility." Both are described with hyperbolic imagery of youth, vitality, newness, potency, freedom, fecundity, aggression, and raw emotion. Thus speakers in *noísmo*'s "Gesto" manifesto speak of their "youthful audacity" and their "fistful of creative energy" (LHA 242), and the "Manifesto antropófago" characterizes its collective speaker as "strong and vengeful like the Jabuti" (GMT 357). Speakers in Chile's "Rosa náutica" manifesto claim to be a new generation of intellectuals, "ascending to the plains of the sun" (*MPP* 121), framers of the *atalayismo* manifesto describe themselves as "warlike spirits" (LHA 247), and the *estridentistas* are members of the "triumphant ranks" (*MPP* 125). The theatricality of these characterizations lies in the imagery's palpable dynamism. We can visualize these speakers in emphatic, even frenetic, motion before us, and this quality is reinforced by the long lists of action verbs that spell out a group's specific artistic program: "let us shout, let us destroy, let us create!" the *euforismo* manifesto proclaims (LHA 228).

A striking feature of the manifesto's speaking "we" is the reliance on its two audiences, the document's directly addressed "you" and its more obliquely invoked "they," for the process of self-definition. Normally, the manifesto characterizes its directly addressed "you" on a grand scale in terms that are simultaneously specific and select, on the one hand (poets, artists, "special" people), and more general and all-encompassing, on the other: "the poets of America," "the youth of America," "the creative spirits," "the men of the universal fraternity," "the youth of the world," "young poets," "all of Mexico's young poets, painters, and sculptors," "the intellectual youth of the state of Puebla," or "the literary youth of Puerto Rico."[4]

The modes of addressing this rhetorical "you" reveal contradictory pulls in the vanguardist project. Specifically, the vacillating between specificity (poets and artists) and a more global generality (the youth of America, for example) manifests the tension in vanguardist discourse between the elitism of the manifesto's speaking voice—a self-selective and privileged "we"—and the impulse to address a mass audience. In his work on the avant-gardes, Andreas Huyssen has recast the term "the great divide" to describe the "volatile" quality that has characterized the relationship between high art and mass culture since the mid-nineteenth century and, more specifically, to designate the kind of critical discourse that distinguishes between the two (vii–viii). In their critique of the previous generation's aestheticism, the European avant-gardes unquestionably attacked such dichotomies but at the same time exacerbated that great divide. For example, although the futurists provoked riots at their *serate,* in Marinetti's "The Futurist Synthetic Theatre," their objective was to instill a "current of confidence" in the audience (*Selected Writings* 128). The dadaists declared that they would "spit on humanity" (Ribemont-Dessaignes 109), and yet Tristan Tzara envisioned in *Seeds and Bran* a utopian, transformational union between artists and a knowledgeable public: "the wisdom of crowds . . . joined with the occasional madness of a few delicious beings" (*Approximate Man* 215).

The Latin American writer who perhaps grasped this tension and expressed it most cogently was José Carlos Mariátegui, editor of the Peruvian vanguardist periodical *Amauta,* who carried out an extensive critical inquiry into the nature of the European and Latin American avant-gardes. In Mariátegui's view, contemporary art would best serve its "hedonistic and liberating function" by incorporating the great divide's polarities. Specifically, this art would be simultaneously "rigorously aristocratic" in its vanguardism and "democratic" in its human spirit, qualities that Mariátegui perceived in the works of Charlie Chaplin (*OC* 3: 74). What sharpens this aristocratic-democratic tension in Latin American manifestos, documents produced primarily in countries with high illiteracy rates and still relatively small reading publics, is the implicit, sometimes confessed, recognition that the desired mass audience the speaker is addressing directly does not really exist as a separate entity but is simply an extension of the speaker's utopian project for change. In part, this admission is manifested in the hyperbolic characterizations of the "you" as an entity far too vast to assume a concrete identity, such as "the men of the universal fraternity" or "the youth of America."[5] But these phrases also manifest the vanguardists' awareness of their common enterprise and the continental spirit, as I have noted, embodied in the university reform movements. In addition, in the manifesto's communicative scheme, verb forms reinforce the mirror identification of this "you" with the manifesto's speaking "we." It is not uncommon for reference to a directly addressed "you" ("young poets") to be followed immediately by a plan for action expressed through the first-person plural imperative form, for example, "let us raise (*levantemos*) our voices," a form in which the second person is absorbed by the first. Such forms are common in political rhetoric ("let us move forward . . ."), but in the vanguardist manifesto, the "you" is repeatedly equated with the "we," as poets seek the support of poets, American youth speak to American youth, and, as in the case of the Nicaraguan Anti-Academy, speakers seek the support of those exactly like themselves: "We count on the goodwill of all anti-academics" (*MPP* 377). Occasionally, a manifesto openly confesses that the separate, supportive audience it addresses does not, indeed, exist and must be conjured up or hammered out from an amorphous mass public. Thus the speaker in the "Apresentação" of *Terra Roxa e Outras Terras* boasts that the journal is destined to a public that does not exist and later adds that this is "a journal in search of a reader" (GMT 341). The speaker addresses this nonexistent audience directly—"the hypothetical and uncertain being for whom we compose this"—and then adds (in the line that provides an epigraph for this chapter), "Comrade reader: A great pleasure and a great honor to discover you" (GMT 342). Thus, to affirm its own existence, the manifesto's speaking "we" advocating a new art must construct the illusion of a live audience to receive and respond positively to its program.

Equally essential for the manifesto's project is the audience that is never directly invoked, those against whom the speaking "we" define themselves. Interestingly, the manifesto characterizes this absent, adversarial audience that it never acknowledges directly in far more concrete terms than the all-encompassing "you." To some degree, this comes about because many manifesto speakers have certain real-life adversaries in mind, artists or critics from the local scene whose names may even sometimes be mentioned. But, more important, in constructing the collective, integrated speaker, the manifesto relies heavily on what it is challenging, and the oppositional stance is inextricably linked to the speaker's own identity. A typical case is the *Martín Fierro* manifesto that, before laying out its own program, enumerates what it opposes with the repetitive "as opposed to." The link between the targets of its attack and *Martín Fierro*'s own identity is reinforced syntactically by blending the list of things opposed into the list of what the journal supports. Similarly, the Brazilian *Verde* manifesto reveals the relative unimportance attributable to the specific object of attack and emphasizes the indispensability of the adversarial stance itself: "We are who we want to be and not those whom others want us to be," and "We are different. Even extremely diverse. Much more different than the folks next door" (GMT 349).

Although the manifestos' lists of what was opposed were meticulously detailed and often seemingly endless, most vanguardist groups opposed fundamentally the same things: social and artistic conventions and traditions in general or, in particular, romanticism, symbolism, and/or elements of Spanish American *modernismo,* particular elements of European vanguardism, or specific writers or critics who somehow stood for these movements. The manifesto's theatrical quality, however, derives from the oppositional stance itself and from the rich, often satirical imagery with which these documents construct an absent, adversarial "they" to complete a triadic communicative scheme. In sharp contrast to the images of youth, vitality, power, and authenticity that characterize the speaking "we," the adversary under attack is constructed with images of fossilization, decay, decrepitude, inauthenticity, and physical and emotional malaise. Thus a sampling of manifestos from numerous countries yields an assortment of similar adjectives used by manifesto speakers to characterize the objects of their attack: "putrid," "rancid," "spongy and sparse," "fossilized," "senile," "sickly," "valetudinarian," "atrophied," and "worm-eaten." Particularly colorful noun designations for adversary targets include an *estridentismo* attack on "ideological rancidolatry" (*MPP* 125–26) and the "Manifesto antropófago" aversion to "vegetable elites" (GMT 356).

The dramatic oppositions constructed by these documents imply a reader who will be drawn into the conflict, who will identify with the directly addressed "you" of the youth of America, and, more important, who will recoil from the pejorative imagery of decay and decrepitude surrounding the adversary under attack. The rhetorical strategies, moreover, imply a reader who is a flesh-and-blood listener and spectator, a live audience witnessing a performance. The nouns and pronouns of direct address, the enumerative declarations of principles, the easily identifiable and simplistic oppositions, and the clipped, telegraphic phrases marked by exaggeration and insult all contribute to the ambience of an oratorical event, scripted in a text to be read aloud, proclaimed, or performed. In addition, the speaker's cultivation of lyrical prowess and verbal cuteness through comical, insulting, and sometimes scatological one-liners coined to attack the opponent and to characterize the new art reinforces that speaker's identity as a linguistically agile performer. "Tupi or not Tupi," quips the speaker in the "Manifesto antropófago" (GMT 353) while addressing the serious matter of Brazil's response to Europe's primitivist representations of the New World.

A theatrical transition from manifesting to performing is also intimated in the word *manifesto,* specifically, in its etymological kinship with the verb *to make manifest:* to make public, to render concrete, to transpose to the sensorial realm, particularly the visual. To manifest is to "make palpably evident or certain by showing or displaying" (*Webster's Third International,* 1986 ed.), an act that presupposes a viewer. One of the fundamental strategies for involving the spectator in the showing is the reliance on enumeration. Perloff notes that this device, a common political strategy for holding audience attention, showed that the futurist authors meant business (96). But I would add that the manifestos' endless lists, itemized by letters, arabic or roman numerals, or simply the repetition of opening phrases such as "as opposed to . . . ," serve other functions as well. Listing is a form of verbal display, a tactic for pulling out, as if from a magician's hat, one item after another and revealing these to an audience. As the list becomes longer and longer, in particular if it includes short, telegraphic phrases, the cumulative effect on the reader-listener is a sensory bombardment reinforced by the verbal aggression in the manifesto's tone. The rapid-fire list also underscores the theatrical sense of visual and verbal motion already constructed through the image of a powerful and dynamic speaker. These lines from the *atalayismo* manifesto typify this image: "We the *atalayistas* ask for the super free power of action because this is the only thing that can coil around our waists the belts of the stars. We want . . . [to] trap the diabolical lightning bolts of danger with the star-spangled lures of our warlike spirits" (LHA 247).

But the manifesto's performative substance derives from more than its oppositional conflict and the ambience of sensorial activity generated by its predilect rhetorical devices. The manifesto's counterposition of divergent attitudes toward art and culture provides the seeds of a story that can be embodied in a dramatic action. Perloff notes that the futurists often surrounded their manifestos' actual proposals with narratives of the group's activities and discoveries. Elements of such site-specific narratives that make direct or oblique reference to the vagaries of a particular group are present in some Latin American manifestos and vanguardist polemical articles.[6] But even when the details are not fleshed out, a potential story underlies each document's oppositional structure, the story of an encounter between the new artists and the old in an environment of conflict, creative energy, and individual or cultural self-affirmation. Through its enactment, this story must imagine its own engaged and informed audience, a spectator who might ultimately play a key role in constructing a new art or culture.

Enacting Artistic Encounters: The Performance Manifesto

The vanguardist manifestos, Poggioli observed, were often written with a prose that was more "fiction and literature . . . than aesthetics and poetics" (71). It is not surprising, then, that vanguardist writers produced manifesto-style creative texts that simultaneously built on the manifesto's performative qualities and developed the narrative seeds that it enclosed. The hybrid creative texts that I call performance manifestos prescribe for concrete public display the new aesthetic relationships and practices espoused in the more straightforward manifestos. Here I examine performance manifestos from Brazil, Mexico, Nicaragua, and Cuba. These works enact the stories of adversarial encounters between conflicting views of culture and art, and while the manifesto incorporates the spectator into its communicative scheme, the performance manifesto recasts the spectator as a character in its story. Not surprisingly, one can often discern explicit connections between these creative works and the authors' more expository writings on art. Generally, however, these performative texts are artistically richer than the average manifesto, and, resisting strict formal or generic classification, they frequently combine poetry, music, dance, narrative, or ritual display. The purpose of these multimedia performances is to spin a palpable tale of cultural encounter that enacts, through metaperformative strategies and metaphors, specific artistic views. In Latin America, moreover, these ostensibly antimimetic works are strikingly culturally specific and make reference to the specific national historical contexts within which modern artistic activity was to emerge.

These texts' performative quality is inextricably linked to their concrete playing out, their "doing," of specific aesthetic positions. Dramatic codes, as Victor Turner argued, are "doing" codes (33), and the performance theorist Richard Schechner has similarly defined performance as an "actualizing" activity, one related to "patterns of doing" (70). In the post-Renaissance, literary Western tradition, Schechner argues, these doing patterns are gradually reencoded as patterns of written words that produced modern drama's reliance on a specialized script. But the avant-gardes, he suggests, refocus attention on the "doing aspects" of a script (71). Vanguardist writers did produce theatrical scripts, and I examine these in a separate chapter. But the more generically hybrid performance texts, with the concretely confrontational quality of a vanguardist manifesto, illustrate an overriding concern with the palpable doing aspects of art. One of the most striking features of the performance manifesto's "doing" of art is its incorporation of the manifesto's speakers and its imagined audiences, both friendly and hostile, into the conflictive story it tells.

PERFORMING *MODERNISMO'S* RECEPTION: "AS ENFIBRATURAS DO IPIRANGA"

An outstanding example is Mário de Andrade's "As enfibraturas do Ipiranga" (translated by Jack Tomlins as "The Moral Fibrature of the Ipiranga"). Subtitled a "profane oratorio," "As enfibraturas" is the lengthy final composition in the 1922 poetry collection *Paulicéia desvairada* (Hallucinated City), a founding text of Brazilian *modernismo*. Significantly, this collection is introduced by the "Prefácio interessantíssimo," one of *modernismo*'s first manifestos, and concludes with "As enfibraturas," a poetic blueprint for the performance of an oratorio in verse. Thus the *Pauličéia desvairada* collection is framed initially by a manifesto that examines the artistic notions underlying its creation and in conclusion by a performance text designed to enact those ideas within the specific socioaesthetic context surrounding the emergence of Brazilian vanguardist activity.

The oratorio's "distribution of voices" is characterized both aesthetically and, as Benedito Nunes has argued, by social status, including the Orientalismos Convencionais (Conventional Orientalisms), "writers and other praiseworthy artisans," played by a "large, imposing, finely tuned chorus of sopranos, contraltos, baritones, and basses"; the Senectudes Tremulinas (Palsied Decrepitudes), millionaires and bourgeoisie, represented by a chorus of castrati; the Sandapilários Indiferentes (Indifferent Pallbearers), workmen and poor people, performed by baritones and basses; the Juvenilidades Auriverdes (Green Gilt Youths), also identified as "we," to be sung by "tenors, always tenors"; and a coloratura soprano soloist representing Minha Loucura (My Madness). With the accompaniment of an orchestra and a band, the oratorio's setting is to be the esplanade of São Paulo's Municipal Theater, a locale that only a few months before *Pauličéia desvairada*'s appearance had served as the real-life site for the Semana de Arte Moderna's three evening performances launching the *modernismo* movement. Although "As enfibraturas" situates the band and orchestra on the theater's terrace ("5,000 instrumentalists under the baton of maestros"), vocalists are to perform from different areas of the city: the Orientalismos Convencionais from the theater's windows and terraces; the Senectudes Tremulinas from various city settings (City Hall, the Hotel Carlton) appropriate to their social class; the Sandapilários Indiferentes from the city's viaduct; the Juvenilidades Auriverdes, their feet buried in the soil, from the Anhangabaú River parks; and Minha Loucura from within the Juvenilidades' midst. In the futuristic spirit, the performance is to be staged "On the Dawn of the New Day."

The oratorio's performers are also characterized by the content of their song and the cues for their performances, and as characters, they represent the adversarial artistic positions embodied in a typical vanguardist manifesto's communicative scheme. Specifically, the piece is organized by an escalating chain of confrontations between the Orientalismos Convencionais (traditional artists) and the Juvenilidades Auriverdes, rebellious youth with creative projects and steeped in the Brazilian soil. Predictably the Senectudes Tremulinas support the Orientalismos Convencionais, while Minha Loucura, identified as the

poet's lyricism, sides with the Juvenilidades Auriverdes. The Sandapilários Indiferentes beg to be left alone. The imagery of their verse identifies the Orientalismos Convencionais with uniformity, unanimity, and
rules in art: "No ascents and no verticals whatsoever! / We love the
boring flatness." "Our choruses are all on the note of 'do'!" they add,
supporting "public sanitation," "moral habits," "ordered productivi-
ties," "regular fecundities," as well as Verdi's music, Phidias's sculpture, Corot's painting, Leconte's verses, and the prose of Macedo
D'Annunzio and Bourget (55, 59, and 61; JT 83, 91, and 93). The
Juvenilidades Auriverdes affirm the aesthetic richness of Brazil, including the "fringed banners of the banana trees" and the "lyricisms of the
sabiás and the parakeets" which seek to join "the thundering glorifica-
tion of the Universal" (53; JT 81).

Against the Orientalismos' orderly world, the Juvenilidades' verse
expresses creative dissonance, passion, and martyrdom for the future
cause of a new art. Minha Loucura's first solo elaborates in more lyric
and less polemical tones an intertwining of poetic yearnings for transcendence with the Brazilianist program posed by the Juvenilidades:
"My voice has shining fingers / which will brush against the lips of the
Lord; / but my raven-black locks / got entangled in the roots of the
jacarandá tree . . . / The brains of the swirling cascades / and the boon
of the serene mornings of Brazil" (57; JT 87). As the confrontation
intensifies, the anger and frustration build until the youths collapse in a
final delirium. The other voices recede, night falls, and Minha Loucura
chants a lullaby celebrating the Juvenilidades' sacrifice for the art of a
new day: "There will still be a sun on tomorrow's gold!" (63; JT 97).
The rebellious youths' martyrdom for their aesthetic cause exemplifies
what Poggioli labels the "agonistic" moment of vanguardist movements, a moment that poses a hyberbolic image of the artist as victim-
hero whose "self-immolation" is the necessary sacrifice for the creation
of future art (Poggioli 67–68).

The oratorio's conflicting aesthetic positions are played out in the
diverse musical styles of their enactment. The Sandapilários Indiferentes scream from the viaduct "in a black salvo." The Senectudes
Tremulinas proclaim, in the measured tempos of a minuet and a ga-
votte, their support for art of the famous, opera subscriptions, and "elegance by precept." The Orientalismos' performance stresses conformity
and power, as their song emerges in a "magnificent tutti," in unison,
and with the full accompaniment of both band and orchestra. They sing
with regularity (*a tempo*) and repetitively (*da capo*), as a "solemn funeral

march." By contrast, when the Juvenilidades Auriverdes begin to sing without sufficient rehearsing, many instruments stay silent during the "soulrendering *rubato*," executed with rhythmic flexibility within a phrase or measure. As their militancy and passion intensify, the Juvenilidades' renditions run the gamut: "pianissimo," "fantastic crescendo," "in a din," "roaring," "now screaming," "shouting in irregular cadence," and, finally, "mad, sublime, falling exhausted." The more lyric Minha Loucura performs in a "recitative and ballad" style, accompanied by "great glissandi" from the harps.

This composition's contextual markers are evident, particularly its connections with early Brazilian *modernismo*'s program for change. As Nunes has explained in his insightful study, the titular reference to the Ipiranga creek where Brazilian independence from Portugal was declared is an ironic allusion both to this event, the centenary for which was being celebrated in 1922, and to the simultaneous declaration of artistic liberty (and linguistic liberty from Portugal's Portuguese) undertaken by the Semana de Arte Moderna ("Mário de Andrade: As enfibraturas do modernismo" 69). The neologistic metaphor "enfibraturas," moreover, encompasses a tone of social and moral position taking as well as the aesthetic "fibratures"—intertwinings of voice, image, and music—of the piece's composition. Thematically, the text itself privileges originality, aesthetic deviation, and passion over tradition, artistic convention, and the socioaesthetic order of things. The allusion through the name Juvenilidades Auriverdes to the colors of the Brazilian flag as well as the youths' choices of imagery place the changes they advocate in the context of the cultural nationalism shaping *modernismo*. In addition, the poet's lyricism, Minha Loucura, situates Mário's own work, specifically, the compositions of *Paulicéia desvairada,* in the context of aesthetic debates surrounding its production and reception.[7]

Beyond these transparent references to *modernismo,* the manifesto quality of this script for a performance is evident on one level in explicit textual connections with the "Prefácio interessantíssimo" introducing the *Pauliceia desvairada* collection. In keeping with Mário's early training in São Paulo's conservatory and forecasting his subsequent achievements as a musicologist, the selection of an oratorio as a performative framework sustains the music-based metaphors of the "Prefácio." Poetic verse, Mário affirmed, had lagged behind musical composition, which for centuries had preferred harmonic over melodic structures. In the *Pauliceia desvairada* poems, he suggested, a sensation of harmonic verse, of the simultaneous overlay of elements, had been created by juxtaposing disconnected phrases, creating a "poetic polyphony" (23; JT 12). In keeping with this model, Minha Loucura's lyricism in "As enfibraturas" is shaped by disconnected phrases, and the oratorio as a whole at times overlays the piece's "distribution of voices." Thus the performative text "As enfibraturas do Ipiranga" explicitly displays what the manifesto text "Prefácio interessantíssimo" affirms. The poet's lyricism (Minha Loucura) provides another link between "As enfibraturas" and the preface's references to "the mad dash of the lyric state" and to a lyric impulse that "cries out inside us like the madding crowd" (18 and 21; JT 8 and 11).

In addition to these explicit connections with the "Prefácio interessantíssimo," "As enfibraturas" incorporates into its structure certain communicative features and strategies typical of the vanguardist manifesto. The most evident of these is the text's employment of the hyperbolic image, the feature that Poggioli associates with the vanguards' futuristic and apocalyptic tendencies. If the vanguardist manifesto defined both its speakers and its audiences on a grandiose scale (the youth of America, the citizens of Buenos Aires, all of Mexico's poets), "As enfibraturas" is conceived as a performance that incorporates, either as active participant or reactive spectator, all the citizens of São Paulo. Some perform openly from the esplanade of the city's Municipal Theater, while others are spread out around familiar city sites—buildings, parks, the river. Essentially, "As enfibraturas do Ipiranga" is a script for a performance that is fundamentally not performable. An oratorio is by definition a traditionally large-scale production. But Mário's script requires participation by more than five thousand instrumentalists who will accompany an even larger number of singers, as we hear in the prelude: "All of the 550,000 singers quickly clear their throats and take exaggeratedly deep breaths" (53; JT 81).

As a performance manifesto, moreover, "As enfibraturas" enacts a concrete story of artistic encounter, specifically, the story of early Brazilian *modernismo*'s conception, self-affirmation, and reception by a diverse São Paulo audience. The characters in that story represent the divergent artistic positions embodied in a typical manifesto's communicative scheme. Specifically, the manifesto's speaking "we" is enacted by the Juvenilidades Auriverdes with the support of Minha Loucura, with whom they identify and associate. Although several of the oratorio's participating groups introduce themselves with the first person ("We are the Orientalismos Convencionais"), only the Juvenilidades are openly identified in the introductory "distribution of voices" with a parenthetical "nós." This privileged first-person perspective is reinforced by the possessive pronoun designating Minha Loucura.

Most important, "As enfibraturas" recasts the vanguardist manifesto's characteristic two audiences (the "you" and the "they") as participating oratorio performers and literally gives them a voice. As a performance text, the work makes tangible what a manifesto only affirms, that is, the relationship between the "doing" of an artistic composition and the work's intended recipients. The piece's visual qualities are essential for bringing this about. An oratorio is by definition a more auditory than visual event (there is traditionally no action, scenery, or costume), but, as in a vanguardist manifesto, Mário's multigeneric script insists on visual components, and the oratorio's performance site, São Paulo's Municipal Theater, implies something one goes to watch. The spectatorly or "watching" component of this performance is underscored in the text's epigraphic quote from *Hamlet* (cited in English): "O, woe is me / To have seen what I have seen, see what I see!" (52; JT 77). In addition, although an oratorio's action is traditionally embodied in verbal and musical exchange, when "As enfibraturas" culminates with the Juvenilidades' frenzied collapse, a scene (to be seen) is described: "The orchestra has vanished in fright. The *maestri* have succumbed. Night has fallen, besides; and in the solitude of the thousand-starred night the *Green Gilt Youths,* having fallen to the ground, are weeping" (62; JT 95).

But who is watching? Who sees the orchestra vanish and the night fall? As with the vanguardist manifesto, the speaking "we" in "As enfibraturas," enacted by the Juvenilidades with support from Minha Loucura, addresses two audiences. The adversarial audience, against whom the speaker assumes a specific aesthetic identity, is defined in the more palpable terms. Embodied in the Orientalismos Convencionais (traditional artists), this group is supported by the bourgeois and millionaire Senectudes Tremulinas, designated with a name that recalls the imagery of malaise and decrepitude employed to characterize the typical manifesto's oppositional "they." The participation of these voices, representing conforming and orderly art, is essential for the "nós" (the Juvenilidades) to construct its antagonistic self-affirmation. Although this adversarial group participates in the performance, moreover, it is also assigned a more explicitly audience-style identity in the city's final response to the Juvenilidades' program for aesthetic reform. As Minha

Loucura concludes the final lullaby to the Juvenilidades, the latter sleep "eternally deaf" to the "enormous derision of whistles, catcalls, and stamping of feet" that bursts forth from around the city (64; JT 99). This negative reception enacts the response by São Paulo's cultural elite (embodied in the oratorio's Orientalismos Convencionais) both to the oratorio itself and to the real-life Semana de Arte Moderna program it dramatizes.

As with the "you" of a vanguardist manifesto, the oratorio's other audience is openly addressed as the reader, defined as a virtual listener and watcher for the performance of "As enfibraturas." Comparable to the explicit audience of a vanguardist manifesto, this spectator is asked to intervene in the performance by taking sides in the polemic. At one point, while the Orientalismos Convencionais enumerate the conventions they favor, the endless series becomes a list of repeated suffixes preceded by blank words: "———— cidades," or, in English, "———— cities." A footnote instructs the reader to fill in the blanks according to personal preferences. If one favors the Orientalismos, the suffixes should be preceded by names of admired São Paulo writers; if the spectator favors the Juvenilidades, names of detested writers may be used. Although here the text offers a choice of allegiances, it subsequently instructs the reader-spectator which side to favor. As the Juvenilidades collapse in exhausted rage, they emit a final outburst against their detested opponents: "Seus ———— !!!" (You ———— !!!) (62; JT 95). The reader is directed to complete the expletive with the filthiest word known, a move incorporating this implicit spectator into the performance that would be witnessed as well as the Juvenilidades' program for aesthetic reform.

Both of these audiences are essential for dramatizing the performance text's story of Brazilian *modernismo*. The negative response to the Orientalismos Convencionais assigned to the oratorio's directly addressed audience casts that reader-spectator as the illusory, supportive audience necessary for the Juvenilidades' program of cultural renewal. In contrast, the final whistling, catcalling, and foot stomping by an adversarial public (extensions of the Orientalismos) plays out a hostile reaction to the poet's lyricism, Minha Loucura, and, by extension, to *Pauliceia desvairada*, the innovative poetic collection of which this performance forms an integral part and the reception to which it forecasts and records.

CONTENDING FOR MEXICO'S AUDIENCES—
MAGNAVOX 1926: DISCURSO MEXICANO

Published in 1926 by Xavier Icaza, a writer with *estridentismo* connections, *Magnavox 1926* prescribes a performance on an equally panoramic scale. Comparable to "As enfibraturas do Ipiranga," this text's generic identity is ambiguous, presenting a synthesis of theater, narrative, and polemic. This generic ambiguity, noted by John S. Brushwood in his study of vanguardism in Icaza's work (10), also characterizes Icaza's most experimental novel, *Panchito Chapopote* (1928).[8] Although *Magnavox 1926* is subtitled a "discurso," in the text's preface, Icaza calls it a farce and notes its theatrical form (16–17). Moreover, lists of the author's literary productions appearing in later works often include the piece under "theater."[9] The work speaks directly of the postrevolutionary context in which it was written. According to the preface, Icaza wrote *Magnavox 1926* when he returned to Mexico after a year's absence and sought to present "the panorama of today's Mexico" (19). Specifically, he explains, the text seeks to dramatize conflicting ideological perspectives vying for control of Mexico's social and cultural future: the idealistic-mystic, the conservative-practical, the leftist-Communist, and the autochthonous-nationalist. In *Magnavox 1926*, these views are played out by individual voices seeking to address Mexico's people. These addresses are physically laid out in the text like the dialogue in a play. The dialogue is intercalated with narrative interventions that provide social background and historical summary. These narrative sections consist of the clipped, synthetic statements characteristic of vanguardist creative works and manifestos but are also, as Brushwood has pointed out, analogous to stage directions in a play (12). Statements such as "Mexico remakes itself" (23), "Elections. The people don't go to the polls" (26), and "Nobody pays attention" (30) are typical of these "stage directions."

As a performance text, *Magnavox 1926* is organized into six scenes separated by these stylized narrative sections. In the initial scene, following narrative stage directions about the state of the nation, various segments of the population, including a reactionary, a missionary teacher, and an Indian, speak to illustrate the point. Each of the following four scenes consists of a "discurso" or speech by a voice representing one of the four ideological positions in contention for Mexico's future. Each speech is followed by its reception among various segments of society. Three of the four speeches emanate from a separate "magnavox" or loudspeaker, each placed inside a different Mexican volcano. A woodcut by the *estridentista* artist Ramón Alva de la Canal precedes the text's preface and spells out visually the written text's performative scenario. A man, humble in demeanor and dress, stands on a pyramid surrounded by cacti and faces a volcano. A periscope-style loudspeaker protrudes from its crater, and two more look out from alongside it. Because of his location facing the volcano with his back to the implicit reader and potential "onstage" spectator of *Magnavox 1926*, this man can be seen as the intended audience of the loudspeaker's performance. In the text, the voice of José Vasconcelos, presenting the idealist-mystic view of Mexicans' future as a cosmic race, delivers the first speech from a loudspeaker inside the Popocatepetl crater. The second voice, that of an Italian journalist urging Mexico to emulate the southern cone countries by encouraging immigration and foreign investments, emanates from a loudspeaker in Ixtlaccihuatl. From the peak of Orizaba, a third loudspeaker projects Lenin's voice amid thunderbolts, proletarian canons, and the notes of the Internationale. These performances elicit various responses from the chorus of scientists, the "indignant" students of America, the chorus of the mediocre, and even from Romain Rolland (from the Alps) and Alfonso Reyes (from the Eiffel Tower). But ordinary Mexican people, the intended audience for the magnavox speeches, only ignore what they hear, yawn, laugh, dance, cry, or shrug their shoulders.

As Icaza spells out in the work's preface, *Magnavox 1926* favors the fourth speech, that is, the autochthonous-nationalist perspective on Mexico's future. Following the first three speeches delivered through loudspeakers, Shakespeare takes the stage to explain the meager response from ordinary people: "Words, words, words . . ." (39). At this moment, the fourth and principal speaker, Diego Rivera (object of the *estridentistas'* great admiration), scales the pyramids of Teotihuacán and agrees: "That old Shakespeare is right. Those are pure talkers" (39). Eliciting sparks as he strikes the pyramid of the sun, Rivera speaks, advocating works over words: "Let us learn from the pyramid builders. Let us continue their interrupted work. Let us realize Mexican works. It is imperative to be of the country. It is imperative to express Mexico" (40). Significantly, Rivera is the only speaker to address his audience without a magnavox and the only one to capture unified public attention and receive a positive reception: "Creative masses have gathered at the foot of the pyramid. Painters, some literati, agronomists, teachers, all resolved to realize Mexican works" (40).[10]

The manifesto qualities of *Magnavox 1926* operate on multiple levels. The piece dramatizes conflicting views on Mexico's future and the reception of those views by an explicit audience, Mexico's people. By enacting the story of that conflict, the work establishes a concrete relationship with debates about Mexican cultural and aesthetic autonomy that provide a context for *estridentismo* activity. These debates, which included Vasconcelos's tributes to cultural *mestizaje,* also surround vanguardist production in the visual arts, in particular the work of Diego Rivera and other muralists. Comparable to "As enfibraturas do Ipiranga" in this sense, *Magnavox 1926* openly advocates an autochthonous position for shaping culture and ideology. In addition, the work acts out the more explicitly *estridentista* position on the engagement of art with life, a view of art as only one of several forms of action that ought to constitute a modern and dynamic Mexican scene. This implicit integration of artistic activity with other kinds of work is often evident in the piece's narrative stage directions: "The students organize themselves. The workers unionize. The farmers unite. The artists don't let go of their paintbrushes. The writers, although nobody notices them, persevere and write" (27–28). As Brushwood points out, the piece also has important connections with Icaza's own more expository writings on Mexico's cultural life, including the work's "Proemio" and ideas delineated in "La revolución y la literatura," a 1934 lecture delivered at the Palacio de Bellas Artes.

The rhetorical strategies employed in *Magnavox 1926* also contribute to the ambience of a performance manifesto. All of the work's speakers, including the external narrative voice that emits the clipped stage directions and the internal voices addressing Mexico's people, speak with affirmative, polemical maxims in the manifesto mode: "It is imperative to make a nation," "It is imperative to create," or "It is imperative to be Mexicans" (28, 40). Similar to the Juvenilidades Auriverdes in Mário's piece, here Diego Rivera assumes the voice of a manifesto's speaking "we," employing one of that genre's predilect communicative forms, the first-person, plural imperative that incorporates speaker and audience into one: "Let us learn from the pyramid builders. Let us continue their work uninterrupted. Let us realize Mexican work" (40). Through its incorporation of the vanguardist manifesto's hyperbolic imagery, *Magnavox 1926* is the script for as unperformable a performance as the Brazilian "As enfibraturas do Ipiranga." Invoking metaphors of modern communicative technology, the work stages a global-scale interaction among distant voices from New York, Paris,

Moscow, the Alps, and Argentina, with interventions from such totalizing characters as "the students of all America." And if Mário's piece incorporates its gargantuan audience, the citizens of São Paulo, into its own performance, *Magnavox 1926* does the same with the equally comprehensive "Mexican people."

But the most marked performative and manifesto quality in Icaza's text is the tension between doing and words, between the dynamically visual and the auditory. Both "As enfibraturas" in its subtitle ("Profane *Oratorio*"; my emphasis) and *Magnavox 1926* in its title invoke communicative forms sustained by sound. But both undermine the auditory mode with the visual imagery of powerful and dynamic speakers (or singers, in Mário's work) typical of the vanguardist manifesto. In Icaza's piece, this speaker is constructed through the image of Diego Rivera whose immediate physical presence contrasts with the distant voices trying to reach Mexico's people through the magnavox: "Those are pure talkers,—Diego Rivera shouts, climbing the Teotihuacán pyramids. Diego Rivera gives his cane an Apizaco strike, producing sparks on the top of the pyramid of the sun" (39). And after his speech: "Diego Rivera descends with a sure step, with his head held high, and with a thick cane" (40).

This performative interaction of the visual with the verbal is further underscored in the text's use of the woodcut to depict graphically its own performative situation. The scene of the Mexican man facing the magnavoxes emerging from the volcanoes emphasizes that the work's performance is something to be seen as well as heard. In the text's privileging of visible work and action over words, moreover, this woodcut lays bare the performance metaphors that *Magnavox 1926* employs to make its point. The image of a loudspeaker inside a volcano is more than an obvious juxtaposition of the modern with the indigenous, or of technology with nature. It also presents a farcical play-within-the-play, a palpable image for the duplicity of the theatrical that embodies something disguised as, playing the part of, or representing something else. Though they might appear to spring forth from the volcanoes, the voices the loudspeakers magnify actually come from somewhere else, as Vasconcelos speaks from New York, the Italian journalist from Argentina, and Lenin from Moscow. More important, the magnavox projects a technological duplication, amplification, and distortion of the human voice; the result lacks that voice's immediacy and presence and also, the text's deceptive imagery suggests, its power. By contrast, Rivera's lightning-inducing voice is cast as unmediated and immediate, visually present and powerful. Like theater that seeks to abolish the theatrical, Rivera's brief speech calls for the end of speeches in favor of creativity and action: "There is no need to talk. The Indian does not pay any attention because he is too intelligent and senses that words are superfluous. One must do things. One must create" (40). Extending the performative metaphor, the reaction to Rivera's speech to the assembled "creative masses," including painters, writers, and farmers resolved to carry out "Mexican work," constitutes a kind of cataclysmic Artaudian visual theater of passionate movement.

Tocotines y Santiagos lo rodean (Rivera), en danza gigantesca. Las pirámides parecen revivir. Algo flota en el aire. El Águila y la Serpiente triunfan desde un sol rojo. Se enciende el holocausto en la pirámide. Una violenta ráfaga lo apaga y aparecen hogueras en lo alto de la serranía que oprime el valle. Las profecías se cumplen. El aire se estremece. Es que ya Quetzalcoatl torna a vivir entre los suyos. (41) [11]

(Tocotines and Santiagos surround him, in a gigantic dance. The pyramids appear to revive. Something floats in the air. The Eagle and the Serpent triumph from a red sun. The holocaust is ignited on the pyramid. A violent gust extinguishes it and flames appear on the heights of the mountains that oppress the valley. The prophecies are fulfilled. The air trembles. It seems that Quetzalcoatl is now returning to live among his own.)

Because Rivera's direct address is the only one to cross the line between speaker and audience and elicit a response, his words undermine the mediated experience embodied in the magnavox and suggest cultural forms that might abolish the distances between performer and audience, art and life. As in "As enfibraturas do Ipiranga," *Magnavox 1926* dramatizes its own reception and poses two different kinds of audience. But the communicative scheme that organizes Icaza's piece is somewhat more intricate than the one shaping Mário's oratorio. Duplicating the tension I have noted in vanguardist manifestos between the desire to speak directly to other artists and the desire to reach a mass audience, *Magnavox 1926* poses two levels of performance and reception. In this vein, it is noteworthy that the Mexican piece was composed during the postrevolutionary era of educational reform and literacy campaigns undertaken through Vasconcelos's leadership in the Ministry of Public Education. Thus, within the narrative frame and at the level of the theatrical dialogue, the piece dramatizes efforts to reach the intended recipients of the four "discursos," that is, the various segments of Mexico's population who alternately ignore and respond to what they hear. Revealing the performance manifesto's ambivalence toward a truly mass audience, this "discurso" audience is cast as both adversarial and friendly. It is mentioned in the narrative stage directions and addressed in the four speeches. When it fails to respond to the magnavox speeches, this audience is described as an indifferent "they." However, it responds ("the masses applaud") when directly addressed through Rivera's imperative "we": "Let us realize Mexican work" (40).

At the level of the narrative frame itself, however, it becomes clear that the authorial voice that provides the stage directions for the piece's performance is speaking not to "the masses" addressed by Rivera but to somebody else. In the work's closing scene, as a cacophony of overlapping voices suggests that Mexico's future remains unresolved, that authorial voice becomes more polemical and delivers its own "discurso," to the simultaneously broadly defined and elite audience typical of the vanguard manifesto: "But the *select* group reacts. It launches its cry of nonconformity" (45; my emphasis). This group, the narrative voice declares in conclusion (and once again echoing a manifesto's futuristic tone), is "that youth of ours" in whose hands lies "the security of a brilliant future, child of its creative impetus" (47). It is this elusive and illusory creative audience, youthful builders of the future, that the principal performer in *Magnavox 1926* dearly desires to reach.

ART OF THE PEOPLE OR ART FOR THE FEW: THE *CHINFONIA BURGUESA*

In the spirit of Mário de Andrade's "profane oratorio," a musical metaphor also shapes the *Chinfonía burguesa* (1931–36; Bourgeois Chymphony), a farcical performance manifesto written by the Nicaraguans Joaquín Pasos and José Coronel Urtecho. First published in 1931 as a dramatic poem but transformed in 1936 into a "farseta," the *Chinfonía* was staged three times by Nicaragua's Anti-Academy. In its parody of bourgeois art and its deployment of musical motifs, this piece resembles "As enfibraturas do Ipiranga," but in combining vanguardist strategies with a multitude of colloquial linguistic forms, it places even greater emphasis on language play in an exaltation of living speech. The piece also embodies the Nicaraguan vanguardists' affirmation of autochthonous art.

Employing an opera buffa style and based on a traditional Hispanic *coloquio*, the *Chinfonía burguesa* gives brief testimony to the tragicomic life of a petit bourgeois couple—Don Chombón (also called Don Trombón, Don Bombón, or Don Bombín) and Doña Chomba (Doña Tromba or Doña Bomba)—whose only daughter, Fifí, "pretty like a tití," marries a younger, third-rate poet, the *pueta*. The issue of this unfortunate union includes endless lines of execrable verse parodying the excesses of latter-day Spanish American *modernismo* and the "nieto garrobo" (iguana grandson), named Jacobo, "producto del robo / que es una mixtura impura / de la poesía y la burguesía" (product of the theft / that is an impure mixture / of poetry and the bourgeoisie) (35).[12] The domestic complacency and aesthetic sterility of this liaison are self-perpetuating; although Doña Chomba fears that the *pueta*'s arrival signals her family's ruin, the longer he stays in the bourgeois ambience, the less poetry he produces and the more contented with his presence the others become. The materialist idyll is abruptly interrupted by death, who whisks them all away in her bag. In contrast to the labored rhymes and banal imagery emanating from the *pueta*, the rest of the piece unfolds in a range of popular verse, repetitive rhymes, wordplays, tongue twisters, and onomatopoetic play shaping the speech of other characters.

On the most evident level, the *Chinfonía* constitutes a comic but acerbic critique of the relationship between conventionalized art forms and bourgeois society and of the specific linguistic formulas such forms generate. The work's literary theme is announced in the opening metatheatrical prologue declaimed by actors portraying individual furniture pieces in Don Chombón's parlor and assuming a narrative role. In turn, they introduce themselves, the other characters, and the subject matter of the performance: the family's "meritorious history / summary and literary" (16). This is, the spectator is clearly told, a literary story, a fact reinforced by Don Chombón's lengthy inventory of personal possessions including a predilect aesthetic object, his beloved "pianola Manola," the player piano who is his "principal muse." This bourgeois reification of the aesthetic is reinforced by the characterization of the *pueta*'s verse as a "rhyme seat" on which he sits while courting Fifí. It is primarily the *pueta* himself and the language of his art that enact the play's critique of conventional art. The young artist seduces the object of his affection with compulsive versification, an unwitting parody of the labored rhyme schemes and overdone metrical patterns, metaphors, and synesthesias of bad poetry:

> Tu mano cálida como el verano
> me da una impresión de pajarito
> chiquito en confesión,
> y ante la porosidad de tu
> sinceridad

se me quita del dedo el miedo
a don Chombón.
Tus miradas cargadas
de babosadas
ponen mi corazón acurrucado
como un puño cerrado
mientras el tuyo está inquieto
como un secreto,
pero tu cabeza está tiesa
con su moña ñoña
y siento en tus piernas tiernas
y en tus pies al revés
las perezas de las patas de las
mesas
y las cosquillas de las ancas de las
sillas. (24)

As a performance manifesto, the *Chinfonía* has concrete connections with the Nicaraguan vanguardists' program for artistic renewal. The group's dual agenda, to modernize literary expression and to create a viable national tradition, was set forth in the Nicaraguan Anti-Academy's manifesto, published in Granada's *Diario nicaragüense* in April 1931. On the one hand, the group's stated goal was to disseminate in Nicaragua "the vanguard techniques that have dominated in the world for more than ten years but are almost unknown in Nicaragua" (*MPP* 378). This enterprise was undertaken through the translation of French and North American poets. The ultimate purpose of this aesthetic modernization campaign, on the other hand, was to enable young writers to "feel the nation," to "express national emotion," to "give free rein to the emotion of existing and being (*ser y estar*) in Nicaragua," and, above all, to "undertake the artistic re-creation of Nicaragua" (*MPP* 377–78). To this end, the young poets affirmed their intention to create national poetry, national theater, and national painting, sculpture, music, and architecture. Because of its concrete emphasis on linguistic performance, moreover, the *Chinfonía burguesa* manifests the Nicaraguan Anti-Academy's focus on autochthonous language, a reaction in part against North American cultural influence. If "As enfibraturas do Ipiranga" and *Magnavox 1926* may be considered performance manifestos, the *Chinfonía* is the manifesto for a particular kind of "doing" with words. The explicitly linguistic nature of the Anti-Academy's search for national art forms was affirmed in the group's polemical "Cartelón de vanguardia" (Vanguard Poster) that embraced linguistic invention (*50A* 173).

Although the Nicaraguan work does not unfold on the panoramic scale that shapes "As enfibraturas do Ipiranga" and *Magnavox 1926*, it, too, is marked by the hyperbolic imagery typical of a vanguardist manifesto. But in the *Chinfonía* the hyperbole unfolds at the level of farce: the bourgeoisie's materialist obsessions that reify aesthetic objects (the pianola Manola, the "rhyme seat"); the sterile bourgeois-*pueta* union that generates an iguana instead of a child; the poet who becomes totally inert through his association with the bourgeoisie; and the characters who literally perish from boredom reinforced by the *pueta*'s verse. Something of the vanguardist manifesto's apocalyptic tone permeates the arrival of the cronely death in the *Chinfonía* as well as the inevitability of her determination that all must be carried away in her bag. Inverting the voluntary self-destruction of the vanguardist poet that unfolds in "As enfibraturas do Ipiranga" and that, Poggioli notes, typifies vanguardism's futurist moments, the death and removal without a trace of Don Chombón's resident *pueta* seems to be the necessary sacrifice for the worthy cause of a future new art.

As a performance manifesto, the *Chinfonía burguesa* puts into play conflicting views on culture and art. Specifically, the piece tells the story of the confrontation between the conventionalized art forms sanctioned by bourgeois society and the playful, linguistic experimentation with which the *Chinfonía* itself unfolds and which is advocated by Nicaragua's vanguardists. As with "As enfibraturas do Ipiranga," the piece's adversarial, indirectly addressed audience—the audience that corresponds to the vanguardist manifesto's "they"—is embodied in major characters. In "As enfibraturas do Ipiranga," the work's "nós," performed by the Juvenilidades Auriverdes and Minha Loucura, defines itself artistically in opposition to the Orientalismos Convencionais and the supporting, bourgeois Senectudes Tremulinas. In the *Chinfonía*'s farcical structure, this oppositional group under attack takes center stage in the form of the *pueta* and the bourgeois family that harbors him. As in a vanguardist manifesto, this unhealthy, iguana-generating adversary corresponds to the bourgeois audience the Nicaraguan Anti-Academy characterized, for example, in José Coronel Urtecho's essay "Contra el espíritu burgués," as "anemic," "feeble," and "consumptive" (*50A* 95). Here, however, the work's implicit, speaking "we" that defines itself in opposition to the *pueta*'s art is embodied not in concrete characters but rather in the work's own parodic form. Although there is no specific character incarnating artistic renewal, through this experimental form, the *Chinfonía* poses an alternative view of art in contrast to the exhausted literary tradition the *pueta's* cumbersome verse is intended to parody.

Ostensibly, the *Chinfonía* is a "farseta" in a prologue, two acts, and an epilogue, scenic demarcations that superficially organize the brief character encounters. But more significant is the play's identity as a *chinfonía*, a metaphor for a creative process described by Joaquín Pasos in "Un ensayo de poesía sinfónica." This concept refers in part to the interweaving of voices in a single composition. Such an interweaving is explicit in the *Chinfonía's* earlier, poetic version that includes seven sections, each with a musical title: Prelude in Bourgeois Form, Domestic Andante, Dialogue a la Sordina, Agitato Furioso, Commercial Moderato, Psychic Piano, and a Final Honeymoon. The creation of a *sinfonía-chinfonía*, Pasos explains in his essay, is analogous to the principles of symphonic orchestration but without musical pretensions (*50A* 54–56). This nonlinear organization of an aesthetic exercise is comparable to the distribution of overlapping voices in "As enfibraturas do Ipiranga." The *Chinfonía's* simultaneity, however, functions on the level of primary linguistic elements, synthesizing words, syllables, and sounds into a symphony of voices. This process can be seen in the *Chinfonía* lines distributed among individual character voices that, if articulated with precise timing, create the synthetic effect of the *chinfonía*.

> (*Se oyen golpes en la puerta*)
> *Una voz adentro*
> ¡Tan! ¡Tan!
> al zaguán . . .
> (*Todos los actores de los muebles esconden la cabeza*)
> *Inmediatamente la voz de doña Chomba—adentro—*
> Ten, ten la puerta Norberta Berta
> tuerta
>   (*Pasa Norberta*)
> *La voz de la puerta—dando un golpe—*
> ¡¡¡Pan!!!
> *La voz de don Chombón—adentro—*
> Pon
> la mesa, Teresa,
> la tortilla tiesa,
> la mayonesa
> la salsa inglesa
> la . . .
> *Voz de doña Chomba* (*adentro*)
> Sssssssssssss . . .
> *Ambos cónyuges a la vez* (*saliendo*)
> ¡¡¡Chó!!!

Una voz adentro
    Chon (16–17)

(Knocks on the door are heard)
A voice inside
    ¡Tan! ¡Tan!
    al zaguán . . .
    (All of the actors of furniture pieces hide their heads)
Immediately the voice of Doña Chomba—inside—
    Ten, ten la puerta Norberta Berta
    tuerta
                                    (Norberta passes)
The voice of the door—slamming—
    ¡¡¡Pan!!!
The voice of Don Chombón—inside—
    Pon
    la mesa, Teresa
    la tortilla tiesa,
    la mayonesa
    la salsa inglesa
    la . . .
The voice of Doña Chomba (inside)
    Sssssssssssss . . .
Both spouses at once (coming out)
    ¡¡¡Chó!!!
A voice inside
    Chon [13]

As I have noted, the image of a dynamic speaker is fundamental for constructing the vanguardist manifesto's speaking "we." In the *Chinfonía,* however, this collective speaker emerges not in the form of specific characters (there are no designated vanguard poets onstage) but rather in the work's foregrounding of the creative and productive verbal activity of dynamic speaking itself. The interaction among characters is a fundamentally linguistic relationship, developed through the symphony of sounds they create together. Thus the collectively elaborated *chinfonía* provides a humorous and rhythmical contrast to the awkward exchanges between the *pueta* and Fifí. Essentially, the work contrasts two views of art by contrasting two kinds of performance. The piece designates the bourgeois family's final exchange a "*tertulia* de la digestión," a digestive gathering, but the tertulia can also refer to a theater's upper gallery. This digestive allusion calls to mind the Brechtian designation "culinary theater" for the tradition his experimental epic theater sought to challenge.[14] On the level of its banal dramatic action, the *Chinfonía* parodies the sentimental story sustaining bourgeois, culinary theater. In contrast, the *Chinfonía*'s linguistic forms present a theater of performance that undermines its rather ordinary script for action with a concrete display of a new kind of art.

But this performance has an audience, and as a performance manifesto, the *Chinfonía* alludes directly to its spectator's presence. As I have demonstrated, the bourgeois family and its poet-in-residence incarnate an implicit audience whose artistic tastes and behavior are attacked (the vanguardist manifesto's "they"). But although it is not embodied onstage, another audience is invoked. A present spectator is directly addressed in the furniture's introductory speeches ("I am Paquilla the Chair"), and this presence is underscored with occasional metatheatrical gestures, for example, when Don Chombón begs for the curtain to fall (on his misfortunes) or takes solace in the fact that this is, after all, only a play. The "you" that this present spectator implies, however, exemplifies the vanguardist manifesto's ambivalence toward the audience it is attempting to reach as well as the tensions in vanguardist discourse between art for the few and art for the many. In its appropriation of popular linguistic forms, the *Chinfonía* both addresses and incorporates into its performance the potential mass audience for whom those forms constitute a familiar and known tradition. By incorporating that familiar "doing-with-words" into a farcical and parodic context, however, the piece also constructs an audience that would share the aesthetic concerns of the *Chinfonía* authors (and of the Nicaraguan Anti-Academy). This audience, implied through such distancing moves as the furniture pieces' introductory and narrating roles, is called on to recognize the work's literary concerns and to participate in advancing the aesthetic program for Nicaragua's cultural renewal that the *Chinfonía* embodies.

CULTURAL COLLISIONS THROUGH PERFORMANCE: *EL MILAGRO DE ANAQUILLÉ*

In a comparably autochthonous spirit, Alejo Carpentier's *El milagro de Anaquillé* (1927; The Miracle of Anaquillé) synthesizes strategies from music, dance, theater, and Afro-Cuban ritual into a performable manifestation of the writer's early ideas about culture and art. Subtitled an "Afro-Cuban choreographic mystery in one act," the ballet was eventually staged in postrevolutionary Cuba, accompanied by Amadeo Roldán's music. The ballet's script constructs a scene and prescribes character actions, movement, and gestures in order to enact a confrontation between two cultural orientations toward performance: the making of a film "on location" in the Hollywood mode and an Afro-Cuban *ñáñigo* initiation ceremony.

Ballet characters include a North American businessman, sailor, and flapper, a *ñáñigo* Diablito (little devil), the Iyamba (supreme leader of Afro-Cuban *ñáñigo* religious cults), a group of *guajiros* (Cuban peasants), eight sugarcane carriers, and the Jimaguas, twin divinities of Afro-Cuban witchcraft who are joined by a rope around their necks. The ballet's set is marked out by two *bohíos* (thatched huts) on either end of the stage: the principal *guajiro*'s hut on one side and, on the other, the Iyamba's. A young boy's fearful face is painted over the door to the *guajiro*'s hut, and a gaudy image of San Lázaro adorns the entrance to the Iyamba's hut. A sugarcane field and palms form a backdrop, behind which three enormous stylized sugar mill chimneys loom over the scene. Movements in each of the ballet's eight scenes correspond to specific musical tempos in Roldán's score. The principal *guajiro* and his companions relax in front of his *bohío* by playing music after work, when they are interrupted by the confrontation between the American businessman-filmmaker and the Iyamba. The unfolding encounter is cast as two competing performances, two plays-within-the-ballet, with the *guajiro* as a captive audience. To underscore this division between actors and spectators onstage, the businessman and the Jimaguas wear masks, move like automatons, and appear "unreal and monstrous" (*OC* 1: 271). By contrast and as spectators of these competing displays, the *guajiros* are to look "natural," wear no makeup, and appear almost pale. The performances they witness enact a confrontation between two cultural orientations toward art in a series of interlocking representations of one culture by another.

In scene 1, the *guajiros* return from work, pulling a toy horse that they shove offstage. While the *guajiros* strum a guitar and begin a gentle *zapateo* (foot-tapping dance), the businessman enters in scene 2 wearing a giant mask that doubles the size of his head. A caricature of the North American tourist, he sports a checkered suit with golf pants, thick wool socks, and an unusual hat. He is also weighed down by paraphernalia: a collection of strange posters, a bicycle tire pump, mysterious packages, and a movie camera tripod slung over his shoulder. The *guajiros* stop their dance to watch him. After carefully inspecting the place and the people, the businessman summons the sailor and the flapper who enter in scene 3, dancing a disjointed black-bottom. While the *guajiros* watch the dance "stupefied," the businessman engages in a flurry of frantic activity. First he plasters the Iyamba's hut and the tool shed with posters advertising products and services, from Wrigley's gum to the "*Church of the Rotarian Christ* (*The biggest in the world*)" (*OC* 1: 273; original in English). Next, "as to inflate an imaginary tire" (*OC* 1: 273), he works the bicycle pump in a row of cane. As he pumps, a skyscraper gradually inflates behind the cane. When the building reaches a certain height, the pump detonates and the black-bottom music ceases. In scene 4, the businessman dresses the flapper as a Spanish dancer and the sailor as a bullfighter. Surrounded by the *guajiros,* they execute a burlesque Spanish dance as the businessman films the scene. As the sailor–bullfighter pins the Spanish dancer to the ground with his sword, the dancers freeze in a "ridiculously" dramatic pose (*OC* 1: 274).

In scene 5, the cane carriers and the Iyamba solemnly enter and deliberately file before the camera, destroying the film-in-progress. Ignoring the businessman's ensuing tantrum, the Iyamba removes the posters from his hut, and when the businessman moves to protest, the Iyamba's forceful glance stops him in his tracks. As the Iyamba places larger-than-life earthen bowls, shells, and feathers on a bench in front of his hut and under San Lázaro's image, the cane carriers squat in a circle around the bench. In scene 6, the Iyamba's group performs a *ñáñigo* initiation ceremony that includes the Diablito dance. With heightened interest, the businessman sets up his camera in front of the Iyamba's hut, dresses the sailor in a tiger skin and the flapper in a Hawaiian dance costume, directs the actors to join the initiates, and begins to film again. In scene 7, as the initiates stop the actors from entering the scene, a confrontation ensues between the two "directors." The Iyamba and the Diablito conjure up flames under the businessman's nose, and he, in turn, throws down his tripod and destroys the San Lázaro altar. As the initiates run to save the altar, they suddenly freeze and bow down, detained as if by "the action of an inexplicable force" (*OC* 1: 276). In the final scene, the Jimaguas emerge from the Iyamba's hut. These gigantic black dolls with cylindrical heads and protruding eyes are connected by a long cord and appear "supernatural and implacable" (*OC* 1: 277). Though the businessman retreats in terror, the Jimaguas advance "in a heavy dance," position themselves on either side, and, with a "brusque movement," secure the cord that binds them around their victim's neck. At this moment, the skyscraper deflates, the sugar mill emits a slow, lugubrious sound, the other characters freeze like statues, and the initiates raise their arms to the sky (*OC* 1: 277).

Certain elements of the ballet (the toy horse, the inflatable skyscraper, the stylized masks) indicate Carpentier's contact with contemporary avant-garde theater and emphasize the piece's assertive theatricality.[15] The toy horse's abrupt departure on wheels in the opening scene underscores that this is make-believe, and the metatheatrical plays within the ballet focus attention on the cross-cultural factors at work in making believe and representation. Frank Janney, who has done the most detailed analysis of *El milagro de Anaquillé* in his study of Carpentier's early work, suggests that the piece is a hybrid work containing elements of the colonial farce, the *bufo,* early 1920s allegorical, proletarian drama, Valle Inclán's *esperpentos,* and Pirandellian devices.[16] But the work's manifesto quality derives from its concrete relationship to early debates about Afro-Cuban culture and art that helped to shape Cuban vanguardist activity. The piece also allegorizes the antipathy toward U.S. involvement in Cuban affairs shared by Cuban artists and intellectuals in the 1920s.

A commitment to "vernacular art" was affirmed in the 1927 "Declaración del Grupo Minorista" manifesto signed by Carpentier and other founders of the *Revista de Avance,* and for the journal this included a recognition of Afro-Cuban cultural presences. *El milagro de Anaquillé* resembles other experimental works produced by the Afro-Cuban movement, including the early poetic experiments of Nicolás Guillén and other writings by Carpentier himself: a small group of Afro-Cuban poems, the novel ¡*Écue-Yamba-Ó!*, *La rebambaramba* (another ballet), and the opera buffa, *Manita en el suelo. El milagro de Anaquillé,* moreover, resembles the Nicaraguan *Chinfonía burguesa* not only in its self-conscious vernacular content but also in its expression of vanguardism's hyperbolic tone through its farcical mode. Compared to the panoramic representations of "As enfibraturas do Ipiranga" and *Magnavox 1926, El milagro de Anaquillé* (like the *Chinfonía burguesa*) unfolds in what seems by comparison a rather small corner of the world. But excessive theatricality in characterizations of the businessman and the Jimaguas, the sugarcane *central*'s enormous, stylized chimneys, the overinflated skyscraper that threatens to pop, the businessman's frenetic activity and abundant, unwieldy baggage, and the work's stylizations of gesture and body movement all contribute to a hyperbolic ambience.

The work's dominant and most evident manifesto quality, however, is the explicit counterposition of two radically different approaches to performative art, a standoff that (at least on the surface) clearly favors one over the other. Because in *El milagro de Anaquillé* those differences are construed in cultural terms, Carpentier's work displays what Austin Quigley has posited in *The Modern Stage and Other Worlds* as a defining characteristic of modern, experimental theater: the counterposition of disparate worlds in which "the notion of a single world with a single set of values is repeatedly brought into conflict with a concern for pluralistic worlds with pluralistic values" (9). In Carpentier's ballet, the primitive and the modern (a predilect, almost cliché, vanguardist juxtaposition) constitute the colliding worlds. But, also in keeping with Quigley's "worlds motif," the collision itself is cast in theatrical terms. Through the plays within the ballet, the cultural encounter between two worlds is played out as an engagement between two modes of performance. The businessman's persona posits a caricature of modernity, a world of material glut, gimmicky appearances, and stereotypical representations, mechanically reproduced and packaged for marketing, like Rotarian religion and Wrigley's gum. As an artistic director, the businessman stages two performances for filming: the Spanish dance by the sailor and the flapper and their invasion of the Iyamba's initiation ceremony dressed as Tarzan and the Hawaiian dancer. The filming process exposes its own mimetic lies, cursory falsifications shaping modernity's portrayal of its others. The art thus (re)produced, the performance suggests, bears little similarity to anyone's lived experience and merely (literally) projects one culture's prior imaginings of the other.[17]

In contrast and resistance to the businessman's approach to art, the Iyamba stages his own manifestation. As a performance event, the initiation ceremony superficially resembles the businessman's activities. Comparable to the actor in the businessman's film, participants in the ceremony undergo a voluntary transformation process. Each performance requires the creation of a framed space, emerging and set apart from ordinary life.[18] The businessman converts the area around the *guajiro*'s hut into the scenario for the Spanish dance and bullfight. Similarly, the Iyamba marks out the initiation ceremony space by setting out the bench and instructing the cane carriers to form a circle around it. Each performance is directed from outside the scene; the businessman stands behind his camera directing his actors' movements, and the Iyamba stands outside the circle while manipulating what transpires within its boundaries. In addition, each performance requires special trappings, including costumes and props for the businessman's film and the bench, earthen bowls, shells, and feathers for the initiation ritual. Both performances point to the power relationships informing the interactions between the two cultures. The visual allusion to a foreign-controlled sugar industry implicates the businessman's film in exploiting the culture he purports to depict. After staking a claim to the Iyamba's hut by plastering it with commercial materials, the businessman also attempts to appropriate the ritual he witnesses and transform it into a more marketable commodity. In the process, he invokes the power of his culture's most imposing reproductive tool, its technological expertise. By staging an initiation ceremony in response to the businessman's intrusive moves, however, the Iyamba brings to bear his own culture's most compelling representational instruments, the *ñáñigo* witchcraft that conjures up the foreboding Jimaguas.

In the spirit of a manifesto, the work's confrontation between modernity's mechanically reproduced representations and the ritual ceremony of a traditional society unquestionably privileges the latter. The title itself invokes a cultural perspective as well as an audience that would experience the Jimaguas' appearance as a miraculous event. While the businessman's conception of art is depicted as inauthentic and exploitative, the Iyamba's ritual is portrayed as a reverent act, shaped by its engagement of believing initiates. If the filmmaker's work displays, in Walter Benjamin's terms, art's loss of aura in the age of mechanical reproduction, the Iyamba's exhibition presents a cultural practice imbued with an aura of presence and a sacred but intimate part of its participants' actual lives. In juxtaposing the primitive and the modern, a pervasive practice in vanguardist discourse, Carpentier's ballet portrays one culture as richer than the other in creative and critical force. More powerful than the camera's eye, the Iyamba's deliberate gaze detains the businessman in his frenetic bustling, and the performance the Iyamba directs is creatively and critically fruitful. As the title's miracle prophesies, the *ñáñigo* initiation conjures up the prodigiously monstrous Jimaguas, next to whom Tarzan and the Hawaiian dancer seem like mere simulacra of representations twice removed. It is the Jimaguas, furthermore, who wage the ultimate critique of the businessman's projections by bringing them to a definitive halt. These contrasts play out the Afro-Cuban aesthetic position that African cultural forms constitute a richer resource for Cuban artistic expression than, for example, an emerging North American mass culture. As an aesthetic form, moreover, Carpentier's ballet is itself portrayed as a match for the "disarticulated" black-bottom executed by the sailor and the flapper and as superior to their burlesque Spanish dance.

But the manifesto qualities that structure *El milagro de Anaquillé* harbor a more intricate communicative scheme, particularly through the construction of an audience, than the other pieces examined here. The most clearly identifiable entity is the work's adversarial "they," the Yankee purveyors of modernity's mass culture who provide the clear target for the ballet's attack and for Afro-Cuban culture's contrastive definition of itself as more powerful, vital, and self-present. The Iyamba, moreover, is posed as the work's "we," the embodiment of a sought-after collective cultural subject. Although the ballet unfolds almost entirely without words, through the power of his gaze and his movements, the Iyamba constitutes the work's dynamic "speaker," or, as in the vanguardist manifesto or manifestation, its virtuoso performer. But the work's implicit "you" is the most ambiguous communicative element, a quality that sends the ballet's audience mixed signals and focuses attention on the communicative process itself, particularly the recipient's role.

On one level, each of the two plays within the ballet constructs its own audience. The initiation ceremony is staged above all for a present, believing, and participatory spectator. The businessman's film in the making, in contrast, implies a future audience whose response will be mediated by distance in time and space from the initial performance. In addition, both the businessman and his actors and the Iyamba and his initiates are spectators of one another's performances, and their mixed responses play out the problems of cultural power at issue between them. But the most important onstage audience in *El milagro de Ana-quillé* is the *guajiros,* not only because their primary function is to witness all that transpires but also because they are explicitly cast as the work's least theatrical and therefore most audiencelike characters. In contrast to the "unreal and monstrous" appearance of the businessman and the Jimaguas, the cane carriers' perfectly synchronized movements, and the sailor's and flapper's exaggerated gestures, the *guajiros* move "naturally," without benefit of masks or makeup. Their unaffected characterization, as well as the reminder through the toy horse that this is, after all, make-believe, distances the *guajiros* from the shows they watch and links them most closely to the ballet's implicit real-life spectators. This connection provides keys for discerning the ballet's ambiguously constructed implied audience.

As the onstage spectators of the ballet's two competing performances, the *guajiros* are cast, on one level, as the dramatized "you" that, as a performance manifesto, *El milagro de Anaquillé* seeks to address. But through the *guajiros'* shifting relationships to events that they witness, the ballet encourages comparable shifts of focalization on the part of its implicit, "real-life" spectator. As a result, the precise nature of the work's directly addressed "you" remains ambiguous, revealing once again the tension in vanguardist discourse between the expansive impulse to reach a mass audience and the simultaneous desire to speak with a select few. As I have noted, the ballet's title invokes a spectator position that would perceive the Iyamba's display of power as a miraculous event and therefore constructs an audience that would be drawn through faith and collective identity into the performative practices that the work openly espouses. On this level, *El milagro de Anaquillé* is addressing the mass audience that a vanguardist manifesto might have invoked as "the Cuban people" and then openly directed to embrace its African heritage and reject the growing cultural influence of the United States characterizing Cuban life in the 1920s. But, in addition to initiating their own performance (the after-work dancing), the *guajiros* witness two performances, and as these unfold, so does their shifting position. First, they are performers of the initial guitar strumming and *zapateo*. Then, as they observe the businessman's activities, they become unwitting, intimidated participants, for he incorporates them through film into a circle around the flapper and the sailor's dance. Finally, spectators outside the circle of the Iyamba's ritual, the *guajiros* are here recast nonetheless as fearful and respectful potential initiates. Through both performance events, they are subject to constant pulls, positioned on the boundaries between participation and estrangement. The *guajiros'* reactions to what they see reinforce this shifting position, for they are alternately amused, incredulous, intimidated, and surprised by the businessman's performance, fearful and respectful before the Iyamba's. However, although they might be drawn by cultural proximity to the latter, the *guajiros* are not, in the final analysis, the participating initiates but, instead, those who watch. The intermediary position of their alternating reactions intimates an awareness of the differences between the two events. By virtue of this awareness, the *guajiros* are, like the implied spectator of *El milagro de Anaquillé* who watches them in turn, on the threshold of a critical position. That critical position implies for this performance manifesto not a faithful public of willing initiates but a more reflective audience of artists or critics concerned with the aesthetic and cultural problems this work poses.

Conclusion

Through the rhetoric of the vanguardist manifestos, Latin American writers mapped out specific positions on culture and art. In the process, they constructed imagined audiences embodying the aesthetic practices and cultural positions under attack as well as the idealized allies for building a future new art. Drawing on the manifesto's intrinsic theatrical substance, manifesto-style performance texts dramatized these positions. As performance manifestos, "As enfibraturas do Ipiranga," *Magnavox 1926, Chinfonía burguesa,* and *El milagro de Anaquillé* display for their recipients' inspection the artistic practices that they openly support. What the avant-garde manifesto or polemic advocates, these works render concrete, transposing a specific aesthetic orientation into the realm of sensorial experience. With the imminence of a vanguard manifestation, the sense of immediacy the works create emerges from the subject matter of the performance, for as exhibitionist works-in-progress they portray the doing of the art they espouse. Thus Mário de Andrade's oratorio exemplifies Brazilianist poetic polyphony and dramatizes *modernismo*'s reception. *Magnavox 1926* exhibits the synthetic verbal economy and directness ascribed to Diego Rivera's privileged speech; the *Chinfonía burguesa* parades a "chymphonically" adroit overlay of rhymes, wordplays, and puns; and Carpentier's ballet displays the visual and kinetic power of Afro-Cuban ritual.

The sensory directness of these works is reinforced by an eschewal of conventional dialogue. With the exception of the businessman's "Ok" as he summons the sailor and flapper onto the scene, Carpentier's ballet characters do not speak at all. The communicative purpose of character exchanges in "As enfibraturas" and the *Chinfonía* is subservient to poetic function and to the works' musically inspired overlaying of voices. And, even though *Magnavox 1926* is subtitled a "discurso," the work itself openly favors the least wordy and most visually absorbing speaker, undermining the magnavox speakers who mold their performances from mere words. More performative than representational, language in these performance manifestos is employed for doing rather than for telling. The effect of these works' musical, linguistic, and choreographic ostentation is to posit the vitality and experiential expansiveness of a specific set of artistic strategies. These are contrasted, in turn, with other cultural practices—orderly bourgeois art, mass media communication, conventional poetry, Hollywood filmmaking—portrayed as somehow less attuned to the fullness of life. This manifesto-style polemical scheme assumes almost Manichaean proportions, for in each work the condition for one kind of art's emergence is the demolition of the other, a nihilistic-futuristic dynamic typical of vanguardist discourse. Thus the *Chinfonía*'s bourgeois poet-in-residence is whisked off by death; Diego Rivera's powerful speech silences the cacophony of magnavox voices and produces instead an Artaudian orgy of visual display; and the power of ritual in Carpentier's ballet diverts modernity's gaze and deflates its cultural monuments. And although Mário's Juvenilidades Auriverdes succumb in their passionate confrontation with the orderly bourgeois world, their martyrdom is only a temporary sacrifice in their cause of a future new art.

Most important, by construing vanguardist aesthetic activity as performance, these works reveal and underscore a momentous concern: the perceived need for a potential new audience in conceptualizing and creating a new kind of art. On one level, these performance manifestos cast a concrete and directly addressed adversary as a protagonist in the performance who is essential for the work's forging, by contrast, of a specific aesthetic identity and position. These adversaries range from traditional artists and the bourgeoisie that supports them to purveyors of the same mass media and mass culture that vanguardist works exploit through satirical and caricaturesque motifs. More significant, however, is the imagined supportive audience that these performance manifestos directly invoke and sometimes openly court. Exemplifying the simultaneous desire to engage a mass audience in the cause of a future new art or culture and to explore self-critically with other artists or critics the aesthetic process itself, these works fancy their directly addressed audiences in seemingly contradictory ways. To enlist participatory sustenance from such vastly conceived entities as the citizens of São Paulo, the people of Mexico, the grass-roots creators of Nicaragua's popular traditions, or the Cuban *guajiros,* these creative texts tap performance's seemingly palpable presence to create engaging sensorial events. At the same time, they deploy metaperformative metaphors to construct a more reflective spectator and to promote in that imagined audience self-awareness of its presence at the performance and, by extension, in the activities of culture and art.

2.

Outward Turns of the Vagabond Eye/I

The Vanguards' Portraits of the Artist

Distant voices, pyrotechnic splendors reach my ears, but I am here alone, held down by my land of misery as if with nine bolts.

—Roberto Arlt, *El juguete rabioso*

We are all images conceived during a calm and supple trot.

—Martín Adán, *La casa de cartón*

At about the midpoint of Mexican writer Jaime Torres Bodet's first novel, *Margarita de niebla* (1927), the narrating protagonist Carlos Borja disengages briefly from his obsessive analyses of Margarita to contemplate himself in the mirror shaving. As the narrator watches himself perform this banal, quotidian act, his attention is simultaneously drawn to the mirror's representation of what lies behind him: a partially open window and, beyond the window, a fragile landscape bathed in dew, a scene, the narrator notes, that the mirror's frame endows with an "almost artistic consistency" (64). Just as the passing years have recorded the gradual changes in his own reflected countenance, the narrator notes, so as the sun rises on the landscape behind him does the "decorative art of the mirror" reveal changes in the "schools of art" dominating the scene: "The dawn's impressionistic canvas has been hardening, cooling until it has attained the skeleton and the temperature of cubism" (65).

The most striking feature of this passage is its evocation of the garden-windowpane metaphor in José Ortega y Gasset's *La deshumanización del arte* (1925; The Dehumanization of Art), a link in Torres Bodet's ongoing dialogue with Ortega's ideas about art.[1] In this well-known extended metaphor, Ortega affirms the incompatibility of focusing simultaneously on the landscape we see through a windowpane and on the windowpane itself. Realist art, he suggests, focuses on the "human content" of the garden; modern art, by contrast, calls attention to the perception of the pane and thus encourages spectator awareness of the artifice. Although the scene from *Margarita de niebla* is certainly reminiscent of Ortega's framed garden, the differences are more interesting than the similarities. Torres Bodet's landscape is not only surrounded by a window but is also reflected with the window through a mirror, a second level of framing that underscores even further art's estranging activity. Changes in the total scene, moreover, are provoked not only by the framing process but also by the shifting quality of the landscape itself—the "human content" in Ortega's metaphor—as the sun travels and time goes by. Most significantly, the self-reflexive narrator observing the window and the landscape also watches himself in the act of contemplation. But, unlike Ortega, Torres Bodet's narrator, rather than favoring the frames over the landscape, focuses on the interaction between the framing process and its raw material, that is, between art and life, as well as on the position and activity of the human subject who constructs the interaction.

Characterized in the novel as a young intellectual with artistic expertise and inclinations, Carlos Borja reflects on his own position vis-à-vis the interaction of artistic representations with the changing world that surrounds him. The scene is emblematic of the vanguards' obsessive self-reflexive portrayal of artists and artistic activity. Artist stories are so common in vanguardist expression that there are few significant works that do not construct an artistic persona of some kind. Vanguardist writers explored through their art possible productive relationships between artists and the world around them. This inquiry is singularly intense in prose fiction and is drawn particularly sharply in the novels I examine in this chapter: *El juguete rabioso* (1926) by Argentina's Roberto Arlt; Jaime Torres Bodet's *La educación sentimental* (1929); *La casa de cartón* (1928) by the Peruvian writer Martín Adán; and, from Brazil, Oswald de Andrade's *Memórias sentimentais de João Miramar* (1924) and *Serafim Ponte Grande* (1933). In tones ranging from anguished to irreverent, these works question the substance and viability of the contemporary artistic persona and explore just what there might be for artists to do in a changing Latin American world.

As the vanguard movements unfolded in Latin America, the self-aware artist hero (or often antihero) was a fairly recently established literary presence. In Spanish America, the crystallization of this presence is associated with turn-of-the-century *modernismo* stressing formal and linguistic innovation in both poetry and prose. As the dominant mode in Spanish American letters in the final decade of the nineteenth century and the first decade of the twentieth, *modernismo* is regarded as a founding event in contemporary Spanish American literature. Saúl Yurkievich has succinctly summed up the widely held view of the aestheticist *modernista* artist emerging both from the lives of writers and from their works. "Aristocratic attitude: the poet is a select being at odds with his surroundings; misunderstood, he isolates himself from the surrounding world that, with its pragmatism, its vulgarity, and its insipidness, produces his revulsion" (*Fundadores* 18). Brazilian literary historiography, as Antônio Cândido points out, attributes such a founding function not to the turn-of-the-century Brazilian Parnassianism and symbolism that, to some degree, parallel Spanish American *modernismo* but rather to nineteenth-century romanticism and (beginning in the 1920s) to early Brazilian modernism that corresponds to the Spanish American vanguard movements (*Literatura e sociedade* 112). Historiographical differences with Spanish America notwithstanding, an aestheticist stance and social disaffection also permeate Brazilian turn-of-the-century symbolism. Recent critical studies have provided a more intricate and ambiguous view of the Spanish American *modernista* artist. Aníbal González, for example, demonstrates in his study of the *modernista* novel that these texts portray an artist vacillating between the desire to retreat to his atelier and the pulls of a problematic social reality in which he must function. Gwen Kirkpatrick's study, *The Dissonant Legacy of Modernismo*, suggests that the work of poets such as Leopoldo Lugones and Julio Herrera y Reissig points to the cracks and contradictions in the *modernista* ideal of poetic perfection.[2] Similarly, recent commentators argue that, under the surface, Brazilian symbolism at times manifested a complex awareness of social context, pointing away from the aestheticist model.[3]

Conventional wisdom about the vanguardist artist who followed these movements has been powerfully shaped by the "small god" of Vicente Huidobro's 1916 "Arte poética" as well as by the high-wire verbal gymnastics of the eponymous poetic voice in his masterwork *Al-*

tazor (1919–31). An extreme version of the aestheticist *poète maudit* that inhabits *modernismo* and Brazilian symbolism and unfettered by contingencies of time or place, this artist figure assumes the stance of a linguistic wizard, forger of "pure poetry" and magical inventor of autonomous worlds. But I would argue that, as with the *modernista* and symbolist predecessors, a more complicated, even contradictory, vanguardist artist emerges from a variety of texts, in particular, prose fiction narratives. In his analysis of Huidobro's work, René de Costa has demonstrated convincingly that *Altazor* documents both the culmination and the unraveling of the aestheticist autonomous artist, a personal trajectory from the 1920s "celestial poetics" of the avant-gardes to the artist's deeper concern in the 1930s with "the world in which one must live, and die" (*Vicente Huidobro* 161). On a similar note, Nelson Osorio suggests that Huidobro's 1932 manifesto "Total," which rejects his prior experiments and searches for a "poet's voice that belongs to humanity," signals the end of the polemical and experimental phase of Latin American vanguardism (*MPP* 383).

The premise underlying these incisive assessments of an individual career is that vanguardism (at least in poetry) is defined by the detached, polemical stance and that gestures toward "humanity" or social context somehow signal the movement's decline. It is true that the shift in dominant modes, from aestheticism to engagement, was gradual. I would argue, however, that a combative, sometimes productive, interaction between "celestial poetics" and a concern with the contingent world permeates vanguardist artistic concerns all along. It is possible to discern within vanguardist activity both an intensification of the detached, superior stance to the extreme and a simultaneous critique of that position. This tension, particularly evident in prose fiction, is different from the tug-of-war that González documents in *modernista* prose. The latter constructs, as González shows, a Flaubertian conception of art as the "fruit of immense and tenacious labor comparable to that of a craftsman in his workshop" (21). Vanguardist prose fiction also portrays art as a time-consuming activity and often characterizes artists as workers of a special kind. But the image of an artist-craftsman in a workshop is gradually replaced by an artist on the move, more circumspect about a personal aesthetic identity, or more overtly critical of the concrete world. Obsessed by both the power and limitations of creativity, this acutely self-aware artist points to the gaps in an elusive selfhood and embodies both radical skepticism and creativity in seeking something viable to do in the world, often a concretely Latin American world with the real-life conditions typical of these countries in the 1920s. The stresses between aestheticism and engagement, moreover, frequently unfold in a critical stance through which even the most seemingly esoteric aesthetic endeavor is somehow construed as a critical act. Though prose fiction works examine these issues most closely, multiform and sometimes contradictory characterizations of the artist also circulate in vanguardist manifestos.

The Artist in Vanguardist Manifestos

To some degree, the manifestos reinforce dominant poetic images of the vanguardist artist. This is particularly true of the all-encompassing Nietzschean super-artist who, like the poet hero of Apollinaire's *Le poète assassiné* (1916), had often "seen God face to face" (*Selected Writings* 259) or was, like Marinetti's futurist artist, "gluttonous for infinity" (*Marinetti* 155). This artist assumes a privileged, cosmic position, with visionary powers in the Rimbaudian tradition of poet as seer, and affirms the totalizing capacity of aesthetic activity to encompass humanity's past, present, and future. In poetic discourse, such an image emerges from the opening sections of *Altazor*. Here, the speaker assumes a superior cosmic position and vision, witnesses creation, and, asserting that he is the "total man" balancing centuries of humanity in his voice, constructs a self-affirmative poetic persona, "the great poet" Altazor who can "give birth to stars" and "see it all" and whose mind is "forged in the tongues of prophets" (*OC* 1: 367; EW 9).[4] A similar cosmic perspective shapes Pablo Neruda's *Tentativa del hombre infinito* (1926), a poetic voyage like *Altazor*, which, according to de Costa, traces a personal "poematic quest for the absolute" (*The Poetry of Pablo Neruda* 54). In the same spirit, the lyric voice in Mário de Andrade's "As enfibraturas do Ipiranga" from his landmark experimental collection *Paulicéia desvairada* (1922) proclaims that the "shining fingers" of his voice will "brush against the lips of the Lord" (*PC* 57; JT 87).

The manifestos reiterate these exaggerated poses of lyric power, most obviously in their deployment of a (primarily first-person) dynamic speaker who also often possesses special perceptual powers. Thus Huidobro's 1921 manifesto "La poesía" anticipates the *Altazor* stance: the poet extends his hand to direct humanity "beyond the last horizon"

(*OC* 1: 656). Many documents characterize their own speaking voices and the new art they advocate with hyperbolic imagery of youth and vitality, for example, the Chilean "Rosa náutica" manifesto speakers, "ascending to the plains of the sun," who affirm that "a hundred planets are born each morning in the horizons of our pupils" (*MPP* 120–21). Similarly, the *estridentista* chronicler Germán List Arzubide describes aerial poetic activity that "shatters the theories of gravity" (*MPP* 237), and the Ecuadorean José Antonio Falconí Villagómez urges poets to be "the antenna that gathers up the vibrations of the Cosmos" (*MPP* 117). These images not only reinforce vanguardist lyric assertions of poetic power but also expand the model of a visionary artist into a kind of perceptual radar, with the ability either to see more clearly or to absorb perceptual stimuli others overlook.

If the artists in these texts are "gloriously isolated" from the rest of humanity, as in Altazor's parachute descent, there is often a simultaneous gravitational pull toward intimate contact with the world. Certainly a more terrestrial lyric domain characterizes the work of César Vallejo. In the context of a "celestial poetics," Vallejo's poetry never takes flight at all. The hermetic linguistic inventiveness of the *Trilce* collection notwithstanding, critics have often attributed a strong "human" quality to Vallejo's verse, the manifestation of a lyric somehow enmeshed in reality.[5] Yurkievich has noted that Vallejo "finds human truth down there, close to the ground" in his intentionally prosaic language (13–14). But other poets are more direct on this issue; for example, the Nicaraguan Pablo Antonio Cuadra urges simply in his manifesto-style "Arte poética" that poets "sing that which [they] live" (*50A* 31). Interestingly, Salvador Novo's brief poem "Ciudad" notes the contrary stresses on aestheticist artists propelled over rooftops by an "infinite thirst" and away from the ground that pulls them back even as they ascend (*INPA* 206). On the sole basis of individual careers, then, it is not inaccurate to conclude that some vanguardist poets assumed the cosmic pose, others were always more engaged with a concrete reality, or some evolved over time from the former stance to the latter. But the interaction between these stances and the critique of the cosmic pose by the more engaged position are present in the vanguardist manifestos as these documents suggest alternatives to the lyric super-artist.

A persistent antiromanticism constitutes a key element in this process. Some manifestos express the reaction overtly. "We are not romantics; we are young," Carlos Drummond de Andrade writes in the "Para os céticos" declaration of *A Revista* (GMT 337). Others oppose pervasive romantic lyric motifs, sentimentality and anecdotal subjectivity, and the notion of individual originality. Thus the journal *Klaxon* opposes Sarah Bernhardt, tragedy, and sentimental and technical romanticism and proposes the elimination of "lachrymal glands" (GMT 296). The *euforistas,* even as they exalt "personality in the lyric revolution" (LHA 232), attack "romantic women," "long-haired poets" (LHA 229), and the "hordes of flutists by the light of the moon" (LHA 231). Contesting the romantic idea of innate, creative originality, Torres Bodet declares in "La poesía nueva" that poets are made, not born, and notes the constructed quality of both poets and their work (*Contemporáneos* 23, 28). In a humorous vein, Puerto Rico's Evaristo Ribera Chevremont parodies in "Motivos de la rana" overblown claims to poetic originality: "I sing the frog / Nobody has sung the frog / Nor has anybody sung it as I have" (LHA 179).

But the critique of individual aesthetic power goes beyond rejecting romantic motifs or questioning poetic originality. While many celebrate their own first-person speaking voices ("We Are," "We Exist," "We are to be," "I am"), the manifestos also seriously question the lyric tradition's reliance on a psychologically integrated sense of self. Some simply suggest this by eschewing personal pronouns, for example, Oswald de Andrade's "Pau-Brasil" and "Antropófago" manifestos. But others, for example, the Argentine *ultraísmo* manifestos, openly question the autobiographical impulse. The *Prisma* "Proclama" manifesto opposes "garrulous anecdotalism" and subjectivist poets who "live in their autobiography" and "believe in their personality" (*MPP* 98). On a comparable note, Torres Bodet censures in "La poesía nueva" the "licentious nudity" with which late-nineteenth-century poets displayed the psychological I in their verse (*Contemporáneos* 26). Vallejo's *Trilce* compositions provide a radical poetic destruction of aestheticism's organic lyric self, as critics note the fragmentation of these poems' language and imagery in the poetic speaker's body and voice.[6]

Drawing on Ortega y Gasset's comments on Mallarmé in *The Dehumanization of Art,* Walter Mignolo has argued persuasively that the figure of the vanguardist poet supersedes, through its overblown motifs, the biological and temporal confines of an actual human person and becomes anonymous and disembodied.[7] The personal pronoun, Mignolo argues, no longer designates a person but now stands for a voice (134–35). In a similar vein, both Gustavo Pérez Firmat and Francine Masiello have explored evidence of a changing fictional self in some vanguardist prose, an idea on which this chapter expands. But while I agree with Mignolo that this process of the vanishing self is antiromantic in substance, I would also emphasize that it results from intensifying often to the point of caricature the subject-centered romantic tradition. In manifestos and poetic discourse, the exaggerated, romantic self becomes so superinflated that it eventually self-destructs. Thus this narcissistic construction that, in the words of the surrealist René Crevel, had "eaten up the universe" (Balakian 139) eventually consumes itself. It is possible to view Altazor's descent in this fashion: in the totalizing desire to absorb and express all linguistic possibilities, the poetic voice disintegrates into the precommunicative utterance. Lines from Pablo Neruda's *El hondero entusiasta* (1923–33) express a similarly expansive moment beyond self: "I want to have no limits and raise myself toward that star," the poetic voice affirms, expressing also the desire to "liberate myself from me. I want to leave my soul" (*OC* 1: 167). This simultaneously self-expanding and self-erasing process is explicitly identified in Vicente Palés Matos's manifesto poem of *euforismo* in which the self-affirming lyric speaker, whose opening words are "I am," records the destruction to any sense of self wrought by his own totalizing nature: "My life / Has expanded so much, has opened in such a way / That I have become lost outside of myself" (LHA 176). Similarly, Oliverio Girondo's speaker in the prose poem *Espantapájaros* calls himself a "conglomerate, a manifestation of personalities" (*Veinte poemas* 107).

My difference with Mignolo and with Ortega whose thinking he incorporates into his analysis is one of emphasis. Mignolo suggests that the vanguardist critique of this lyric subject leads to a voice of detachment, a "select mechanism" for "processing information" (144). While I agree that this change signals a disintegrating concept of self, I would argue that the destruction of a cosmic lyric figure also poses a critique of the isolation and superiority that construction embodies, that is, of the lyric persona's larger-than-life stature and of the idea that artists are, in appetites and capacities, superlative versions of other humans. If this disembodied voice replaces an integrated human character, it also undermines that lyric persona's propensity to speak from a world apart. Stripped of an identifiable personality and reduced to a dynamic voice or, I would add, a sharp eye, the textually constructed vanguardist artists often conduct their activities not from stratospheric heights but from within a contingent world.

Vanguardist manifestos evoke this sense of immersion by situating the artist in a concrete place and time. Thus, although the lyric persona in Mário de Andrade's "As enfibraturas do Ipiranga" has "brushed the lips of the Lord" with his voice, his black locks are also "entangled in the roots of the jacaranda tree," and he contemplates "the serene mornings of Brazil" (57; JT 87). Even *Altazor*'s high-flying poetic speaker measures himself by his times. Born under the "hydrangeas and the airplanes of the heat" (*OC* 1: 365; EW 3) and opening his eyes in the century when "Christianity was dying," Altazor springs forth from the World War I era.[8] But if lyric discourse always maintains at least an element of the inwardly turning voice and eye, as a public-seeking genre, a manifesto by definition fosters engagement. In proposing a specific aesthetic position, the manifesto turns the lyric impulse outward to construct a public ars poetica that dilutes the lyricist's separatist stance. For example, Mário de Andrade's lengthy 1924 manifesto, "A Escrava que não é Issaura," argues that the contemporary poet is reintegrated into the life of his times (GMT 302–8), and the speaker in the *A Revista* manifesto affirms the imperative of "entering into a collision with real life" (GMT 338). Writing on the new art for Cuba's *Revista de Avance,* Martí Casanovas argues that artists, as an integrated part of society, should be stirred by the "same problems that agitate all people" (HV 137). And in a similar tone, José Carlos Mariátegui, editor of *Amauta,* writes that "the artist who does not feel the agitations, the uneasiness, the anxieties of the people and of the times is an artist of mediocre sensibility, of anemic comprehension" (*OC* 15: 222).

Vanguardist real-world activism, as I have noted, often emerged in cultural rather than explicitly political arenas. Thus, Mariátegui's own political activism notwithstanding, being in touch with one's times is expressed in vanguardist discourse not necessarily through advocacy of overt social action but, in part, by reconceptualizing artistic activity through modernity's dominant motifs, embracing, in the futurist spirit, technology and hyperactivity. Disrupting the contemplative mood of a cosmically situated artist, the manifestos often represent art as dynamic action, as if to legitimize artists by demonstrating that they have something important to do in tune with what is happening around them. Many vanguardist groups drew attention to their own labors by characterizing what they did as broadly defined cultural and intellectual activity, not exclusively aesthetic. It is common for these artists to describe themselves collectively, in manifestos or little magazine editorial statements, as a study group or an intellectual gathering rather than as an assemblage of aesthetes.

Vanguardist expression reinforced this self-defining image of artists as workers by portraying artistic work with technological or athletic motifs, a poetics of airplanes, automobiles, elevators, bicycles, and trampolines. Little magazine titles were frequently drawn from this repertoire: *Klaxon* (Brazil; Horn), *Antena* (Chile and Mexico), *Dínamo* and *Gong* (Chile), *Irradiador* (Mexico), the *Trampolín-Hangar-Rascacielos-Timonel* series (Peru; Trampoline-Hangar-Skyscraper-Helmsman), *válvula* (Caracas; valve), *Motocicleta* (Ecuador; Motorcycle), and from Puerto Rico, *Faro* (Lighthouse) and *Vórtice* (Vortex). These motifs also abound in poetry titles that seek to immerse artists in the machinery of contemporary life: "Song to the Airplane," "Express," "*Simplista* Train," "Velodrome," "Sidecar," "Poem of the Elevators," "A Sensation of Velocity," "Superplane," "Aerial Poems," and "Looping the Loop."[9] The thematic evocation in this poetry of a world of technology, movement, and work is often reinforced through the predominance of nouns and transitive verbs (to construct an ambience of objects in motion), the suppression of adjectives and adverbials excluding those derived from verbal forms, and the use of short, telegraphic statements typical of the vanguardist mode. Such poetry often constructs the poetic voice by intertwining its activity with a specific city's dynamic life, for example, of Buenos Aires, Rio de Janeiro, and various European cities in Girondo's *Veinte poemas para ser leídos en el tranvía* (1922), of São Paulo in Mário de Andrade's *Paulicéia desvairada* (1922), of Rio de Janeiro and New York in Ronald de Carvalho's *Toda a América* (1926), of New York, Antwerp, and nameless ports in Carlos Oquendo de Amat's *5 metros de poemas* (1927), or of Managua in José Román's "Preludio a Managua en B Flat."[10] And although cityscapes dominate in this kind of poetry, the less common vanguardist poetry of rural scenarios also identifies poetic speakers with dynamic scenes, for example, in Leopoldo Marechal's "Canto para una segadora" or the Peruvian *indigenista* vanguardist poet Alejandro Peralta's "Jornaleras" or "Siembra," compositions that link innovative poetic creation with agricultural cycles in the Andean highlands.

The manifestos, even more than the poetry, project an explicit conception of artists as activists. These documents construct their vigorous speakers through the same rhetorical strategies—action verbs, clipped statements, and verbal wit—that typify much vanguardist poetry. Technological motifs characterize the artist figure here as well, as in Huidobro's portrayal of the poet in "Manifiesto de manifiestos" as a "motor of high spiritual frequency" (*OC* 1: 670), in the "Rosa náutica" manifesto that pledges to place the speakers' hearts in gear with "the great nervous system of future machines" (*MPP* 120), or in the *atalayistas*' self-portrayal as "the coachmen of the car of the world" (LHA 248). But in their more confrontational style, the manifestos spell out the idea of art as active work. Thus São Paulo's *Klaxon* artists compare themselves to engineers, and the first Puerto Rican *atalayista* manifesto evokes a comparable engineering poetics: "We want to exploit the quarry of free thought in order to construct new highways" (LHA 246).

This insistence on art as action in tune with the times raises the obvious question of what artists were concretely to do. Addressing this issue, manifestos often suggest a kind of critical persona, embracing both the aestheticist, contemplative artist and the engaged, activist artist, without resolving the stresses between them. In an ambience of science and technology, the manifestos often portray artists as people who generate or find new things. As Poggioli observes in *The Theory of the Avant-Garde,* the international vanguards sought to imbue creative activity with the aura of scientific pursuit and experimentation. Huidobro spelled out this connection in "Vientos contrarios" by comparing Shakespeare, Góngora, and Rimbaud to Galileo, Copernicus, Newton, and Einstein (*OC* 1: 752), but, more generally, the words *invention* and *discovery* (or their synonyms) are also two of the most common in Latin American vanguardist manifestos. Through these concepts, which embody both spontaneous and intentional inventiveness, the "new" is generated by turning the artist's special lyric vision on the external world. Thus the manifestos combine in the figure of the new artist creative and intellectual activity to affirm a critical perspective. Even Borges, who as an *ultraísta* often assumed an aestheticist stance, suggested that artistic renovation requires the ability to "see with new eyes" (*MPP* 75). This essentially critical notion is echoed in Oswald de Andrade's "Pau-Brasil" manifesto that also calls on young poets to "*see with open eyes*" (GMT 330; SMSR 186; emphasis in original).

Most important, numerous manifestos affirm that the artist's work in an active, modern world will require a synthesis of creative and intellectual endeavors. These documents are almost unanimous in their attack on existing artistic critics and often suggest the new artist might fill the critical void by turning the lyricist's sharp inner eye outward. As early as 1921, the Dominican Republic's *postumismo* manifesto forecasts an "intellectual aristocracy" based on critical skills that will bring artists closer to their contexts: "Poets will not continue to be privileged beings, unknown by the multitude and on the path to daydreams, but rather sighted beings on the path to the truth, thinkers and philosophers" (*MPP* 110). Puerto Rico's *noístas* call themselves America's first intellectuals and express the desire to "sharpen" the aesthetic sense and make their thinking "more agile" (*MPP* 164). In his manifesto, "A esclava que não é Issaura," Brazil's Mário de Andrade advocates "the maximum of lyricism and the maximum of criticism" (GMT 306), and the manifesto speakers in *A Revista* seek to embody both in a "labor of creation and of criticism" (GMT 338). In Argentina, *Martín Fierro* establishes in its opening manifesto a creative and a critical agenda through the fusion of "*Martín Fierro* artist" and "*Martín Fierro* critic" (*MPP* 135). Broadening the creative-critical synthesis into a more activist agenda, Cuba's Grupo Minorista manifesto designates its signers (who include founders of the *Revista de Avance*) simultaneously as a group of artists and "intellectual workers" (*MPP* 249). Similarly, Mariátegui's *Amauta* in Lima identifies its aesthetic goals in the context of a comprehensive intellectual program dedicated to study "all of the great movements of renovation—political, philosophical, artistic, literary, scientific" (*MPP* 192).

The artist figure posed by vanguardist manifestos in dialogue with prevalent poetic discourse, then, embraces a range of images. Still marked by the aestheticist tradition of the lyricist's visionary interiority and cosmic detachment, this artist is recast through modernity's technological and activist motifs as a figure of movement and action. Though the artistic persona's individual solidity may be stripped down at times to a dynamic voice and a perceptive eye, the lyric vision and verbal virtuosity are often directed toward a concrete world. Situating this less self-centered artist on the boundaries of contemplation and engagement, a conceptually stressful space, the manifestos often construe art as a form of activity in step with vigorous times. That activity is conceived as a kind of creative intellectual work, synthesizing the lyric and the analytical into an artistically self-critical position, simultaneously detached from and critically engaged with the surrounding scene. In a similar spirit of skepticism toward the power and limits of artistic projects, vanguardist novels of the same period undertake a more intricate investigation into the substance of a contemporary artistic persona by constructing complex artist characters as central figures in their fictions.

The Artist in Vanguardist Prose Fiction

With its lengthy tradition of inquiry into how the self is to tell its story, the novel provides a propitious setting for examining artists and artistic activity. The novels I analyze here—*El juguete rabioso, La educación sentimental, La casa de cartón*, and (together) *Memórias sentimentais de João Miramar* and *Serafim Ponte Grande*—provide significant insights into the multiple portraits of the artist emerging from Latin America's vanguardist period. Artists' stories are so numerous that many must be omitted from this discussion, including, from Chile, Pablo de Rokha's *Escritura de Raimundo Contreras* (1929) and Huidobro's *Cagliostro* (1934); from Mexico, Salvador Novo's *Return Ticket* (1928), Gilberto Owen's *Novela como nube* (1928), and Xavier Villaurrutia's *Dama de corazones* (1928); and from Cuba, *El laberinto de sí mismo* (1933) by Enrique Labrador Ruiz.

The works I examine here, from Argentina, Mexico, Peru, and Brazil, exhibit diversity in regional context as well as style, tone, and narrative strategies, from the still reasonably discursive *El juguete rabioso* to the fragmented scenarios of *La casa de cartón*, from the lyric prose in *La educación sentimental* to the radically parodic collage compositions of *Serafim Ponte Grande*. Evident differences notwithstanding, these novels explore significant common ground. Each presents the story of a would-be artist in a narrative framework that conjures up and alters the *Bildungsroman* and *Künstlerroman* heritage. Each work possesses autobiographical markers that have provoked critics to note connections with the authors' lives, a quality reinforcing the artist's story ambience. Although each novel antimimetically displays its own artifice, each one also evokes a temporally and site-specific "real-world" urban referent, a mode that reflects the involvement of actual vanguardist artists and groups in significant developments in the cities in which they worked. Each novel is also structured at least partially through an ulterior, autodiegetic narration, ironically distanced from the protagonizing artistic self. Through this self-contemplative position, each work undertakes a critical dialogue with both traditional and vanguardist notions about art and artistic activity.

ART AS LARCENOUS FABRICATION: ARLT'S *EL JUGUETE RABIOSO*

As Argentine writer Roberto Arlt's first novel, *El juguete rabioso* (1926; The Rabid Toy) is less radical in narrative structure and style than his later works, *Los siete locos* (1929; The Seven Madmen) or *Los lanzallamas* (1931; The Flamethrowers). But the novel is clearly a product of the vanguard years in its overtly artistic theme, its generic and linguistic heterodoxy, and its inquiry into the artistic self. The novel also synthesizes concerns shaping activities of the two principal Buenos Aires artists' groups of the time, Florida and Boedo. Its aesthetic theme recalls Florida's approach to artistic innovation, while the class and cultural conflicts of its Buenos Aires characters evoke the concrete time and place in which the novel was written as well as Boedo's call for a socially concerned art. Through an ulterior, autodiegetic narration, the novel presents in four chapters episodes from four years in the life of its protagonist, Silvio Astier, a petit bourgeois adolescent with creative ideals who seeks a viable vocation in a rapidly expanding Buenos Aires. Although the narrator identifies the story being told as his written memoirs, the temporal relationship between the story and its telling remains vague. Narrated by an older Silvio-writer, the story is focalized primarily through Silvio the adolescent. Nevertheless, occasional temporal markers and focalization shifts from the acting to the narrating Silvio establish the ironic distance typical of this narrative structure. While the narrating self remains elusively situated in time and place, the acting Silvio provides the story's primary center of consciousness. But the two come together in the protagonist's ultimate emergence as an artist defined by his talent for creative fabrication and a critical outlook on his world.

The story consists of key moments in Silvio's life between his fourteenth and seventeenth years. A youth with inventive talents, literary experience, and dreams of fame seeks a coherent sense of self and transcendence over the persistent need to make a living in a sordid urban world. Chapter 1 presents adolescent escapades of Silvio and his friends: readings of serial bandit literature, experiments with poetry and homemade explosives, and, as the "Club of the Midnight Gentlemen," a larcenous excursion to a school library. In chapter 2, family economic needs send Silvio to work as a live-in servant for an avaricious used bookstore proprietor. Though eager to be around books, Silvio is humiliated by the menial work and unsuccessfully attempts to burn down the store before abandoning the job. In chapter 3, Silvio seeks to develop his inventive talents as an aviation mechanics apprentice in a military school. Dismissed because the military needs workers, not thinkers, Silvio wanders the city and attempts suicide. In chapter 4, Silvio achieves limited success as an itinerant paper salesman and begins to master city life. But, reunited with Rengo, a rogue from his thieving days, Silvio plots a robbery with his friend whom he then denounces. Conceived as a perverse deed necessary for self-affirmation, this event coincides with the youth's decision to become the "future teller" of the city's stories. Impressed by Silvio's zest for life, the would-be victim of the failed robbery offers to find him a job in the southern Neuquén, where, most critics have surmised, Silvio will retreat to write the memoirs we are reading.

Recent criticism of *El juguete rabioso* has focused on its representation of a literary apprenticeship and its anticipation in content and style of Latin America's new narrative; on Silvio's recourse to inventive models for self-transformation and to treason as an existentially self-affirming response to an alienating modern life; and on the novel's interaction with inherited literary forms aimed at exploring the status of character in modern fiction.[11] Recent studies have generally addressed the social and aesthetic implications of the novel's literary and cultural thematics and the work's relationship to a variety of narrative genres, including the picaresque, the *Bildungsroman*, serial fiction, and the Dostoyevskian memoir, among others. Here I examine the work's attention to artistic activity, but I am particularly concerned with its construction of a specifically vanguardist artist who has a contentious relationship both to artistic tradition and to a concrete Buenos Aires world.

On the surface, the novel's *Bildungsroman* markers are evident: adolescent initiation into the world; friends and mentors as models for that process; conflict between protagonist values and the surrounding society; and a plot structured by the search over time for a meaningful adjustment within the conflict.[12] In addition, Silvio's characterization as a creative figure, repetitive references to his readings, and his gradual decision to become the recorder of the city's stories further define the work as a *Künstlerroman*. In fact, Silvio's final decision to retreat from the city to compose stories about the problematic world he is leaving recalls Stephen Daedalus's decision in Joyce's *Portrait of the Artist as a Young Man* to leave his land and forge "the uncreated conscience" of his people (253). The work's abundant literary allusions and Silvio's attempts to model his life on his readings situate the novel in the narrative tradition identified by Mikhail Bakhtin as the "auto-criticism of discourse," that is, a testing of literary discourse (often parodically) against a given reality through a hero who, like Don Quixote or Madame Bovary, sees the world through literature and attempts to live accordingly ("Discourse in the Novel" 412–13). What is unique about this process in *El juguete rabioso* and typical of the context in which it was written is the specifically vanguardist models being tested, the focus on Silvio's emerging artistic persona, and the work's response to the conflictive relationship it poses between art and life.

In this novel, the protagonist's trajectory over time embodies the vanguardist problematic of the relationship between aesthetics and life, specifically, the limitations of an elitist "celestial" poetics within an insistently ordinary world. Affirming intellectual superiority to his surroundings, a stance underscored through a gallery of uncomplimentary characterizations, Silvio yearns not only to improve his social circumstances but also to be "admired" and "eulogized" (173). Like the real-life vanguard artists who formed select gatherings, Silvio and his friends organize a club, "a true society of intelligent young men" (101) with a multiform agenda. As in a vanguardist group, the club constitutes a site for experimental pyrotechnics (in this case, scientific) and members seek to employ "the most modern procedures" (103). And although it is a tiny, self-selected assemblage, the club is motivated, like the vanguardist artist, by an expansive, grand design to engage a mass public. Just as the speakers in a vanguardist manifesto seek to reach the youth of America, this group will organize other clubs throughout the country. Drawn to stealing and playing with explosives, the group embodies irreverence toward conventions and rules. And, as their principal larcenous act, the boys raid an established literary institution, a school library, to remove the imposing *Diccionario enciclopédico,* an act emblematic of the vanguards' assault on academic tradition. Evoking Don Quixote's selective perusal of the books of his times, the club recontextualizes this act in the book-stealing scene with jabs at Argentine poet Leopoldo Lugones, a favorite target of the Buenos Aires vanguardists.[13]

As Francine Masiello and Aden Hayes have pointed out, Silvio's attempts to build a viable self constitute a principal focus in this novel. I am concerned more specifically here with how that self in the making interacts with the artist figures constructed through vanguardist manifestos and poetic discourse. Silvio's models in constructing his artistic persona are Baudelaire, Rocambole, Edison, and Napoleon. Known to the youth through his readings, these larger-than-life creative figures incarnate multiple features of the artist as imagined in vanguardist discourse. Baudelaire evokes the vanguards' inheritance of the aestheticist tradition of subjectivity and a select artistic stance. Rocambole, the outcast hero of Ponson du Terrail's popular serial novels, provides remnants of the romantic hero embedded in the vanguards' overblown poetic persona. He also points to the movement's challenge, in Andreas Huyssen's terms, to the "great divide" between high art and mass culture, a critique embodied in the manifestos' invocation of a mass audience as well as some artists' attention to popular art forms. Edison evokes the vanguardist portrayal of art as work with a scientific aura and artists as inventors or discovering explorers who produce or find new things. Napoleon suggests the militaristic tone of the vanguards' polemical manifestos and the vanguardist artists' expansive desire to encompass all.

Heroes in their respective specialties, these four figures are commensurate with the imposing destiny Silvio envisions for himself, and he invokes his models in ways underscoring their vanguardist connections. The theft of Baudelaire's biography coincides with the emergence of Silvio's interior, lyric voice. Rocambole provides the bedrock of his literary education (he has read all forty volumes), and the bandit's presence shapes the youth's melodramatic reveries and rebellion against social institutions. Edison inspires Silvio's chemistry achievements and modest reputation as an inventor. Napoleon incarnates the protagonist's desire for superiority over others, for example, when, as an apprentice, he adopts "the military position" and imagines his glorious future, far from the "penurious life that the majority of people naturally sustain" (173). Although Silvio ultimately assembles attitudes and skills from each, none of the four models can provide a direct path from a difficult life to a grandiose destiny. On one level, Silvio's life marks the failure of expansive vanguardist goals. The club's Rocambolesque banditry ends abruptly under the imminent threat of capture. The need to work constantly interrupts Silvio's immersion in readings as a would-be aesthete, and, in his "literary" bookstore job, art becomes a commodity. Finally, Silvio's hopes to combine scientific and Napoleonic aspirations in the military are dashed because he is deemed too creative for the practical tasks. In search of a poem he cannot find, Silvio vents his frustration in the lines that provide an epigraph for this chapter and that could well serve as the Latin American vanguard artist's lament, calling to mind once again the stresses between cosmic aspirations and the pulls of a contingent world: "Distant voices, pyrotechnic splendors reach my ears, but I am here alone, held down by my land of misery as if with nine bolts" (153).

Silvio's failure to construct a viable self from heroic models is accompanied by a growing proclivity for self-analysis with a decidedly theatrical quality. In the book-stealing scene, Silvio first hears what he calls his "other voice." But a theatrical process of shifting focalization accompanies this heightened subjectivity, as Silvio pictures himself in specific roles and imagines how others see him. A critical element in Silvio's formation is realizing that these two perspectives do not coincide. Thus key moments in the protagonist's interiorization are paralleled by shifts projecting how others might see him. For example, when Silvio attempts to set fire to the bookstore, he rejoices in how manly the act must have made him appear. But at this key moment of private liberation, he literally explores his exterior self, running his fingers over his face to fashion an exterior representation: "What painter will make the portrait of the sleeping shop assistant" (159). In dealing with others, Silvio actively creates these self-portraits from his models as he would assume a theatrical role but with close attention to his audience's reactions, as in the military interview: "I gazed at the countenances of hard lines and inquisitive eyes . . . of men who observed me between curious and ironic." Calling to mind one of his role models, he fashions a self appropriate to the scenario: "I thought of the heroes of my favorite readings, and the appearance of Rocambole . . . with a rubber visored cap and a riffraff smile on his twisted mouth, passed before my eyes, inciting me toward confidence and the heroic attitude" (168).

The compelling sensation of being watched, at times by an unidentifiable source, characterizes Silvio's experience of city life. In one hallucinatory moment, for example, he discerns through a chaotic scene of suspended cement buckets a fragmented countenance held together by a single, enormous, winking eye. This image forecasts the sensation of a Foucaultian panoptic gaze, a paranoia, as Masiello has suggested, that sometimes pursues both characters and reader in Arlt's later novels (*Lenguaje e ideología* 210). But the significance of this phenomenon for Silvio's self-analysis in *El juguete rabioso* derives from the protagonist's humiliating intimation that the selves he imagines himself to be portraying may not coincide with what others see. For example, although he fancies himself as a poet in his literary job, Silvio concludes that others see only a *pícaro*. His growing adeptness at playing roles for an audience obscures any coherent selfhood residing beneath, as he wonders at the military school who he really is underneath the uniform.

Thus the increasing subjectivity that accompanies Silvio's agility with theatrical roles only intensifies feelings of fragmentation, reducing overwhelming emotion to physical sensations: for example, anger at his employers, a "red fog" within his cranium (156). This stripping down of the self becomes particularly intense in Silvio's most subjective moments, for example, as he calmly contemplates suicide and sees himself as nothing but a heartbeat and "an eye, lucid and open to the extremely serene interior" (192).

The fragile selfhood that the protagonist finally achieves is tied to his mastery of the city, to the ability of that lucid and open eye to turn outward, and to the concomitant vocational choice as a storyteller. It is crucial for this work's portrait of an artist that the decision to write coincide with growing skills in urban life, as the contentious encounter with his city unfolds in Silvio-protagonist's artistic persona and Silvio-narrator's literary style. Though he never stops dreaming of distant places and his imagination is forever populated by literary presences, Silvio the character confronts his surroundings rebelliously as he wanders throughout the city. These forays to recognizable Buenos Aires locations reinforce the sense of direct engagement between an artist and his world, an engagement as crucial for the character's artistic development as heroic models or constant readings.[14]

The urban roaming itself constitutes Silvio's personal learning style and shapes his artistic apprenticeship. Arlt himself lauded the virtues of this approach in a 1928 journalistic sketch, one of his *Aguafuertes porteñas,* entitled "El placer de vagabundear" (literally, the pleasure of vagabonding). The Buenos Aires wanderer, especially a would-be artist, Arlt observed, would be awed by "the extraordinary finds of the street" (*OC* 2: 446). We should recall that in the novel, Silvio's single successful job is as a wanderer, a traveling salesman. Imbued with the exploratory spirit of his mentors Edison and Napoleon, Silvio and his friends approach their environment through larcenous expeditions, "organized to rob fruit or discover buried treasures" (93), as when they experiment with homemade explosives and imagine that they have actually discovered a new continent and become "owners of the earth" (94). This discovering attitude, similar to Peter Bürger's characterization of the surrealists' marvel-seeking forays through Paris (Bürger 71), marks Silvio's critical eye and estranging perceptions that ascribe newness to the most ordinary things. Silvio becomes aware of this discovering attitude just as he chooses a storytelling vocation and imagines that he is a recent arrival on earth for whom everything is totally new.

The urban meanderings also constitute Silvio's education as an inventor, as artistic and life apprenticeships coincide, for he learns to conceive mechanical projects during what he describes as observant hours of vagrancy. He explains to the military interviewers where he has studied. "Everywhere, sir. For example: I go along the street and at a mechanics shop I see a machine I don't know. I stop, and I tell myself studying the different parts: this must work like this and like this" (170). In fact, it is the ability to construct, to put things together, that Silvio gleans from his urban surroundings. Although he yearns to become an inventor like Edison, the method he employs is *fabrication,* a word frequently used in the novel which, in the spirit of both Rocambole and Edison, combines the deception of larceny and the creativity of invention in a concept that, in its allusions to construction, also connotes the activity of a workaday world. In his study of *El juguete rabioso,* Christopher Towne Leland analyzes the relationship between the concept of inventing and Silvio's efforts at self-transformation. But my interest here is in fabrication as a kind of inventing with additional connotations. On the material level, *fabricar* means to construct (often by mechanical means), as a building, a bridge, or a wall. But on the figurative level—"to make or make use of something not material"—the word carries long-standing connotations of deception, as in the example provided by the Real Academia Española's example of this usage: "fabricar una mentira" (to fabricate a lie; *Diccionario de la lengua española,* 20th ed.).[15] This combination of creative construction and deception or artifice is reinforced by dictionaries of contemporary Spanish usage that define *fabricar,* for example, as "inventar cuentos, mentiras, historias, líos" (to invent stories, lies, histories, intrigues; Moliner 1267). Silvio's real-life mentors reinforce this synthesis of imaginative construction and deception, including Irzubeta, the "Falsifier" who progresses from faking toy flags to forging checks, and Hipólito, who can "fabricate" airplanes from bamboo. Silvio's own inventive method relies similarly on fabrication, as he creates something new—a homemade culverin, for example—by piecing together miscellaneous fragments gathered around the city. His mentor-friend Rengo perfects this method, for he can fabricate a sumptuous beefsteak meal from leftover marketplace scraps, a little grease and a few meaty bones here, a bit of potato and a slash of liver there. Silvio himself masters this technique in assembling a mediocre but viable clientele, pieced together, he explains, from miscellaneous market tenders, pharmacists, booksellers, and merchants.

Silvio also succeeds in creating a viable, functioning self when he realizes the fabrication required to construct a believable character. Assuming a real-life role such as that of a salesman, he learns, works best not by imitating a single model like Rocambole but by self-consciously assembling a persona from miscellaneous gestures and words in order to become "multiple, flexible and charming" (208). Significantly, Silvio also ultimately suggests that even his more interiorized self, the "real" self under theatrical representations, possesses a similar collagelike quality, like a god made from "pieces of mountain, of woods, of sky and of memory" (205). This pieced-together self undermines the novel's organic models of personal development, including the *Bildungsroman* structure of integrated personal formation and the work's references to character "regeneration," a concept Silvio's friend Rengo explains in Darwinian terms. It is true that in his story Silvio is forever new, as each chapter signals an inauguration into a new profession, a new part of the city, a new way of life. And at the end, Silvio, leaving the city to write, will begin a new life yet again. But he begins again each time not through a clearly plotted development but through a process of self-fabrication, of artifice by piecing together. This process challenges organic models of personal formation or biological regeneration as well as romantic notions of individual artistic originality and, in the vanguardist mode, favors character construction that is openly nonorganic, as in Bürger's term for describing the vanguardist work of art.[16]

As I have noted, the model of artist as fabricator emerging from Silvio's urban wanderings ascribes, in the vanguardist spirit, a legitimizing aura of work, of construction, to artistic activity. But Silvio himself abhors work with only material ends, and his daily doings are often marked by a tone of gratuitous play. The boys concoct explosives because they enjoy the pyrotechnics, and the club is a childlike, if larcenous, organization, an elaborate game of make-believe. And Silvio plays a variety of roles, sometimes merely for pleasure. Significantly, his inventions are notably impractical; they include a machine for counting stars and, in keeping with the vanguards' linguistic experiments, one for transcribing words into writing. Although his bitter work-world encounters do much to curb his playfulness, the frolicsome attitude toward life returns with the decision to write. Having matched his perverse environment with his own perversity, as an artistic persona descended to the level of the sordid world, Silvio reaffirms the ludic impulse as he explains the decision to write so that he may teach people to be happy, "to play pirates . . . , to build marble cities . . . , to laugh . . . , to shoot off fireworks" (238).

As Silvio-protagonist and Silvio-narrator begin to merge in the choice to become a writer, parallels become evident between the apprenticeship in life and the one in art, between the character's skills forged from his urban encounters and the emergent artist's style in the memoirs we are reading. The decision to become a writer appears to coincide with a relinquishing of the heroic artistic persona. Thus Silvio's uphill struggle to fashion an integrated self is paralleled by the narrator-Silvio's elusively situated voice, as if, once having decided to write, the artist as a forceful individual presence in his work consciously begins to disappear. But we recognize him through his style. The peripatetic structure of the narrator's tale, for example, reflects Silvio's hours of vagrancy through the city. Although it follows a rough temporal sequence, the story is marked by frequent narrative vagaries. Paralleling the character's fabrication of ingenious inventions from miscellaneous gathered parts, the narrator, in a synthesis of larceny and creativity, fabricates the character's story by irreverently piecing together, as critics have documented, heterogeneous traditions and sources: the picaresque, the *Bildungsroman,* the serial novel (each chapter could be a self-contained issue), the Dostoyevskian interiorized confession, Baudelairean lyric subjectivity, and stylistic bits and pieces akin to the work of Hispanic writers such as Pío Baroja and the nineteenth-century Argentine writers Esteban Echeverría and Domingo Faustino Sarmiento. As Rita Gnutzmann has carefully documented, a comparable pieced-together assemblage constitutes the narrator's linguistic repertoire, a heterogeneous amalgam of Argentine *lunfardo,* colloquialisms, foreign words, invented words, and scientific terms (Introducción 50–64). In addition, incorporating the protagonist's discovering attitude, the narrator subjects the city to a critical eye, turning characters into grotesque caricatures and ordinary scenes into defamiliarized landscapes: "the enormous oblique chimneys, the unfolding of the chains in somersaults, with the shouts of the maneuvers, the solitude of the svelte masts, the attention already divided in a countenance that looked out at an eye of an ox and an iron bar suspended by a crane over my head" (191).

Silvio's decision to tell stories coincides with his awareness that he can fabricate a scene by juxtaposing styles stolen from others with his own lucidly critical vision. Adjacent passages describing city scenes, for example, evoke and ironically juxtapose two versions of nineteenth-century Argentine romanticism, Echeverría's grotesque portrayal of gaucho life and Sarmiento's expansive descriptions of the pampas' unending horizon. Thus, on the one hand, Silvio describes a butcher's floor, evoking Echeverría's *El matadero:* "covered with sawdust, the smell of tallow floated in the air, black swarms of flies seethed in the chunks of yellow fat, and the impassive butcher sawed the bones" (203). And, on the other, in the passage immediately following, the narrator focuses on a Sarmiento-like endless sky, which in this case also reflects the sea: "the smooth space like a celestial porcelain in the blue frontier, with the depth of the gulf in the zenith" (203). The artist's "originality" in this case consists in piecing these inherited images together. The resulting passage, moreover, subjects to the narrator's critical eye not only the Buenos Aires landscape itself but also the ways in which others have seen it.

The irony in the juxtaposition also reveals stresses in the narrator's style, as well as in the vanguardist project, between the playful and the serious. For just as Silvio the character's inventive activity is sometimes cast in a playful mold, so does the narrator play with his sources. He also plays with the reader's expectations through the sources he evokes and the generic scraps he assembles like Rengo's beefsteak meal. Pérez Firmat has affirmed in *Idle Fictions,* his study of the Hispanic vanguard novel, that vanguardist prose fiction plays with its ancestors, a phenomenon that, according to Bakhtin, characterizes the entire Western novelistic tradition.[17] But that play has a serious purpose in critiquing the worldviews implicit in the genres it steals and, in keeping with Bürger's characterization of vanguardist activity, in its irreverence toward the stylistic hierarchies posed by artistic tradition (Bürger 63). The placement of Baudelaire and Rocambole on equal footing underscores such irreverence in Arlt's case. It is important to note, moreover, that in *El juguete rabioso,* the literary critique encompasses the vanguardist project itself, played out in Silvio's four models that evoke, as I have demonstrated, elements of vanguardist discourse about art. The image of art as both gratuitous play and serious critique is already implicit in the novel's title. Significantly, the "toy" refers to the activity of play by focusing on the object constructed for this purpose and reinforces the idea of creative fabrication in the objects (rockets, explosives) that Silvio and his friends build for their own entertainment. But the qualifier "rabioso," furious or raving, gives this invention an oxymoronic quality, juxtaposing play and raving. The combination underscores the artist-in-the-making's conflictive interaction with his surroundings and undermines the possibility of regarding the toy, the artistic fabrication, as a totally autonomous, gratuitous, or disengaged object.

Silvio Astier's project for a magnificent destiny and personal transcendence notwithstanding, the figure constructed by *El juguete rabioso* through the interaction of its narrating voice with its acting protagonist poses quite a different view of the vanguardist artist. The *Bildungsroman* ambience promises an individual's integrated formation. But the protagonist's shaky interior solidity and need to fabricate a viable self as well as the elusively situated narrating voice signal an artist defined less as a biographical personality and more as a singular form of interacting with his world. An urban rambler saturated by a heterogeneous literary heritage, he cloaks himself in an aura of scientific and exploratory action and fabricates art by assembling the scraps taken from both his literary and his lived environment. Irreverently critical toward artistic traditions, this artist contentiously focuses the inner eye of a lyric inheritance on the limits of his own aesthetic power and on the problematic surroundings through which he moves.

THE ARTIST'S "DISORDERLY HUMANITY": TORRES BODET'S *LA EDUCACIÓN SENTIMENTAL*

Through his literary criticism and experimental novels, Jaime Torres Bodet, a member of Mexico's Contemporáneos group, participated in vanguardist debates about the interaction between art and human experience. Specifically, he initiated, as I have noted, a dialogue with Ortega y Gasset's *La deshumanización del arte*. These concerns are fully explored in his second novel, *La educación sentimental* (1929; The Sentimental Education), the story of a would-be writer who studies the interaction of art and life that shapes individual styles. But the debate had already been joined in Torres Bodet's first novel, *Margarita de niebla*, through the protagonist's self-contemplative scene evoking the Orteguian windowpane-garden metaphor, a scenario I have described in this chapter's opening lines. In a 1928 critique of Ortega's work explicitly entitled "La deshumanización del arte," moreover, Torres Bodet took issue with Ortega's assessment that modern aesthetic sensibility derived from a "triumph over the human" and defended a place in contemporary aesthetics for contact with the very "disorderly humanity" that, the Mexican writer asserted, Ortega would "exile from the work of art" (*Contemporáneos* 127, 123).[18] There is no art, Torres Bodet insisted, without a "struggle" with the "human matter" that it stylizes (*Contemporáneos* 127–28). On the same note, he affirmed in the 1928 essay "La poesía nueva" that "reality itself will always be the support and the pretext for the work of art" (*Contemporáneos* 29).

In his own prose fiction, but most explicitly in *La educación sentimental,* Torres Bodet explored these issues further, reinforcing the position that art and experience interact with and shape one another. In his study of the Hispanic vanguard novel, Pérez Firmat suggests that this work may be read either literally as a "slight" *Bildungsroman* or allegorically as a response to Ortega's ideas on the lack of transcendence in modern art (76).[19] Pursuing the second of these options, he then argues that *La educación sentimental* shows how the "perfect poem" produced by an autonomous conception of art "cannot shield itself from the impure substance of life" (77) and, conversely, that the novel protagonist's life experience is shaped by what he reads. I propose a reading that expands on Pérez Firmat's work and, at the same time, shifts its emphasis. I am particularly interested here in how the novel's narrating artist protagonist seeks to construct an artistic self by analyzing how his mentors' life experiences are marked by a particular artistic style. "Style" in this novel's idiom refers to a means of artistic expression that is both individual and marked by historical periods and generic conventions. Bürger argues that the absence of a characteristic style constitutes a distinguishing feature of the historical avant-gardes. Instead, the vanguards made available the artistic means of all periods, and it is only through this "universal availability" that artistic means, or styles, become recognizable as such (18). Torres Bodet's protagonist in *La educación sentimental* manifests this recognition, as he draws on his mentors' styles and examines how different artistic styles—neoclassical, romantic, or Spanish American *modernista*—interact with ordinary experience.

On the most accessible level, *La educación sentimental* presents the account of an adolescent friendship critical for its autobiographical narrator's maturation. The more experienced and literate Alejandro provides a model for the overprotected and unformed narrator-protagonist. Key moments include a separation between the friends when the narrator, vacationing in Cuautla, seeks to construct a more solid sense of self and the discovery when he visits Alejandro's home uninvited that this cultured young man is a prostitute's son. As in *El juguete rabioso,* *Bildungsroman* markers are evident: adolescence, school, parental and peer mentors, separation and self-contemplation in an idyllic setting, and loss of innocence. The narrator-protagonist's artistic aspirations also suggest the artist's story or *Künstlerroman,* a context reinforced by discussions of his readings. But despite these familiar elements reinforced by the title from Flaubert's novel, Torres Bodet's work devotes scant attention to the narrator's development as an individual. If *El juguete rabioso* undermines the artist's solidity through an elusively situated narrative voice, here the nameless narrating protagonist is enveloped by unanswered questions. Instead of clarifying identities, an ambiguous Cervantine "preamble" cloaks the artistic persona in anonymity and directs the reader's attention to the problem of literary style. Here an unidentified publisher-narrator introduces the work and its nameless narrator-protagonist. The latter, a childhood friend and a "failed poet," has been rediscovered as a fifty-year-old teacher in the school where he was once a student. This teacher, the reader surmises, embodies the autobiographical voice that speaks in the chapters that follow. The work itself is introduced as the teacher's youthful diary, turned over to the preamble's narrator to be published at its author's request.[20]

The preamble draws significant links between this "found manuscript" and its "found" author. Both are cloaked in the ambiguity of the preamble's opening line: "I don't know if I might affirm that the author of this notebook—biographic?—might really have been my friend" (101). Both are texts to be read, moreover: the diary is enclosed in a notebook (a *cuaderno*) and its author's face, "bookish and positive like Spencer's" and "scrupulously bound" *(encuadernado)* by sideburns, exhibits a comparable learned facade (101). In addition, discrepancies between the preamble and the text it introduces—entitled *La educación sentimental*—suggest that both the manuscript and its author have undergone change. Though the preamble's narrator-publisher reports that he has found his childhood friend unaltered, he also characterizes the diary's author paradoxically as capable of "a permanent apprenticeship" (101). If Silvio Astier's failed dreams of grandeur in *El juguete rabioso* yield to fabricating a personal style, opening assertions in Torres Bodet's novel intimate that this learning process is also a stylistic apprenticeship. Although the preamble describes the volume as a diary, for example, the actual telling of *La educación sentimental* unfolds not through the alternating intercalated narrative of a diary but through an ulterior narration of youthful moments, a temporal structure reinforced by such references as "in those years" (118) contrasting with allusions to "in our time" (104). Thus, if the work really began as a diary, it has been subjected to subsequent editorial intervention, and its autobiographical narrator hints retrospectively that he is responsible, with a reference to his expressive development: "if I had known how to express myself then with the words with which I do now" (111). Intimating the evolution of a literary style, this comment suggests that, through maturation, the narrator, like his notebook, has been "rewritten." The possibility of a stylistic apprenticeship is reinforced by a contradiction the reader immediately perceives between the "honorable poverty" of style attributed by the preamble to the manuscript and the stylistic richness of the document that follows. In fact, the marked stylistic similarities between the preamble and the manuscript it introduces suggest that the preamble's narration represents a self-reflexive doubling on the part of the manuscript's autobiographical narrator, a move that reinforces the self-contemplatory stance of *La educación sentimental* itself.

In keeping with the preamble's focus on style, the text's principal narrator engages in meticulous retrospective readings of the mentors, his parents and Alejandro, who have shaped his own stylistic apprenticeship. Like Silvio in *El juguete rabioso,* the narrator is immersed in his surroundings, the city streets he wanders with Alejandro, and engaged with the people he encounters in the neighborhood and his parents' home. But his focus on style mediates this interaction with his environment. In contrast to the Argentine novel and in keeping with the Contemporáneos group's eschewal of overt social commentary, this work includes few concrete Mexico City referents. Like *El juguete rabioso, La educación sentimental* also plays with its sources through literary allusion, parodic appropriation, and the same Bakhtinian "autocriticism of discourse" that pits Silvio's idealized models against his life. But here this "ancestral critique," to paraphrase Pérez Firmat, becomes the center of the artist's story and manifests Torres Bodet's concern with the interaction of art with life. The narrator in *La educación sentimental* examines, with a humorously critical eye, how each of his mentors stylizes ordinary experience by filtering it through specific aesthetic traditions. His mother provokes the narrator's initial awareness of this process. She selects her children's associates with care, "until . . . having completely assimilated them . . . to the particular mode of the house and the fundamental norms of her style" (110). Faithful to her French origins, the mother embodies a neoclassical spirit, and the narrator sees in her the source for whatever degree of tidy classicism he may possess. Although she seldom writes more than letters, she has inherited "the rigor of good prosody" (110), a talent she applies to everyday life. His mother, the narrator notes, engages in a very specific strategy: "to reduce the human material to the perfect—but undoubtedly impoverished—proportions of the too strict Ars Poética, in whose angles I later recognized, upon reading Boileau, their unquestionable origin" (110). The mother privileges style over content, for she accepts adversarial viewpoints if they are forged with "the elegance of correct elocution" (111). Her tutelage, the narrator suggests, has best prepared him to be a piano tuner, for the "mechanical uniformity" of her expressions (117) and her "typographical voice" (125) have served not only to censor his youthful readings but also to eliminate any false notes he might emit. In the neoclassical spirit, she tolerates idiosyncrasy by assimilating troublesome difference into generality, recognizing in the "singularities" of all people "the appearance of a general virtue" (110).

Also a product of the Enlightenment, the narrator's father exhibits more of its romantic spirit and modern tensions. In contrast to the mother, the father approaches the raw material of life with the zeal of a modern collector. As a "man of the Encyclopedia," he sometimes does bring to his collections the "minutiae" of the entomologist and "the systems and the fever of the cataloguer" (108–109). But although he began by collecting stamps, the father's assemblages begin to manifest the tensions between order and chaos that Walter Benjamin ascribed to all collections ("Unpacking My Library" 60). Thus the narrator compares the disorderly state of his father's collections to a novelist's style, a conception reminiscent of Silvio Astier's vanguardist talent in *El juguete rabioso* for larceny and assembled fabrications: "that vague aptitude to gather poems, figures, objects, cigarette rings, medallion profiles, comedies of manners, women, dates, keys and fans that lies dormant in the depths of every good novelist and constitutes the charm of *every good thief* (108; my emphasis).

The father's most serious collection, the anthology of his friendships, exhibits his talent for discerning the exotic within the banal. Unlike his wife, who assimilates friends into the neoclassical order of her household, the father seeks out eccentricities in his friends' most mundane habits, qualities amenable to the caricature of a critical eye. Thus one friend is selected for the "perfect bad taste" of his jackets, another, a golfer, for the singular way in which he lands four lumps of sugar in his tea at a single swing (109). In keeping with romanticism's primitivist mode, the father singles out his female friends as replacements for his own "lost animality" and selects them not for their beauty but for their "fury, sensuality, or gluttony" (109). While the mother tolerates and even erases difference by absorbing it into her worldview, the father possesses a modern propensity for exposing difference through curious juxtapositions. Thus the narrator greatly admires his father's novelistic gatherings of miscellany or his collection of rare tuberoses with obscure Latin names that might be provocatively combined, the narrator notes, by surrealist poets. Similarly, the narrator concludes that his father's singular storytelling style derives from the ability to superimpose temporal planes into a single simultaneous moment.

But the mysterious Alejandro presents the narrator's most important model, and deciphering his friend's style is critical in identifying and constructing a style of his own. Decidedly unique, Alejandro is the only one to appear "handwritten" among the other students, "an ensemble of mechanical copies" (104). Still, his style resembles the mother's in its propensity for order. He is "tidy," "moderated," and "orthographic" (144). He shares the mother's correct elocution, and she admires his "precise lucidity" (112). Alejandro writes clean and "modest" school compositions (122), and his prose, which the narrator attempts to imitate in his youth, is "transparent, temperate and angularly cerebral," his style "logically mature" (121). He selects exact topics for his compositions and applies to them the "precise sharpness" of titles almost modern in their succinctness (122).

For the narrator, however, there is much in Alejandro, including the inexplicable reserve about family, that simply does not coalesce. Alejandro is, in fact, the character in *La educación sentimental* who most palpably embodies Torres Bodet's focus on the interaction between art and human experience. The narrator is most intrigued by an apparent incongruity between Alejandro's style and his substance, and this quality intensifies the narrator's concern with the interaction between a style and a life. This gap is manifested in Alejandro's physical demeanor with imagery that suggests a form-content tension. His fragile heels are too thin for his very thick shoes, and, in the boxing ring, his body seems to disguise his great strength. In addition, there is something too natural in his modesty resembling an "artful spring," a quality that for the narrator seems to blur the boundaries between artifice and spontaneity, imposing the strategies of art on life (106).

While the parents embody the narrator's classical and romantic stylistic inheritance, with the latter pointing toward its legacy to the vanguards, Alejandro's qualities recall more immediate antecedents, the Spanish American *modernista* tradition. Changing from camaraderie to eventual distance, the narrator's connection with his friend embodies the would-be artist's coming to terms with the *modernismo* legacy. Alejandro's conversation is peppered with obscure aesthetic allusions, his name hints at one of the *modernista* poet's favorite verse forms (the *alejandrino*), and his physical description harbors a paradigmatic *modernista* motif, the interrogating neck of a swan: "He sustained an abstract head . . . on the bough of an elegant but indecisive neck, like a vague question mark" (103). In addition, Alejandro wants to be an architect and, like the *modernista* writer, is concerned with ornamentation and formal perfection, qualities the narrator ascribes to his voice, his expressive means: "every inflection now seemed to me the project of a form: the unfolded fan of a staircase, the charming perspective of a window, the arc and the foliage, dense, of a column" (116). The title's allusion to Flaubert and the preamble's invocation of the French novelist as a mentor reinforce Alejandro's modernist aura, for, as I have noted, Aníbal González has documented convincingly that *modernista* prose writers, like Flaubert, compared the "immense and tenacious" labors of art to that of "the craftsman in his workshop" (21).[21] But Alejandro's most intriguing quality in the narrator's eyes is the disjunction between the "great calligraphic pulchritude" of his personal presence and the "eternal litigation of languages" and the "confused urban paragraph" that define the neighborhood of his origins (143). This discordant note in Alejandro's persona points precisely to what Gwen Kirkpatrick has termed *modernismo*'s "dissonant legacy" to developments in art that followed. The contradiction also reiterates Torres Bodet's own concern with the interaction between art and life. As González has shown, *modernista* novels portrayed artists engaged in anguished vacillations between aestheticist, intellectual strivings and life in a turbulent world (31–52), stresses that were laid bare and intensified in vanguardist experience.

Through this retrospective scrutiny of his mentors' styles, the narrator begins to identify an emerging style of his own. He calls attention to this process of constructing a self through the contemplation of others, as he stares at his mother's aging photograph and perceives in it "the gallery of my successive images as a child, as an adolescent and as a mature man" (107). But, as with Silvio's self-fabrication in Arlt's novel, the developmental process intimated here is again more a matter of personal style than of individual substance. The narrator recalls that during the Cuautla vacation he first became aware of his own lack of originality and (like Silvio's thievery) his plagiaristic proclivities. As Pérez Firmat has noted, the narrator worries about his propensity for imitation (*Idle Fictions* 79). His speech, his toys, even his illnesses, he recalls, are identical to those of his friends, and he once even pilfered his language teacher's collection of tildes. This imitative dexterity was responsible, he feared, for his lack of "interior consistency" (126). In this novel's expressive system, however, interior consistency is grounded in a personal style. Significantly, the narrator's emergent sense of self in Cuautla is manifested in narcissistic hours of staring into a well, and the intensification of a highly subjective narration is accompanied by a growing "will to style" (to borrow Ortega's term). The narrator imagines, for example, altering the surrounding landscape with a "touch of shade" here or "a bit more green" there (139). This stylistic awareness becomes a fundamental component of the mature narrator's own style. Thus he appears at times to be more of an artistic critic than the artist he aspires to be, a critic who foregrounds the process of stylization itself in which experience is constructed through the worldviews of specific styles. By exposing this process and bringing varied styles into contiguity, the narrator engages in a typically vanguardist activity that, like Silvio Astier's fabrications, undermines stylistic hierarchies and emphasizes a process over a product or finished-work conception of art.[22]

This narrator is also an aspiring novelist, however. He seeks a narrative style through which to filter his experience as he reflects on "how difficult it would be to explain all of this in the chapter of a novel" (137). Steering away from the maternal example, the narrator seeks to avoid an over stylization of experience that might impoverish the raw material of life. He notes, for example, the importance of alternating in his own expression "the improvised pleasures of the fantastic" with "the delicious sense of the true" (115). He is bothered by Alejandro's austere literary allusions that, because of "the protective simplicity of the words," seem to be lacking in "the minimum of human meaning" (119-20). And it is precisely his overly formalized dialogues with Alejandro—"a closed world like the perfect poem" (116)—that lead him away from his friend and this *modernismo* goal for aesthetic perfection. Significantly, the narrator has been most intrigued by his friend's "dissonant legacy," that is, those features of his Alejandro experience that will not fit into the perfect poem's closed world: the fragile heels that the thick shoes will not accommodate, his friend's preference for unbound books, the mysteries of his background, and, most important, the rambling "incoherences" and "contradictions" harbored by the deceptively perfect poem of their conversations (138).

Concerned that his own style maintain some of these disorderly incongruities of experience, the narrator produces a text, *La educación sentimental,* that combines a penchant for unusual metaphors with a digressive baroque narration, a text that points to its own lack of perfection. Dominant metaphors render characters as material, often graphic, elements of language. These include the handwritten Alejandro, the mechanically copied (typewritten) students, the confused urban paragraph of Alejandro's world, a misplaced character identified as an "erratum" (146), and the family's vacation time female neighbors, the "five vowels" of Cuautla (128). Grounded in orthography, calligraphy, and phonology, these metaphors suggest a circumscription of experience through linguistic norms and representational modes. But with a proclivity for baroque syntax and metaphoric accumulation, the narrator's prose, like the narrator himself walking the city, tends to wander away from such tidy comparisons. Thus, although Alejandro is originally depicted as handwritten like a penmanship exercise, a subsequent image suggests a more idiosyncratic, languid motion, still reminiscent of writing on a page but distorted as through a slow-motion film. The narrator describes how each of Alejandro's movements "displaced in the air the volume acquired from the previous ones, letting the following ones slide, without haste, down the slope of a velocity that went and came neutral, isochronous, gentle, from one side to the other of the contest, like the hammock of a languor" (104).

Interestingly, the narrator appears to cultivate these metonymic meanderings to preserve in his prose something of the disorderly urban world that he and Alejandro have explored. Although he hails from a far more comfortable milieu than Silvio Astier, as in *El juguete rabioso,* the narrator's wanderings about the city with his friend—to poorer sections and the red-light district—provide a key element in his education. And although concrete geographic references are infrequent, the sense of a recognizable ambience as in Cuautla also reinforces the notion of an artist's engagement with a surrounding world. As with Silvio, moreover, these vagaries metonymically shape this narrator's metaphors.[23] Thus his own conversation disrupts the friendship's perfect poem: "I liked to . . . depart from a point established beforehand and move away from it, little by little, thanks to a series of conclusions without continuity" (118). The father's conversational style, a fundamental model for the narrator, manifests a similar tension between poetic image and rambling impulse: "his conversation flowed in the manner of the picture on those kimonos in whose silk people's names do not suppress them but rather contain them with the discretion of a portrait that is, at the same time, a monogram" (134–35). This graphic image, the monogram, embodies a spatial figure that, in contrast to *modernismo*'s closed poem, is simultaneously open and closed. The image also suggests a flowing prose style that, like the kimono's silk writing, will contain life's "disorderly humanity" without totally enclosing it. A similar tension between poetic containment and proselike digression is expressed through the image of an arabesque, a form not unlike the monogram in its ambiguous circumscription of space.

Y es que la educación, un poco escolástica, en que las conversaciones con Alejandro me habían ido envolviendo estaba tan llena de incoherencias y de contradicciones sutiles que yo mismo me extraviaba en ella como en el plano de esas ciudades del centro de España con cuyo trazo, de *musicales arabescos,* no pude abstenerme de compararla cuando las conocí. Antiguas, abandonadas y en *desorden, ninguna simetría las contiene, pero ningún sistema las sacrifica.* (138; my emphasis)

(And it seems that the education, somewhat scholastic, in which the conversations with Alejandro had been enclosing me was so full of incoherencies and subtle contradictions that I myself would become lost in it like in the map of those cities of central Spain with whose outline, of *musical arabesques,* I could not refrain from comparing it when I made their acquaintance. Ancient, abandoned and in *disorder, no symmetry contains them, but no system sacrifices them.*)

A comparable language of boundaries and digressions informs Torres Bodet's essay "Reflexiones sobre la novela" (1928). Modern novelistic writing had a debt to poetry, he observed, in a new kind of metaphoric description, "rich in oppositions." But through the modern novel, he asserted, the issue of style in art had shifted its center from a "form of expression" to a "form of exploration" (*Contemporáneos* 15), that is, from product to process. Through the poematic prose of *La educación sentimental,* the artist follows such an exploratory path. In the work's final scene, while walking slowly homeward, the narrator selects a strolling couple to follow at a distance. The description of this act points directly to his own emerging style: "And I continued to follow them in a kind of *leisurely, vagabond play* that—despite the journey—possessed nothing of the active risks of the hunt but rather the immobile risk of fishing that like the dream—or like poetry—does not pursue but waits for its discoveries" (153; my emphasis). Thus the narrator's style combines the chance metaphoric discoveries of his lyric inheritance with the "leisurely vagabond play" of a meandering prose that, like an arabesque or a monogram, seeks to stylize life without containing it.

Although the works are quite different in language and tone, the portrait of an artist constructed by *La educación sentimental* possesses meaningful points of contact with the artistic persona emerging from *El juguete rabioso.* This nameless protagonist remains elusive as an identifiable personality and lacks "interior consistency." Instead, the novel presents the "formation" promised by the *Bildungsroman* markers as the construction of a literary style. As in the development of Silvio Astier, this process includes a critical confrontation with the protagonist's surroundings as well as with inherited traditions. But here the confrontation with sources is more direct, as the narrator, with the sharp eye of a literary critic, displays and disassembles his role models to discern how each filters experience through style. The effect is an often humorous, critical view of the characters themselves and of the styles they embody.

The artist figure that emerges here engages in the activity of a discerning reader and critic who scrutinizes the styles of others. This portrayal of the artist as reader, moreover, establishes parallels with the novel's own implied reader, characterized by this work as one who would undertake a similar critical enterprise. Although in vanguardist novels the relationship is usually more subtly drawn, this conflation of artist and reader is also typical of the vanguardist manifesto. As I show in the chapter on manifestos, these documents simultaneously assault and court an imagined audience and often construct a recipient in the speaker's own image. Implicitly anticipating contemporary debates about art, its contexts, and interpretive activity, *La educación sentimental* poses a model for critical reading that is exclusively neither extrinsic nor intrinsic. More concretely, the model calls for the critic (the narrator-protagonist) to focus solely on neither the text (the mentor's style) nor the context (the mentor's experience and times) but rather on the interaction between the two.

To construct his own literary style, then, the artist narrator in *La educación sentimental* draws on those qualities of his antecedents that maintain something of a "disorderly" context: the *modernista* "dissonance" in Alejandro between his overformalized style and his substance, the father's miscellaneous collections and the temporal superimpositions of his storytelling style. In the same mode, the narrator selfconsciously absorbs into his own style something of his incongruent life in the very world he is scrutinizing, including the "leisurely, vagabond play" of his own meanderings through the city. At the heart of this narrator's activity is the work's refusal to separate sharply the domains of art and life. *La educación sentimental* reveals the dynamic relation between the Orteguian windowpane and garden through eyes that, optical limitations notwithstanding, struggle to focus on both. Thus as he critiques the styles of his mentors, the would-be artist narrator constructs his own tenuous interior consistency through a poematic prose style that exposes both the artifice shaping his human models and the irrepressible "disorderly humanity" impinging on his aesthetic ones.

THE TACHYGRAPHY OF A WAYFARING OBSERVER: ADÁN'S *LA CASA DE CARTÓN*

First published in 1928, *La casa de cartón* (The Cardboard House) is the only novel written by the Peruvian poet Martín Adán (born Rafael de la Fuente Benavides). The work's forty loosely linked, poematic prose fragments constitute one of the most radically antimimetic pieces of Latin America's vanguards. Pérez Firmat does not address this work in *Idle Fictions,* but, of the texts analyzed in this study, *La casa de cartón* most closely coincides with his conception of a "pneumatic aesthetics" to describe narrative works with diffuse characterization, nebulous form, and content resistant to plot reconstruction (Pérez Firmat 40–63). The text's forty lyric segments, interweaving subtle humor and nostalgia, present subjective visual evocations of scenes and people in Barranco, an ocean resort outside Lima, and in the city itself. Stressing the possibilities more than the tale, *La casa de cartón* intimates the ingredients for a story that is never quite told.[24] The identifiable setting is Barranco and Lima, the time a recent vacation interlude in the narrator's past. Principal characters are the nameless youthful narrator and his close friend and mentor, Ramón, whose death has apparently provoked the recollections we are reading. Additional characters include other male companions, the young women with whom the youths form sentimental attachments, and caricaturesque snippets of Barranco inhabitants, Peruvian and foreign. In general, character activities, never organized into a conventional plot, include oceanside interludes, trolley rides and walks in Barranco and Lima, discussions of readings, erotic encounters, and the narrator's peripatetic, penetrating observations of the world and the people around him. Thirty-nine of the forty sections present a primarily autodiegetic poematic narration sliding from present to past tense and often directly addressing a narratee, that is, a "you" sometimes specifically identified as Ramón. The twenty-seventh segment, appearing as an insertion into the work, consists of the "Poemas Underwood," found, the narrator explains, in a book of Ramón's.

Critics of *La casa de cartón* have aptly noted its innovative features: Luis Loayza, its generic ambiguity; Mirko Lauer, its cinematographic and "kaleidoscopic" imagery, ironic stance toward the modern, and introspective examination of Peru; and John Kinsella, its eschewal of chronological progression, subjective constructions of time and space, and shifting cubist and surrealist imagery. My own specific concern is the image of an artist that the piece constructs, an issue also briefly addressed by Kinsella but with conclusions different from my own.[25] As with *El juguete rabioso* and *La educación sentimental,* this work harbors numerous *Bildungsroman* markers: adolescence, schooldays and vacations, mentoring friendship, ironic portrayal of elders and teachers, erotic initiations, conflict between an unconventional youth and a rule-driven world, and a narrating self looking backward. Other elements in the work suggest an artist's story in the making. The first is the nebulous identity boundaries between the dominant narrator and his mentor-friend Ramón, who is described as a poet. The narrator's scenes are presented as a synthesis of his own recollections and excerpts that he has culled from Ramón's diary. The text's slippage in personal pronouns underscores the ambiguity. Although the first-person voice dominates the narration, in the opening scene a voice addresses an ambiguous "you," either a self-contemplative doubling or a constant companion. The narrator's first concrete recollection of an afternoon with his friend further conflates their identities: "And there is nobody who isn't you or I" (9; KS 9).[26]

The narrator's reports of literary odysseys and debates contribute to the *Künstlerroman* ambience and suggest the story of an aspiring modern artist with an ambivalent relationship to modernity. There is little overt presence in *La casa de cartón* of the social concerns, *indigenismo* in particular, that shaped much of Peru's vanguardist activity. But in presenting artistlike characters simultaneously immersed in and humorously critical of a recognizable Peruvian urban world, the novel actually epitomizes Mariátegui's model for the new artist: engaged but always heterodox. Specifically, with remnants of aestheticist superiority, the narrator casts an irreverent eye toward the interaction between Latin America's literary life and the modern European cultural scene. Section

11 parodies the Latin American writer's obligatory European pilgrimage in a comic, oneiric account of a young novelist friend's transcontinental leaps: one minute he is strolling through Latin American consulates in Paris, and the next moment, he awakens in Barranco. The following section comments ironically on Peru's cultural environment: "frenetic and infantile, experienced and weary, critical and dilettantish" (23; KS 27). This mood is linked to the fascination with Europe, ascribed to the general post–World War I travel frenzy characterizing modernity, with references to globe-trotting modern writers fashionable in Peru (Blaise Cendrars, Paul Morand, Panait Istrati) as well as to characters, foreign and local, creating an international atmosphere in Barranco. These characters include secretaries, foreign owners of Peruvian companies, students in European schools, and female tourists drawn to the resort for both salutary and erotic ends.

The skeptical portrait of a provincially tinted international modernity notwithstanding, the narrator's critical reports of the youths' readings identify this as the story of an experimental artist, a vanguardist in spite of himself. The narrator recounts the youths' guarded reactions to harbingers of European modernism such as Pirandello, Joyce, Shaw, and Wilde. Instead, he notes with irony, they adhered to the "moldy stew" of Spanish literature, a target for the narrator's vanguard-style, scathing critique of his literary ancestors for failing to challenge their readers: Benavente's "clichéd conversations," Fernán Caballero's literature with "ecclesiastical license," Pardo Bazán's writings "full of sins that are never committed," Pereda's "withered and uncouth literature," and Galdós's "practical and perilous literature with consumptives and the insane and criminals and the diseased, all of whom the reader sees from afar at no risk to himself" (45; KS 54–55).

The narrator's focus on the problems of representation and of the relationship of experience and art further identifies La casa de cartón as the story of an artist in formation. Concretely, the narrator informs us, he wonders about the connections between a character he constructs through writing and his vague recollections of the original. This inquiry seems particularly apt in a work filled with fragmented but highly memorable satirical character sketches: Herr Oswald Teller, a German boarder in Ramón's house; the gringa photographer Miss Annie Doll; the schoolteacher Señorita Muler; and Catita, girlfriend to both the narrator and Ramón. Reading the description in Ramón's diary of a man they had seen at the beach, the narrator seeks to reconstruct his image from the written fragments: an index finger "yellowed by tobacco," an "ashen moustache with golden handlebars," trousers that are "empty holes, with large bulges at the knees" (41; KS 48). Was this simply their own invention, the narrator wonders, or did the man actually exist? This type of disjointed description permeates the narrator's own character constructions, including the *beatas* who are merely swaying black bulks or old men who are creaking bones enveloped in empty cloth.

Just as Ramón attempted to reconstruct the man on the beach through writing, the narrator now seeks without success to construct an "iconography" of Ramón in his memory. But what remains, the narrator laments, are only fragmentary lines and images, as lacking in solidity and dimension as the title's cardboard house. Still, the narrator insists, challenging the knowability of originals, these disconnected character constructions (dehumanized, in Orteguian terms) bear a strong similarity to his lived experience of the self's fragile consistency. The narrator considers this creative image-making process a fundamental quotidian experience, for just as he constructs images through the characters he encounters, so, he observes, are others, including wandering Lima dogs and mules in Barranco streets, constructing him in their imaginations. This specularly interactive process further challenges concepts of individual formation and solidity. Addressing Catita after Ramón's death, the narrator denies the *Bildungsroman* notion of individual formation—"life is not a river that flows"—and affirms instead the simulacrous process of representation through image making that construes life as a stagnating puddle in which unknown faces are reflected, a "turbid and interceding mirror" (64; KS 77).

If the narrator (re)constructs Ramón and other characters through interactive contemplation and image making, the reader is challenged to discern through the work's own "turbid and interceding mirror" the portrait of the artist the narrator-Ramón construct embodies. While the image that emerges is shifting, it displays certain identifying marks. One is the sense of a tenuously (dis)integrated self that permeates, as I have shown, all of the character representations in *La casa de cartón*. If *El juguete rabioso* and *La educación sentimental* reveal their narrators' lack of interior consistency, in Adán's work, this absence takes center stage. The narrator's own elusive solidity is manifested not only in the identity blurrings with Ramón but also in the fragmented quality the narrator ascribes to himself. Thus the initial scene's first reference to a speaking human presence, identified solely by physical and psychological sensations, is marked by the absence of any personal pronoun at all: "Breakfast is a warm ball in the stomach, the hardness of the dining room chair on the buttocks, and the solemn desire in the entire body not to go to school" (5; KS 1). As anonymous as the enigmatic narrator in *La educación sentimental*, this speaker circumvents the romantic notion of an artist's psychological self.

As I have noted, despite an ambivalent relationship with modernity, this narrator manifests traits of a deliberately vanguardist artist, most specifically, in the merciless critique of his literary ancestors, particularly their failure to discomfit their readers. The portrait of a vanguardist artist is reinforced by Ramón's Underwood poems and their title that echo the self-affirming rhetoric, the clipped, direct style, and the modernity clichés of a manifesto. In a series of "I am" pronouncements that, like the narrator's text, sometimes unfold into a "you," the verse's poet-speaker cloaks aestheticist claims to singularity and a rebellious, unconventional spirit in vanguardist metaphors of modern life. "Your heart is a horn prohibited by the traffic regulations" (50; KS 61), the speaker declares, cautioning further that those who reveal themselves as poets will be arrested. In addition, these verses and the narrator's text also manifest the stresses that I have noted in vanguardist manifestos between a cosmic vision and engagement with the very ordinary world. The narrator's prose shifts frequently from an all-encompassing perspective to the minutiae of his own everyday reality. Facing Barranco's oceanside cliffs, he imagines in the rock old men's faces that are simultaneously global and concretely Peruvian, evoking, on the one hand, the four cardinal points of the world, but looking, on the other, simply like old Lima men. In a comparable perspective shift, the narrator portrays himself as a global being, pointing in all four directions. From this totalizing image that encompasses a human composite of Turkish, Spanish, French, Roman, German, Belgian, Russian, and Jewish, the focalization moves abruptly toward the very local: Barranco's beach, fig trees, and beast-drawn carts.

Reinforcing these stresses between the global and the quotidian, the speaker in Ramón's Underwood poems vacillates between aestheticist distance and identification with ordinary people. He contrasts himself with discontented people encountered on city streets. Whereas they are "calloused by offices" (50; KS 62), the speaker is unconventional, happy, and doubtful of his own humanity. "Humanity" in the work's expressive system denotes, in an Orteguian spirit, institutionalizations of the ordinary. Thus domesticated donkeys on city sidewalks are portrayed as "municipalized, bureaucratized, humanized" (74; KS 89).

While setting himself apart in this fashion, however, the Underwood speaker underscores his own banality: he has no great thoughts, denies any personal exceptionality, and pledges to love his fellow humans.

His inward-turning subjectivity notwithstanding, the artist embodied in the narrator-Ramón pair is intensely involved with his surroundings, the concrete Barranco and Lima context. The characters' principal activity, after all, is traversing beaches and streets. The textual effects of these wanderings led Mario Vargas Llosa to affirm in an early study that this radically antimimetic work is characterized by a type of subjective realism and Mirko Lauer, in agreeing with Vargas Llosa, to observe that *La casa de cartón* presents the first interiorized recording of Peru's reality (Lauer 30–31). As with *El juguete rabioso* and *La educación sentimental,* the reader of *La casa de cartón* who has actually walked through Barranco or Lima streets may experience, even considering the city's radical changes, an uncanny sense of déjà vu. The Barranco-specific motifs are constant: the streetcars, the carts, the fig trees, the jacarandas, the *garúa* (misty rain), the bathing resort, the promenades, the breakwaters. The work also presents striking Lima scenes of sticky asphalt streets, filthy movie houses, and belching oil factories.

The profound connections between the novel's artist figure and his site-specific context are manifested most sharply through the metaphoric links between the narrator's wanderings and his own artistic style. These metaphors suggest that the narrator's creative activity, the textual movement of *La casa de cartón,* has been literally extracted from the surrounding world. From a position on the roof of a house, the narrator in one scene shifts from peering into the house itself to contemplating the street scene below. There he spots a young girl fabricating a toy from the scraps of her environment (like Silvio in *El juguete rabioso*), an activity the narrator compares to the arduous movement of his own writing: "A ragged youngster strings spools naked of thread onto a cord. I string wooden adjectives onto the rough and thick cord of an idea" (73). The striking feature of this comparison is the interaction it suggests between narrative flow—the activity of stringing together—and creating a poetic image, that is, the spools or the adjectives strung onto the cord, an apt model for a poematic prose text.[27] A similar prose-poetry dynamic is established in the opening lines of Ramón's Underwood poems, which evoke two kinds of textual activity: narrative movement, embodied metaphorically in the "hard and magnificent prose of the city streets," and the weaving of lyric images through creative watching, the "spectacled poetry of the windows" (50).[28] Toward the work's end, moreover, the narrator suggests that this very kind of creative activity constitutes his legacy from his mentor-friend Ramón. All that remains of Ramón, he notes, in addition to the bitterness of the loss and the privilege of perusing his diary, is "*a trail of cigarette butts along the city's longest street, and a way of thinking and seeing* that makes it possible for me to live in the midst of this amorphous group of houses" (77; KS 93; my emphasis).

The narrator's rejection of life as a river notwithstanding, this passage reinforces the conception of his own art as a synthesis of narrative vagrancy that, like writing, leaves its mark—the trail of cigarette butts along the longest street—and poetic image making derived from a unique vision, a particular way of thinking and seeing, as he calls it. This synthesis of city wanderings and special visions presents interesting parallels with Francine Masiello's analysis of Argentine vanguardist poets, whose work, she demonstrates, is marked by "an eye that sweeps" the city "extracting disparate images of the urban panorama" (*Lenguaje e ideologiá* 111). This combination is succinctly encapsulated as the narrator attempts to reconstruct the man on the beach. These efforts, he concludes, may be nothing more than the "*tachygraphy of a wayfaring observer*" (42; my emphasis), a phrase encompassing both narrative meandering and close observation into "shorthand" descriptions typical of *La casa de cartón* itself.[29] In a metaphor that provides an epigraph for this chapter, the narrator ascribes a similar poetic image making and narrative vagrancy to the donkey he imagines imagining him: "We are all *images* conceived during a *calm and supple trot*" (83; KS 99; my emphasis).

These qualities mark the artist figure's own creation, *La casa de cartón*. Narrative meanderings shape many scenes' vanguardist-style lists, images accumulated, like spools on a cord, by a metonymically wandering eye. The lyric vision of *beatas*, for example, is constructed through a linking of images metonymically derived (with adolescent imagination) from the context enveloping the religious women: smells, sensations, fantasies, prayers, and discarded objects. Critics have noted a static quality in the work, and *La casa de cartón* does in fact display pulls between time as sequence and time as Bergsonian duration. The narrator evokes this tension just as he acknowledges Ramón's death. The vacation with Ramón he would relive becomes an expansive moment detaining the flow of time. But even the most static scenes manifest the pulls of a narrative flow embodied in a hyperactive narrative consciousness and a restlessly wandering eye, as, for example, on an otherwise still afternoon, when the narrator sees the countryside crossroads under his feet take on the meandering life of infants.

In addition to its vagabond narrative flow, *La casa de cartón* is also pervaded by the peculiar way of seeing ascribed to its artistic persona. Lauer has described the work's strikingly original imagery as "kaleidoscopic" (31), an adjective also applied to Roberto Arlt's prose,[30] and Kinsella notes the "surrealist" and "cubist" imagery ("La creación de Barranco" 90, 93). Many images do seem constructed from typically surrealist juxtapositions of elements from disparate spheres: romping clouds like "award winners" at an exposition or winds transformed into a "swinging young dandy" (36; KS 43). But a closer look at other images reveals a more contextual than unconscious or random affiliation, metonymic metaphors in which both terms of the comparison are derived from a contiguous world. Thus the statement that "the world is a potato in a sack, . . . little, dark, gritty as if just harvested in some unknown agricultural infinity" (36; KS 42) seems less surreal as one realizes that the speaker emitting it stands at a Peruvian countryside's edge, contemplating clouds and alfalfa. Similarly, the image characterizing the English photographer Miss Annie Doll as a "moving road, sun-blind, leading to the tundra, to a nation of snow and moss" (14; KS 16) is derived from the narrator's preconceptions of her context.

The narrator's peculiar way of seeing is also derived from constant shifts in the focalizer's position. The critical edge of this vision derives, in part, from the narrator's fascination with boundaries, both spatial and temporal. The work's time focus is not only the vacation period itself but, in many scenes, the days just before and just after the interlude, transitional moments when the memory of the prior mode lingers on. Similarly, many scenes unfold neither in Barranco nor Lima exclusively but through movement between the two, and Barranco itself is a suburban boundary space. In addition, several scenes are situated on the boundaries between Barranco and the countryside or on the margins of the beach and the water, with the narration focalizing in at least two directions. Thus the text constructs the ocean or Lima from the beach or the promenade: "the city [is] an oleograph we contemplate, sunken under the water" (8; KS 6). But it also projects a fish's-eye view of Barranco from the water, perceived through "round ichthyological eyes" (12; KS 15).

The narrator is drawn to these boundary spaces as undefined sites of transformation, harbingers of what is yet to unfold. For example, as he views with fascination an area at the end of an urban street where the countryside begins abruptly, he imagines in minute detail the expanding city and its people in the future. The focus on boundaries also blurs the lines in the narrator's world between the human and the non-human, as with the face of an aunt divined in a clod of earth, the old men's countenances emerging from a Barranco cliff, or a chair's cane work that takes on the form of a spinster. Reinforcing the text's focus on image making in the creation of individual selves, the narrator spells out this process as he imagines himself in harmony with the mule that is imagining him. But these blurred positions are also fundamental for the artist figure's ambivalent engagement with a changing world. This boundary position points metaphorically to the artist's desire in the vanguardist spirit to maintain a distance from his surroundings and to immerse himself within them. Most important, this position generates the plurality of shifting focalizations that shape the narrator-artist's construction of his world and its people.

As an individual, the artistic persona in *La casa de cartón* is as fragile as the shifting walls of a cardboard house. The work's title suggests the self-consciously fabricated quality of artistic works and the artistic self, and, as in Arlt's *El juguete rabioso,* it also evokes the vanguardist artist's childlike propensity for play. But as Elaine Scarry has suggested, the physical shelter (room, house), as a metaphor for the human body, is emblematic of the individual's protective efforts at integrated self-containment, the attempt to secure a "stable internal space" (39). But the shelter simultaneously invokes the human being's interaction with the world, the "impulse to project himself out into a space beyond the boundaries of the body in acts of making, either physical or verbal, that once multiplied, collected, and shared are called civilization" (Scarry 39). The shelter, then, serves metaphorically as the meeting place of body, locus of the individual, and world (38–40). In *La casa de cartón,* as I have shown, the sites of those meetings and the boundaries that define artist and world are constantly shifting. Vacillating between aestheticist image making and interaction with others, the artist portrayed in this work is defined neither by name nor by autobiography. We recognize him instead by the shifting walls of his cardboard house: the contentious and ambivalent relationship with his literary antecedents and, through the vagaries of a critical vision, with the changing Peruvian world through which he moves.

FROM IDLE PURSUITS TO CRITICAL VORACITY: *MEMÓRIAS SENTIMENTAIS DE JOÃO MIRAMAR* AND *SERAFIM PONTE GRANDE*

Because of the connections between them, critics have often regarded Oswald de Andrade's two novels of the 1920s as a pair: *Memórias sentimentais de João Miramar* (Sentimental Memoirs of John Seaborne), published in 1924, and *Serafim Ponte Grande* (Seraphim Grosse Pointe), written between 1924 and 1928 and published in 1933. Radically experimental in structure and style, together these works display the gamut of strategies from the vanguardist repertoire. They also present unremittingly acerbic critiques of Brazilian bourgeois society of their times. But, as tales of two men with literary pretensions, they also constitute a notable contribution to the Latin American vanguards' exploration of new artistic personas.

Memórias sentimentais de João Miramar recounts in a fictionalized editor's preface and 163 brief segments the unfinished life story of its bourgeois protagonist. The segments sequentially encompass episodes from João Miramar's childhood and familial upbringing; early schooling, adolescence, and erotic initiations; meetings and wanderings with São Paulo friends; European travels and contact with the Parisian vanguards; the return to Brazil and his mother's death; courtship, marriage, and the birth of a child; the search for a vocation and work as a journalist; marital problems and infidelities, divorce, and the death of his wife; and the decision to abandon writing the recollections we are reading. Presented as memoirs in an autodiegetic narration, the numbered and titled segments, some containing only a few sentences, consist of brief poematic and prose statements. The scenes are populated by the protagonist and a wide array of relatives, friends, and acquaintances as well as contemporary Brazilian and European cultural and historical figures. The memoirs also incorporate other materials including postcards and letters, speeches, obituaries, public announcements, poetic experiments, and an interview. These extend the narrative perspective and put into play a register of linguistic styles broader than the principal speaking voice. The memoirs' tone, more irreverent and satirical than nostalgic, is reinforced by brief titles that point discursively to a segment's content ("High School"); establish ironic distance ("Eden" for a two-sentence description of São Paulo); or encourage the reader to focus on stylistic or structural issues ("Direct Object," "Past Perfect").

Though it possesses strong thematic and structural connections with

João Miramar, Serafim Ponte Grande radicalizes the first novel's innovations, loosens remaining bonds with mimetic and generic conventions, and intensifies the focus on the telling as opposed to the tale.
Exhibiting much in common with its predecessor, Serafim's story includes his childhood, education, and early marriage; the banalities of his
social life, marital conflicts, and infidelities; his rebellion against societal
norms through divorce and theft of money during the 1924 São Paulo
barracks revolts; and his flight to Rio de Janeiro and Europe. Imbued
with a hyperbolic quality, Serafim's travels and erotic encounters are
more extensive than João Miramar's, as he traverses Europe and the
Middle East. His eventual return to Brazil is marked by a final speech
to posterity, his death and commemoration by friends, and the initiation by an "anthropophagous" peer of a permanent voyage of rebellion.
This second novel greatly expands the Bakhtinian "autocriticism of discourse" already present in *João Miramar*. The work's eleven major sections and smaller fragments within them constitute parodic appropria-
tions of varied literary traditions and styles. Major literary genres and
forms parodied include romantic poetry, the personal diary, the bourgeois drama, nineteenth-century realism, the cloak-and-dagger romance, Renaissance travel literature, and the picaresque. In addition,
the novel provokes a willful heteroglossic interplay of other literary and
nonliterary forms, with parodies of the textbook primer, futurist poetic
recipes, society page journalese, dictionary entries, aphorisms, epigraphs, epilogues, letters, film scripts, newsreels, and wills as well as a
range of linguistic idioms.[31]

These novels have generated outstanding critical responses over the
years, and, within the daunting Oswaldian bibliography, studies by Antônio Cândido, Haroldo de Campos, and K. David Jackson in particular
stand out.[32] This work has underscored the novels' sharp satire of Brazilian society and the critical function of Oswald's radical parody of
genres and styles. In addition, strong connections have been drawn between the novels' rebellious spirit (intensified from *João Miramar* to
Serafim) and the author's concept of *antropofagia* as, in de Campos's
terms, a "permanent and vivifying nonconformism" ("Seraphim" 129).
My interest here is neither in duplicating nor in contradicting this work
but rather, while building on it, to shift the focus to these novels' portrayal of an artistic persona and to their connections with works by
Oswald's Spanish American contemporaries.

As these critics have aptly noted, both structurally and at the story-
line level these novels possess *Bildungsroman* markers that shape reader

expectations toward accounts of individual formation. Although in *Serafim* these elements have become mere remnants of a narrative tradition, both works evoke the sequential repertoire of youthful education and friendship, sentimental and erotic initiations, and contentious encounters between an emerging self and a problematic social environment. *Bildungsroman* structural leftovers include the narrative sequencing that parallels a life and a narrating protagonist retelling his own tale. *Serafim*'s autobiographical framework seems more fragile, in part because the novel places less emphasis on the protagonist's early years and also because, in its ubiquitously parodic spirit, the work undermines the sequence it evokes by placing certain episodes out of order.

Beyond the *Bilgdungsroman* markers, both novels identify their eponymous heroes as artists. This designation is reinforced by the storyline parallels critics have drawn with Oswald's own life, and *João Miramar* has been explicitly compared with Joyce's *Portrait of the Artist as a Young Man*.[33] But biographical links notwithstanding, these novels create artist figures as pivotal mechanisms in their fictions. In *João Miramar*, the artistic persona is first established with the device of a preface signed by one Machado Penumbra, spokesman for literary tradition, who introduces the young writer and his work to the reader: "John Seaborne has momentarily abandoned the field of journalism to enter as a man of his age upon the thorny path of letters" (9; RN 112). In addition, an epigraphic quote from the eighteenth-century writer Basílio da Gama creates the ambience of apprenticeship: "That I might meanwhile / Accustom to flight my newborn wings" (5; RN 112). These memoirs, then, are recollections of the recent past by an artist in the making. Machado Penumbra portrays this artist as an innovator, moreover, for, while revealing his own nineteenth-century affiliations, he begs the reader's indulgence for the "beginning novelist" and his "satirical essay" with its "telegraphic style," "stabbing metaphor," and peculiar "glottology," that is, "a new modernist language born from the mixture of Portuguese with contributions from other, immigrant languages" (10–11; RN 113). These allusions invoke Brazilian *modernismo*'s emergence in a historical period of intense cultural and linguistic nationalism. In the same artist's portrait vein, the novel ends as João Miramar reveals in an interview his decision to discontinue writing his memoirs. Here the interviewer notes the protagonist's nervous style and the jeopardy in which the young writer's precipitous decision has placed his country's nascent literature. This ending parodically inverts the formative genres on which the novel draws. Although both the

Bildungsroman and the *Künstlerroman* often close with the protagonist's decision to become a writer, as we still see in Arlt's *El juguete
rabioso, João Miramar* concludes with the choice not to write anymore.
Allusions to literary contacts and friends and to the Parisian vanguards
reinforce the protagonist's artistic characterization, and the narrator
specifically calls himself a young poet. João Miramar also exhibits a proclivity to filter experience through literature, for example, as he characterizes his divorce as a naturalist novel in the making.

The process of Serafim's artistic characterization is more circuitous.
Readers learn that he is an artist through an intricate narrative structure
and in the connections between the two works. As in *João Miramar,
Serafim* is filled with literary allusions and references to artist friends,
and the novel also immerses its hero in a Parisian vanguardist world. In
one of many seduction scenes, Serafim actually boasts that he is a poet.
But the narration also designates Serafim as a geographer and a gymnast, giving him an identity with connotations of the world of letters
and allusive to vanguardist travel motifs. An autodiegetic narration does
not dominate *Serafim;* after the protagonist's flight from São Paulo, a
more distanced, heterodiegetic narrative voice emerges. But there is
much to suggest that this text, like João Miramar's memoirs, constitutes the protagonist's own artistic creation. Paralleling Machado Penumbra's presentation of the young writer João Miramar, Serafim introduces himself in the novel's opening "Recitative" segment: "I
appear to the reader. A ball player. Character in a display window"
(137; KDJ 8). This introduction's theatrical quality—its presentational
rather than representational mode—anticipates the novel's seemingly
unmediated style, often divested of personal and temporal markers.
More significant for Serafim's characterization as a specifically vanguardist artist, however, is the passage's similarity in rhetorical directness and theatricality to a typical vanguardist manifesto. Like a manifesto's first-person speaker, Serafim "presents" himself to the reader,
performative and dynamic, and the exhibitionist move rests on connections between the verbs *to manifest* and *to display.*

Although Serafim's autodiegetic voice controls the novel's early sections, particularly the diary excerpts, as the second novel parodies a
greater array of genres and forms, this voice generally disappears. In the
section "In Sedative Seas" that documents Serafim's ocean voyage in a
parody of travel literature with picaresque tones, a confrontation ensues
between the protagonist and his friend Pinto Calçudo, whom Serafim,
affirming authorial control, evicts from the novel. In addition, the novel

presents an aesthetic filtering of experience that reinforces the protagonist's identity as an artist and also explains, in part, the disappearing
autodiegetic narration. In João Miramar's memoirs, as I have noted,
the narrator consciously reprocesses his life through literary constructs,
as in the "naturalist novel" of his divorce that documents the "dac-
tylated dossier" of his infidelities (80; RN 151). The diary section of
Serafim, "Conjugal Tales or Seraphim at the Front," most closely parallels *João Miramar* in both form—the daily personal notations—and
content—the minutiae of ordinary life. Although in *João Miramar* the
memoir structure provides a chronological sequence, in *Serafim*'s more
parodic diary, portion titles—"Thursday, Tuesday, Wednesday, Fri-
day"—set this chronology loose from any referential moorings. In addition, Serafim, like his predecessor, alludes to his life as a literary phenomenon and expresses the desire to construct works by filtering his
experiences through parodies of literary conventions. An accumulation
of literary references follows, in which the protagonist compares his
deteriorating marriage to "a social drama in four frightful acts" (155;
KDJ 21), to a Dostoyevsky novel, and to a tragedy of which he is the
critic and which is moving toward a burlesque ending. Cumulatively,
these references suggest how *Serafim* goes beyond the earlier novel. As
a would-be writer, João Miramar alludes to the process of filtering his
life through a literary style and pokes fun both at the life event itself
(divorce) and at the particular style (naturalism). Thus João Miramar
initiates a work of stylistic parodies, but Serafim executes this project
with greater vigor. Though still the protagonist of his own work, moreover, the shift away from an autodiegetic narration underscores the resulting critique by providing Serafim with a greater authorial distance.

Although João Miramar and Serafim both create their own works, at
the story-line levels, the protagonists' artistic identities prove strikingly
empty. Being a poet or an artist becomes a sign of respectable exceptionality, a part to be played rather than something substantive to do.
Drawing on Mário de Andrade's *Macunaíma*, which features a hero
"without any character," K. David Jackson suggests that João Miramar
is a "hero in search of a character" ("Vanguardist Prose in Oswald de
Andrade" 173). I would add that he is also an artist in search of a
vocation. In wanderings through São Paulo and Europe, this character
dedicates his time to gatherings with friends and erotic exploits. As an
artist, João incarnates a strange kind of idle mobility, hyperactivity without any purpose. The protagonist himself admits to a vapid existence:
"Celia thought I should have an ennobling vocation. I had none at all.

I vaguely pondered joining a boxing club after having had my physique appraised by a trainer from Catete street" (42; RN 129). This pugilistic allusion suggests the vanguard artist's athletic proclivities, a reference the second novel reiterates in Serafim's portrayal as a gymnast. But João Miramar informs us that, as an aspiring bourgeois artist who is also a home owner with a pregnant wife, he has nothing important to do. His undertakings with another artist strike a similar note: "On Saturdays, I and the poet Phileas would britannize the week in sorties along sunset roads the other side of the suburbs" (46; RN 132). This trivializing of the artist's social role is reinforced in *Serafim Ponte Grande*, particularly in the diary sections that most closely parallel the narrative of João Miramar. Here, a totally self-involved Serafim spends his time meeting with friends, undertaking extramarital exploits, and thinking about the book he would like to write. His life, exceptional only in its mediocrity, includes gossip, detested social appearances, and creative avoidance of conjugal obligations. Even in the work's later sections, in which an intensified parodic critique suggests a new artistic vocation, Serafim the character devotes significant time to hyperactively trivial pursuits.

As artists, João Miramar and Serafim embody a changing social role and, through their unorthodox works-in-progress, seek to redefine the artistic vocation. In a way, the two protagonists still share remnants of the romantic tradition that culminates in the extreme aestheticist stance. At the story-line level, after all, these are malcontent nonconformists who, though mired in ordinary life, acquire through the titles "poet," "artist," or "beginning novelist" a measure of social respectability and an air of superiority over their peers. In their appetites for accumulating travels, women, and experience, moreover—and this is particularly true of Serafim—the two artists still embody the vanguards' totalizing impulse, the all-encompassing artistic persona we find in Huidobro's *Altazor* and Neruda's *Tentativa del hombre infinito*. But, as I have noted, such a stance marks both the culmination of aestheticism's powerful artist and the beginning of that figure's demise. Thus, like their counterparts in Spanish American novels of the artist, João Miramar and Serafim, even as they exaggerate the romantic pose, manifest the vanguards' relinquishing of the romantic rebel's psychological self.

If the other artist figures I have examined suffer from a fragile interior consistency, Oswald's characters possess almost no interiority at all. This is particularly noticeable in *João Miramar*. The title *Sentimental Memoirs* provokes expectations of intimate, confessional revelations, but the narrator's focus rarely turns inward, as he records instead the people and situations around him. The rare moments when João Miramar does speak of feelings are marked by a matter-of-fact tone and an exteriorized perspective, for example, when he visits his deceased father's hometown: "I moistened dry eyelashes for the hunchback glen that had seen my father born" (38; RN 127). This absence of interior reflection undermines the *Bildungsroman* formation; the sequence of events constituting João Miramar's experience is cumulative, not causal, in a life that lacks the self-evaluation that reflection would provide or the hierarchy of experiences it would establish. As Jackson notes, João Miramar's account of his life becomes a "non-memoir" that fails to "explain the core of his experience" ("Vanguardist Prose in Oswald de Andrade" 187). Thus the hero's self acquires the same nonorganic and collected quality shaping the work itself.

Serafim intensifies this quality, although the character seems more interiorized than João Miramar. Serafim does express emotion and, evaluating his situation, assumes a more openly self-critical air. But the work's consistently parodic tone permeates this scene as well, as Serafim addresses his life simply because that is what a memoir writer is supposed to do. Thus his apparent turn inward openly parodies the memoir's confessional moves: "I isolate myself to meditate on the events. . . . I look back on my past" (161–62; KDJ 27). Parodic effects are also achieved through abrupt contrasts in tone. The narrator's flip and graphic allusion to a sexual conquest punctuates his description of the great despair and anguish he has suffered. Like João Miramar, moreover, Serafim embodies a point moving through time around which experiences simply accumulate but fail to organize themselves into the highs and lows that could shape the contours of a *Bildungsroman* styled self. We remember these two protagonists not for their sketchily developed personalities but through the types of activities they embody and that alter the artistic identities they inherit.

These artists' interaction with their contexts constitutes a major feature of the change. As with the artists portrayed by vanguardist manifestos (and through some poetic discourse), these novels immerse João Miramar and Serafim in their times and their place and define the two Brazilian protagonists in culturally specific terms. This feature coincides with the marked nationalist spirit characterizing much Brazilian cultural and political life of the time. In the first novel, Machado Penumbra's opening phrase affirms the connection directly. João Miramar, he explains, is a modern man, a product of the postwar era. This new era, Penumbra asserts, calls for a new artistic mode, as the work's "telegraphic style" and "stabbing metaphor" are linked not only to this violent time but also to their Brazilian source. The time is right for Brazilian artists, Penumbra intimates in the spirit of *modernismo*'s cultural nationalism, because the modern era of discord has something Brazilian about it: "Our very nature, like our beloved flag of glaucous green and golden yellow, tends toward a marvelous violence in color" (10; RN 113). The novel's ending reiterates the artist's link with his nation as the interviewer notes that João Miramar's decision to abandon his memoirs, "a sumptuous monument to Brazilic life and language" (94; RN 60), will threaten the country's emergent literary tradition. The memoirs themselves contextualize the artist in his times. A description of the city in which he lives immediately follows an opening childhood scene of the protagonist with his mother. Ironically entitled "Eden," this segment describes São Paulo as a book lacking the expected illustrations of a child's story. From childhood on, then, the city becomes a book for João Miramar to read, the site of his literary apprenticeship and the subject matter of his satirical observations. In the Latin American tradition, moreover, the protagonist's encounter with a Parisian Bastille Day vanguardist scene, parades with Picasso, Satie, and Cocteau, provokes a profound reengagement with things Brazilian.

Serafim Ponte Grande intertwines its artistic persona with his context in similar ways. In the "Recitativo" introduction, a decadent and rotting São Paulo provides the background from which the protagonist steps forth to present himself, manifesto-style, to the reader. The following segment portrays Serafim's "encounter with malice" in lines from a primer that signal the child's learning to read. The segment "MEMORY OF MY COUNTRY AS AN INFANT" that follows shortly reconstructs Brazil through a child's language and perspective as Serafim begins to "read" his city: "The car puttputts on the streets. / The train speeds seeing Brazil. / Brazil is a Federative Republic full of trees and of people saying good-bye" (142; KDJ 10). Serafim's identity is even more tightly interwoven with that of his country, target of the work's scathing critiques. Thus, on São Paulo streets during the 1924 barracks revolts, a real-world encounter initiated by army officers seeking political and social reform, Serafim's inadequacies and his country's converge in the impotence (figurative and literal) of both. During his European travels, Serafim, affirming his identity, explains his cultural origins time and again; he advises one woman he seduces that she should feel proud of having been loved by a genuine Brazilian. As in *João Miramar*, the Parisian vanguardist encounter triggers a coming to terms with Brazil and leads to the parodically primitivist construction of his country's identity that marked Oswald's own "anthropophagous" manifesto.

These protagonists' relationships to the worlds from which they emerge shape their artistic identities. Like the manifesto artists who cloak their artistic practices in technological and activist motifs, João Miramar and Serafim, products of what Penumbra calls the "clangorous attacks" and "human outbursts" of the postwar era, are characters obsessively on the move and imbued with an aura of hyperactivity. They traverse São Paulo and Brazilian society and European capitals with rapidity and ease, and, in contrast to the disengaged aesthete, they become compulsive consumers of experience. Like Silvio in *El juguete rabioso* and the nameless narrators in *La educación sentimental* and *La casa de cartón,* the Brazilian artists are nomads, though the pace and scope of their wanderings, Serafim's in particular, are far greater than, for example, the "leisurely, vagabond play" in *La educación sentimental.* The Brazilian novels also exaggerate the proclivity in other works to traverse literary texts and traditions, landmarks on these vagabonds' itineraries as crucial as the geographic stops. These artists' attitudes toward what they encounter in both arenas are thoroughly irreverent and critical, as they subject contemporary bourgeois existence to a scathing satirist's view and a vast range of literary and popular discourses to parody's critical mimicry. As critics both social and literary, João Miramar and Serafim gradually discard the superior psychological self that marks the aestheticist tradition they inherit. Rather than remove themselves to a life of reflective contemplation, they plunge headfirst into the banalities—experiential, literary, and linguistic—that surround them. In the process, these two Brazilian artists in the making construct their works nonorganically and, like Silvio's plagiarized toys in *El juguete rabioso,* with the materials plundered from that confrontation.

Conclusion

In his extensive writings on European and Latin American vanguardism and his assessment of the contemporary artist's possible role in modern life, Mariátegui, editor of the vanguardist journal *Amauta,* explored how writers, specifically, in their artistic roles, might have an impact on social life. A Marxist, "convicted and self-confessed," Mariátegui attacked aestheticism and artistic self-involvement. But he insisted on reserving a privileged position for art, artists, and intellectuals, although one less isolated than that occupied by the turn-of-the-century aesthete. He defined the artist's relationship to the world paradoxically as one of engaged autonomy: "Art's autonomy, yes, but not the reclusion of art" (*OC* 6: 47–48). Although artists in the modern world might reengage with the problems of the times, however, their perspective should always be critical. Because art was "substantially and eternally heterodox" (*OC* 6: 64), Mariátegui argued that even politically engaged artists had a duty to provoke debate and question the beliefs to which they were committed.[34]

In a 1932 article on Mexico's Contemporáneos group, Jorge Cuesta sought to characterize that country's "vanguardist generation," and, although the political context was different, Cuesta coincided with Mariátegui in his portrait of the modern artist as critic. Mexico's innovators, Cuesta explained, had emerged in a "rachitic intellectual environment" and faced a literary milieu almost "totally lacking in criticism" (HV 97). The activities of these writers, he added, were directed toward filling this void, and, in fact, a "critical attitude" provided the common bond of the Contemporáneos artists. Manifestations of such an orientation included mistrust of any single aesthetic program, idol, or "false tradition"; a rejection of so-called original artists subscribing to a single doctrine or temperament; and an eclectic voracity and openness toward all literatures and cultures. This attitude, he explained, accepted "any influence," including cultural and linguistic knowledge, meeting people through travel, and confronting any reality, "even the Mexican" (HV 99).

Although this piece is enmeshed in debates about Mexican art that dominated Mexico's cultural scene in the 1920s, Cuesta's identification of a vanguardist "critical attitude" echoes Mariátegui's account. But his description of the Contemporáneos writers also coincides with the portraits of the Latin American vanguardist artist constructed by the movements' manifestos and creative texts, particularly the novels. The artist figures these novels create embody nonconformist individuals for whom art constitutes a direct response to the problematic contexts in which they live and work. These artist protagonists all inherit an aestheticist legacy that shapes their initial orientation as would-be poets and writers. But rather than adopt the aesthete's detached life of cultured pursuits, they immerse themselves critically in the disorderly worlds around them. In the process, they seek to piece together their own elusive and fragmented identities from the products of that en-

counter. They become, to paraphrase Cuesta, voraciously eclectic consumers of both literature and experience, as they transform the banalities of both into the substance of their art. In search of viable artistic
vocations, they turn an irreverent eye toward a vast range of literary
traditions: from the Baudelairean to the Rocambolesque in *El juguete
rabioso;* from the neoclassical and the romantic to the Spanish American
modernista in *La educación sentimental;* from the "moldy stew" of
Spanish peninsular literature to the latest European modernists in *La
casa de cartón;* and from a showcase of styles from canonical Western
literary modes to conventions of contemporary mass media in *Memórias
sentimentais de João Miramar* and *Serafim Ponte Grande.* Significantly,
all of these artist figures are irreverent toward modernity itself, and,
even as they insistently identify themselves as artists, their experiences
point to the limits of an artistic vocation. Thus, although Silvio in *El
juguete rabioso* initially sees art as a path to personal liberation, and his
Mexican, Peruvian, and Brazilian counterparts bear aestheticist remnants of exceptionality, ultimately their artistic activity assumes a more
modest tone. No longer an avenue either to personal glory or to cosmic
transcendence, "art" becomes for these artists, to quote the narrator in
La casa de cartón, a way of "thinking and seeing" that allows them to
function in a chaotic world, critically engaged with human experience,
both literary and lived.

3.

"Surely from his lips a cockatoo will fly"
The Vanguards' Stories of the New World

Patience brothers! No! I won't go to Europe, no. I'm an American and my place is in America. European civilization will surely shatter the integrity of our character.
　　　　　　　　—Mário de Andrade, *Macunaíma*

Europe . . . decadent and fatigued . . . still rigorously demands of every stranger his own task. She is bored by the rhapsodies of her thought and her art. She wants from us, above all, the expression of ourselves.
　　　　　　　　—José Carlos Mariátegui, "Waldo Frank"

In the final chapters of Mário de Andrade's 1928 novel *Macunaíma*, the work's eponymous hero "without any character" returns with his brothers to the virgin forest of his origins following a peripatetic São Paulo sojourn. Macunaíma cuts an impressive figure. His beloved *muiraquitã*, the amulet he has retrieved from the city of "the children of Manioc," hangs from his lower lip. But the hero also displays on his body predilect artifacts of the great São Paulo civilization he leaves behind. A Smith and Wesson revolver and a Swiss watch dangle from his ears, and in his hand he carries two caged leghorn fowl. Defined by his folkloric origins but also portrayed as a tourist in his own land, Macunaíma is cast as a "primitive" being who discovers, conquers (after a fashion), and manipulates the technological marvels of the modern world. Although he is described as explicitly Brazilian, Macunaíma, especially at this moment of his return, simultaneously epitomizes and parodies the principal issues shaping the Americanist component of Latin American vanguardist activity. His destiny at birth is to become a Brazilian national hero, but in conception and development he is also an American. In the words that provide an epigraph for this chapter, Macunaíma abandons his dream of a European tour, and later, while searching for the conscience he had discarded on the island of Marapatá, he decides to "seize the conscience of a Spanish American" and shape himself "in that fashion" (148). In a similar spirit, the novel that ironically poses the problem of a Brazilian national character constitutes a deliberate and self-conscious geographic and linguistic amalgam, a composite of folkloric sources expressed in a collagelike language nobody actually speaks.[1]

In the preamble to *The Voice of the Masters: Writing and Authority in Latin American Literature,* Roberto González Echevarría affirms that from the romantic period until the 1950s, modern Latin America and its literature were conceived as "a metaphoric field whose ground is nature," a field through which it was posited that "Nature, the landscape, created through its own uniqueness and originality a new and original being who expressed himself or herself in the form of a new and different literature" (4). Founded on classical and romantic notions of the organic, this idea, according to González Echevarría, envelops Latin American literature and culture like an enormous vine, is most forcefully expressed in the organicist metaphors of José Martí's "Nuestra América" (1891), and is not profoundly undermined until Alejo Carpentier's 1953 novel *Los pasos perdidos* (*The Voice of the Masters* 41–43). The widespread Americanist activity within Latin America's vanguards, particularly in the manifestos and little magazines, builds on and even exaggerates organicist myths of America. As González Echevarría notes, however, the organicist notions, present in Latin American thought since Independence, had never been totally lacking in irony and had always implicitly questioned themselves. I would argue that during the vanguard period this critique is particularly intense. While vanguardist rhetoric in manifestos may have reinforced long-standing myths of the New World, the vanguards' Americanist creative texts, predating *Los pasos perdidos* by more than two decades, seriously questioned the organicist conception of Latin America's cultural integrity.

America in Vanguardist Manifestos

During the century's early decades, Latin America's search for a sharper regional and continental understanding neither originated with nor was limited to the literary vanguards. Serious inquiries into the cultural specificity of New World experience constituted an influential political and intellectual current, a fact evident from the most superficial perusal of major essayists' work: Ricardo Rojas's *La argentinidad* (1916) and *Eurindia* (1924); Gilberto Freyre's *Manifesto regionalista* (1926); Franz Tamayo's "Carta de americanos para americanos" (1926); José Vasconcelos's *La raza cósmica: Misión de la raza iberoamericana* (1925) and *Indología, una interpretación de la cultura iberoamericana* (1926); Antenor Orrego's "¿Cuál es la cultura que creará América?" (1928); Pedro Henríquez Ureña's *Seis ensayos en busca de nuestra expresión* (1928); and Juan Marinello's "Americanismo y cubanismo literarios" (1932). European and North American thinkers with New World concerns had an impact on this work, for example, Oswald Spengler (*The Decline of the West,* 1918–22), Count Hermann Keyserling (*Meditaciones suramericanas,* 1933); José Ortega y Gasset (in particular, "Carta a un joven argentino que estudia filosofía," 1924, "Hegel y América," 1928, and "La pampa . . . promesas," 1929); and Waldo Frank (*The Re-discovery of America,* 1929).[2] In addition, Ortega's journal *Revista de Occidente* circulated widely in Latin America and played a critical role in disseminating Spengler's ideas about the future significance of non-European cultures.[3]

Many of the Latin American works manifest certain broad attitudes in common. Most reverse the nineteenth-century civilization versus barbarism dichotomy and celebrate cultural difference and *mestizaje* as sources of national energy capable of overcoming an enervated European civilization. In the spirit of José Martí's "Nuestra América," these works often reaffirm a link between humanity and nature as a positive determinant of Latin American experience, and some explore essentialist notions of an emergent American character or soul. Literary historiography has traditionally ascribed the impact of these currents to the Spanish American *novela de la tierra,* or "novel of the land" (for example, *La vorágine,* 1924; *Don Segundo Sombra,* 1926; and *Doña Bárbara,* 1929), and to other regionalist writing such as Brazil's Northeast novel of the 1930s. But New World concerns and Americanist rhetoric are also widely evident in the activities of vanguardist groups and writers who addressed questions of aesthetic modernity.

As I have observed in the introduction, cultural nationalism was common in Latin America's vanguards, and literary experiments were often marked by the deliberate reclaiming of autochthonous traditions. Mariátegui's well-turned phrase "Peruanicemos al Perú" (Let us Peruvianize Peru), the title for his 1925–29 column in Lima's *Mundial,* also informed the agenda for intellectual modernity in his influential vanguardist journal *Amauta* (1926–30). In Brazil, the term "Abrasileirar o Brasil" (Brazilianize Brazil) was coined in the editorial inaugurating the 1927 magazine *Verde,* and the question of cultural self-definition dominated major manifestos and magazines in Brazil's *modernismo* movement. In Nicaragua, signers of the first manifesto of the Anti-Academy outlined a program to disseminate vanguardist techniques while giving free rein to emotions of *being (ser y estar)* in Nicaragua (*MPP* 378; emphasis in original). In addition, vanguardist groups or writers throughout Latin America expressed similar interests in indigenous cultural experience, concerns that also emerge in numerous innovative creative works, for example, Oswald de Andrade's *Pau Brasil* poetry (1925); Mário's *Macunaíma* (1928); Brazilian Raul Bopp's *Cobra norato* (1928–31); Mexican Xavier Icaza's *Panchito Chapopote* (1928); Pablo de Rokha's *Escritura de Raimundo Contreras* (1929) from Chile; Miguel Angel Asturias's *Leyendas de Guatemala* (1930); Carpentier's *¡Écue-Yamba-Ó!* (1927–33); Cuban Nicolás Guillén's *Motivos de son* (1930) and *Sóngoro cosongo* (1931); Pablo Antonio Cuadra's *Poemas nicaragüenses* (1930–33), Peruvian Carlos Oquendo de Amat's *5 metros de poemas* (1927); Luis Barrios Cruz's *Respuesta a las piedras* (1931) from Venezuela; or Peruvian Alejandro Peralta's vanguardist *indigenista* poetry collections *Ande* (1926) and *El kollao* (1934). But beyond this attention to regional culture, many of these works are also framed in broader Americanist contexts, while manifestos and literary magazines, including some openly eschewing regionalist concerns, often affirm explicitly Americanist positions.

As I have noted in my introductory comments, the continental university reform movement enacted an Americanist agenda in the political and intellectual arenas. Thus, although it is more a political than an aesthetic document, the June 1918 proclamation from the Argentine "youth of Córdoba" to the "free men of South America," marking the historic student congress in that city, may well have set the ecumenical tone for many of the literary manifestos that followed (*MPP* 64).[4] A comparable mood characterized the earliest calls for artistic innovation, for example, in the Dominican Republic's 1921 *postumista* manifesto that addressed the youth of America in polemical tones, Puerto Rico's second *euforista* manifesto (1923) proclaiming "the Great Euphoric American Republic" (LHA 232), or the 1925 *noísta* manifesto celebrating "the great Republic of American Thought" (LHA 245). In Cuba, the "Declaración del Grupo Minorista" (1927) lobbied "for Latin American cordiality and union" (*MPP* 250), a position subsequently developed in the *Revista de Avance* (1927–30).[5]

Almost all of Lima's magazines of the "new art," including *Flechas* (1924), *Guerrilla* (1927), and the *Trampolín-Hangar-Rascacielos-Timonel* series (1926–27), assumed an Americanist posture, typified, for example, in *Guerrilla*'s forecast of a new America's birth. Among regional publications, Arequipa's *Chirapu* (1928) published a piece on "Latin American continental citizenship," and Puno's *Boletín Titikaka* (1926–30) included articles on "aesthetic Indoamericanism." Most important, Mariátegui's skepticism about an emergent American culture notwithstanding, *Amauta* committed itself to a continental exchange of ideas and published copious materials with Americanist content including portions of Waldo Frank's *Re-discovery of America* in translation.[6] Elsewhere, Enrique Terán wrote of an "Indoamerican soul" in "El arte de vanguardia" for Quito's *Elán* (128), Montevideo's *La Pluma* (1927–31) called for the "intellectual autonomy of America" (*MPP* 258), and in a Nicaraguan manifesto, Pablo Antonio Cuadra supported preserving an "Indo-Spanish" spirit (*50A* 27).

An Americanist mood emerged even in those vanguardist endeavors that generally avoided cultural nationalism and ostensibly cultivated more internationalist goals. Argentina's *Martín Fierro* (1924–27) underscored the country's debt to European culture, decried the "stupidities" perpetrated in the name of Spanish Americanism, and defended itself from attacks for its use of a national masterpiece for its name. Still, the journal's inaugural manifesto celebrated America's intellectual contributions and praised its creative assimilatory capacity (*MPP* 135). The landmark anthology *Indice de la nueva poesía americana* (1926), edited by Alberto Hidalgo, Vicente Huidobro, and Jorge Luis Borges and including poetry from Argentina, Colombia, Chile, Ecuador, Mexico, Nicaragua, Peru, Uruguay, and Venezuela, manifested editorial ambivalence toward the Americanism implicit in its selection criteria. In the volume's introduction, Huidobro remained silent on the subject, and Peru's Hidalgo declared that Spanish Americanism repulsed him.

But Borges, who would later distance himself both from his early vanguardism and from cultivated cultural autochthonism, cited examples from Argentina, Mexico, and Chile to suggest that "the poetifiable truth no longer lies only across the sea" (*INPA* 15).[7] Although both *Martín Fierro* and Mexico's *Contemporáneos* (1928–31) consistently refrained from openly nationalist or Americanist posturing, both journals frequently published writers from Argentina and Mexico, respectively, as well as other Spanish Americans, and both participated in a continental exchange with magazines with an Americanist agenda. And, though it was not a vanguardist publication, Joaquín García Monge's widely circulated *Repertorio Americano* (San José, Costa Rica, 1919–59) facilitated these continental contacts and published significant Americanist pieces.[8]

In Brazil, Americanist concerns were more openly evident in creative works such as *Macunaíma,* Oswald de Andrade's 1925 *Pau Brasil* poetry collection, and Ronald de Carvalho's poetic composition *Toda a América* (1926) than in most manifestos or little magazines. Occasional references to Spanish American writers appeared in *A Revista* of Belo Horizonte (1925–26) and the *Revista de Antropofagia* (São Paulo, 1928–29), and a broader interaction with Spanish America was documented in Rio de Janeiro's *Festa* (1927–28 and 1934–35), including an exchange with *Repertorio Americano*. In 1927 and 1928, Mário de Andrade reported on Argentine aesthetic innovation for São Paulo's *Diário Nacional*. These articles and Mário's annotations in the Spanish American works in his own library document a concern with the questions of American cultural specificity being debated in other countries.[9] Although focused on Brazil, Oswald de Andrade's "Manifesto antropófago" (1928) presents the most provocative Americanist position in Brazilian modernism. The manifesto stresses Europe's debt to the New World for its conception of natural man, as set forth in writings by Montaigne and Rousseau, and proposes instead the "bad savage," an all-consuming cannibal, as a New World model of cultural critique and capacity for creative assimilation.

In general, the polemical Americanist discourse in vanguardist manifestos and magazines celebrated the continent's humanism, energy, "ancestral" spirit, and radical newness as powerful antidotes to European cultural exhaustion. With echoes of Whitman, Nietzsche, and Spengler and doses of Bergsonian elán vital, vanguardist documents forecast an energetic new day, a potent new human species, and a powerful new art. But, although these pronouncements sometimes cast aspersions on the "sterile ultraisms" of Europe's avant-gardes, they were often saturated themselves by the futurist rhetoric of international vanguardism that proposed, as Renato Poggioli observed in *The Theory of the Avant-Garde*, an "artistic palingenesis" paving the way for a future new art (75). Thus Martí Casanovas's affirmation in the *Revista de Avance* piece "Arte nuevo" echoed throughout Latin America: this generation's art would require a "profound humanism" to be found in the "virgin essence" and "inexhaustible fecundity" of Indo-Latin America (HV 137). Essential for this new culture would be the emergence of a new American being, variously designated as the new "cosmic fetus" (*engendro cósmico*), the "new human soul," the "matrix race," and the "Atlantic shoulders of the formidable creators of beauty."[10]

A striking feature of this Americanist language is the penchant for organicist metaphors, telluric and anatomical, through which America, portrayed as the earth or as a living, breathing human body, would engender the new American art. The *postumistas* proclaimed that the new art would be molded from America's "grotesque clay" (*MPP* 109), and Peru's Antero Peralta Vásquez proposed similarly that a new art could be forged from the "clay of the soil" and the "breath of the race" ("El uno y vario del arte vanguardista" 2). With comparable telluric language, the Brazilian modernist painter Tarsila do Amaral conceived the *antropofagia* agenda for cultural transformation as a kind of psychodynamic archaeological dig: "Let us descend to our prehistory. Bring up something from that immense, atavistic depth. . . . Remix the roots of the race, with psychoanalytic thought. From that reencounter with our things, in a creative climate, we will be able to achieve a new structure of ideas."[11] Calls for American cultural unity were often expressed through metaphors of an anatomically explicit body-continent with a spinal column and vascular system traversing the Andes and a speaking voice embodied in the new American intellectual or artist. Thus Luis Valcárcel declared in Peru's *Amauta* that "just as the mountain range running from South to North gives unity because it serves as column and axis, so is there a common desire among youth: create American Culture" ("Hay varias Américas" 39). Similarly, editors of Ecuador's *Elán* proposed that a new creative impulse was to be found in "the profound pulsating of a single aorta spread out along the length of the Andes" ("Editorial" 59), and Puerto Rican *noístas* used similar body language in their "Gesto" manifesto: "Let us put our aesthetic into harmony with Niagara Falls and may the emotion open out like the mouth of the Orinoco" (LHA 243).

But the most striking feature of this Americanist rhetoric was the claim that vanguardism itself was a fundamentally New World event. The manifesto-style preface to Oswald de Andrade's novel *Memórias sentimentais de João Miramar* affirmed that the time was right for the art of "Brazil in America" because this New World (Brazil in particular) had always been shaped by the "human outbursts" and "clangorous attacks" cultivated by European literary modernity (9–10; RN 113). Peruvian Federico Bolaños affirmed that "the birth of the word VAN-GUARDIA belongs to America which has centered in its 10 letters all the directions of the European movement" (*MPP* 330). Venezuela's Uslar Pietri argued that America had not only not plagiarized the European vanguards but had made its own considerable contribution to the movement (*MPP* 273). And Peruvian poet Emilio Armaza claimed that "vanguardism in Europe was a fetus; here it is a sturdy, thoroughbred specimen" ("Confesiones de izquierda" 1).

These hyperbolic claims for future American culture and art did not escape sharp contemporary criticism, even from within the vanguardist ranks, for example, from Peru's César Vallejo. In 1926, he deplored the paucity of Latin American cultural leadership but conceded that the vanguardist generation might serve as a source of creative hope (*MPP* 188). But he also insisted that modern motifs alone (telegraphs, skyscrapers, lowercase typography) could not create a modern spirit, and he indicted his generation for creative impotence and for a "false and epidermic Latin Americanism" that still aped Europe by dancing the "vanguardist charleston" (*MPP* 189 and 242–44). Autochthonism, Vallejo explained, did not consist in saying that one is autochthonous but rather in being it without saying it. As a major promoter of vanguardist activity and of exploring Americanist concerns, Mariátegui, like Vallejo, was guarded in his assessment of both. Under attack by more nationalist contemporaries, in the *Siete ensayos de interpretación de la realidad peruana* (1928), he defended his interest in European thought as the "only salvation for Indo-America" (*OC* 2: 12). Mariátegui supported intellectual and cultural exchange among Latin American nations and argued that most South American countries had experienced comparable processes of national development, but he turned away from the ideal of a unified Spanish American cultural experience or of an incipient new American culture.[12]

In Brazil, even though Mário de Andrade's hero Macunaíma adopts a Spanish American conscience on the island of Marapatá, if we recall that Macunaíma was a hero *without* any character, it is not surprising that Mário himself was also guarded about Americanist rhetoric. In an article on Argentine literature, he recoiled from the concept of Pan-Americanism and argued that "continental psychological or ethnic unity" did not exist (de Andrade in Antelo 165). However, in an otherwise highly critical review of André Sigfried's *Amérique Latine*, Mário agreed with Sigfried's identification of a persistent Latin American "savage" quality but insisted, as his novel *Macunaíma* explores, that this "primitivism" was historically and culturally complex (de Andrade in Antelo 193).

The Americanist component of Latin America's vanguardist activity was also always ironically intertwined with European expectations of an imagined New World. The European sojourn, actual or literary, had become a standard step in a would-be artist's formation, and for many writers of this period—Mariátegui, Asturias, Carpentier, Oswald de Andrade, Evaristo Ribera Chevremont, and Luis Cardoza y Aragón—the transatlantic experience had provoked a "discovery" and reengagement with Latin American culture. Not surprisingly, the transatlantic is a frequent motif in Latin American manifestos and poetry. Through writers such as Spengler and Keyserling as well as through the expectations of European vanguardists, the agenda for Latin American self-discovery was closely intertwined with a European rediscovery of what was imagined as the non-European world. Pilgrimages in search of an autochthonous America were eventually undertaken by some European vanguardists, including Blaise Cendrars, André Breton, and Antonin Artaud. Mariátegui notes in the article on Waldo Frank (cited in an epigraph to this chapter) that Europeans wanted from America the expression of itself (*OC* 3: 194) rather than "rhapsodies of European 'isms' " (*OC* 12: 73). But European artists' expectations for American art were often problematically shaped by primitivist quests and by romantic and vitalist conceptions of America as the organic. Even as their own work was marked by these same ideas, Latin America's vanguardists were also ambivalently aware that their own New World stories manifesting these conceptions were often exactly what European artists wanted to hear.

"We are still the land of Columbus 'where people are born with tails.' Victims of the Europeans' literary hysteria," Oswald de Andrade observed in 1929 (Costa, "Revisão necessária" 6).[13] In a similar tone,

Mariátegui lamented absurd demands by exoticism-seeking Europeans that Peru's Parisian-based surrealist poet César Moro produce work with indigenist themes (*OC* 2: 329). Other writers documented European expectations of Latin America and its art. In "Las posibilidades de un teatro americano," written from Paris for Guatemala's *El Imparcial,* Asturias noted that the performance of a European-style South American play had been received critically by an audience "anxious for exoticism" and seeking a spectacle of "American substance" (*Paris 1924– 1933* 476–77). Similarly, in his aphoristic composition *Membretes* (1932), Argentina's Oliverio Girondo noted Europe's projection of its exoticist desires onto Latin America: "Europe is beginning to be interested in us. Disguised in the feathers or the *chiripá* that she attributes to us, we could achieve clamorous success! What a shame that our sincerity obliges us to disenchant her, . . . to introduce ourselves as we are" (*Veinte poemas* 95). In a 1931 article, "América ante la joven literatura europea," Carpentier summarized a survey of young European vanguardists, including Philippe Soupault, Nino Frank, Robert Desnos, Georges Ribemont-Dessaignes, and Georges Bataille. Carpentier had asked how they imagined Latin America, and he noted the anti-European tone of their answers that proposed Latin America as the site of the West's cultural and political future. The contemporary reader is also struck by the penchant for organicist language, as in Desnos's affirmation that America's "effervescent virgin and fertile land" would be the scene of formidable events (Carpentier, *OC* 9: 299). Latin American writers needed to pay attention, Carpentier suggested, to European clamorings for a New World vernacular art (*OC* 9 303–4).[14]

America in the Vanguards' Experimental Texts

A humorous critique of such transatlantic expectations was constructed by Peruvian Carlos Oquendo de Amat's brief poem "Amberes" from his *5 metros de poemas* (1928). As a collage of images from that port, "Amberes" records the city's expectations upon the arrival of "passengers from America": "The curious read American landscapes in his eyes / and the puma that embraces the Indians with his boots. / fountains of gold / Surely from his lips a cockatoo will fly" (n.p.). But even as they noted the ironies in European expectations, Latin American writers rigorously investigated the possibilities such a vernacular expression might present for affirming a peculiarly American experience and art. Americanist manifestos and little magazines generally portrayed America as the new, the primordially telluric, or the organic. In a critical forum, as I have noted, writers such as Vallejo, Mariátegui, and Mário de Andrade, among others, seriously questioned these images. But a more nuanced critique of these New World stories unfolds in experimental literary works that either address Americanist questions directly or cast their vernacular content in New World frames. Five works that exemplify this critical process are Mário de Andrade's *Macunaíma* (1928); Gamaliel Churata's *El pez de oro* (1927–57) from Peru; Carpentier's *¡Écue-Yamba-Ó!* (1927–33); Asturias's *Leyendas de Guatemala* (1930); and, from Guatemala, Luis Cardoza y Aragón's *Pequeña sinfonía del nuevo mundo* (1929–32). Similar works not encompassed in my analysis include the Brazilian writer Ronald de Carvalho's poetic collection *Toda a América* (1926) and, from Chile, Pablo de Rokha's surrealist poematic prose composition *Suramérica* (1927–28).

Macunaíma, subtitled *The Hero without Any Character,* draws its narrative substance from the "Myths and Legends of the Taulipang and Arekuná," from German ethnologist Theodor Koch-Grünberg's *Vom Roroima zum Orinoco* (1916–24). The work recasts these tales into the story of Macunaíma's life of heroic misadventures, erotic encounters, and dirty tricks. By mating with the queen of the Amazonian Icamiabas, Macunaíma becomes Emperor of the Forest, but his wife and son die from a curse, and she leaves him a magical amulet, the *muiraquitã.* The giant Piaíma, alias the huckster Venceslau Pietro Pietra, steals the amulet, which Macunaíma and his brothers travel to São Paulo to retrieve. Back in the virgin forest, the hero encounters new antagonists, loses the amulet again, and is mortally wounded by the sun goddess Vei. After telling his life story to a parrot, Macunaíma willfully ascends to heaven and is transformed into Ursa Major. One day the work's nameless narrator, wandering in the vanished tribe's land, encounters the parrot, who repeats Macunaíma's story. As the parrot flies off to Lisbon, the narrator begins to sing in "impure speech" Macunaíma's tale.

A hero of enormous appetites and a trickster of Pantagruelian proportions, Macunaíma defeats his adversaries with his wits. As a Brazilian hero, he learns spoken Brazilian and written Portuguese, and the language recording his story incorporates regionalisms, colloquialisms, puns, and indigenist and Africanist elements into a singular idiom. The work's New World substance derives from Macunaíma's adoption of a

Spanish American conscience and from the discovery and encounter motifs woven through his story.[15]

A prime mover of Andean vanguardist activity, Gamaliel Churata (née Arturo Peralta) wrote significant portions of the 501-page *El pez de oro* (1957; The Fish of Gold) between 1924 and 1930.[16] Subtitled *Retablos del Laykhakuy* (referring to a traditional Aymara healer) and divided into eleven *retablos*, the work narrates a young writer's journey to a pre-Columbian past where he seeks to resolve the conflict of competing cultural traditions that hampers his creativity. With a fragmented structure and multiple narrators, the story is told in a surrealist prose of modern and baroque Spanish with frequent inclusions of Quechua and Aymara, neologisms, and linguistic hybrids of the author's invention. The inchoate work, highly uneven in quality, includes rambling narrative prose, indigenous poetry and songs, polemical essays, dramatic dialogues, short tales, and stories within stories. Essayistic musings on metaphysical, historical, linguistic, ethnographic, and indigenous issues weave through the autodiegetic frame narrative. Countless references to America's contested cultural, linguistic, and artistic identity situate the work's engagement with Peruvian indigenous culture within a broader American context.

¡Écue-Yamba-Ó! was published in 1933, but Carpentier wrote a first draft in 1927. Originally subtitled *Historia afro-cubana*, the work narrates the life story of its Afro-Cuban protagonist, Menegildo Cué. The story includes Menegildo's birth and childhood in a sugarcane *central* (mill) community, initiations into Afro-Cuban customs, his murder of his lover Longina's mate, imprisonment in Havana, initiations into Havana street life and Afro-Cuban *ñáñigo* cults, and his death in a fight with a rival group. The novel ends with Longina's return to the *central* community where Menegildo's son is born and the life cycle begins again. Though it draws on the naturalist novel and the *Bildungsroman*, critics have noted that *¡Écue-Yamba-Ó!* is a strikingly heterogeneous work.[17] In addition to sometimes disconcerting shifts in narrative tone and focalization, the novel incorporates Afro-Cuban songs, ethnographic accounts of *ñáñigo* rituals, samples of vernacular speech, and jarring vanguardist metaphors. Although Menegildo's story unfolds in an unmistakably Cuban world, as with *Macunaíma*, discovery and encounter motifs insert his tale also into an Americanist mode.

The first (1930) edition of Asturias's *Leyendas de Guatemala* contained five lyrical prose narratives based on colonial and pre-Columbian folklore as well as tales from the *Popol Vuh*.[18] These tales are framed by two introductory pieces. "Guatemala" situates the reader in the world to be explored, as a first-person speaker returns to the land of his origins. Through ephemeral voices and lost shadows and with the help of *el Cuco de los sueños* (the phantom bogeyman of children's dreams), he constructs an imaginary journey through the layers of a pre-Columbian and colonial past searching for the substance of his stories. "Ahora que me acuerdo" presents a narrative proving ground for deciding who shall tell these tales and in what voice. Here, the narrator displays his lyric prowess to the town's *güegüechos,* centenarians with magical powers, by assuming the form of the mythological Cuero de Oro (Cuculcán or Quetzalcoatl) and recounting his people's beginnings. The collection creates profuse sensorial imagery through vanguardist accumulations of metaphors coupled with rhetorical strategies such as responsive repetitions of key words and phrases. Key references to the Spanish-indigenous encounter place these Guatemalan stories in a broader Americanist context.[19]

Although the work was not published until 1948, Luis Cardoza y Aragón composed the 100-page prose poem *Pequeña sinfonía del nuevo mundo* (Small Symphony of the New World) between 1929 and 1932. The composition's twelve sections present in a baroque, surrealist style the poetic discovery of the modern and the primitive New World, in New York, Havana, and Central America's pre-Columbian past. Three poetic perspectives organize the poem's profuse material. In response to modernity's technological jungle, an adult poet recreates an autochthonous world of his childhood and of America's prehistory, what Cardoza y Aragón termed the "universe of the animal and the flower" (245). Two other perspectives are embedded in this experience: that of a child poet who reclaims an innocent vision and that of Dante in New York's modern inferno, a focus that links the adult poet's journey to a Western poetic tradition. These perspectives intersect in a search for a poetic language to express what the poet himself called the "recondite feeling of the New World" (246).[20]

These five works differ markedly from one another in genre, style, and quality, and they register a multitude of narrative and poetic voices. But even at first glance, they share certain obvious features. Each work presents itself as a self-consciously vanguardist text. Although they all seek to address a specific cultural reality, they all ignore, alter, or parody inherited mimetic conventions. With varying degrees of effectiveness, each work mobilizes specific literary strategies commonly associated with the literary vanguards: parody, linguistic free play, and the inter-

play of the primitive and the modern in *Macunaíma;* multiple narrators, stream-of-consciousness narration, and the inclusion of diverse literary and nonliterary genres in *El pez de oro;* variations in narrative style
and focalization, startling metaphors, and the interplay of the modern
or the urban and the primitive in *¡Écue-Yamba-Ó!;* lyrical prose, ambiguous voicing, and linguistic free play in the *Leyendas;* and the cultivation of logical incoherence and the baroque proliferation of surrealist
imagery in the *Sinfonía*'s poematic prose. In addition, each work is
marked by a generic indeterminacy or voracity, invading generic
boundaries and incorporating multiple genres. The *Sinfonía* plays with
the boundaries between poetry and prose. The *Leyendas, El pez de oro,*
and *Macunaíma* combine prose fiction with folklore. And *¡Écue-
Yamba-Ó!* alters its *Bildungsroman* infrastructure and incorporates collagelike descriptions and, as both González Echevarría and Frank Janney have noted, somewhat static visual scenarios with the quality of
religious *retablos.*

Beyond a studied experimentalism, each of these works is emphatically culturally focused in vernacular content and expression. These are
site-specific texts that seek to evoke the sensorial, linguistic, or cultural
environments of known New World locations: from the Amazonian
world to São Paulo in *Macunaíma,* the Lake Titicaca *kollao* in *El pez de
oro,* the sugarcane *central* setting and the Havana underworld in *¡Écue-
Yamba-Ó!,* the overlapping pre-Columbian and colonial worlds in the
Leyendas, and New York, the Caribbean, and Mesoamerica in the *Sinfonía.* Most strikingly, in all of these texts, New World specificity is
equated with non-Western cultural presences, some indigenous, some
transplanted: the Quechua-Aymaran in *El pez de oro,* the West African
in *¡Écue-Yamba-Ó!,* the Amazonian and the legendary Tapanhuman in
Macunaíma, the Maya-Quiché in the *Leyendas,* and the West African
(in Harlem) and the pre-Columbian Mesoamerican in the *Sinfonía.*

It would seem logical to attribute this primitivist mode to the general New World climate that produced the less overtly experimental
novela de la tierra. This is particularly tempting because most of these
writers were no mere dabblers in Latin America's vernacular cultures.
Carpentier and Mário de Andrade undertook serious work in ethnomu-
sicology, and Mário promoted the study of Brazilian folklore. Asturias
studied Mesoamerican myths and legends at the Sorbonne and, under
the tutelage of Georges Raynaud, translated the *Popol Vuh* and *Los ana-
les de los Xahil* into Spanish. Gamaliel Churata collected ethnographic
materials from the indigenous cultures of Puno, Peru, and Bolivia, and

Luis Cardoza y Aragón translated Raynaud's version of the play *Rabinal Achí* into Spanish. But these writers' use of vernacular materials for aesthetic purposes must also be considered in the context of international vanguardism. The avant-gardes' ethnographic impulse has been carefully explored by James Clifford in a study of Parisian-based "ethnographic surrealism." Vanguardists' ethnographic activities included the self-conscious collection and recontextualization into experimental projects of non-Western visual artifacts and the cultivation of what were regarded as "primitive" verbal forms. The widely traveled 1985 Museum of Modern Art exhibit, "Primitivism in 20th-Century Art: Affinity of the Tribal and the Modern," focused on this process in the visual arts. But primitivism was also common in verbal and performing arts, for example, in Dada's "African Nights" in Zurich and Tristan Tzara's inventions of a pseudo-African language; in works such as Apollinaire's "Zone," Cendrars's *Anthologie Nègre*, Marinetti's *Il Negro*, Fernand Léger's and Cendrars's theatrical ballet *La Création du Monde;* and in materials on non-Western cultures published in magazines such as *Documents* and *Minotaure*.

Drawing on emergent practices of psychology and cultural anthropology and operating in an intellectual climate influenced by James George Frazer's *The Golden Bough* (1890–1915), Freud's *Totem and Taboo* (1913), and Lucien Lévy-Bruhl's *La mentalité primitive* (1910), European vanguardism conceived through its primitivist discourse a link between "precivilized" experience and primary or nonrational states of mind and being. Vanguardists sought such primary experience as an antidote to what was perceived as the mediated quality of modern life. In the study of ethnographic surrealism, Clifford suggests that the Parisian vanguards' ethnographic concerns were different in kind from romantic exoticism because they emerged from a "reality deeply in question." Other cultures, according to Clifford, "appeared now as serious human alternatives; modern cultural relativism became possible" (*The Predicament of Culture* 120). It is true that the vanguards turned to non-Western cultures for divergent modes of thinking and interacting with the world. But in her groundbreaking study of Western primitivism, *Gone Primitive: Savage Intellects, Modern Lives,* Marianna Torgovnick argues that, until recently, Western primitivism has been a projection of the West's own cultural constructs (leading at their worst to racial, ethnic, or gender stereotypes) and has seldom been based on substantive information about the societies defined as primitive. Even in the postmodern era, she suggests, cultural relativism has been painfully slow to develop. André Breton himself conceded in the 1950s that surrealism's pursuit of the primitive was a questionable activity because it was based on such "partial knowledge" of ancient cultures (*Surrealism and Painting* 333).

But in Latin America, the vanguardist encounter between Western society and its imagined "others" affirmed a historical specificity and cultural proximity that the European avant-gardes could not claim. Even though many Latin Americans might have had relatively little personal contact with the non-Western cultures present within their own and even though most vanguardist writers participated little in those cultures, what Antônio Cândido said of Brazil could be applied to many parts of Latin America: "in Brazil, primitive cultures mingle with everyday life or are living memories of a recent past." Primitivism, therefore, was "fundamentally more coherent" with Latin American cultural heritage than with the European (*Literatura e sociedade* 121). In this spirit, the Americanist texts of the vanguards present their vernacular material not as something foreign and remote but rather as palpable experience that might serve as resource material for a new Latin American art. For this reason, these works interweave their vernacular material with thematic explorations of the artistic process. Usually this connection is established through a potential artist or creative figure with privileged connections to America's "Americanness" or cultural specificity. As I have demonstrated in the chapter on portraits of the artist, the vanguards constructed an artist figure more immersed in the contingent world than aestheticist predecessors. In the works with an Americanist orientation, that contingent world assumes a vernacular substance.

Thus, *El pez de oro*'s principal narrator is a would-be writer searching for a language that will express his culturally conflictive experience, a quest that leads him to the Andean indigenous underworld. Here, a debt to Lucian, Homer, and Dante is superseded by the vernacular connection, as he descends, "strumming not the heptachord but the Laykha's *khirkhinchu*" (an Aymara healer's *charango*; 264). The *Leyendas'* frame narrator is a storyteller who finds his creative voice in Guatemala's multilayered cultural world and by retelling Mayan cosmogonic myths. Other *leyendas* address the creative process, through stories of transformation in "Leyenda del Cadejo" and "Leyenda de la Tatuana" and a tale of art's gratuitous and playful qualities in "Leyenda del Sombrerón." Menegildo Cué is not an artist in *¡Écue-Yamba-Ó!*, but through Afro-Cuban cultural practices, he and his people are cast as intimately linked to sources of aesthetic creation. Menegildo is intuitively "doctorate in the gestures and cadences" of music, dance, and improvisation (*OC* 1: 46), and the *ñáñigo* rituals into which he is initiated require performative and linguistic agility, linked to the natural world: "animal instruments" and "black litanies . . . coupled under the sign of an invisible jungle" (*OC* 1: 47–48). The *Sinfonía* invokes the aesthetic process in epigraphs from Nerval, Shelley, de Chirico, and Pound, in its structural musical metaphor, and in the poetic voice centering the work's perceptions and openly addressing poetic issues. The work's multifocalized artist speaker finds a poetic voice in America's "universe of the animal and the flower" (245). Though *Macunaíma*'s unnamed narrator is cast as a singer of tales, the novel's most imposing artist figure is the crafty hero himself, capable of radical linguistic inventiveness and dramatic, instantaneous transformations, into a "comely prince," a French prostitute, a drop of water, a leaf ant, or varieties of fish.[21]

Each of these works claims direct connections to America's non-Western substance, through a narrator, a character, or a specific cultural practice, as a source for creative power and a new vernacular art. At this level, these works do indeed appear to sustain an organic notion of cultural wholeness and the idea of a new and different literature emerging from Latin American experience. But these organicist links and authenticity claims become more complex as one examines carefully just how these texts represent that vernacular American substance and, most important, the impact on this image of the vanguardist motifs with which it is framed.

AMERICA AS THE VANGUARDS' GROUND ZERO: A CHALLENGE TO THE DISCOURSE OF ORIGINS

A resolute pursuit of the new is vanguardism's defining feature and its greatest cliché, even as this search unfolds, as Matei Calinescu suggests, in the parody or the critique of modernity itself (141). More than a youthful gesture or a willful breach with tradition, the obsessive cultivation of novelty provoked inquiries into the nature and substance of newness. Sustaining the avant-gardes' relentless quest for the original, or the very new, was the paradoxical fascination with the originary, the very old, that is, with a time-before-time of experience harboring the mysteries of the creative process. This search for beginnings is characterized by Poggioli as a "disturbed nostalgia for a new primitiveness" (76). Paraphrasing futurist Massimo Botempelli, Poggioli notes the avant-gardes' will to re-create a "primitive" or "primordial" condition that would pave the way for a "grand future renascence" (75). Peter Bürger notes similarly in *Theory of the Avant-Garde* the surrealists' quest for "pristine experience" (71). In her essay "The Originality of the Avant-Garde," Rosalind Krauss states this idea more boldly: "Avant-garde originality is conceived as a literal origin, a beginning from ground zero, a birth" (157).

In Latin America, originary discourse was widespread even in vanguardist writings that eschewed an autochthonous agenda. Poets, Huidobro wrote in "La poesía," are "those who carry the memory of that time, only those who have not forgotten the cries of the universal birth, nor the accents of the world in formation" (*OC* 1: 655). And according to the "Manifiesto del Ultra" signed by Borges, among others, the aesthetics of *ultraísmo* required of each poet "a vision, as if the world were arising dawnlike before his eyes" (HV 269). A similar language has often characterized the critical language applied to vanguardist works.[22] But in the Americanist context, the vanguardist link between the very old and the very new was often expressed as a return to vernacular sources. Thus, in his memoirs of Nicaragua's vanguardist movement, Pablo Antonio Cuadra explained that "the formula was clear: the original was the originary" ("Los poetas en la torre" 188). Because of its ongoing engagement with what were perceived as originary cultures, indigenous or, as with West African presences, more recently imported, Latin America was depicted through the primitivist motifs of its vanguardist texts as the originary site of the original, the place of first times and of a new language, a new art, and newness itself.

In a sense, of course, this representation of America is not new at all. González Echevarría affirms in *The Voice of the Masters,* as I have already noted, that Latin American literature from Independence until Carpentier's *Los pasos perdidos* is marked by a romanticist "anxiety of origins" (4). And Djelal Kadir argues persuasively in *Questing Fictions* that an obsession with "making it new" was inscribed into Latin America's cultural imagination both by the proleptic Old World texts forecasting the New World's discovery and by the "errantry" that led to the discovery itself. This determination, according to Kadir, manifests itself in Latin America's "perpetually unfolding fictions that endlessly re-make the New World anew" (6). Although he sees this process already at work in colonial texts, Kadir traces in key modern works an elusive quest for beginnings that, he suggests, locates its "perpetually dislocated" home in the homelessness, or exile, of "originary ciphers" (5 and 3).

I would argue, however, that what is singular in the originary quests undertaken by the vanguards' Americanist works is the primitivist mode in which they are framed. The concept of exile, geographic or metaphoric, has always been implicit in twentieth-century primitivism, often characterized, as Torgovnick has observed, by recurrent metaphors of finding a home or being at home. Using Georg Lukács's concept of "transcendental homelessness," Torgovnick underscores a "sense of cultural void" and "a fear of the fragility of the self" that often motivate modernism's primitivist projects (190). Taking this idea, I would suggest that even as originary textual quests cast American experience as the homelessness of a cultural void, vanguardist notions of the primitive offered a way of imagining that elusive home as a ground zero of artistic creation to be forged through autochthonous sources. In his deliberative study of Spanish America's twentieth-century regional novel, Carlos Alonso suggests that Latin America's founding cultural myths predicated on a "radically new beginning" foreclosed the possibility of defining national cultural identities on the necessary identification with a "fathomless past" (33–34). But within the vanguards' primitivist discourse, the fathomless past and the "future renascence" coincided through the equation of artistic originality with origins, providing a way for imagining that past. Thus, because of its continuing engagement with non-Western cultures, Latin America was portrayed by the Americanist texts I have been describing as the very old that was also very new: a primeval world of unprocessed experience where inaugural events, like Macunaíma's birth in the virgin forest, had happened once and could therefore, paradoxically, happen again and again, always for the very first time.

These creative works simultaneously affirm and undercut this image. All portray America as the locus of very first times, through characters construed as originary beings, through primal scenes and events, or through cosmic creation stories or humbler accounts in the folktale mode of "how things came to be." Thus the frame narrators in the *Leyendas* and *El pez de oro* derive their expressive originality from the ancient creation stories of America's indigenous worlds. The narrator in the *Leyendas*' "Ahora que me acuerdo" transforms himself into Cuero de Oro and journeys to the ancestral jungle where life began and to the "uncreated" sensory jungle where his own sense of being emerged. Here he hears echoes of the original errant tribes—"This is where their life began!"—and invocations to their creators, as he witnesses the creation of the paths of the land and the beauty of the colors and of language that provides the source for his artistry. In the *Popol*

Vuh's originary spirit, the *leyendas* that follow present founding tales, such as the arrival of the Quiché world's original inhabitants in "Leyenda del Volcán" or accounts of how things came to be: the *Cadejo* (night-stalking animal) and the opium poppy in "Leyenda del Cadejo"; the almond tree in "Leyenda de la Tatuana"; the Maya-Quiché love for ball playing in "Leyenda del Sombrerón"; and the emergence of a new volcano on the shores of Lake Atitlán in "Leyenda del tesoro del lugar florido." The comparable originary motifs in *El pez de oro* include its title and the semantic field of its most repeated words—germ, genesis, seed, avolue, root, genesic cell, generate, and nest. The narrator seeks his expressive system in the "lacteal point" of humanity in the depths of the earth and, descending to the Andean underworld, hears its inhabitants' stories of America's beginnings. The title's fish of gold, or Khori Challwa, a cosmogonic being associated with origins of life and whose birth in Lake Titicaca is reenacted in a dramatic dialogue, provides the work's sustained metaphor for America's beginnings and for human creative energy derived from this source.

Menegildo Cué in *¡Écue-Yamba-Ó!* does not enjoy the same geographic proximity to his roots as the inhabitants of indigenous worlds do. But possessed of an "unpolished humanity" (*OC* 1: 81), he is cast as an originary being, and the community to which he belongs is portrayed as an early world. Its physical dwellings for the *zafra* (cane harvest) evoke humanity's first shelters (*OC* 1: 34); its inhabitants are said to experience "primary" emotions, and their music is characterized as "elemental" and of "primary rhythms" (*OC* 1: 152). The music of Menegildo's world reenacts what is portrayed as that art form's birth, and the Afro-Cuban ritual dances keep him and his people in contact not only with the continent of their origins but also with their secret knowledge of "remote eras, pregnant with intuitions and with mystery" (*OC* 1: 47). In addition, the novel casts Menegildo as a perpetual initiate, forever new through repeated losses of innocence, a role his newborn son will resume through the continuing cycle of beginnings. The comparably repetitive originary motifs in the *Sinfonía* are based on creation images from the New World's multiple traditions, European, indigenous, and African. A return to beginnings is enacted through repeated allusions to the birth of Venus, through pre-Columbian sacrificial scenarios, and through the "primal" music and dance of Harlem. An epiphanic moment in the lengthy prose poem is provoked by the adult poet's discovery of nature's artifact, horse manure, in New

York's mechanical jungle. This scatological Proustian device evokes a flood of memories, of the world of "sensible chaos," of his "double infancy as a poet," of a childhood in Antigua, Guatemala and of the pre-Columbian past (264–65). Here, the child poet assumes the identity of one about to be sacrificed and experiences the convergence of the very old and the yet to be born: "My past, so ancient, and my future, so remote, suddenly combine some of their threads, intertwine them" (269). At the moment of sacrifice, the poet participates in the "creation of a world" (276).

Significant differences of style and tone notwithstanding, each of these works evokes originary events, situating a speaker or character in a position privy to special knowledge harbored at the sources of things. Each work records beginnings: initiations, transformations, births of characters, of a people, of a country, of a continent, or of a world. Most important, the creative inventiveness of speakers or characters derives from this originary activity. As the founding story of a people embodied in their hero, *Macunaíma* shares many of these features. The hero's birth in the depths of the virgin forest, surrounded by the enormous silence of the murmuring Uraricoera River, has the aura of a primal event. Dislocated in São Paulo like Menegildo in Havana or the *Sinfonía*'s poet in New York, Macunaíma and his brothers yearn for the land of abundance they have left behind. Macunaíma is a being perpetually (re)created, even returning several times from the dead. Like the *Leyendas,* moreover, *Macunaíma* employs the folkloric how-things-came-to-be mode ("And it was thus that . . . ") to describe the emergence of something new: a plant, a word, or a custom.

But *Macunaíma* is a radically parodic work, and by exaggerating these originary motifs or placing them in curious contexts, the novel performs a critical mimicry of originary discourse, pointing to its flaws and bringing into focus similar though less conspicuous critiques in the other works as well. The primal ambience of Macunaíma's birth offers a case in point. As I explore in detail in the chapter on language, in the other works, originary moments are construed as prelinguistic events. Cuero de Oro witnesses language's emergence in the *Leyendas;* the Khori Challwa's birth precedes language in *El pez de oro;* the *Sinfonía*'s speaker alludes to a time before things had names; and in *¡Écue-Yamba-Ó!,* through their music and dance, Menegildo's people conjure up a time before song had been invented. *Macunaíma* renders this idea literally, providing a humorous twist. For six years after his birth, Macunaíma fails to emit a sound, and when he speaks at last, it is only to complain, "Ai! que preguiça!" (5) ("¡Ay, que flojera!" in Spanish, or, literally, "Oh, what laziness!" in English).

The originary creative capacities Macunaíma derives from the natural world of his origins are extended to São Paulo's land of technology, as when he transforms his brother into a "telephone-machine" on cue. Macunaíma's proclivity for self-(re)creation is exaggerated even more as he and his brothers recycle themselves to the point of obscuring their origins. Before they enter São Paulo, Macunaíma bathes in the shoals of a magic river and becomes white-skinned and blue-eyed, and his brothers lighten their skin and limbs. Speaking of the vanguardist link between origins and originality, Rosalind Krauss notes the movement's parables of "absolute self-creation," for example, Marinetti's account of his (re)birth as a futurist: "thrown from his automobile one evening in 1909 into a factory ditch filled with water, [Marinetti] emerges as if from amniotic fluid to be born—without ancestors—a futurist" (157). But Macunaíma's frequent experiences in self-(re)creation are portrayed not as birthlike primal events but as self-conscious reconstitutions, for example, when the giant chops him up into a stew and his brother hastily reassembles his parts. In addition, *Macunaíma*'s folkloric accounts of originary occurrences often commemorate banal accidents of modern life rather than sacred natural events. The story of a new plant emerging from the grave of Macunaíma's son preserves the aura of a legendary tale, but other such "and that is how . . ." tales expose their constructed quality. Thus, when Macunaíma slings a brick at his brother, the soccer ball is born.

Macunaíma's most significant critique of originary discourse unfolds in the ambiguity of the novel's own telling. Combining references to countless geographic sites, colloquialisms not limited by time or place, and a multiplicity of folkloric sources, *Macunaíma* resists delineation as the founding story of one place or one people. The work's narrative structure also avoids such boundaries. If *Macunaíma* is a story of origins, the origin of its own telling remains obscure even as the novel ends. From the opening reference to the "hero of our people," the nameless narrating voice identifies with the group whose story is being told, and though he does not arrive on the scene until the story has ended, this initial participatory tone is maintained by the colloquial expressions and linguistic inventiveness the speaker shares with the characters he describes. Close to death, Macunaíma tells his story to a talkative parrot, and once the hero dies, his tribe and its language vanish until a man wandering along the Uraricoera stumbles upon the parrot, who repeats Macunaíma's tale in a marvelously new language. That man, the speaker confesses to his "dear reader," is the narrator himself who has stayed on to repeat the story. But *Macunaíma*'s originality is only in its (re)telling, for the narrator is repeating a story he has heard from a parrot. Though the parrot has allegedly heard it from the hero himself, a parrot is not a creator but a repeater of the words of another. And everything we know about the parrot's source, Macunaíma himself, suggests a radically unreliable narrator. Thus, although *Macunaíma*'s teller shares a supposedly original account of a people's beginnings, the work portrays him as the repeater, twice removed from unreliable sources, of the words and stories of others.

The other Americanist works are not overtly parodic. But like *Macunaíma*, they also expose uncertain origins, through ambiguous narration and poetic voicing or through obscure or multiple sources. Thus, while drawing on creation myths, the *Leyendas* undermines the primacy of first times through its ambiguous and multiple origins. The speaker in the two initial narratives assumes a variety of forms—the returning native son, Cuero de Oro—and vacillates from singular to plural with the result that we do not always know who is speaking or from where. Though as Cuero de Oro the narrator returns to Mayan sources, the *leyendas* that follow are presented less as primary experience than as a retelling of what was already there. The initial native son narrator culls his tales from "lost shadows and phantoms with empty eyes" that populate the air (13), and the world from which they emerge, like Guatemala's layered pre-Columbian and colonial past, is a palimpsest of voices in which the original layers are obscured. In addition, these lost stories are inscribed in the oral tradition that is repeatedly invoked in their telling. The narrator participates in this tradition not only by explicitly quoting from it but by reminding us that he, too, is in the process of retelling: "And it happened that . . . , and it happened, I repeat in order to take a breath" (35). And although it is a story of beginnings, the *Leyendas* itself has not one but two beginnings, the narrator's return to Guatemala and the storytelling test with the *güegüechos*. Curiously, the narrator has asked them to tell him stories, but transformed into Cuero de Oro, he becomes the teller, an ambiguity of speaker and audience that poses the problem of how to begin and of who shall begin. Significantly, the second section's title, "Ahora que me acuerdo" ("Now that I remember," or, more colloquially, "Now that I think of it") provokes a sense of interruption and digression, of a beginning in media res.

As in the *Leyendas,* one is often unsure in *El pez de oro* exactly who is speaking, as the principal narrative voice unfolds into three perspectives: the voice of experience remembering, a youthful voice, and an authorial voice that examines in an essay style cultural and linguistic questions. A multitude of additional voices intermingle with the principal narration without warning or accountability for their sources: poetic voices reciting indigenous verse, a teacher and student debating linguistic *mestizaje,* Aymara healers arguing with Western doctors, biblical-sounding voices telling stories of Khori Challwa and Khori Puma, and the disembodied "gutturalizations" reminiscent of "old voices" (267) that the narrator hears in the land of the dead. The narrator's "originality" derives from collecting these voices and transmitting them without comment to the reader. More important, in his underworld sojourn, rather than the unified originary account he seeks, the narrator unearths a polyglot cacophony of classical European, Spanish, and indigenous versions of America's beginnings.

In a comparable mode, as the *Sinfonía*'s poetic speaker searches for originary experience, the focalizer for that voice shifts continually from adult poet to child poet to Dante, and the work incorporates other voices that emerge from the natural world. Even as it accumulates images of first times, the poem also addresses the difficulty of ascertaining beginnings, as the child poet seeks primary explanations in vain through the fossilized framings of blackboards, maps, and philosophy: "The philosophers finished reading the libraries, closed the last volume and began to write a new one for future philosophers who on rereading the libraries would write another volume, that one they didn't find, which would be read by future philosophers who on not finding the volume they were seeking would write another" (257–58). Seeking to create lyrically what could not be found in philosophy, the adult poet poses to the reader directly the problem of aesthetic originality. The work espouses an antiartifice approach to art. Thus, through the child poet's freshness of vision that transforms the familiar into the unknown, the ordinary will become new: "Habitual the bewilderment, renewed, strange, and familiar" (337). But by making explicit its own intention to seek out the primary experience of the unintentional, the poem exposes the artifice of originary searches.

Over the years, critics such as Juan Marinello, Joseph Sommers, and

González Echevarría have noted disconcerting vacillations in narrative perspective in ¡Écue-Yamba-Ó!, a feature that, as in the other works here, makes the speaker's position difficult to pin down. Portrayed as a nonreflexive, self-present, and originary being, Menegildo is paradoxically situated by this novel in vanguardism's self-reflexive context. The actual source of Menegildo's story is never clearly identified, but the voice that tells it speaks in different registers, sometimes detached and ostensibly objective, sometimes critical of social conditions, and, particularly while describing Afro-Cuban rituals, sometimes seemingly yearning for participation in Menegildo's world.[23] I would suggest that this voice parallels the ambiguity James Clifford describes in the ethnographically inclined Parisian avant-gardes, as it combines ethnography's intentions to make the strange familiar with vanguardism's impulses to make the familiar strange (The Predicament of Culture 121). As in some ethnographic narrative, the voice speaks from the interstices of participation and distance, seeking to describe from within a fullness of experience that it desires and projects from the outside.[24] Narrator observations, at once condescending and admiring, are multiple. Thus, though neither Menegildo nor his companions "had ever undertaken the arduous task of analyzing first causes," the narrator notes that "they possessed, through atavism, a conception of the universe that accepted the possible magical nature of any event" (OC 1: 68).

The tension bred by such a split focus accounts for the "crack" that has been noted in the novel's structure, but this crack produces the text's critique of its own originary discourse and is manifested in Menegildo himself.[25] He is characterized as a man imbued with the fullness of being but with no self-reflexive "gaps," no "lost space" to disturb this plenitude. Menegildo, the narrator asserts, "felt himself, complete, solid, filling his skin, with no lost space, with that same essential reality possessed by the heat or the cold" (emphasis in the original). He had a "sensation of living that excluded all metaphysical anguish" (OC 1: 162). These affirmations or the observation that Menegildo feels overcome by a sense of grief that he is incapable of analyzing construct a feeling and yet unreflective being who is paradoxically both aware and unaware of his condition. But as the work repeatedly suggests, there are indeed gaps in Menegildo's being, as he repeatedly experiences estrangement and, indeed, suffers at times from the very sense of "transcendental homelessness" that Western yearners for the primitive have sought to resolve by inventing beings like Menegildo. Thus in a crosscultural context that parallels the position of the novel's ethnographic speaker observing Menegildo's world from outside, Menegildo attends a festive gathering, feels "strange among so many blacks of other customs and other languages," and is reassured by the sight of one of his own who at least speaks "like a Christian" (*OC* 1: 73). The most self-conscious and willful split in Menegildo's persona unfolds theatrically when he adapts to city life by joining an amusement park sideshow. With turban and red robe, Menegildo portrays the ghoulish executioner of Saint John the Baptist, a part he plays with care and gusto and fully "aware of his role" (*OC* 1: 167). Throughout *¡Écue-Yamba-Ó!*, Menegildo spends far more time adjusting to things foreign to his experience than he does partaking in the existential fullness of his ancestral primal world.

All of these works represent America as a primordial ground zero of human experience and creation. But through the multiplicity and ambiguities of their sometimes obscure, sometimes mediated sources, these works also undermine the creative primacy of first times, that is, the vanguardist notion of the originality of originary events. By suggesting that there are no purely originary beings, no univocal or "unifocal" experiences, and no absolutely new stories to be told, these works explore the elusive nature of newness and suggest that the originality of artistic creation—American or otherwise—resides elsewhere than in the imagined original moment. Through shifting voices and focalizers and by emphasizing their own repetitions, these works cast doubts on the originary substance of characters or narrators and make evident the constructed nature of originality. And even as they posit an ahistorical time-out-of-time of human experience, these works also reveal the contextual and historical contingencies of the new, evident particularly in its dependence on the eye of its beholder.

COLUMBUS'S EGG: DISCOVERIES IN THE EYE OF THEIR BEHOLDER

The vanguardist image of artistic discovery harbors a profoundly paradoxical idea, and in part this paradox emerges from the meaning of the word itself. To discover is to obtain for the first time, through purposeful search or by accident, sight or knowledge of something previously unknown to the discoverer. In vanguardist artistic practice, this interaction between purpose and accident is exemplified in the artist who deliberately sets out to discover a new effect with the hope of being dazzled by the surprise of his or her discovery. The paradox is intensified by the word's aura of scientific pursuit. Poggioli notes that the avant-gardes' idea of discovery was imbued with the spirit of scientific experimentation, as artists tested new modes. But to be open to the process of discovering, artists, like scientists or explorers, needed to be properly disposed. They needed to cultivate a discovering attitude or a propensity for divergent thought, what Haroldo de Campos has called an "inaugural inclination" ("Uma poética da radicalidade" 25), or what Bürger calls a "pervasive openness to impressions" (65). The paradoxical combination of the willful "inaugural inclination" and the surprise encounter it should generate also underlies the geographic meaning of discovery and its historical allusions to the encounter between the Old World and the New. This historical context is embedded in the vanguards' quest for "original effects" among artifacts of non-Western cultures. As Poggioli points out, the deliberate search for such effects sometimes became a Faustian "search for Eldorado and the fountain of youth" (135). Breton made this historical allusion explicit while expounding on the creativity of the insane: "Christopher Columbus should have set out to discover America with a boatload of madmen," he observed (*Manifestoes of Surrealism* 5–6).

Recent assessments of Columbus's widespread appearance as a literary symbol in Western literature have revealed the discovery concept's problematic substance.[26] His appearance in vanguardist discourse in particular embodies those aesthetic problems of special concern within the avant-garde projects. In Latin America's vanguards, discovery references were common in the context of "inaugural inclinations" and the innocence of vision they implied. "We want to discover life. We want to see with new eyes," Borges wrote (*MPP* 75). "*See with open eyes,*" Oswald de Andrade affirmed in the "Pau-Brasil" manifesto (GMT 330; SMSR 186; emphasis in original). But references to Columbus's venture and to the cross-cultural conflicts it provoked were also quite common in writings on aesthetic discovery. On one level, writers identified with and admired the discoverer. Thus Vicente Huidobro compared "theoretical adventurers" or discoverers (such as Galileo, Copernicus, Newton, Einstein, Shakespeare, Góngora, or Rimbaud) to "practical or dynamic adventurers" who discover or conquer new lands (for example, Columbus, Cortés, Napoleon, Livingstone, Cook, or Magellan) (*OC* 1: 752). Columbus, he argued, had provided "a new poetic sustenance" for the world (*OC* 1: 779). Puerto Rico's *atalayistas* claimed Columbus as one of their own (LHA 104), linking the idea of Columbus's farsightedness with the group's name derived from *atalaya*, a watchtower or lookout point. Oswald de Andrade dedicated his experimental *Pau*

Brasil poetry collection to Blaise Cendrars "on the occasion of the discovery of Brazil" (*Poesias reunidas* 65). And Paulo Prado's introduction to that edition compares the work (in which the "História do Brasil" section presents a rediscovery of that land) to "Columbus's egg," that is, something doubted by others but ultimately enriching the discoverer.

This expression, "o ôvo de Colombo," underscores the tension in the vanguardist idea of discovery between chance and intention as well as the role of divergent thought. The saying "É como o ôvo de Colombo" (literally, "It's like Columbus's egg," but more figuratively translated, roughly, as "It's easy when you know how") emphasizes the change in perception provoked at the moment of insight.[27] But the expression refers also to the apocryphal story of Columbus's response to the skeptics. Declaring that an egg could be stood upright, he is said to have challenged the doubters to figure out how. After their futile efforts, Columbus then flattened the egg's curved bottom (by smashing its shell against the table) and stood it up straight, an unconventional solution to the problem, obvious once it was revealed.[28] This story underscores the interaction between intention and chance. The answer to the riddle, moreover, shows not only a determination to solve it but also a predisposition to divergent thought. A similar idea was posed by Mexican Contemporáneos group member Jaime Torres Bodet. The genius, Torres Bodet suggested, cannot foresee all the results of his work but consciously finds the direction to follow. "What was admirable in the history of the discovery of America," he wrote, "was not the discovery, a mere finding in which nature got to know herself a little bit better, but rather the *will* of Christopher Columbus placed at the service of a route *wisely intuited*" (*Contemporáneos* 108; my emphasis).

But invoking Columbus's discovery points to another problem as well, for the word *discovery* harbors the paradox of seeing for the very first time something, or somebody, that was already there. Thus allusions to Columbus's discovery foreground the conflict of perspectives between those who discover and those who are discovered. In fact, this problem is already embedded in Breton's suggestion that Columbus needed madmen to discover the New World. We know that for Breton and other vanguardists, madmen were grouped with "primitives" and children as repositories of the unmediated experience and divergent thinking that vanguardist artists were seeking. Making a truly grand discovery, then, would require the "wisely intuited," willful plan of a Columbus combined with the "inaugural inclination" of the "primitives," that is, of those he believed he had discovered and onto whom (we know from his writings) he projected prior imaginings of who they would be. This paradox is fully exploited by vanguardist works that portray America as a site of the inaugural disposition required for discovering and as a place for seeing for the very first time things that are already there, wisely, or foolishly, intuited. Through exaggerations, inversions, and parody, these Americanist vanguard works play with the interaction of discoverer and discovered, exposing the ironies of such meetings as well as their historical and cultural contingencies.

The *Sinfonía* tightly interweaves perspectives of discoverer and discovered, as the New World is perpetually reinvented through the perception of the one who beholds it. The poem emphasizes the power of a radically innocent vision by reiterating the phrase "the child sees" to provoke floods of accumulated imagery and by lauding childhood's creative focus: "Poetry and reality, simultaneous, ubiquitous, without guile, without age" (346). Evocations of an Antigua childhood and of Mesoamerica's pre-Columbian past link the child poet's discovering eye to America's "universe of the animal and the flower." But the *Sinfonía* also reveals discovery's purposeful mode, for the adult poet willfully conjures up the child poet and Dante to evoke alternate experiences of a single encounter. Imagining Columbus's discovery of indigenous sacrificial rites from the navigator's perspective, for example, produces one kind of response: "From the deck of his caravel he could contemplate a procession bathed in blood, that wailed monotonous songs" (268). But by shifting the focus through the child poet to the position of the sacrificed, ascending a pyramid flanked by obsidian-bearing priests, the poet imagines a sacred, time-defying experience: "all is Present, all, even past and future" (268–69). Later, perceiving Harlem as a primeval world and feeling a connection with its displaced inhabitants, the poet relives the arrival of America's discoverers through the discovered's fearful gaze: "He saw from the depths of his infancy white men, with thin noses and fine curly lips, who were looking for something as if demented" (319).

A similar transformation is brought about when the child poet recasts Dante's New World discovery, providing two different visions of New York. Dante discovers a modern inferno, an urban world of "dense subterranean rivers, [which] capillarily irrigated the metropolis's body laid out in the night, soft and translucent like a great lizard," and of houses like "skulls with empty sockets" and with "slate craniums" over which "the crystallized crocodiles stuffed with sugar warm themselves"

(256). But a shift in perspective willfully rediscovers New York in the spring, projecting onto the city the child poet's animal and flower worldview: "New joy in the typewriter keyboards, in the automobile horns, in the firemen's polished bells . . . , Spring of the air" (282). These perpetual rediscoveries seek to bring the ordinary reality of one world under the estranging perception of another.

In the same way that the child poet fearfully recalls the white men's arrival in the *Sinfonía,* the *Leyendas'* initial lines invoke the specter of prior encounters in the land the narrator has returned to find: "The road sinks like the blade of a broken sword in the plaza's fist" (11). But the "Leyenda del Sombrerón" examines in a more playful mood how the encounter's creative impulses interfered with its ideological goals. Here Guatemala is the land of the historical encounter—"that remote corner of the world promised to a queen by a crazy navigator" (34)— and initially the story seems to emerge from the conqueror's perspective. Thus religious leaders inhabit a beautiful temple raised side by side with monuments to the "idolatry of man" (34). But those charged with eradicating idolatry are overcome by the very "inaugural inclination" that led the crazy navigator to the New World and devote their time instead, the narrator notes ironically, to sinfully creative pursuits: the fine arts, science, and philosophy. One particularly devout monk resists these temptations only to be discovered and captivated himself by a magical rubber ball that bounces his way, emblematic, Asturias observes in a note, of the indigenous love of the ball game. As the story inverts the hierarchy between discoverer and discovered, the monk charged with converting the infidel is transformed by the creative power of the discovered culture, a conversion facilitated by the very "openness to impressions" that led the discoverers to this land.

The "Leyenda del tesoro del lugar florido" enacts a more profound inversion by recounting don Pedro de Alvarado's attack on Lake Atitlán from the perspective of the indigenous world. But here, too, the conqueror's "inaugural inclination" helps those he finds to outwit him. Santiago de Atitlán and its market present an alluring profusion of sensorial abundance. As high priests read signs from the nearby volcano, the town prepares for attack with a multichromatic display of warriors. This "centipede rainbow" parade of deception serves as a weapon: "May the white men be confused by seeing our arms!" (41). As the white men advance in a rigorous silence contrasting with Atitlán's vociferous color, the fleeing Indians abandon their treasures, and the conquerors crossing the lake on a boat are dazzled by the artifacts they behold. But before they can seize a thing, the erupting volcano reproduces itself, covering the Indians' tracks and their abandoned treasures. The conquerors are left to contemplate the illusory riches afloat in the water, and the reader is left to speculate whether the wonders bedazzling these discoverers were mere projections of their "wisely intuited" desires.

The fourth *retablo* of *El pez de oro* enacts a similar inversion as it recreates Columbus's discovery from the perspective of the non-Western world. From the heights of the Andean *kollao*, Pachamama and her son the Khori Puma watch the Spaniards arrive in the Caribbean and unmask Columbus's mistake. Recast as the catastrophe foretold by indigenous myth, the event is precipitated by the willful intention of Pachamama herself who (through a momentary lapse in judgment) tricks the lost explorers to America's shores. Indigenous narrative voices interspersed with archaic Spanish from Columbus's writings create a step-by-step account of the Caribbean landing. "And this sublime dreamer discovered us!" the indigenous voices announce (143). The natural world responds with a cosmic concert of Andean verse, reaffirming Pachamama's power. By turning the explorer's "openness to impressions" against them, the New World version of the encounter underscores that what the travelers believe they behold (Marco Polo's land of the Great Khan) is not what they are actually seeing (the Khori Challwa's indigenous world). Instead, it is the "primitives" Columbus believed he had found who see clearly, as the lines of a traditional *haylli* record: the "discovering of discoverers" was all simply the magic of Aymara healers (147). Thus, when Columbus discovers a nova in the sky, it is only Pachamama herself giving the disoriented dreamer a hand, as "compassionately she went out to meet him" (147).

¡Écue-Yamba-Ó! and *Macunaíma* undertake more radical inversions of discovery motifs by repositioning the non-Western beings, traditional objects of discovery, in the discerning role of discoverer. Both Menegildo Cué and Macunaíma contemplate the modern urban world with the eyes of the newly arrived. And each dazzled discoverer scrutinizes this new world's banalities through the lens of the first encounter, shaped, as with Columbus and the chroniclers, by the frame of his own worldview. Menegildo becomes an infant discoverer when he explores the wonders of his family's *bohío*. Focusing through the toddler's innocent eye, the narrator imbues this ordinary event, designated "Initiation (a)," with the awe of a momentous revelation, as Menegildo moves beyond the "civilized world" of his cot. The child willfully undertakes

the journey on all fours, propelled like all explorers by the lure of the yet to be known. His discovery of "the great mystery . . . in the base of the wardrobes" is charted in a language reminiscent of the chroniclers first contemplating America and anticipating the baroquely prodigious natural world that Carpentier's nameless narrator finds around every bend in *Los pasos perdidos:* "The dust transforms those regions into ancient caves, with stalactites of animal threads that oscillate like soft pendula . . . [and] the world displays itself as a jungle of pillars that sustain platforms, plateaus, and cornices populated by discs, sharp edges, and fragments of dead beasts" (*OC* 1: 41). Although this panorama unfolds in words beyond Menegildo's expressive powers, the passage is focalized from his position and that position's relationship to the world he observes. Thus the physical limits of Menegildo's lived experience shape his perception of the new world he beholds. As with many exploratory journeys, Menegildo's most "marvelous discovery" is an ostensibly human scene. The "magical theater" of the family altar filled with colorful figures and objects presents a world separated from Menegildo by its theatrical frame but one that he desires to enter and, as with the treasure seekers of Lake Atitlán, one that he reaches out to seize.

Menegildo's second major new world encounter, his trip to Havana as a prisoner, is not a willful endeavor. But although he is initially passive in the hands of his captors, on the train his "openness to impressions" takes over. Thus, although the landscape he surveys is identical to the world he is leaving behind, very small variations, say, in the shape of a tree or the course of a river, assume the aura of a discovery. Just as Columbus and the chroniclers often compared what they saw to what they had known so too does Menegildo seize on the familiar, for example, when the landscape dotted with novelty is interrupted by a group of blacks at work. This penchant for reframing the new into a context already known shapes Menegildo's most basic perceptions as he "hears" the train car's wheels as the words and rhythms of a popular refrain: "Huye alacrán, que te pica el gallo. . . . Huye alacrán, que te pica el gallo" (Run, scorpion, or the rooster will sting you) (*OC* 1: 121). In the city, Menegildo is once again dazzled by his surroundings, objects and people as "exotic" in the young man's eyes as the New World's inhabitants to arriving Europeans. But at this very moment, Menegildo is brought back to earth by a child who recognizes him as a black prisoner. This shift underscores Menegildo's marginality from the world he has discovered, a position that generates the work's open critique of modernity's cultural leveling. Marginal as Menegildo may be, however, the novel credits his culture with the critical power of resistance: "The bongo, antidote for Wall Street!" (*OC* 1: 115).

As a folkloric and Rabelaisian creation unfettered by the lingering naturalist conventions that shape *¡Écue-Yamba-Ó!,* Macunaíma undertakes his São Paulo journey voluntarily and in a more powerful position than Menegildo to subject the urban world to the condescending scrutiny of his own discovering eye. Macunaíma is portrayed as a conqueror as the narrator recalls "so many conquests and so many past deeds" (36). In São Paulo, Macunaíma reacts with "surprised contemplation," his intelligence "very perturbed" (40). Initially he processes the fantastic and strange *paulista* "world of beasts" through the frame of his own experience. But he soon learns to rename what he sees though continuing to identify it with his own world. Thus wild animal roars and shrieks turn out to be the city's sirens and horns, and the flora and fauna perceived by Macunaíma are actually signs, chimneys, buses, and cars. Even so, Macunaíma remains outside of the culture he observes, as he demonstrates in his approach to machines, a feature of São Paulo life, he quickly intuits, that dramatically distinguishes it from his own. Thus, although São Paulo's "Children of Manioc" have many different words for their machines, in Macunaíma's mind they form a single category that sets them apart from the nonmachine (nature, animals, humans, and gods), and he persists in referring to the telephone-machine, the taxi-machine, and the elevator-machine. In his customary augmentative fashion, moreover, he broadens the category to encompass all artifacts of São Paulo life foreign to his own world, including the rouge-machine, the shoe-machine, the dress-machine, and the newspaper-machine.

The work's most acerbic critique of the discourse of discovery and the power relationships surrounding it develops in Macunaíma's notorious letter home to the Icamiabas (Amazonian women). Imitating the chroniclers' style and parodying the language of travel and ethnography, Macunaíma describes the banalities of modern life as exotic features of São Paulo civilization (its sexual habits, its materialism, its insects) and reports on the quaint and picturesque customs and mores of its people. Macunaíma's description of street-cleaning machines as monsters recalls the chroniclers' accounts of America's fantastic creatures. The city itself is the edenic, abundant "ground zero" of origins for urban life; the water is so magnificent, the climate so mild, the earth so healthy that "one could well affirm, in the manner of the chroniclers," that . . . "the urban fauna was spontaneously generated" (80).

São Paulo's filth is ironically recycled through the bedazzled discoverer's eye; its streets are "adorned" with litter and fruit peelings and a "delicate dancing dust" full of germs that contaminate the city's people. And as in the chroniclers' accounts of the New World's inhabitants, Macunaíma assumes an ethnographic distance from the city's people, recasting them as the "primitives" imagined by their discoverer: "The *paulistas* are a bold and plucky people, inured to the hardships of war. They live in singular and collective combat, all armed from head to toe" (81). They have "curious" and "original" habits, and they speak in a "barbarous and multifarious chatter" (84).[29]

This letter interweaves various levels of perception. The "primitive" being contemplates the modern through the lens of his own worldview, refracted through the distancing language of discovery once elaborated by those who constructed their own representations of the primitive and his world. As the object of the modern world's primitivist discourse, Macunaíma simultaneously embraces and celebrates his own primitiveness and turns that discourse against its creators. It was this process that led Oswald de Andrade's *antropofagia* group to regard *Macunaíma* as the anthropophagic work par excellence. A polemical document that radically inverts European texts of discovery, the "Manifesto antropófago" constructs, as critics such as Benedito Nunes and K. David Jackson have affirmed, the "ignoble savage," never successfully "catechized" by the conquest, to consume primitivist fictions and turn them around as critiques of European culture and social institutions. "I only want what is not mine. Law of man. Law of the anthropophagic," the manifesto's cannibal voice declares against "all importers of canned consciousness" (GMT 353–54). As a guide for aesthetic practice, this primitive ingests all foreign models, recycling them as his own and launching a "Caraíba Revolution" against Western cultural institutions.[30]

In the spirit of the *antropófago* manifesto, all of these Americanist works employ the vanguardist discovery motifs for purposes of cultural critique. On one level, this critique unfolds as a celebration of vernacular cultures through the voices of those who claim them as their own, as if enacting *El pez de oro*'s admonition that "nobody can discover a world already discovered" (143). Claiming a cultural proximity to the discovered, these works invoke Taulipang and Arekuna myths, Andean cosmology, Afro-Cuban ritual, Mesoamerican rites, Harlem's music and dance, and America's untamed song as prodigious aesthetic resources, cultural worlds constructed not as the outsider imagines them but as capable of telling their own stories. Beyond celebrating the creative power of the vernacular, however, these works reveal the process of projection at work in one culture's discovery of another. In a specific critique of Western primitivism, they suggest that original effects in art may be provoked by subjecting any group or practice to a discoverer's gaze, focused through anybody's eye. Estrangement, aesthetic or cultural, may be generated through the clash of one world with another, and, as Bürger points out, the surrealists in search of estranging effects cultivated an innocent eye as they wandered like primitives through the "enigmatic nature" of Paris (71). But the discovery inversions enacted in these works suggest that, though one may cultivate a "primitive" perspective with the hope of seeing for the very first time, there is no radical purity of vision, primitive or modern, for what the discovering eye "wisely intuits" is always shaped by its prior experience. Thus the "seeing with new eyes" that these works portray derives not from an originary innocence of vision but from experiences of personal or cultural estrangement, fortuitous or by design. This idea blurs the primitive-modern dichotomy as well as the nature-culture opposition that sustains it. Latin America becomes the site of discovery not because it presents the more pristine, natural world the discoverer seeks or because it harbors the "inaugural inclination" the discoverer ascribes to and seeks from the discovered but rather because Latin American experience brings into focus the estrangement provoked when one culture encounters another, an effect that Latin America's history repeatedly reenacts. Such a conception of America poses an emergent cultural pluralism and reconceives the New World not as the site of vernacular or modern culture but as an all-encompassing space where all cultures potentially encounter and interact with one another.

AMERICA'S NEW WORLD RHAPSODY: FROM TOTALITY TO THE NONORGANIC

Art in the early twentieth century, according to Arnold Hauser, was seized by a "mania for totality" (4: 237),[31] and the international avant-gardes gave this impulse free rein to the extreme. But at the same time, vanguardist art undermined wholeness by attacking classical and romantic models of art's organicity, that is, the idea that a work's constituent parts form a complete and unified whole. Bürger affirms in *Theory of the Avant-Garde* that the organic work of art seeks to appear as a work of nature and to make "unrecognizable the fact that it has been made" (72). Challenging the organic model, vanguardists constructed what Bürger terms "nonorganic" art, creations that under-mine any sense of wholeness and focus attention on their own incom-pleteness and the decontextualized quality of their parts.

In Latin America, the impulse to encompass all was evident in the manifestos' hyperbolic language and grand schemes that I explore in chapter 1. It was also manifested in the vanguards' portraits of the artist, as I show in the chapter on that topic, particularly in the aestheticist inheritance of an all-encompassing grand poetic vision. But this totaliz-ing drive was particularly evident in the vanguards' Americanist vein, not only in manifestos that imagined a colossal continent of the fu-ture but also in creative texts inclined to represent America as an all-encompassing whole. But in the construction of this portrayal, these works employ strategies of containment that undermine the notion of New World integrity and reveal an overflowing and disconnected American experience, simultaneously too out-of-bounds and too frag-mented to be comfortably inscribed within an organic whole.

In part, this revelation takes shape by exaggerating the organic model in an America so full and complete that it exceeds its own whole-ness. The title of Ronald de Carvalho's *Toda a América,* a work that I have mentioned but have not analyzed in detail here, presents the most obvious example. De Carvalho's America, moreover, is a world of "all imaginations" that "merges all cosmologies" (45). In vanguardist works, this perception of an all-inclusive world emerges in spatial con-structions as well. But if the Americanist manifestos cast the New World as an organically integrated body-continent, the creative works gener-ally construct a "baggy monster" geography that overflows its own boundaries, organicity out of control. This view relies in part on charac-ters, narrators, or poetic speakers who traverse hyperbolic distances. The frame narrator in the *Leyendas* moves freely from layer to layer of his country's geographic and temporal past, and in the body of Cuero de Oro, he roams the Mayan jungles and mountains to their prehistoric beginnings. *El pez de oro*'s principal narrator executes similar tours of the Andean world, and in the discovery *retablo,* indigenous characters embrace at a glance a vast reality in which the Caribbean and the An-dean *kollao* are contiguous. The *Sinfonía*'s poetic perspective encom-passes Florence, Pompeii, and China along with New York, Havana, and Mesoamerica. Here a sense of physical expanse is produced by repe-titions of the word *recorrido* (traversal), and as the child poet's "travers-ing the maps," by land, by sea, or by air. Macunaíma traverses space on a comparably grand scale in repeated adversarial chases, on foot, by stallion, or on the back of an insect, that take him all over Brazil and from Venezuela to Argentina and back through São Paulo.[32] But this New World's uncontrollable size disorients its travelers, as the *Sinfonía*'s child poet and Dante become lost traversing the city, Macunaíma forgets where he is going, and *El pez de oro's* frame narrator becomes geographically and temporally disoriented. Even Menegildo Cué in *¡Écue-Yamba-Ó!*, who as an islander and a prisoner experiences geographic and existential confinement, contemplates the threat of an uncontainable world in the ocean, an open expanse onto which he cares not to venture.

If geography fails to chart America's totality, music provides another option. The symphony metaphor, with the artist as conductor, provided an early vanguardist totalizing motif, as in Apollinaire's essay on modernity's "new spirit," which, he forecast, would dominate the entire world. The new artists, the French poet proclaimed, would be "like conductors of an orchestra of unbelievable scope" and would "have at their disposition the entire world, its noises and appearances, the thought and language of man, song, dance, all the arts and artifices . . . with which to compose the visible and unfolded book of the future" (227–28). The New World was also being portrayed through symphonic metaphors, not only in some poetry's Whitmanesque "I hear America singing" imagery but also, for example, in Waldo Frank's *The Re-discovery of America*, which, as I noted earlier, was translated and disseminated by *Amauta* and other vanguardist magazines. Frank described America, which he defined in continental terms, as a symphony of voices (259–61). Symphonic imagery was not uncommon in vanguardist manifestos, for example, in the second *estridentista* manifesto seeking poetry with "orchestrally synthesized" images (*MPP* 125). Creative texts employed global musical constructs as well, either as organizing principles or as recurrent motifs. These include, for example, Mário de Andrade's oratorio in verse, "As enfibraturas do Ipiranga," the *Chinfonía burguesa* by Nicaragua's Joaquín Pasos and José Coronel Urtecho, and the poetic "Orquestación diepálica" by Puerto Rico's *diepalista* poets J. I. de Diego-Padró and Luis Palés Matos.

The Americanist vanguard texts employ a variety of musical motifs to evoke America's "murmurous world," to borrow José María Arguedas's characterization of Andean experience, in which sounds, human intervention notwithstanding, seem to assume a life of their own. But in general these motifs underscore music's multiplicity, improvisational potential, and unlimited scope, playing down its reliance on orderly synthesis. The 100-page *Sinfonía*, for example, is symphonic in scope, but chains of surrealistic imagery orchestrate the multiple voices and perspectives. Cardoza y Aragón explained the poem's title as a "single and vast metaphor" for the endless growth of the poem's music (245). A scenario in which the child poet and Dante witness a New York opera performance alludes to a symphony's potential to organize the world. But the performance of a "disproportionate" composition that follows unleashes a disorderly string of surreal connections, in which hippopotamuses are changed into swallows and cacti sprout irises (309).

Mário de Andrade subtitled *Macunaíma* a "rhapsody," and numerous critics have addressed the work's rhapsodic qualities. In music, a rhapsody is sustained by improvisation and an irregular form, and a literary rhapsody stitches together a medley of miscellaneous pieces with effusive incoherence or a nonorganic, fragmentary style (*Princeton Encyclopedia*, 2d ed.). The cacophonous medley of disconnected sounds provides a recurrent motif in *Macunaíma*, both in the collage of urban noise that disorients the hero in São Paulo and in the jungle's pandemonium that greets him on his return. The musical performances in *¡Écue-Yamba-Ó!* are usually more symphonic than this in their orchestration. But the music assumes an extemporizing life of its own at times, and the sounds enter the round "successively like voices in a fugue" (*OC* 1: 47), as the improvisation becomes potentially boundless, repeatedly enacting new counterpoints (*OC* 1: 154). The cosmic symphony in *El pez de oro* that marks Columbus's arrival presents a stylistic medley of Andean verse forms in a range of styles and a responsive musical exchange among constellations. The principal narrator also often alludes to spontaneous sound-medleys emerging from the Andean *ayllus'* "tranquil disorder" (286). Asturias's "Leyenda del Sombrerón" combines in a similar disorder an expansive medley of human and animal sounds that open out "like lassoes in infinite rings, *encompassing it all*" (36; my emphasis). And Atitlán's rhapsody of bird songs and human sounds in "Leyenda del tesoro del lugar florido" helps to lure and deceive the discoverers.

These disconnected and improvisational New World medleys are often organized into lists, a common mechanism in all of these works. List making is a favorite vanguardist strategy, in manifestos that inventory their attacks and their goals and in prose and poetic writing employing the clipped synthetic phrase or even surrealism's cumulative metaphoric flow, adding image upon image.[33] Because of its reliance on enumeration, a list always implies additional entries and is thus an openly nonorganic construct that resists the possibility of wholeness. Citing the "sequence of isolated events" typical of surrealist automatic writing, Bürger suggests that though these items lack cumulative coherence, their repetition of identical structures (as with items in a series) adheres to language's paradigmatic mode. Unlike the syntagmatic mode in which the end is always reached, the sequence in principle possesses no end (79).

Lists are common in the *Leyendas,* for example, for creating the sense of abundance in the Atitlán market's "florid place." Its penchant for stream-of-consciousness flow notwithstanding, *El pez de oro* incorporates lists of Andean sounds, objects, birds, dances, songs, and verbal obscenities. And although the *Sinfonía* is also written in baroque, poematic prose, its paragraph-long sentences present inventories without syntactical pauses of the New World's surreal images. The one-word, all-noun chapter titles in *¡Écue-Yamba-Ó!* organize the novel as a list of scenes with the vanguardist manifesto's enumerative quality. Though Carpentier's incipient baroque prose might seem antithetical to the clipped style of the vanguardist list, many of the novel's descriptions enumerate the contents of Menegildo's world. It would not be an exaggeration to describe *Macunaíma* as a book of lists, of bird sounds, bugs, trees, wild animals, fishing paraphernalia, precious stones, and dirty words. The list's open-ended resistance to organic completion is underscored in some works in run-on sentences incorporating inventories of items (the *Sinfonía, El pez de oro*), in some by accumulating phrases or sentence fragments (*Leyendas, ¡Écue-Yamba-Ó!*), and in *Macunaíma* by the suppression of commas in many lists. *Macunaíma* alludes explicitly to its inventories' limitless substance as it describes the forest with "close to fifteen times a thousand" animal species and "so many millions of trees that nobody could count them" (96; EAG 90).

List making in Americanist works did not begin with the vanguards, and such inventories build on the chroniclers' representations of the New World's unending abundance. But a list is a verbal collection, and the inventory syntax in these works creates the sense of a vast material medley of countless curious collections, assemblages of objects, images, forces, and beings. Walter Benjamin suggested in "Unpacking My Library" that collecting is a childlike mode of acquisition intertwined with the process of renewal, and at some level the numerous collections these works incorporate support the construction of America as an elusively originary world. But, as James Clifford has outlined in "On Collecting Art and Culture," in modern Western societies, the assembly and display of collected items is closely tied to cultural identity formation and notions of cultural authenticity (*The Predicament of Culture* 215–51). The modern development of collecting is also associated with the Western world's engagement with non-Western cultures. Thus, in São Paulo, Macunaíma quickly grasps that collections have something to do with power and that one can somehow define one's relationship to other cultures through the force of one's own collections. When he learns that the modern giant Venceslau Pietro Pietra owns an impressive collection of precious stones, Macunaíma quickly assembles an equally imposing assortment of obscenities that he eventually deploys as a weapon. It is not inappropriate that works addressing Latin America's cultural specificity should engage in verbal collecting as a syntactical mode, gathering and displaying artifacts to affirm a culture's authenticity and creative power.

But the integrity of a finished collection derives from its aura of completion, its incorporation of a last missing item, and from its modes of arrangement as well. Traditional collectors arrange their goods—geographically, chronologically, by topic—to produce an impression of wholeness. Even so, all collections harbor a tension between order and chaos, or, in Benjamin's words, an underlying "disorder to which habit has accommodated itself to such an extent that it can appear as order" ("Unpacking My Library" 60). Vanguardist collectors, particularly those with ethnographic pretensions, exploited this underlying disorder through the (dis)organizing strategies of collage, producing rhapsodic, nonorganic collections of items decontextualized and rearranged. It is precisely in this spirit that these Americanist vanguard works construct a New World of disorderly collections, seemingly randomly assembled artifacts from an ever-expanding sphere in which cultural specificity becomes difficult to define. Such a process of random assembly, Clifford points out in his study of ethnographic surrealism, avoids the "representation of cultures as organic wholes" (*The Predicament of Culture* 146). Thus many of the lists in these works possess a collagelike quality that presents the American world as an unsynthesized "fleamarket of images,"[34] created like the surrealists' startling metaphors through the juxtaposition or superimposing of items from conventionally dissonant spheres.

Ronald de Carvalho's *Toda a América*, the poetic work I have mentioned briefly, presents an outstanding example of America's flea market of images in vanguardist works. Here America is portrayed as the world of "all the imaginations" (Aztec, Germanic, Hispanic, Guaraní, Latin, Incan, Aimoré, Saxon, Slavic, and African) and presents an assemblage of "indisciplines" as it brings together the descendants of pre-Columbian heroes with the children of Isis, Minos, Eleusis, and heirs to the Bible, the Koran, of the Sagas, the dolmens, and the Magdalenan caves (47). Similarly, the curious mixture of styles and materials in ¡Écue-Yamba-Ó! has been repeatedly noted by its critics, as vanguardist metaphors juxtapose nature and technology. In a world of telephone poles with "a thousand porcelain artichokes glistening on their arms," locomotives expel bull-like snorts and peacocks honk their "lugubrious horns" (*OC* 1: 33). The novel's collagelike collections also display similar cultural medleys, as in the *zafra* scenes that bring together multiple nationalities for work and for a polyglot musical performance. Similarly nonorganic collections fill the city's storefronts, as in the *espiritista* center of Cristalina Valdés: "a photograph of Allan Kardek cohabited with a Masonic triangle, an Italian Christ, the classic Cuban St. Lázaro '*printed in Switzerland*,' a Maceo effigy, and a Victor Hugo mask" (*OC* 1: 164).

Described in the collagelike Portuguese that juxtaposes countless regionalisms into a composite that nobody speaks, *Macunaíma*'s profuse collections are comparably heterogeneous. Thus Pietro Pietra displays in his home objects from all over Brazil, a stone collection that includes a potpourri of artifacts—including arrowheads, stones, jewels, petroglyphs, and stelae—such as one might have found in the twenties at the Parisian Trocadero museum. Macunaíma's countercollection of obscenities constitutes a linguistic museum of expletives from all living languages, Latin and Greek, and an obscure Hindu phrase for a centerpiece. Most impressive is the culinary medley Pietro Pietra dishes up to entertain Macunaíma disguised as a French woman, including shrimp bisque and tapioca, a cannibal soup from the body of a meat porter, alligator shinbone stew, Spanish and Peruvian wines, and São Paulo champagne. In the mode of the curious collection, the *Leyendas'* sources superimpose the natural sounds with human oral and written creation; the *Cuco de los sueños* weaves the spoken tales, as the king's chroniclers record stories of the Indies, accompanied by a chorus of psalmodies and the croaking of frogs (15). Here cultural juxtapositions are organized in a montagelike spatial and temporal palimpsest, in a city constructed of buried cities. The juxtapositions in *El pez de oro* suggest a similar verticality, as the narrator descends to the Aymara underworld to unearth a linguistic medley of indigenous idioms and a mixture of literary and intellectual sources: Andean cosmology, combined with bits of Dante, Lucian, Saint Paul, and Horace. The novel's glossary lays out a similar mélange of Quechua, Aymara, neologisms, plebeianisms, and Quechua-Aymara-Spanish hybrids. The *Sinfonía*'s surprising juxtapositions construct an American poetic world in which swans dance at a ball with divers and butchers dressed in armor from the Crusades enter forests to waken Sleeping Beauties.

As a nonorganic construct, the collagelike collection always reveals the absence within it of a unifying principle or center. But in some of these works, the absence these profuse collections harbor is openly laid out before the reader. According to Cardoza y Aragón, for example, he sought to give the *Sinfonía* the structure of an artichoke, an apt metaphor for its layers of imagery. But this artichoke has no heart, as it encloses a world of uncertain substance. Significantly, what the poetic speaker values most in the symphony is the empty space, "that vacuum that follows the perfect performance of a concert" (346), and the work presents repeated tributes to "grandiloquent silences" (292). Similarly, the material abundance in the "Leyenda del tesoro del lugar florido" serves to deceive the conquerors by concealing an absence, the illusory jewels in the water. Hyperbolic accumulations also cover up voids in *Macunaíma,* for example, when the hero laments in São Paulo that he cannot go fishing because he lacks the proper gear and lists, item by item, not the paraphernalia he possesses but that which he lacks. Here, as in the *Leyendas,* accumulation provides adversarial protection. Incarnating the *antropófago* manifesto's credo "I only want what is not mine," the hero's body becomes the site of material overabundance as he devours all the edibles around him in order to regurgitate and hide in his own vomit.

This body reference is not incidental, for as Clifford points out, the fact that the body has traditionally provided a "privileged image of order" made it a favorite vanguardist target (*The Predicament of Culture* 132). In a similar vein, Elaine Scarry in *The Body in Pain* points out that the human body becomes emblematic of the human being's desire to define a "stable internal space" (39). While the collagelike, rhapsodic collection challenges the notion of an integrated cultural order, the instability of the body—its absence, its transformational propensity, or its fragmentation and disintegration—constitutes a further negation of wholeness. Thus disembodied voices populate the *Sinfonía* in which human bodies are often unstable (the child poet returns through a mannequin's hand to his past as an Indian) and in which images of human and statue decapitations abound. Human bodies in the *Leyendas, El pez de oro,* and *Macunaíma* are subject to instant transformation, into other human bodies, mythological beings, animals, trees, or (in *Macunaíma*) machines. Although he is described as a human with no "gaps" in his being, even Menegildo Cué in *¡Écue-Yamba-Ó!* transforms himself with relish into John the Baptist's executioner, and the bodies of *ñáñigo* ritual participants become agents and voices for supernatural beings. Macunaíma's quintessentially nonorganic body is the most radically unstable, as the dismembered and reconstituted hero returns several times from the dead. Tristan Tzara provided a recipe for the composition of a Dada poem by cutting out words from a magazine, mixing them up in a paper bag, and reassembling them in the order in which they left the bag. Following an interestingly similar procedure, when the giant chops Macunaíma up into his stew, the hero's brothers reassemble him by fishing out the scraps of flesh and bones, wrapping them in banana leaves, and blowing smoke on the concoction from which a reconstituted Macunaíma—a bit weak in the knees—emerges.[35]

Conclusion

The image with which I began this chapter—Macunaíma returning to the virgin forest—suggests a more composed and self-possessed being than the hero whose brothers retrieve him piece by piece from the giant's stew. But this collagelike portrait of the Brazilian hero, adorned with artifacts juxtaposing the world of his origins with the "great São Paulo civilization," also underscores its own constructed substance. This picture of Macunaíma presents a fitting emblem of the confrontation in Latin America's vanguard movements between a continuing search for vernacular art and the cultivation of literary modernity, as well as of the tensions produced by multiple cultural and historical registers within Latin America's lived experience. And this image of Brazil's Amazonian hero turned São Paulo tourist calls to mind many other images these works project: Dante strolling with the *Sinfonía*'s child poet surveying the "craniums of crystallized crocodiles" adorning houses in New York's inferno; Menegildo Cué, child of an ancestral early world, dispatching Saint John the Baptist with gusto in a Havana carnival sideshow; the narrator of *El pez de oro* unearthing the voices of Lucian, Homer, and Dante among the "gutturalizations" of the Aymaran underworld.

In *Theory of the Avant-Garde,* Bürger suggests that by juxtaposing elements from many eras and cultures, the avant-gardes undercut the validity of a hierarchy of techniques and styles derived from historical succession or tradition and sought instead to legitimize the "simultaneity of the radically disparate" (63). Calinescu also notes that the avant-gardes constructed a "blunt rejection of the principle of hierarchy in all walks of life and primarily, obviously, in art itself" (143–44). A similar idea is developed by Edward Said, who observes that modern works cultivate "random appetites" and establish with other works relationships of "adjacency" rather than of dynastic succession (9–10). "Beginnings" within this context require not the establishment of a dynastic origin from which an individual work or a body of literature descends but rather the marking out of a space *alongside* other works and other traditions. The Americanist vein of Latin America's vanguard movements addressed the problem of the origins and genealogy of a Latin American artistic tradition. The manifestos with an Americanist vein generally perpetuated romantic, organicist myths through images of an integrated, telluric, body-continent rooted to its ancestral origins, a body for which the new American artist would provide a voice, as I explore further in the chapter on language. Although they address similar issues, the vanguardist creative texts propose a different view. On the occasion of a new edition of *¡Écue-Yamba-Ó!* in 1979, Carpentier noted the apparent contradiction many of his generation had faced: "It was necessary to be 'nationalist,' trying at the same time to be 'vanguardist.' . . . A difficult aim given that every nationalism rests on the cultivation of a tradition and that 'vanguardism' of necessity signified a rupture with tradition" (*OC* 1: 26). This apparent contradiction is worked through when the tradition that one is constructing denies the hierarchy of traditions, as the vanguardist creative texts do by posing a more collagelike American culture of the fragmentary and the displaced.

These texts' exaltation of America as a quintessential originary space always ripe for new beginnings serves to reveal the mediated quality of such origins and the difficulties to be encountered in attempting to pin them down. If Latin America provided fertile ground for the endless generation of new discoveries, this potential derived less from the integrity or perfect presence of its originary cultures—indigenous or imported—than from the dislocating heterogeneities generated by multiple cultural collisions. On one level, these works do enact the search for an "authentic" tradition in the distant past of the continent's non-Western cultures. But instead of the definition of America's "essence" affirmed by the manifestos or the clear line of cultural descent implicit in the search for national traditions, these works embody, as Haroldo de Campos has said of Brazil, a "refusal of the essentialist metaphor of gradual, harmonious natural evolution" ("The Rule of Anthropophagy" 45).[36] They propose instead a tradition of "random appetites" and "adjacency," to borrow Said's terms, or, to employ Bürger's, of the "simultaneity of the radically disparate." By appropriating vanguardist motifs as the idiom through which to explore Latin American cultural specificity, these writers create sometimes bizarre "hybrid works," as Carpentier said of *¡Écue-Yamba-Ó!* Through these unusual works, these writers also laid claim to the vanguards' dislocations, fragmentations, and nonorganicity as peculiar to and definitive of Latin American lived experience. If one lends any credence to such claims or simply recognizes their presence in Latin American literature, it is not surprising that contemporary theoreticians of the postmodern have not infrequently directed their attention to Latin America's new narrative, as several writers of the past three decades have been credited with postmodern writing. As European vanguardists in search of the primitive looked to the Latin American artists for the cockatoo that would surely spring from their lips, so contemporary theorists of the eighties expected them to speak in "postmodern." In his meticulous typology of postmodernist fiction, for example, Brian McHale suggests that because of the continent's mosaic of dissimilar cultures, languages, worldviews, landscapes, and ecological zones, Latin America's condition might well be described as "*intrinsically* postmodernist" and the worlds that its literature constructs as "heterotopias" (52–53; emphasis in the original). It is certainly true that Latin American literature's time has come, and perhaps this is partly because it has been paradoxically in step and in tune with the cacophonous dislocations of our postmodern times. But if we look carefully at these Americanist vanguard writings, we may discern that the experience of radical discontinuity is a story that Latin American literature has been trying to tell about itself and its world already for quite some time.

4.

On the Interstices of Art and Life
Theatrical Workouts in Critical Perception

The theater still remains the most active and efficient site of passage *for those immense analogical disturbances in which ideas are arrested in flight at some point in their transmutation into the abstract.*
　　　　　　　—Antonin Artaud, *The Theater and Its Double*

We inhabit a city without direct light—the theater.
　　　　　　　—Oswald de Andrade, *A morta*

In the opening scene of Vicente Huidobro's 1934 play *En la luna,* the implied spectator is confronted by a theater door. Maese López, a carnival barker–style master of ceremonies, addresses the onstage passersby as well as the play's live audience, successfully convincing an occasional stroller to stop, buy a ticket, and enter. What they are about to witness, Maese López proclaims, is different from anything they have ever seen before, a "unique spectacle in its genre, in its content, and in its form" (*OC* 2: 1566). Forty years after this play was written, the contemporary theater worker and performance theorist Richard Schechner has noted that while Western post-Renaissance mimetic drama sought to reactualize onstage what had occurred elsewhere, traditional theater, a category in which Schechner includes the experiments of the avant-gardes, is transformational, "creating or incarnating in a theatre place what cannot take place anywhere else" (*Perfor-*

mance Theory 166). Despite the Huidobrian carnival barker's ironic promise of novelty (the play is as much about crippling repetition as about positive change), Latin American vanguardists assigned performative and theatrical activity a unique place on their agenda, seeking to express through theater what they could not demonstrate as effectively elsewhere. Particularly in Argentina and Mexico, contemporary Latin American theatrical achievements can be traced directly to the vanguardist period.[1] But in other countries as well, vanguardist groups engaged in performative activities and addressed theatrical issues in their little magazines, while individual writers composed a variety of theatrical exercises and plays.

Theater and Performance in the Vanguardist Project

In addition to the multigeneric audience-engaging events that I examine in the chapter on manifestos, some vanguardist groups organized more explicitly theatrical projects that have been more extensively documented in Latin America's dramatic history. In 1926, for example, Leónidas Barletta, Alvaro Yunque, and Elias Castelnuovo, members of the Buenos Aires Boedo group, and theatrical director Octavio Palazzolo founded the Teatro Libre for the avowed purpose of creating a theater of art. After losing its director, this group reassembled in 1927 as the Teatro Experimental Argentino, an enterprise that lasted for one year. In 1930, Barletta and members of both groups established the Teatro del Pueblo dedicated to developing a modern Argentine theater. In keeping with the Boedo group's social goals, initial objectives were to construct a new relationship between theater and its public and to bring theater and art into ordinary people's lives. To this end, the group brought performances to city neighborhoods. The Teatro del Pueblo endured into the 1940s and made a fundamental contribution to modern Argentine theater, staging innovative plays by both international and young Argentine writers. In the early 1930s, Barletta's encouragement was instrumental in the turn from narrative to dramaturgy by Roberto Arlt, whose early work constitutes the best example of Argentine vanguardist theater.[2]

In Mexico, short-lived but significant efforts at theatrical renovation were undertaken by Mexico's *estridentistas*. In 1924, Luis Quintanilla organized the Teatro del Murciélago project dedicated to developing

Mexican cultural life. The theatrical endeavors of the later Contemporáneos group had a more lasting impact, however.[3] Group members Celestino Gorostiza, Xavier Villaurrutia, and Salvador Novo organized the 1928 Teatro Ulíses experiment, followed by the more enduring Teatro Orientación (1931–34). On a modest scale and in a private salon under the patronage of Antonieta Rivas Mercado, the Teatro Ulíses performed contemporary European plays in translation, including works by Jean Cocteau, Charles Vildrac, and Claude Roger-Mark. As a more formal, public, and enduring enterprise, the Teatro Orientación was supported by the Secretaría de Educación Pública y Bellas Artes. While its members continued to stage selected European plays, they also performed experimental work by Mexican writers, including pieces by Gorostiza, Villaurrutia, Carlos Díaz Dufóo, and Alfonso Reyes. Like the Teatro del Pueblo in Argentina, Orientación's activity posed more direct relationships between performer and audience—but a very different kind of audience. One contemporary spectator described the scene as a play ended: "The actors maintained their positions and nobody moved forward to receive the public's applause. The spectators were friends among themselves and intellectuals. . . . The communication between actor and public was evident" (Mendoza-López 31).

The founding members of Nicaragua's vanguardist Anti-Academy affirmed in their 1931 inaugural manifesto their intentions to overhaul every aspect of Nicaragua's cultural life, a project that would include a little theater. Here they would perform every kind of play: Hispanic and European, traditional and experimental, popular and high art. Although this ambitious project was not realized in all of its detail, the group's theatrical efforts did include the establishment of the Teatrito Lope in 1936. Here, the dramatic version of the *Chinfonía burguesa,* written earlier by Anti-Academy members Joaquín Pasos and José Coronel Urtecho, was staged three times.[4]

Although vanguardist drama was more limited elsewhere, a concern with theatrical renewal was expressed in many little magazines, including Mexico's *Contemporáneos,* Havana's *Revista de Avance,* Lima's *Amauta,* and São Paulo's *Klaxon* and *Revista de Antropofagia.* Some of these published critical articles on theater, and others published new dramatic pieces. In addition, during the 1920s and 1930s, several vanguardist writers created their own experimental theatrical exercises and plays: Huidobro in Chile, Mário and Oswald de Andrade in Brazil, Roberto Arlt in Argentina, Villaurrutia, Novo, Bernardo Ortiz de Montellano, and Xavier Icaza in Mexico, Pasos and Coronel Urtecho in Nicaragua, Pablo Palacio in Ecuador, Alejo Carpentier in Cuba, and Miguel Angel Asturias in Guatemala. While drama is only one element in these writers' creative endeavors, this work constitutes a significant component of the vanguardist project's critical inquiry into artistic practice, as artists drew on theater's singular qualities to examine specific aesthetic problems.

For the vanguardist artist, the most evident appealing features of theater and performance are the temporal immediacy and spatial palpability they bring to the relationship between performer and spectator. As I have demonstrated in the chapter on performance manifestos, vanguardist writers exploited this relationship to construct an ideal audience for their work and to focus that imagined audience's attention on the "doing" of aesthetic activity. The same concern with work in progress characterized vanguardist theatrical texts. But in vanguardist plays, the examination of aesthetic concerns became far more intricate through abstract dramatic texts that investigated the theoretical implications of dramatic activity itself. Even in its most highly codified forms, theater as a genre has always inclined more toward a process than a finished-work conception of art. Both in conception and execution, theater constitutes a work in progress, for the dramatic text is a prescription for a performance, a plan for something to be done. This quality in particular attracted vanguardist artists. Because it focuses on its own construction and materials, the vanguardist artwork, as I have noted, can aptly be called nonorganic in the terms of Bürger's *Theory of the Avant-Garde*. But by these terms, theater is already virtually nonorganic, not only because as a " '*doing*' code" (Turner 33; emphasis in original) or as an "actualizing activity" (Schechner 35–67) it calls attention to process over product but also because of the lengthy tradition Herbert Blau has fittingly called "theatre's profoundest mixed metaphor" (*Blooded Thought* 32), that is, the play within the play that employs theater's own mechanisms to expose itself. Always potentially metatheatrical, theater poses the means for art to talk about art, not as an isolated curiosity but in its constant interplay with that which is not art: a posited real world or life.

Vanguardist nonorganic works posed questions about the category art and its relationship to experience. This concern with the interaction between art and life, I have argued, was manifested precisely in those features Ortega y Gasset had called "dehumanized," that is, in the antimimetic impulse and the self-reflexive focus on the process of representation. Theater's palpable connection with that process offered singular possibilities for vanguardist inquiries. Theater in performance fuels anti-mimetic yearnings for immediacy and presence, but it is simultaneously a reminder of separation and deferral. As Jacques Derrida affirms in his exegesis of Artaud, theater presents the possible "primordial and privileged site" for a destruction of imitation, an alluring opportunity for that "closure of representation" that Artaud imagined (and Derrida put into words) (234). But in performance, as Blau insists, theater is always a reminder of an "*initiatory breach,*" a constant "testament to what separates" (*The Eye of Prey* 174, 183; emphasis in original). Theater is a deliberate act of play, a conscious pretense about something that might have or will perhaps have happened at another time, before or after. It functions, as Victor Turner argued time and again, in the subjunctive or "liminal" mode. Any performative act requires a framing, a setting apart in time and space from ordinary reality. But in the execution, there is always the potential and temptation to abolish theater, to step out of the frame, discard the mask, and cross over the boundary. Theater and performance operate, in Blau's words, in that "interstitial moment crossing art and life" (*Blooded Thought* 78), a crossing in which the spectator's role is complicitous. Thus theatrical experiments offered vanguardists the opportunity not only to explore the mimetic boundaries but also to make evident the spectator's complicity in the performance and to provoke that spectator to question the representations constituting both theater and ordinary life.

Experimental plays produced by Latin America's vanguardists probed deeply into the nature and substance of art itself and examined how what are conventionally designated artistic experience, on the one hand, and life experience, on the other, interact with and shape one another. The desired reengagement between art and life was manifested in works that, through divergent theatrical strategies, examined the aesthetic process and explored its relationship to the activity of living and its potential for transforming both perception and experience. Latin American vanguardist writers were drawn to the transformational potential in theater we have subsequently come to associate, in different ways, with Bertolt Brecht and Antonin Artaud. Both saw theater as a means for a structural alteration of experience and as a path toward a qualitative reengagement with life. Both perceived the possibility of a liberation through theater's transformative powers, though Brecht sought social liberation through the transformation of perception and Artaud sought a metaphysical liberation through the alteration of experience and being. In the vanguards' utopian spirit, Latin American writers turned to theater because, like Brecht and Artaud, they were interested in change—social, ontological, or both—as well as in comprehending the nature and mechanisms of change itself. Specifically, plays such as Arlt's *Trescientos millones,* Villaurrutia's *Parece mentira,* Huidobro's *En la luna,* and Oswald's *A morta* scrutinize connections between artistic invention and the representational practices of ordinary life. These works also openly address the spectator's or recipient's role in the workings of theater and art as well as that spectator's critical position in art's transformational promise both for the ways that we see and for the ways that we live.

THEATER IN THE SUBJUNCTIVE MODE: ARLT'S *TRESCIENTOS MILLONES*

Conceived in 1927 and first staged in 1932 by Leónidas Barletta's Teatro del Pueblo, Roberto Arlt's *Trescientos millones* (Three Hundred Million) in a prologue and three acts uses the metatheatrical metaphor to investigate human creative activity and the continuities and disjunctions between a creator's represented and lived realities. Spanish immigration for low-paying work was a common feature of Buenos Aires life in the 1920s, and, according to Arlt, the play was inspired by an impoverished Spanish immigrant maid whose real-life suicide the writer had documented as a police reporter. The play reconstructs the elaborate daydream created by the Sirvienta (servant woman) during a solitary vigil in her empty room the night before she dies. Her intricate fantasy assumes the structure of a play performed by phantom actors and draws on her readings of pulp fiction, in particular, the eighteenth-century writer Ponson du Terrail's forty volumes starring the roguish Rocambole. Through her dream-play performance, the Sirvienta seeks a life more palatable than her servitude to the Patrona (employer) and her son. In the opening scene of act 1, the Sirvienta contemplates herself in a mirror and expresses distress at what she sees. Declaring that if only she were rich her life would change, she worries that in her present state even death will not want her. Death, the first phantom character, enters on this cue. A composite of female picaresque literary types, she reassures the Sirvienta that people die only when they are ready. The Sirvienta then enacts her will to live through a dream-play melodrama reflecting its creator's readings: Rocambole brings news that she is the rightful heir to *trescientos millones;* the Sirvienta takes an ocean voyage and meets the noble Galán; their child is kidnapped and put to work in a Buenos Aires slum; with Rocambole's help, the Sirvienta rescues her grown daughter, who in turn seeks her mother's blessing in a marriage to the Galancito. The "real-life" Patrona's calls for service periodically interrupt the dream-play's action, and the fantasy is brought to a halt when the son, seeking sexual favors, repeatedly knocks on the Sirvienta's door. To escape his demands, the Sirvienta shoots herself, and her dream-play's phantom actors celebrate their emancipation from her service. Only Rocambole grieves her death. Dispersing the other phantoms with a crack of his whip, he kneels before the dead Sirvienta, sadly kisses her forehead, and begs God's mercy for the suffering servant. As the Patrona's son continues to bang on the door, the curtain falls.

The melodramatic action of the Sirvienta's dream is not *Trescientos millones'* central concern, and the dream itself actually constitutes a play within the play. The play *without* the play that frames the Sirvienta's dream and is also enacted during its "intermissions" includes the preparations for and the process of staging that event. The piece's preface shows a secret gathering of the phantom actors who are traditionally summoned by human dreamers to portray individual creations like the Sirvienta's dream-play performance. Here, these "protagonists of dreams," including Rocambole, the Cubic Man, the Byzantine Queen, the Galán, and the Devil, assemble in the "astral zone" of human dreams to discuss the rigors of their work. At the mercy of their creators' whims, they must often play roles beneath their artistic dignity. Of this group, only Rocambole and the Galán are slated for roles in the Sirvienta's dream-play. The others will be summoned by diverse human creators, and the Sirvienta's own dream will include additional phantom actors. But those in the initial gathering spell out their theatrical callings. "Actually," the Galán explains, "one plays all the parts." "Just like actors," the Byzantine Queen adds (*OC* 3: 243). This self-conscious exchange ceases when the actors are summoned by their respective human dreamers, but it resumes during the Sirvienta's dream-play intermissions when her mistress calls and the actors use the break to talk. In addition, throughout the dream-play, both the Sirvienta and her actors step out of their roles to comment on the performance in progress.

Critics have aptly noted this work's Pirandellian quality, its Freudian allusions to the theatrical nature of dreams, and the pathos and social critique implicit in its opposition of a "happy-ending" dream world with the impoverished "real world" of the Sirvienta's tragic life.[5] The work's metatheatrical structure and deployment of explicitly theatrical strategies, however, foreground a concern with the process of human invention and its interaction with actual experience. The theatrical texture of the Sirvienta's dream-play permeates the demeanor and performances of those who enact it. The actors assembled in the preface are not only the phantoms of individual dreamer-playwrights but also the products of diverse traditions in human artistic creation, many with performative or theatrical qualities. The protean Rocambole appears in the same elaborately stylized outfit with which he is represented in woodcuts and chromolithographs illustrating early Barcelona editions of Ponson du Terrail's work. The Byzantine Queen resembles a carnival queen, the Galán has the air of a strolling player, and the Devil, with his caricaturesque Mephistophelian cape, looks like a circus devil. A parody of cubism's dehumanized representations, the Cubic Man resembles the homunculi and mechanical men of assorted human inventors. Regardless of the parts they will enact in individual dream-plays, therefore, the phantom actors are themselves already representational, the progeny of human creation, including popular fiction, chromolithography, carnival and circus dramatics, cubist art, and the Frankensteinian and Promethean humanoids of romanticism's mad inventors.

But the dream-play's theatricality goes beyond the representational substance of its actors or the artistic sources of its plot. The Sirvienta is portrayed as the work's spectator, actor, and, above all, director, and her role shifts intensify the sense of a work in progress. In her role as spectator, the Sirvienta sits on her bed and watches the visions unfolding before her. She becomes an active performer in her own drama when Rocambole delivers the money that transforms her from servant girl to orphan-heiress. In the following scene, the Sirvienta enacts the transformation. As the lights dim in her tiny room, a greenish hue permeates the scene, and one end of the room grows, "*its wall prolonging itself into the bridge of a transatlantic ship, with an oblique, yellow smokestack and the winches' feathers opened in a fan. Orange clarity rolls over the ship and the silvery and bright green perspective of the chimerical ocean*" (*OC* 3: 255). In a scene that blurs the play's boundaries between the mimetic space the audience sees and the diegetic space the characters imagine, representing a crossing from life to art, the Sirvienta moves from her bed to the ship and becomes somebody else. "*The maid, timid and sad,*" the stage directions indicate, "*has been transformed into a voluptuous and elastic creature who smiles with delectation at the scene that surrounds her*" (*OC* 3: 255).[6]

But the Sirvienta's role as author-director is the most critical for the dream-play's theatrical structure. Acknowledging the authorship of human dream builders, the phantom actors critique the play in progress. Although they denigrate her artistic sensibility, they grudgingly acknowledge the Sirvienta's status as the work's creator: they are the actors, she the author. The Sirvienta's involvement is instrumental, however, not only for the dream-play's conception but also for its performance. Her physical presence and mental attention trigger the play's action, and her absence, in body or spirit, brings it to a halt. As the author, she gives birth to its characters and shapes its plot, and as the director, she oversees the creation of its sets from the extension of her bare room and instructs the actors in executing their roles, for example, in her first meeting with the Galán. As the dream-play's central love scene, this encounter alternates between attempts to perform a lovers' assignation and arguments as to how it ought to be played. James Troiano has noted that this Pirandellian procedure gives the scene the quality of a dramatic rehearsal, intensifying the experience of a work in progress (38). As the Galán declaims his lines, the Sirvienta affirms her directorship, calling for more expressiveness. She explains to the Galán how she would play his role, as each draws on prior artistic experience for interpreting the scene. He volunteers the procedure of a German novel, but, explaining that she has read only the forty volumes of Rocambole, the Sirvienta demonstrates the interpretations she desires. This directorial exchange continues in the final scene with her daughter Cenicienta (Cinderella), an episode marked by an impoverishment of the Sirvienta's imagination. In contrast to the elaborate fairy-tale settings for the dream-play's prior scenes, this set's golden porticos and red curtains give it a conventional theatrical ambience, and, in contrast to the multicolored, ethereal lighting of prior scenes, this one is bathed in a "sad clarity." "You don't like to dream," the daughter, who yearns to fly, tells her mother (*OC* 3: 283). But even as she faces a diminution of creative energy, the Sirvienta maintains control of her play, for example, when the daughter steps out of her role to ask how it should be performed.

David William Foster argues that *Trescientos millones* dramatizes the striking differences between the Sirvienta's represented world of escapist dreams, which evolves from the pulp fiction she reads, and the real world of her poverty, an interpretation in which neither her dreaming nor the money of the play's title can solve the protagonist's dilemmas. It is up to the spectator, Foster continues, to think of viable solutions to the problems of people like the Sirvienta (16–17). But although the work's social commentary is indeed profound, the interaction of the

play *without* the play and the play within the play as well as the sometimes ironic distance between them focus attention on the process, not
the content or validity, of the dream and point as much to the continuities as to the disjunctions between represented reality and lived reality.
Trescientos millones is not so much about the possible concrete solutions
to the Sirvienta's difficult life as it is an enactment of the will to change
manifested in the problematic representational inventiveness with
which she lives it. This focus simultaneously exposes and obscures divisions between art and life as well as between high art and popular culture.

To begin with, the *trescientos millones* of the play's title calls for more
than a literal reading. No actual money ever changes hands (it is only a
dream), and the issue of how real money might actually improve the
Sirvienta's life is never posed by the work. In their preplay exchange, in
fact, the phantom actors note the arbitrary nature of the amount, as
one says it will be thirty million and another asks why it could not
simply be thirty thousand. In the context of the dream-play's theatrical
structure, the *trescientos millones* functions as a kind of preperformance
deus ex machina that sets off the Sirvienta's fantasy. Signing for
the money, as I have noted, converts the servant girl into the orphan-
heiress protagonist of her dream-play. But when the Sirvienta first appears onstage, even before that exchange with Rocambole, the money
incarnates the will to transformation that sets the performance in motion. Thus, reclining on her bed in the dark, she observes, "If I were
rich, this wouldn't be happening to me." Sitting up, she insists, "I say
that if I were rich, this wouldn't be happening to me." Then moving
toward the mirror, she turns on the light and observes, "I'm thin and
ugly, . . . even death wouldn't want me" (*OC* 3: 249).

This scene forecasts the theatrical function of the *trescientos millones.*
It is while standing before the mirror, the most literal representation of
herself, that the Sirvienta expresses her wish for a different life. Like the
actor in a play, she seeks a self-portrayal different from the one reflected
before her. More important, the key statements in this scene are expressed in the subjunctive mode. "If I were rich, this wouldn't be happening to me," grammatically encompassing both the condition contrary to fact that she desires and the potential of its fulfillment, is a
fundamentally theatrical construction that provokes the creation of a
virtual scenario. Dramatic activity, as Turner pointed out, operates in
the subjunctive mode, or in what Herbert Blau calls, invoking Turner,
the *"as if"* condition of performance (*The Eye of Prey* 164; emphasis in

original). Thus theater simultaneously denotes the separation (of fact from fiction) in the conditions contrary to fact it enacts and the possibility of actualization (of uniting fact and fiction) implied in its subjunctive mode. In *Trescientos millones,* the money is a theatrical mechanism pointing both to the fiction of the Sirvienta's desire and to the possibility of its transformation into fact. Her performance is the potential "*site of passage,*" to use Artaud's term (109; emphasis in original), between the reality of her lived experience and the fiction of her dream-play, the site of "marking and merging" of horizons posed by Austin Quigley (22 ff.), or that "interstitial moment crossing art and life" of which Blau speaks (*Blooded Thought* 78).

As the work's title suggests a possible site of passage between the two worlds, so does the piece's interplay between them obscure the boundaries of that site. The dream-play's scenarios present the most visible example. The ocean liner deck, a mountain scene, a carbon shop, and an opulent room are all extensions of the Sirvienta's tiny quarters, visible diegetic theatrical spaces emerging from the mimetic, and her movement between the edge of her bed and the imagined scene reminds the spectator of *Trescientos millones* that the dream-play is at once separate from her real life and a part of it. Although certain theatrical devices (the Patrona's bell, the pauses when the phantom actors freeze, the ethereal play of lights over the dream scene) indicate transitions from a theatrical mode to a "reality" mode, the Sirvienta's self-awareness and that of her actors underscore the continuity between the two spheres. Always aware that the dream-play is make-believe, its participants are simultaneously their "real" selves and their performed selves. In an intermission scene, for example, while the phantom actors exchange disparaging remarks and knowing glances about the Sirvienta's artistic tastes, they abruptly return to their dream-play roles, and it becomes "*impossible to discern if they are comrades or enemies*" (*OC* 3: 263). Thus they are at once (and indistinguishably) the adversarial actors who disdain their director and the comrades enacted in her fantasy. The Sirvienta makes similar willful choices, as when the Galán enters for their love scene and she "*resolves to follow the game of the amorous comedy*" (*OC* 3: 259). But like the phantom actors, she plays it with awareness, "*always with her little ironic mode*" (*OC* 3: 259). This ironic distance points to the Sirvienta's simultaneous existence in both worlds, a dual identity made palpable by the "laborer's duster" she wears throughout the performance, even as she is transformed in demeanor and expression.

In the same vein, the dream-play actors' Pirandellian independence, while ostensibly denoting art's autonomy from life, in fact emphasizes the mutual contamination of the two realms. Drawn from the discourses of theater, circus performance, cubist art, and pulp fiction, the actors' physical demeanors, gestures, costumes, and language embody multilayered references to accumulated repertoires of human invention. The site of the play's opening secret meeting is described as an *"astral zone where human beings' imaginations fabricate with force lines the phantoms that pursue them or that they re-create in their dreams"* (*OC* 3: 241). This astral zone constitutes a repository of human representations, a storehouse of surplus intertextuality that humanity has collectively produced and from which individual dreamers unconsciously draw in their creations. Just as the Sirvienta's tiny room unfolds into the set of her dream-play, accentuating the contiguity of the two worlds, so is the astral zone of accumulated artistic artifacts created by human beings in the process of living. More important, the work's "real" protagonist and her immediate surroundings are cut from the same intertextual cloth as the "smoke characters," or her phantom actors. The Sirvienta's room is described by an ostensibly objective authorial voice as imbued with *"the desolate polychromatic perspective of a serial novel by Luis de Val"* (*OC* 3: 249). Although designated a "real character," when she first appears, the Sirvienta is in the act of *re*presenting herself, a process that draws from her readings of pulp fiction: *"A hard and insolent expression that is suddenly tempered in a voluptuous childishness of a cheap fantasy. It is reminiscent of Rina, the Angel of the Alps, or any other harlot destined to endear the burlap hearts of the female readers of Carolina Invernizio or Pérez Escrich"* (*OC* 3: 249).

Like a Don Quixote or a Madame Bovary, the Sirvienta seeks to reinvent herself in keeping with what she reads, forging a lived identity out of a fictitious mold. But as a hyperbolically fictitious character (his exploits fill forty volumes), Rocambole inverts this process: "Whenever I play the character of some drama, I like to suffer and dream *as if* I were a man of flesh and blood instead of a phantom" (*OC* 3: 247; my emphasis). Thus the phantom actor approaches the theatrical event *as if* he were real, and the "real" character, the Sirvienta, approaches it *as if* her life were make-believe. What unites Rocambole and the Sirvienta in the subjunctive theatrical space on the interstices of art and life is the desire for transformation, an inventive impulse to create a different self—and a different life—from the ones they must represent at the beck and call of others. The Sirvienta's struggle to free herself from the roles assigned by her masters is repeated and reflected in the phantom actors' autonomous gestures, seeking to loosen the representational bonds securing them to human dreamers. The process of representation made palpable by the theatrical event is thus portrayed, like theater, as an ambivalent force. Although it promotes a liberating impulse for transformation, it also makes manifest the power plays at stake in the representations that, as if from the prompter's box, we impose on one another. Significantly, neither the Sirvienta nor Rocambole achieves the desired representational autonomy. Rocambole is always Rocambole, no matter how many volumes of his exploits are produced, "always the same character through different names" (*OC* 3: 245). Similarly, notwithstanding her elaborate production, the Sirvienta fails abysmally to transform her life.

Foster suggests, as I have noted, that the Sirvienta's failure to change is attributable to the paucity of her lowbrow literary sources, a reading that would ascribe to Arlt himself the phantom actors' disdain for the Sirvienta's tastes in art (16–17). But I would argue for the need to consider the work's ironic distance from all of its characters, the origins in popular culture of the phantom actors themselves, and the blurring of divisions between high art and popular culture that characterizes much of Arlt's fictional world. While it is certainly true that the Sirvienta's creative sources lie in the realm traditionally labeled low art, the actors' profound social snobbery embeds their aesthetic critiques within an ironic frame. Complaining that the Sirvienta as orphan-heiress has the audacity to address them as "tú," they decry, in terms recalling Walter Benjamin's account of art's loss of aura, the harm they have suffered from art's reproduction through film and disparage the lower classes' creative pretensions: "The next thing you know, the lowliest dishwasher will think he has the right to an imagination" (*OC* 3: 265).[7]

But in Arlt's artistic world, the lowliest dishwasher does indeed presume to dream, and creative self-representation is a feature of human existence not limited to a particular class. This is true, for example, of Silvio Astier, the protagonist of Arlt's first novel, *El juguete rabioso* (1926), which I have examined in the chapter on artists. Silvio's models for the transformation he seeks (Rocambole, Baudelaire, Edison, and Napoleon) are drawn from a range of aesthetic and cultural contexts. In Arlt's subsequent and more radically experimental novels, *Los siete locos* (1929) and *Los lanzallamas* (1931), characters from lower echelons of Buenos Aires society seek to transform themselves and their world by acting out elaborate fantasy games.[8] In the same spirit, regardless of their aesthetic class origins, all of *Trescientos millones*' phantom actors are described as "puerile and ingenuous" products of human imagination.

What *Trescientos millones* suggests is that the impoverishment of imagination paralleling the Sirvienta's loss of the will to live derives not from her scant artistic background but from the nature of human invention itself and its relationship to lived experience. In its prefatory scene, Arlt's piece calls on its implicit spectator to see what the work's characters, "real" or phantom, cannot: the exposed, connecting tissue between *Trescientos millones*' actual reality and its dream-play reality. The Sirvienta does not perceive the phantom actors' astral zone when they are not performing in her play, and they cannot see her when she retreats "offstage" to serve her real-life Patrona. But in its opening secret meeting, the play suggests these things ought to be seen, not only by individual dreamers who construct them but by all people: "If people had more sensitive vision, they would see us . . . like they see the birds and the clouds" (*OC* 3: 247).

The play's implied spectator, possessing a "more sensitive vision," does indeed see the astral zone phantoms as clearly as the birds and the clouds, an analogy drawing attention to the duplicitous reciprocity of the real and the fictitious. This perspective undermines turn-of-the-century aestheticist notions of art's autonomy from life and, in the Sirvienta's specific story, exposes a dynamic interaction between a work in progress and a life in progress. In the play's dramatic world, life and art are intertwined by the process of human invention. The phantom actors rely for their existence on the activity of human dreamers, but the dreamers' creative powers, in turn, are inextricably tied to their will to live, as the depletion of one parallels a loss of the other. But in addition, here both art and life are representational, intertextually prone to repeat what has been said and done before. Thus human dreamer-playwrights like the Sirvienta forge their work from lived experience, but that living in turn is shaped by art, not only by the specific pulp fiction constituting the Sirvienta's artistic training but also by the cadre of phantoms inhabiting the astral zone repository of prior representations. But even as human creative activity, like theater, is weighted down by a persistence of the mimetic, it is also motivated by a desire for liberation. In employing the metatheatrical metaphor to enact the dream-play's performance, Arlt's work exposes theater's mechanisms to display a tension in human invention between the previously said and the urge toward the new. As Blau has aptly noted, there is something in the nature of performance (in this case, a dramatic dream-play *re*presentation) that requires "doing it as it has always been done . . . even when it appears to be done as if for the first time" (*The Eye of Prey* 164). Weighted down by what has always been done, the limits on her life and her art, the Sirvienta fails to transform her world. But even in the face of her failure, *Trescientos millones* privileges the "as if" implicit in its title, encompassing, in the vanguardist spirit, the human impulse in even the "lowliest dishwasher" to transform reality through invention, to alter life through art.

THEATER OF THE THRESHOLD: VILLAURRUTIA'S *PARECE MENTIRA*

A comparable tension between the actual and the virtual shapes Xavier Villaurrutia's *Parece mentira* (That's Incredible), first staged in 1933.[9] In the Teatro Ulíses (1928) and the Teatro Orientación (1931–34), Villaurrutia did extensive work as a director, translator, and promoter of theatrical experiment. But *Parece mentira* is his first staged play and the first of five one-act pieces written during the Orientación years and published in 1943 as the *Autos profanos* (Profane Autos). The play's deceptively simple dramatic action harbors a conceptual complexity of aesthetic problems posed and explored.

Parece mentira strips the dramatic situation down to its primary elements. Subtitled an "enigma in one act," the six-scene play takes place "today" in the minimally furnished waiting room of a lawyer's office. Characters include the Empleado (employee), the Marido (husband), the Curioso (curious one), a lawyer, and three apparently identical women. The careful use of light and limited sound effects (a doorbell and a telephone) manipulates the limited, visible theatrical space. In the opening of the first scene, a ringing doorbell announces the nervous Marido's arrival. He is formally received by the Empleado who, with "mechanical courtesy," summons him to a seat. The ringing bell signals the Curioso's arrival at the beginning of the second scene. Although the Empleado is initially equally businesslike, the Curioso's constant questions alter the direction and the nature of the conversation. As the Empleado opens up, the Curioso suggests he is more of a poet than a secretary, and the two briefly discuss creative activity, the multiple nature of the human personality, and the importance of an examined existence. Excluded until now from what stage directions describe as a pact between the other two characters, the Marido anxiously intervenes and hints that the unrevealed motive for his presence in the office has made him painfully aware of his existence.

The ringing doorbell leads into a third scene, punctuated by the Empleado's confession to the Marido: "I know situations like yours, and, although fortune has not given me the opportunity to experience them firsthand, I have lived those situations intensely . . . through others" (25). Three identical sequences follow: a young woman, veiled and dressed in black, enters the room, hands the Empleado a business card, and enters the inner office to which he directs her. The Curioso watches intently as the sequence is enacted three times, activated each time by the ringing bell and the Empleado's statement ("I know situations like yours . . ."). Responding to the Empleado's directions, the third woman instructs him, "Don't trouble yourself, I know the way" (27), a remark that elicits an anguished moan from the Marido, frozen in his tracks. In a fourth scene, the distressed Marido pumps the Empleado for information about the woman and her visits. As a secretary, the Empleado reveals nothing, but, shifting into his poet role, he intimates knowledge of the situation. When the Marido confesses he has been summoned to the lawyer's office by an anonymous letter suggesting infidelity, the Empleado successfully guesses the letter's contents, explaining that his knowledge derives from contact with similar situations and from similar texts he has written. When the Curioso exclaims that this all seems incredible ("parece mentira"), the Empleado explains that these enigmatic events have given the Marido the opportunity to realize a new self-awareness: "You find yourself on the threshold of an existence that you will be able to discuss, to correct, and construct as you please, in the same way that the artist discusses, corrects, and constructs his work in progress" (38). With the Marido now ready to "construct his work in progress," the Curioso departs.

As a fifth scene opens, the Empleado and the Marido seem frozen in time, hesitant about how to proceed. In this static, theatrical moment, once again the doorbell sets the scene in motion: "*One has the impression that this will continue indefinitely unless something distant, indifferent, casual arrives to break up this immobility, to put into motion the scene of a wind-up theater. Finally one hears the bell of the inner office*" (40). Urging the Marido to be "the creator, the actor, and the spectator" of the following scene, the Empleado adjusts the lights to an "opaque aquarium light," removes the phone from the hook, and quietly departs.

A final scene reverses the third one, with the Marido now in an active role. Three times a veiled woman emerges from the inner office into the dark waiting room, tries unsuccessfully to respond to the Marido's pleas, muffles a scream, and exits. In each case, the Marido responds differently, asking for an explanation of her presence, urging her to come with him, expressing his anguish. As the third woman exits, the Marido remains immobile until the lawyer enters, turns up the lights, and hangs up the phone. In the final brief scene, the lawyer urges the Marido to enter, and although the latter indicates that he will, instead he departs quickly, much to the lawyer's surprise.

Critics have noted this work's existential and artistic themes, its Pirandellian qualities, and its manifestations of the French influences in Villaurrutia's theater.[10] But my interest here is in the two distinct but intertwined levels that constitute this play as well as in the artistic issues they pose. On one level, the work presents ingredients for a somewhat traditional and banal dramatic action, the story of the Marido and his wife. A vague outline is traced for this scenario that never actually unfolds, a process similar to what Gustavo Pérez Firmat has identified as a feature of the Hispanic vanguard novel (*Idle Fictions* 57–58). Contributing elements for this possible action include an anxious husband, a mysterious veiled woman resembling his wife, an anonymous letter hinting at betrayal, and a problematic encounter in a lawyer's office. Interwoven with this level of potential action is the scenario of an abstract conversation about life and art primarily between the Empleado and the Curioso and later incorporating the Marido. Although the work opens and closes with the husband-wife story, the metatheatrical level quickly takes over with the Curioso's arrival in the second scene. At the level of artistic and philosophical discussion, the Empleado and the Curioso dominate; at the level of a potential dramatic action that would tell a story, the Marido, that story's virtual protagonist, takes center stage. But the two levels are tightly intertwined. In contrast to the somewhat abstract concerns explored by the Empleado and the Curioso, the Marido's situation, though verging on melodrama, presents the work's possible mimetic connection. The Marido is, after all, the only principal character possessed of a "real" life, diegetically constructed offstage. But *Parece mentira* enacts, as the Empleado takes pains to tell us, the analogy between a life in progress and a work in progress, linked, it should be added, through the theatrical metaphor that poses a desire for transformation.

At the level of artistic discussion, the three principal characters are defined by their active participation in a theatrical event and, by extension, in a work of art: the Empleado assumes an authorial role, the Marido becomes a potential self-conscious protagonist, and the Curioso becomes an impertinently active spectator. The Curioso notes a sharp difference between the Empleado's secretarial role and the more expansive, open-ended quality of his poetic mode. In both roles, however, the Empleado possesses the authorial quality of one with information and authority the others lack and one who somehow controls the action. The Empleado reveals his artistic proclivities and power to the Marido: "I have the knack, the secret, or the ability, sometimes very painful, for making things and beings speak. From their words I make my poetry, from their confessions my novels" (33). Identified by his inquiring attitude toward the events that unfold before him, the Curioso assumes a spectatorly role. But at the metatheatrical level, he becomes an active and involved spectator, one who, the stage directions emphasize, establishes a "pact" with his interlocutor, the authorly Empleado (22). Like the work's implied spectator, the Curioso struggles to resolve the work's posited "enigma," asks the obvious questions about what is going on, and voyeuristically "devours" the Marido's anonymous letter, seeking to determine its author's identity. Reinforcing his spectator role, it is the Curioso who reacts with surprise ("It's marvelous!") and incredulity ("It's incredible!") to the perplexing events and ideas exchanged.

Through the interaction of the work's two levels, the Marido's possible story, on the one hand, and the artistic discussions, on the other, *Parece mentira* poses more open-ended roles for authors and spectators as well as an interactive conception of art's relationship to life. In contrast to the opening scene's mechanically scripted Empleado role, the play presents an author who talks directly to his potential spectator (the Curioso) about art. Stage directions emphasize that this author behaves in an increasingly more "humanized" fashion toward his protagonist, that is, toward his human subject matter, and, having set the stage by lowering the lights and disconnecting the phone at the end of the fifth scene, he disappears from the scene to allow the work in progress to unfold. In the same spirit, the Curioso spectator constitutes an active, onstage presence. And the authorial Empleado's knack for making others speak notwithstanding, he will not, he explains reassuringly, write the Marido's novel. The Marido protagonist, moreover, is constructed not as a stable dramatic figure with identifiable characteristics but as a being on the "threshold," with the potential for unfolding in a variety of possible situations.

This play's concentration on the threshold, in fact, constitutes its most important theatrical metaphor. Like *Trescientos millones*, *Parece mentira* enacts a tension embodied in the theatrical impulse between what has already ended and what is about to begin. The work presents multiple images allusive to a theatrical tradition and to theater's mimetic claims to *re*present what has occurred before: the Empleado's (pre)scripted behavior in the opening scene; the Marido's melodramatic situation; the Empleado's ability on the basis of prior texts to discern the anonymous letter's contents; and, most notably, the repetition of the three almost identical veiled woman scenes as the Marido and the Curioso look on. On one level, this has all somehow happened before, and the Empleado author has written about it so many times that he knows the hackneyed scenario by heart, just as the veiled woman in the three identical scenes already "know[s] the way." But this play concentrates not on what has been done before but rather on what might yet unfold, on the Marido's possible selves, on the possible interactions with the veiled woman, on the works the Empleado may write. In contrast to these prior representations, *Parece mentira* creates a Marido "on the threshold" of a new existence, ready to undertake theatrically the doing of his lifework in progress. Significantly, although the Marido engages in three "rehearsals," the repetitions with variations of the veiled woman's exit scene, his work is never completed but, like a curtain ready to rise, remains poised on the boundaries of possibility.

The play's most powerful sign of the theatrical tension between repetition and transformation is the doorbell. As it functions in *Parece mentira*, moreover, this sign also points to the interaction of art with life. An auditory cue that is literally activated from a position on the threshold, the doorbell repeatedly functions as a prime mover of the dramatic action, not only because it initiates most of the play's scenes but also because it continually marks transitions from the actual to the virtual and back, from the Empleado's aesthetic discussions to the Marido's lifework in progress. The Empleado himself underscores the bell's ambivalent quality: "The same bell that reminds me of my quotidian death calls you to a new life" (40–41). The bell assumes additional connotations if one recalls the traditional use of bells (true in Mexican theater) to call spectators back to the performance at the end of an intermission.[11] The association suggests that the doorbell in *Parece mentira* functions also as a self-referential theatrical sign that insistently beckons its spectator to that "interstitial moment crossing art and life," in which, as Blau would have it, all performances emerge. The play's focus on possibility is accentuated by its title, *Parece mentira,* which translates as "that's incredible" in idiomatic English, or, more literally, "it seems like a lie." This highly colloquial, almost banal expression highlights the extraordinary perceived from within the ordinary, a perspective that blurs boundaries between fiction and life. Notably, it is the Curioso, the work's metatheatrical spectator, who emits this remark and directs attention to the transformation of the ordinary through theater, on the threshold of the possible self, the possible work, the possible life.

A THEATER OF CRITICAL MIMICRY: HUIDOBRO'S *EN LA LUNA*

The potential of artistic experiment to disrupt the quotidian and the ordinary and transform human experience also marks the work of Vicente Huidobro. His 1934 play *En la luna* (On the Moon) recasts this issue in a theatrical context. Huidobro's early poetic work was shaped by the aestheticist tradition of the *poète maudit,* and his first *creacionismo* manifestos posed the most militant Latin American manifestation of the "art for art's sake" stance. But although his 1914 "Non serviam" manifesto urges young poets to create an autonomous artistic world, Huidobro's own creative work gradually directs attention to the interaction of art with life.[12] A provocative example is the mordantly satirical and linguistically rich four-act *En la luna;* this is one of Huidobro's most engaged works, both in its openly political theme and in its examination of the connections between representation and experience. Like Arlt's *Trescientos millones, En la luna* explores the theatrical impulse for transformation. But while *Trescientos millones,* notwithstanding its broad societal critique, focuses on an individual's desire to change her life, Huidobro's play, written when its author's political engagement had intensified, speaks more openly about the transformation of society. In addition, as it uses the play within the play to expose the dynamics between art and life, *En la luna* addresses more directly the relationship of theatrical performance to language and to the spectator-recipient role in shaping theatrical and artistic events.

Subtitled a "small guignol," *En la luna* dramatizes political change on a fictitious planet, Luna, from a superficially participatory democracy to a totalitarian monarchy. Following a polemical introductory address by Maese López, the sideshow barker who presents himself to the audience as the creator of the performance they are about to witness, a multitude of stylized and verbose puppetlike characters engage in rigged elections and undergo a vertiginous sequence of political coups, by the military, the firemen, the dentists, the secretaries, and the tailors. These changes of government culminate in the tyrannical rule of Rey Nadir and Reina Zenit. The pomp, empty proclamations, and overt greed marking the changes of leadership and the inane solutions to national problems that characterize each leader's rule are interrupted by increasingly intense offstage demands for bread and work. The piece culminates with a play within the play. Rey Nadir and Reina Zenit witness the performance of a puppet show, *En la tierra* (On the Earth), representing a world with language and leaders that, to the amazement and delight of the lunar monarchs, strongly resemble their own. As the mirror images of moon and earth blend, the performances of both plays are interrupted by the intensified demands for bread and work and the invasion of both scenes by the collectivists: workers, students, and an artist. When the puppet monarchs of *En la tierra* are captured, Luna's Rey Nadir and Reina Zenit attempt a futile escape beyond the curtain and into the audience of *En la luna*. Following the offstage execution of all four, there is a radical shift in the play's satirical tone, as a voice, more of a poet than of a revolutionary, proclaims the utopian dream of a changed world: "the great smile of a new world, of a newborn landscape" (*OC* 2: 1640). In the final scene, Maese López reappears and asks Colorín Colorado, the proverbial concluder of Hispanic children's stories, to bring the play to an end. Declaring that the story has now ended, Colorín fires a shot into the air as the curtain falls (*OC* 2: 1640).

On a literal level, this play parodies Chilean political events of the 1920s, which included a series of short-lived governments. But, in keeping with Huidobro's concerns by the time it was written with both aesthetic and political activism, the piece skillfully intertwines the questions of change through politics and change through art. Like *Trescientos millones* and *Parece mentira*, *En la luna* draws attention to its own character as a work in progress, not only through the obvious metatheatrical metaphor of the *En la tierra* play within the play but also through devices that create an ambience of aesthetic inquiry characteristic of Huidobro's previous work. The astronomical-terrestrial imagery of the title and character names is reminiscent of the interplay of motifs that shaped Huidobro's poetic universe.[13] This imagery, as George Yúdice demonstrates, establishes a correlation between scientific investigation and artistic creation (102), and although the astronomical-terrestrial motifs in *En la luna* unfold in a satirical vein, their use situates the play in a familiar Huidobrian cosmos of literary adventure and experiment. In addition, the play's guignolesque theatricality, with an acknowledged debt to Alfred Jarry's *Ubu Roi*, destroys mimetic convention through blatant acts of making believe.[14] These include the use as a model of the guignol or puppet show; the exaggerated stylization of characters through costume, movement, gesture, and voice; the simplified hand-painted sets and ingenuous props such as toy weaponry (the head tailor carries a giant pair of scissors); and character references to the curtain and the ultimate transgression of its borders by a fleeing king and queen.

The most important element in the play's development as a work in progress, however, is its overt obsession with performance, with the "doing" of its script and the process of creative activity. The carnival barker Maese López calls attention to the execution of the show. Standing before the door of a theater, he urges passersby to enter, directing the spectators' attention, as in a circus sideshow, to the dexterity of the performers and promising a spectacle of spectacles. The performance metaphor is sustained throughout the piece, not only in the final play within a play but also in the successive appearances of heads of state whose assumptions of power are portrayed as exhibitionist displays of their persons and prowess. "I will go out on the balcony to show myself to my people" (*OC* 2: 1614) declares one leader of the tailors' revolt. Although on the most obvious level this explicit concern with performance constitutes the play's portrayal of political life as a repetitive and farcical grand guignol, the piece's sustaining performative metaphor is also tied to Huidobro's continuing aesthetic concerns. The puppets of *En la luna* are performers of a special kind, as Maese López explains, because they are endowed with words. The spectacle the audience will witness is, above all, a display of linguistic dexterity, a manifestation of Huidobro's ongoing interest in the power and limits of language, recast here in their performative mode.[15]

In *En la luna*, words and voice become concrete material of the performance with Maese López's insistence on his puppets' verbal facility as well as his allusions to previous sideshow stars, assorted jugglers of the word, including a ventriloquist who "removed the voice from the most distant spectator's pocket" (*OC* 2: 1566). The disorienting sequence of political coups that follows is marked by an endless parade of public acts of linguistic dexterity—proclamations, declarations, public announcements, and acceptance speeches—and each section of the play is introduced by a speaker preparing an audience for the verbal display to follow. Similarly, there are constant references to each new ruler's exhibitionist desire to "offer a word," "have a word," or "make use of the word." But in Huidobro's lunar world, the reception of these verbal performances is as significant as their execution, as the play draws more insistent attention than *Trescientos millones* to the spectator's part in the performances in progress, and groups of onstage spectators are represented in *En la luna*'s enactment. Maese López's opening speech ("Ladies and Gentlemen and all the passersby") is directed both to the play's real-life audience and to the onstage stroller. In addition, each of the play's subsequent flights of linguistic virtuosity is punctuated with an enthusiastic reception by a pliable onstage audience. This performer-spectator dynamic is reinforced visually through a scenic backdrop silhouette of an orator and his public.

This relationship between the work's endless parade of performers and the audiences they address is marked by an ironic tension between the promise of originality with which the performances are billed and the redundancy shaping their execution. The virtuosity of individual performers, in fact, derives not from their generation of something new but from their dexterity in the arts of illusion. Although Maese López insists on the radical novelty of his show, his promise is undercut by the literal and figurative duplicity of his puppet's names (Fifí Fofó, Lulú Lalá, Memé Mumú) and by his own repetitive discourse: "All of these magnificent magnificences, all of these marvelous marvels, that I am going to present to you are only the delirious delirium of an imaginative imagination" (*OC* 2: 1567). In addition, Maese López's allusions to his previous sideshow stars, like the able ventriloquist, point to both their verbal skill and their talents for deception. The carnival barker's own capacity for deceit is hinted at in the allusion through his name to his literary predecessor, the puppeteer Maese Pedro who employed a prognosticating monkey to swindle Don Quixote and his companions. But in *En la luna*, the legerdemain is linguistic, and each exhibitionist "use of the word" that accompanies an assumption of power is an act of verbal prestidigitation designed to create the impression that something new has been done to address Luna's pressing problems. President Juan Juanes's acceptance speech, a parody of the paradigmatic political address, is the most creative example, a Huidobrian invented language:

Señores y conciudadanos: La patria en solemífados momentos me elijusna para directar sus destídalos y salvantiscar sus princimientos y legicipios sacropanzos. No me ofuspantan los bochingarios que parlantrigan y especusafian con el hambrurio de los hambrípedos. No me ofuspantan los revoltarios, los infiternos discontifechos que amotibomban al poputracio. No me ofuspantan los sesandigos, los miserpientos, los complotudios. La patria me clamacita y yo acucorro a su servitidio cual buen patrófago, porque la patria es el prinmístino sentimestable de un coramento bien nastingado. (*OC* 2: 1578)[16]

Although superficially unique, however, Juan Juanes's language is roughly comprehensible to the theater audience, not only because it conforms to Spanish in syntax and morphology and in rhetorical device to the paradigmatic political address but also because of its recognizable constitutive elements. "No me ofuspantan," for example, a ritual statement of imperviousness to opponent pressure, links *ofuscar* (to obfuscate) and *espantar* (to scare away), an integrative procedure Huidobro had employed extensively in *Altazor*. Thus what is billed as a novel verbal display is actually a rearrangement of familiar patterns, as redundant as Maese López's "marvelous marvels." For the spectator of *En la luna*, however, the speech's productivity derives from its critical mimicry of the recognizable models it reflects. Juan Juanes's successors execute comparable acts of linguistic redundancy to tackle Luna's ills. "Problems are solved by solving them," affirms Grifoto, head of the firemen (*OC* 2: 1609). Thus Maese López's assurances of a unique spectacle notwithstanding, the play's action, characters, and language are strikingly deficient in originality and, like a moon that cannot generate its own light, marked by their reflective quality. Their interchangeability is skillfully represented in a scene depicting the simultaneous plotting of four coups. Here, a large structure is divided into four identical rooms, two above and two below. In each cubicle, a group of three conspirators plots the following day's events, and a light flashes on in the corresponding room as each group recites its nearly identical plan. The reflective quality of lunar life, moreover, is epitomized in the final production of its mirror image in the onstage enactment of the puppet show *En la tierra*. This specular relationship of the lunar and terrestrial theatrical sites is also played out on the linguistic level, not only in the doubling of character names but also in an explicit parody of verbal invention, as one character creates "so much poetry in so few words" simply by reversing his love's name from Fifí Fofó to Ofof Ifif (*OC* 2: 1600). The mirrored structure of this transformation is analogous to the mirror imaging of the play within and the play *without*, a comparison linking theater and language, in their proclivity for mimetic doublings as they enact the already-done and repeat the already-said.[17] The visual reproducibility of Luna and Tierra through duplications of scenarios, characters, and events is repeated in the mechanical reproduction of verbal invention. Thus, when a photographer records for posterity an agreement between military leaders, he is struck by the wit of a phrase and asks to take its picture. Holding the camera to the side of his mouth, the photographer simultaneously repeats the phrase and visually records it. The spectator's role in the play's endless doublings is comparably reproducible, for each of the endless verbal performances is greeted by the same approving "bravos" and "vivas."

Despite the specular redundancy of its verbal performances, however, *En la luna* is an enactment of the impulse to transform both the "real-life" circumstances dominating Luna's social scene and the artistic and social relationships organizing the theatrical event itself. Like Arlt's *Trescientos millones*, Huidobro's play employs theater's specific qualities to expose the interaction of performance and experience, linked, as in Arlt's play, by a propensity for representation. In *Trescientos millones*, the inventive desire to re-create the self permeates both life and art, as both astral zone phantoms and humans generate dream works designed to control their own lives. In *En la luna*, a performative proclivity links Maese López's sideshow actors with the "real-life" political leaders seeking to control Luna's fate. Maese López apologizes for the compulsive mimetic doubling and endless proliferation of Luna's exhibitionist leaders compromising the brevity of his show: "Yes, my ladies and gentlemen, they multiply themselves like rabbits and they lengthen my piece" (*OC* 2: 1567). The marionettes' multiplication recalls the accumulation of phantom actors in the astral zone of *Trescientos millones* or the repetitive veiled woman scenes in *Parece mentira*. In all three plays, these accumulated representations undermine the will to transform. Just as the Sirvienta's efforts to reinvent her life or the Empleado's urge to create a new work and the Marido's impulse toward an authentic existence are weighed down by prior representations, so the offstage demands for bread and work are drowned out by the endlessly reproductive power of Luna's rulers' performances.

Huidobro's play, however, foregrounds performance's narcissistic cast, establishing a bond between mimesis and self-contemplation that implicates the spectator. Just as Maese López's marionettes and the political leaders they represent yearn for public display, so does the puppet monarch of *En la tierra* thrive on the power of his own exhibition: "I present myself and everything is illuminated," or, as he contemplates his image, "Leave me alone, for I want to meditate on my greatness. Give me a mirror" (*OC* 2: 1632–33). On the most evident level, the king's specular self-admiration underscores the mirror relationships between the lunar and terrestrial monarchs and suggests that, in watching Tierra's puppet leaders, Luna's royalty basks in its own reflection. But as the monarchs do this, they become spectators of a play, onstage proxies for *En la luna*'s audience, whose implied presence suggests the artistic recipient's participation in the narcissism of mimesis. The dramatized spectators of *En la luna*, both the audiences who applaud political displays and the lunar monarchs who watch *En la tierra*, are so captivated by the virtuosity of those who perform that they fail to perceive the performance's specular substance and to recognize that as long as they participate in its terms, the scenario before them will reflect their own exhibitionist desires and projected fantasies of power.

Unlike *Trescientos millones*, however, *En la luna* does enact a transformation, but the change occurs both beyond the illusionist virtuosity of linguistic display and outside the theatrical event's mimetic frames. Significantly, Luna's leaders call those who revolt the "disassociators of the human order" (*OC* 2: 1582), and it is precisely their *dis*association that disrupts the play's social and aesthetic worlds. Just as each ruler's oral exhibition is interrupted (if only briefly) by offstage demands for bread and work, both dramatic representations, *En la tierra* and *En la luna*, are disrupted with the invasion of a theatrically constructed space by nonparticipants in its deceits. In the process, the implied spectator of Maese López's production who is attentive, as directed, to the "doing" of the show will witness three interlocking levels of performance and reception: the display by Maese López for that implied spectator, the illusory verbal acts of Luna's politicians and the responses of the planet's citizens, and, finally, the enactment of *En la tierra* and its reception by Luna's king and queen. In the process, that primary spectator will also see the disruption of all levels of performance in which some of the actors (Maese López, Luna's king and queen) become the audience and the viewers of the "funniest spectacle in the world," the people who revolt, become the performers as the play careens between the "real" and the theatrical. For the principal spectator of *En la luna*, who must perform complex feats of auditory and visual perception, the invasion of all three performance centers by Luna's revolutionaries transforms more than the social scene of the imaginary planet. As an aesthetic event, the play breaks out of the physical frames and communicative relationships that have defined it to invade the audience's world, a disassociation of the aesthetic order and a literal engagement of art with life.

The play's exposure of the limits of verbal display and its exaggeration of the performative impulse also implicitly address the vanguardist project, particularly its early fascination with linguistic pyrotechnics and its propensity for public display. Although Huidobro openly attacked the writers hawking their wares whom Maese López's character parodies,[18] his own *Altazor* (published only three years earlier) is one of Latin American vanguardism's most linguistically performative texts. The occasional jabs at *Altazor* in *En la luna* are evident in the similarity between the play's verbal strategies and the language games showcased by the poetic work's seven cantos. The play's critical mimicry of these moves and of the illusionists—theatrical or political—who deploy them suggests that radical change, the abolition of art that is "split off from the praxis of life," requires a rearrangement of the mimetic associations informing artistic and linguistic events and a critical perception of art's inner workings. On one level, the play's utopian vision for a new social order is cast in the discourse of origins that characterizes vanguardism's futuristic visions, "the great smile of a new world, of a newborn landscape" (*OC* 2: 1640). Interestingly, the securing of this inaugural world, the destruction of repetition and creation of a "first time," is cast not only outside the mimetic doublings of the theatrical frame but also as an implicit closure of linguistic representation. In contrast to the duplicitous verbiage of Luna's leaders, the collectivists are described as characters with a more unified relationship to language: "They believe what they say and say what they think" (*OC* 2: 1583).

Although the play portrays true change as contingent on a unity of thought and action, however, through its own parodic mimicry of mimetic drama and linguistic play, *En la luna* encourages spectators to maintain a critical disunity. The fictive status of the play's utopian conclusion is denoted both by the storybook quality of its visual presentation—a green field with trees, flowers, a rainbow, people dancing, and a banner depicting "socialized work"—and by Colorín Colorado's storyteller role in bringing this scene and the play to an end. This conclusion enjoins the spectator from subscribing uncritically to the fiction, and, although the play's collectivists include a participating artist, like the play's implied spectator, he too is cast in a special role. As an alternative to the writers who, like Maese López, are masters of illusion, the young poet Vatio who joins the collectivists in their quest for change provides a prophetic vision of a "harmonious life," a world without hunger or war, an artistic and cultural life shaped by "inexhaustible inventiveness" (*OC* 2: 1629). The myth of the poet as a small god had been dismantled in Huidobro's poetics through Altazor's parachute journey, and, as I have demonstrated in chapter 2, this image was also widely undermined in vanguardist manifestos and novelistic portraits of the artist. But the ideal of the artist as an explorer with unique skills, in particular, a radical vision of reality, persists in Huidobro's work.[19] In *En la luna,* however, that unique vision is no longer the exclusive province of a privileged artistic being but is shared with the spectator, encouraged by the play's parodic structure to radicalize his or her perceptions. If change implies a unity of thought and action beyond the mimetic frames, it also, paradoxically, requires the disassociation necessary to keep the frames in view. In a scene shortly before the final collectivists' invasion, Luna's high priests celebrate a mass consecrating the monarch's reign. Lamenting the changes threatening the lunar status quo, one of them defines the problem: "It is the century's demolitionary spirit, the terrible critical spirit" (*OC* 1: 1622). It is precisely that critical spirit that informs *En la luna,* engaging the spectator through its critique of theatrical mimesis in an exposé not only of life on the fictitious planet but also of the inner workings of a performance in which that spectator has been conspiring.

A THEATER OF AUTOPSY: OSWALD DE ANDRADE'S *A MORTA*

Oswald de Andrade's *A morta* (1937; The Dead Woman) also openly engages those who watch in an inquiry into the interaction of theater with life and even, as the title suggests, with death. Oswald, like Huidobro, was far better known for work other than theater, including his experimental poetry, his virtuosity as a manifesto writer, and the experimental novels that I examine in the chapter on portraits of the artist. Like Huidobro's, his turn to theater in the 1930s coincided with the engagement of his radical ideals in politics as well as art. Theater became his medium for exploring art's potential role in social change, but his theatrical writing was as experimental as his prior work. While *En la luna* examines a bond between aesthetic and social change emerging from art's transformation of its recipient's perceptions, *A morta* looks more closely at the social implications in an artist's relationship to art. Specifically, Oswald described in the play's "Prefatory Letter of the Author" his project for the artist's emergence from the "lyrical catacombs" to which a century of aestheticism had condemned him and his return, still as an artist, to effective social involvement. Thus *A morta* was to present the drama of a poet, the "coordinator of all human action" (3).[20] Significantly, this work was contemporaneous with Oswald's turn in the 1930s toward more direct political engagement and his critical reaction against his earlier aesthetic endeavors.

Subtitled a "lyric act," *A morta,* like *En la luna,* is framed by initial and final encounters with its own implicit audience. In a prefatory scene, the Hierophant, one initiated in art's sacred mysteries, urges the spectators, as they view the "mixed ruins" of their own expiring world, not to flee from their seats in horror (7). The following three scenes enact the ambivalent and highly abstract struggle of the Poet seeking more immediate involvement with the world to disengage from his lover Beatriz, a rebellious corpse who refuses to remain dead. With the allusion to Dante's beloved, Beatriz's character suggests the idealization of creative activity, forged, like the inspiration for Dante's *La vita nova,* from the subliminal recasting of earthly passion into aesthetic inspiration. In the ruinous modernity of Oswald's play, Beatriz constitutes the cadaverous object of the Poet's desire, a persistent presence he cannot shake even as he rejects the traditions and ideals of bourgeois aestheticism to return to the Agora of human activity.

Scene 1, "The Land of the Individual" and a "panorama of analysis," unfolds in an explicitly theatrical space, as the Hierophant and the Poet on one side, Beatriz and her "Other" on the other side sit in the audience's first row inside facing theatrical boxes. From here, they simultaneously deliver their lines and watch their own performances, executed onstage by four huge, spectral, and mute marionettes who sit on high thrones. As the offstage characters recite their lines "statically," without gestures, and in slow motion, their voices emerge from microphones above them, while the marionettes enact the words, "gesticulating exorbitantly" (13). The darkened theater is illuminated only by spotlights over the offstage characters and a fire burning in the background of the onstage setting, a "marble cenacle." Here a "somnambulant Nurse," described as the scene's only character in "live action," sits on a metal bench, as if exhausted from an all-night vigil (13). In a fragmented and abstract exchange, the four main characters discuss the Poet's conflictive relationship with Beatriz, the latter's imminent demise, and the nature of the theatrical space they inhabit. The presence of the Nurse, who makes occasional remarks about the state of the patient or the progress of the performance, suggests a hospital vigil, while scattered character remarks intimate a wake, an autopsy, or the scene of a crime. "It is imperative to undo all signs of the drama," the Nurse states as the vigil ends. "There's no danger," the Hierophant reassures them, "we'll recompose the cadaver, . . . we'll put together her scattered members" (21). These indications of her demise notwithstanding, Beatriz declares that it is only her Other who has expired and urges the Poet to flee with her as the scene ends.

Scene 2, "The Land of Grammar," presents a raucous linguistic bat- tle between the dead—characters incarnating fixed phrases, grave inter- jections, lustrous adjectives, and seignorial archaisms—and the living— gallicisms, solecisms, and barbarisms. Advocates of both social and lin- guistic renewal, the living are supported by the cremators in a struggle against the rules, fossilized forms, and authority of cultural tradition encompassed in the dead. A policeman maintains order on behalf of the dead to preserve the "most dignified funerary enterprises" (31), including industries, the press, and politics, as well as powerful cultural cadavers: the "heavens of literature," the "stagnant waters of poetry" (30). A Salvation Army band marches by, led by the Hierophant whose signboard for God, Country, and Family situates this vanguardist strug- gle for linguistic renewal in the context of bourgeois traditions. Against this parodic scenario linking aesthetic renewal with the political avant- gardes, the Poet's private conflict persists. Beatriz, resisting interment and with distant eyes and a wrinkled mouth, wears the "mask of a scat- tering being" (32). Accompanied by the Roman satirist Horace, the Poet has returned to renew his artistic language in the street and, like Huidobro's poet in *En la luna*, to participate in the utopian "world that is beginning" (38). But he is still pulled by the desire for Beatriz, needy of her warmth and adoration, and he urges her to join him in life where his "practical and heroic actions" will save her (37). Ignoring warnings from Horace that death will entrap him (39), the Poet vows to rescue his dearly departed.

Scene 3, "The Land of Anesthesia," presents a modern underworld, a landscape of aluminum and coal with an airport that serves as a morgue for arriving cadavers. The audience's first row remains vacant. Parodic characters from the bourgeois world (the Mother, the Father, the Enamel Kid, the Minister's Wife, and the Complete Athlete) con- verse from a center-stage family tomb, and a defoliated Tree of Life in the form of a cross alludes ironically to Western culture's sacred tradi- tions. Edgar's Vulture, a parodic allusion to Poe's raven, and the Lady of the Camellias provide lingering reminders of romanticism's morbidi- ties, and the Hierophant's comments implicate religion, private prop- erty, and family in the construction of Western life. When the mytho- logical Charon arrives in a helicopter bearing Beatriz's body, the Poet, exalting action, follows him in a glider. Although he now seeks to speak "the language of life" (52), the Poet is still erotically drawn to Beatriz, who is now a disintegrating corpse. As the play's final erotic struggle unfolds, the voyeuristic cadavers follow a radio-patrolman into the audience's first row to watch the climactic "big scene" (52). In a life-and-death struggle, the Poet recognizes the funereal nature of his liaison, and as the cadavers reassemble upstage and Edgar's Vulture spreads its wings over the Tree of Life, the Poet sets fire to this cemetery, the "nocturnal passage" (56) of his existence. Reapproaching the audience, the Hierophant suggests a response more appropriate than applause. "If you wish to save your traditions and your morals, call the firemen or if you prefer the police. We are just like you," he adds, "an immense gangrenous cadaver. Salvage our rottenness and perhaps you will save yourselves from the blazing inferno of our world!" (56).

Although this play has received diverse critical readings, my interest here is in how *A morta,* like the theater of Arlt, Villaurrutia, and Huidobro, exploits theatrical metaphors for aesthetic investigation.[21] Specifically, the Poet's struggle with Beatriz unfolds in an explicitly theatrical space, as transformations in the theater event alter the relationships to art. The play's Dantesque allusions underscore Beatriz's role in the Poet's creative life. Contemporary interpretations have characterized Dante's Beatrice as "the source of his power of invention" and the "essence of his art" (Bloom 7), and her function in the *Vita nova* sonnets has been tied to the poetic persona's maturation and personality (Quinones 26–27). Similarly, the relationship between *A morta*'s Poet and Beatriz defines the Poet's isolated interiority and the subjective artistic identity he seeks to cast off. Scene one's "The Land of the Individual" most closely scrutinizes these connections. Based on the Hierophant's allusion to the play's enactment of the "individual in slices," this fragmented scene's characters have been seen by Fred Clark and Ana Lucía Gazolla de García as diverse components of the Poet's being ("*A morta*" 38–39). But because the play's dismembered character is not the Poet but Beatriz, I would argue that the subject of its analysis is that specific facet of the Poet, his artistic persona, embodied in the tie to Beatriz.

Throughout *A morta,* the Poet himself is characterized by images of social and physical isolation compromising his poetry's vitality. Expelled from effective action and forced to live "outside the social" (21), he is a "spurting cloistered soul" (19) living in a cave, and his life, "reduced, imprisoned, entombed" (21), is like a "closed abscess" (19), ready to burst forth in the Agora of public life. Although he seeks a dialectical poetry with a combative idiom, in his current exile, the Poet can only emit "the nocturnal cry of the walled in" (22). This isolation is embodied in Beatriz, defined as the subjective space he inhabits: the "cavern of the individual" (31) and the mute world of stone to which the Poet has been exiled. Beatriz provides both refuge and incarceration: the Poet is reborn in her "motherly womb" (20), but the nurturing space that shelters him from hope and despair also immobilizes and enshrouds him. Like Dante's inspiration in the *Vita nova,* moreover, Beatriz is portrayed as the site of the Poet's psychodynamic formation and of the emergence of his culture's desires, values, and beliefs. "I began to palpitate with your childhood religion," she observes, "with your adolescent culture! I was the heraldic coffer of your traditions, the cradle of your people" (37). This association casts the Poet's struggle to emerge from Beatriz's cavernous interiority as a separation from childhood in which he is loath to discard his transitional object, his "dear toy" (38).

But the most productive element in Beatriz's characterization is her association with the play's explicitly theatrical metaphors. With the emphasis on its own execution realized through the spatial separation of actors and marionettes, the play's first scene presents a performance in the process of examining itself. The site of this analysis, theater, is repeatedly defined in terms analogous to those denoting the Poet's subjectivity embodied in Beatriz. Theater in *A morta* is described as a doorless and windowless room, a "marble cenacle" (13), a "washed out necroterium" (17), a subterranean and unhealthy place, like the closed abscess of the Poet's interiority, "encrusted with fevers" (15). This link between a moribund Beatriz and a theatrical *huis clos* is repeated through the Poet's references to his lover as "my drama" or a "dramatic interior" (21). "The construction of romanticism inhabits this room," the Poet declares, "the unrecognizable psyche" (20–21), a reference tying both theater and Beatriz to the hypersubjectivity of his poetic persona and echoed in the third scene's parodic, romantic allusions to Edgar's Vulture and the Lady of the Camellias.

But the status of theater and Beatriz as interactive metaphors for the Poet's subjectivity is founded not only on images of enclosure and romanticist references but also on the identification of both theater and the dead woman with fragmentation, disassociation, and division. If Beatriz is the disintegrating corpse whose fragments other characters seek to reassemble, theater is also cast as a dismembered land. This quality is initially exposed through the graphic split in scene 1 between the human actor-characters and the marionettes that embody their lines, a deferral of utterance and gesture that exaggerates the artificiality of the actor-character connection and of theatrical mimesis. As with Huidobro's Luna-Tierra opposition, mimetic drama is portrayed in *A morta* as a closed, specular world. "We inhabit," Beatriz's reflective Other explains, "a city without direct light—the theater" (14). The spatial separation of a world with indirect light is reinforced by the temporal deferral implicit in repeating the already said: "Where are we, in what chapter?" (15) the Hierophant asks in the midst of scene one's execution, a question presupposing a performance of the scripted, an enactment of the already-done. But as a being initially divided, Beatriz and her Other in scene one incarnate the fragmented, specular quality of theater's representations. Like scene one's actor-marionette characters, Beatriz is the Poet's "fractured muse" (15), with a "gap" in her image (16), he notes. She is, as her Other points out, always "buried in [herself] before the mirror" (16), or, as described by the Poet, like a headless sculpture, her "eyes and hair imprisoned by a bottomless horizon" (17). Beatriz's fractured, reflective quality is a corporeal manifestation of the aesthetic persona the Poet seeks to abandon. Her dismembering demise is manifested in her "unity's decay" (52), she is the source of his "creative dissymmetry" (52), and the art she inspires is a "disconnected song" (22), beset by shadows and memories.

Beatriz is also, however, the quintessentially sexual, the substance of desire, or, as she repeatedly points out, "the want-because-I-want-of-life." As the voluntary projection of his own desires, Beatriz's wants reflect what the Poet wants. But what Beatriz wants, buried in herself before the mirror, is to be a "spectacle for myself" (18), a profoundly theatrical metaphor for the narcissism of mimesis and for the self-contemplative psychodynamics shaping subjectivity in the Western tradition. The Poet struggles to escape this tradition, for as long as he resides within it, he will be marked like Beatriz by theater's infinite doublings, its shadows and remembrances, selling, through art, the fragments of his spectacle. But the play's disclosure of mimetic theater's projections of desire also implicates the spectator in its narcissistic project. While Beatriz and the Poet whose art she embodies remain spectacles for their own scrutiny, *A morta*'s spectator is constructed and unmasked in an analogous position of self-observation. They should not leave their chairs horrified by their own autopsy, the Hierophant initially warns the spectators, and the cadavers' departure from the stage into the audience further implicates those who watch in the moribund tradition *A morta* critiques. The play portrays the act of watching as both voyeuristic (one cadaver eagerly expresses her curiosity) and narcissistic, as the spectators contemplate a scenario of which they form a part. In addition, the psychodynamic dimensions of the spectator-performer construct are intimated during the cadavers' departure from the stage. In the precise moment that he crosses the proscenium boundary dividing stage and audience, the Hierophant asks, "What's the use here of the subconscious? Where do the two planes unite here, the latent and the manifest?" (53). Thus, just as *Trescientos millones* enacts the Sirvienta's dream-work wishes, *Parece mentira* plays out the Marido's possible scenarios while the voyeuristic Curioso looks on, and the puppet performance *En la tierra* displays the lunar monarchs' projected desires, so does *A morta* construct a complicitous spectator-voyeur whose self-contemplative impulses are mirrored in the Poet's fascination with Beatriz.

But like the other three plays, *A morta* also employs theater's metaphors to enact a fundamental impulse toward change, specifically, the will to reengage art in the doings of everyday life. While theater is cast metaphorically as a moribund cultural tradition, an entombed, specular world of self-pondering mimesis, it is simultaneously recast as the instrument of its own transformation. Like the artist who joins *En la luna*'s collectivists, the Poet in *A morta* expresses his participation in "the world that is beginning" (38) through vanguardism's originary discourse. The Land of Grammar in scene 2 specifically associates the hypersubjectivity of the Poet-Beatriz connection with linguistic sterility and stagnation, as the Poet seeks a more productive art through renewal in the idiom of the streets. His companion in this enterprise is Horace, identified in the classical tradition with deliberately unmajestic language and with the satirist's critical approach. At the same time, the Poet seeks a language beyond the theatrical, more than a mere spectacle unto itself and more productively related to the action he would coordinate. Similarly, the cremators cleansing the world of its diseased traditions look beyond theater's subjectivist doublings. They are brought to the scene by hunger, they declare, "much more than the *will to represent*" (35; my emphasis).

On one level, the search for a new world manifesting more than the "will to represent" is marked by an impulse to abolish the theatrical, to wipe out the specular, interiorized expression separating the Poet from an activist life. In setting fire to the funereal enterprise Beatriz incarnates, the Poet seeks to heal the schisms of his dramatic interior and forge a more unified drama, "the development of the real universal being" (33). Similarly, the cremators' objective in the Land of Grammar is not simply to encourage the solecisms and barbarisms of linguistic production but to lay the foundation of Esperanto, the "language of one single humanity" (34). The Esperanto metaphor simultaneously suggests the expressive unity that combines roots of diverse languages, the maintenance of the very diversity this invented language blurs, and the creation of something new. Similarly, *A morta*'s theatrical metaphors express both the impulse to abolish the interior fragmentation that theater embodies and the contradictory urge to exploit the theatrical schism's critical edge in altering the relationship between life and art. And I quote again from the first scene: "It is imperative to undo all signs of the drama," the Nurse warns. "There's no danger," the Hierophant reassures her, "we'll recompose the cadaver. . . . We'll put together her scattered members" (21). Through the images of morbidity weaving its expressive webs and in the fragmented quality of its own form, *A morta,* as an alternative to the drama of subjective interiority, proposes a theater of autopsy that reconstructs the act of watching as a critical dismemberment. By engaging the spectator in the play's "panorama of analysis," theater, far from the unifying projects of the "universal self" or the "language of one humanity" the Poet openly espouses, is recast as a conceptual taking apart, an etymologically literal autopsy: a "seeing with one's own eyes."

This is precisely what the carnival barker urges spectators of *En la luna* to do: to see in person the wonders of the performance. As in *En la luna, A morta*'s implicit spectator is summoned to perform his or her own potentially unpleasant perceptual feat. In contrast to Beatriz's passive self-contemplation, *A morta*'s pathologist-spectators will actively participate in their own autopsy, a conceptual analysis of themselves and their institutions. While the Poet's utopian yearnings would abolish the theatrical schisms separating art from human action, *A morta* deploys these very schisms to develop its own aesthetic critique. Artaud's designation of theater as a *"site of passage"* for the "cartilaginous transformation of ideas" (*The Theater and Its Double* 109) evokes a space that both unifies and fragments, depending on how you view it. In its visible crossings between those who perform and those who watch, Oswald's play reveals that proscenial site of passage and positions the spectator within it. If the Poet who abandons the catacombs of self-reflection will seek to create an art that can, in André Breton's words, "face the breadth of the street" ("What Is Surrealism?" 116), theater's spectator, conceptually resituated on the interstices of art and life, will be compelled to perceive new things, above all, his or her own position.

Conclusion

While vanguardist manifestos and performative events display and endorse specific types of art, plays such as *Trescientos millones, Parece mentira, En la luna,* and *A morta* explore art's potential for altering human experience. Specifically, these works tap theater's mimetic properties and transformational substance to thematize art's interaction with life. Each play enacts a situation calling for change: the Sirvienta's lonely life in *Trescientos millones;* the Marido's unexamined existence and the Empleado's prescripted art in *Parece mentira;* Luna's endless political corruption in *En la luna;* the Poet's isolation from the world in *A morta.* In dramatizing efforts to alter these conditions, the plays expose theater's bond with the mimetic to express a pervasive anxiety of repetition and of mimesis's power over both art and life. Thus the Sirvienta's theatrical dream-play is marked by prior representations; the search for change by both the Marido and the Empleado is weighted down by prescripted scenarios; the lunar leaders' performative dexterity creates the illusion of change from interminable duplications; and the self-contemplative doublings of the Poet-Beatriz connection unfold in a specular, theatrical space. Each of these plays denaturalizes the mimetic by unmasking its illusory mechanisms. In *Trescientos millones,* the dream-play is a blatant fabrication; in *Parece mentira,* doorbells, lights, repetitive character gestures, and the play's title signal shifts to the theatrical; both *En la luna* and *En la tierra* are billed as puppet performances; and *A morta*'s fragmented actor-marionettes disclose their own synthetic substance. Make-believe reality, announcing its own artifice, is revealed for what it is, and it is not life. But at the same time, each play manifests an antiaesthetic impulse, if not to seal completely the gap between art and life, to make evident the seams of their intersections in the "as if" condition of performance, that is, in the desire for transformation. Seeking to reinvent their worlds, like the vanguardist artists with their illusions of inauguration, the Sirvienta, the Marido and the Empleado, the collectivists, and *A morta*'s Poet are trapped in theater's mimetic cycle, in repetitive representations, the inertia of human invention. As a means of breaking out of that cycle, these works tamper not with the lives of their characters, for they are only make-believe, but with the relationships and terms of the performance, exposing art's inner workings and radicalizing its real-life recipient's role. In the course of these works-in-progress, the lived experience of watching a play is reconstructed as an exercise in critical perception, a provocation to change the way we see and think and even, these artists would imagine, to alter the way we are.

5.

From Early Words
to the Vernacular Inflection

Vanguard Tales of Linguistic Encounter

We must return to silence / To the silence of the words that come from silence.
> —Vicente Huidobro, *Altazor o el viaje en paracaídas*

Let's play with words!
> —Miguel Angel Asturias, Guacamayo in *Cuculcán*

In the poematic prose preface to Vicente Huidobro's masterwork *Altazor o el viaje en paracaídas,* the poetic speaker temporarily assumes a narrative stance. Here he provides biographical information—"I was born at the Equinox, under the hydrangeas and the airplanes of the heat"—and tells of initiating the poetic quest that constitutes the long poem's seven cantos—"One day I gathered up my parachute . . . " (*OC* 1: 365; EW 3). Altazor's lyric pilgrimage of descent is frequently viewed as a progressive dismantling of language in search of a pure, original word. On the journey's first day, the work's eponymous verbal wizard encounters his Creator, "lovely as a navel" and a simple "hollow in space," and is privy to a direct account of the creation of the universe, of the world, and, after a sip of cognac, of human language: "'I created the tongue of the mouth which man diverted from its role to make it learn to speak'" (*OC* 1: 366; EW 5).[1]

Although *Altazor* was first published as a completed work in 1931,

Huidobro conceived the project in 1919 and first published the preface in 1925. In 1923, Miguel Angel Asturias began writing the *Leyendas de Guatemala* collection that first appeared in print in 1930. Asturias's lyrical prose pieces are framed by an autodiegetic narration in which the nameless speaker recounts his return to Guatemala to recover and retell its stories. In the work's second piece, "Ahora que me acuerdo," the speaker meets with village elders and demonstrates the linguistic prowess that qualifies him to tell these tales. For this test, he recounts his own transformation into the mythical Cuero de Oro and his journey into the pre-Columbian past. Like the preface to *Altazor*, this is a story of beginnings. The narrator, as Cuero de Oro, travels to the dense Guatemalan jungle and encounters his ancestors and their makers celebrating the original creation. A key moment in this "delirious night" enacts the coming into being of primal sounds, song, and language out of the silent void that had preceded them: "In the darkness nothing exists. Grasping my one hand with the other, I dance to the rhythm of the vowels of a scream ¡A-e-i-o-u!" (*Leyendas* 19).

The striking differences between these two stories reveal the tensions that dominated tales of linguistic encounters and broader polemics about language in Latin America's vanguard movements. I will return to these differences in a moment, but equally important common features provide a point of departure. In the context of the works from which they are drawn, each of these stories constitutes a tale of aesthetic legitimation and of affirming artistic power by identifying with the initial formation of language. In both cases, the source of linguistic legitimacy is a cosmogonic story of prelinguistic beginnings. Both stories evoke the immodest vanguardist enterprise of (re)creating language from the void. In each story, the speaker embodies the avant-garde artist whose claim to engage in this ambitious task derives from a special connection to the origins of words. This connection is clearly related to the obsession with origins I explore in the vanguardist portrayals of America, but these particular tales are more narrowly focused on language itself. For avant-garde writers, internationally and in Latin America, language constituted both the means and the ends for vast innovative projects. Thus *Altazor* may be read simultaneously as a bountiful showcase of linguistic virtuosity and as a poetic treatise on the potential and limits of language. Similarly, the *Leyendas de Guatemala* lays out an array of lyrical possibilities, storytelling modes, and rhetorical strategies derived from the self-consciously modern tapping of indigenous sources. Language also becomes an implicit theme in the work, and the dramatic piece *Cuculcán* that concludes the collection openly enacts Asturias's concerns about language.

But for comprehending the linguistic inquiries that unfolded within Latin America's vanguards, the differences between these two texts are as significant as their convergences. Huidobro's version of the formation of language possesses no overt vernacular inflections, although, even with *Altazor*'s parodic tone, certain elements—one God creating one world—imply a generic Western, monotheistic, Old Testament situation. Linguistic creation in the *Leyendas*, by contrast, is insistently culturally specific, as it evolves within a pre-Columbian, non-Western, and indigenous Guatemalan context. Altazor's poetic encounter with his creator, moreover, launches a search (some would say a failed one) for an autonomous, linguistically pure idiom, divested of history and immediate referents. Asturias recasts this very idea of linguistic origins and re-creation as a cultural project that implicitly disputes the image of a verbally pure poetic space and sets forth instead an artistic practice of linguistic complication and difference. In the shift from *Altazor* to the *Leyendas*, the creative odyssey of an individual poetic persona observing the world from a cosmic perspective becomes the artistic pursuit of a collectivity rooted in pre-Columbian forests. Neither of these works alone can provide an adequate account of the linguistic explorations undertaken by Latin America's vanguardists; both constitute an intense and multivocal dialogue of texts and ideas.

This dialogue emerged through a wide variety of literary exercises and language-oriented activities. As one would expect, language is a clear, often dominant concern in manifestos and poetic collections. Avant-garde verbal experiments and thematic inquiries into language characterized the work of numerous poets in the 1920s and early 1930s. But language themes and experiments appeared in vanguardist prose fiction and dramatic works as well. In addition to the linguistic investigation undertaken through literary texts, a number of vanguardist groups and writers made spoken language their object of study by self-consciously collecting an array of linguistic artifacts to be recontextualized in artistic experiments but also simply for the sake of collecting. The points of contact and diversion I have highlighted between *Altazor* and the *Leyendas de Guatemala* typify the dialogues about language that permeated these endeavors. If the similarities between Huidobro and Asturias affirm the centrality of language in avant-garde activity, my juxtaposition of their work here underscores the distinct linguistic debates that characterized Latin America's vanguards: the search for linguistic purity, for a "ground zero" of verbal expression that becomes entangled with vernacular concerns; the affirmation of ethnic or national linguistic identities within a vanguardist mode; and the elaboration of a cultural critique that includes exploring cultural differences through language and developing artistic practices that will foreground linguistic difficulty and estrangement.

Language in the International Vanguards

I have suggested, and will demonstrate more fully, that in Latin America vanguardist inquiries into language were often marked by concrete cultural problems. Moreover, an awareness of language as the site of cultural and social tensions often characterized the historical avant-gardes in general. Although the European movements are not my central concern, they provide the basis for contemporary theories of the avant-gardes, and it is pertinent to look briefly at what those theories suggest about language. The fundamental position of linguistic issues in international vanguardism is widely recognized and virtually unquestioned. But critics and theorists of the vanguards differ noticeably in the degree to which they perceive that language was conceived in vanguardist polemics as a social and cultural problem. In his exploratory piece "Language and the Avant-Garde," Raymond Williams cautions against attributing a specific theory or ideological position on language to the vast array of experiments and attitudes that actually made up the vanguards' approach to the subject. Still, it is difficult not to discern certain attitudes toward language that run through the manifestos and artistic practices of the European avant-gardes. These include a rejection of the cognitive power and experiential viability of rational thought and discourse; a consequent antipathy toward conventions of representation, particularly those associated with narrative; and the exercise of what were construed as prediscursive verbal strategies, oral and written, that would somehow provide a more immediate apprehension of experience. By liberating words from the chains of tradition (grammar, genres, and literary conventions), artists would forge new creative principles, including language practices more in touch with an imagined primary experience and the juxtaposition into nonorganic works of decontextualized words and images. But language was portrayed in vanguardist polemics not only as an issue of style or a path to fuller apprehensions of reality but also as a phenomenon of social life, heavily implicated in the autonomous claims of aestheticism and in a perceived disunity between representation and experience, dream and action, art and life.

This multifaceted characterization explains in part why vanguard practitioners expressed such radical ambivalence toward language, which constituted for them the greatest obstacle to original artistic expression and the greatest hope for renewal as well. In short, language was to be torn apart and rebuilt. The new art, according to writers like Apollinaire, would seek a scope "vaster than the plain art of words" ("The New Spirit and the Poets" 228), and Tristan Tzara's infamous "NO MORE WORDS!" announced Dada's campaign to pulverize semantic units into primary elements of sound and rhythm (Motherwell 84). At the same time, Tzara saw language—when properly used—as a utopian path. Demolishing the academy would yield a "fabulous form of action," and this, in turn, would reintegrate art and life and provide an antidote to literature, "a notebook of human imbecility to aid future professors" (*Approximate Man* 169). And André Breton portrayed the unleashing of words as a continuing critical activity with an antihierarchical spirit: "The hordes of words which . . . Dada and Surrealism set about to let loose as though opening a Pandora's box . . . will slowly but surely make their way into the silly little towns and cities of literature . . . and here confusing without any difficulty the poor and the rich sections, they will calmly consume a great number of towers" (*Manifestoes of Surrealism* 152).

Raymond Williams has cogently noted the double-edged quality in vanguardist approaches to language. Language, he observes, "was being simultaneously identified with the blocking of 'true consciousness' and, to the extent that it could emancipate itself from its imprisoning everyday forms and, beyond that, from the received forms of 'literature,' as itself the medium of the idealised 'pure consciousness' " (40). But Williams's short piece on the subject is also exceptional in addressing, albeit briefly, the fact that some vanguardists saw language also as "material in a social process" (Williams 43). Most recent studies of the language of the avant-gardes, however, attend to the relationship between linguistic experiment and the quest for new levels of consciousness through the desired primary experience of created languages.[2] Renato Poggioli and Peter Bürger, two major theorists of the vanguards, have relatively little to say about language at all. Poggioli notes briefly the social significance of the linguistic revolt: a childlike secret language that constitutes "simply one of many forms of avant-garde antagonism toward the public" (38). But he directs more attention to the search for "linguistic purity" and "transrational languages" that, in his view, aligns the avant-gardes with the nineteenth-century aestheticist tradition and twentieth-century European modernism in general.

Although Bürger also says little about language directly, his work suggests how vanguardist linguistic investigations may be addressed as cultural critique. In contrast to Poggioli's elision of the differences between the avant-gardes and modernism, Bürger insists that the former constitute a break with the aestheticist tradition precisely in their focus on the social status of art. He proposes that vanguardists challenged the autonomy of art from life and the nineteenth-century aestheticists' efforts to resacralize art by restoring its aura.[3] Generally, however, Bürger subsumes the problem of language under artistic style and technique. Jochen Schulte-Sasse, in his foreword to the English translation of Bürger's work, examines differences between Poggioli and Bürger and notes that, for the latter, "the development of the avant-garde has nothing to do with a critical consciousness about language; it is not a continuation of tendencies already present in Aestheticism" (xiv). While aestheticism and modernism as defined in the Anglo-American tradition, Schulte-Sasse asserts, might be reduced to an "attack on traditional writing techniques" and to a "*purely linguistic negation*," Bürger shows that the avant-gardes can only be understood as an attack on art as an institution (xv; my emphasis).

I have no argument with this reading of Bürger's differentiation between modernism and the avant-gardes, but Schulte-Sasse's phrase "purely linguistic negation" harbors a limited view of language and of the uses to which vanguardists put it. Bürger's own work implies a broader perspective. Although he may subsume language under artistic means, his views on the latter point to a more complex conception of language as a socially shaped phenomenon. Bürger asserts that, by making available the artistic means of all periods, the avant-gardes challenged an evolutionary hierarchy of styles. This idea may be logically extended to the avant-gardes' exploration of language as socially and culturally constructed. Juxtaposing languages from multiple realms and inventing new languages from scratch were similarly antihierarchical activities that underscored the existence and significance of those socially constructed hierarchies. Returning to Williams's work, moreover, he insightfully perceives this very quality in the vanguards' varieties of verbal performance: "The relapse to the rhythms of the mass in the middle of an outraging Dadaist spectacle," he argues, is a "reminder of how deeply constituted socially language always is, even when the decision has been made to abandon its identifiable semantic freight" (36).

In Latin America, avant-garde language activities were inventive as well as recuperative, as artists sought to dismantle old languages and create new ones from the void but also to recover "lost" languages from imagined national and ethnic pasts. A close reading of these projects reveals an image of language as the site of historically grounded cultural tensions and the move toward new ways of thinking about language and culture. Paradoxically, the vanguardist trope of a primal verbal universality provides the context and sometimes the direct stimulus for projects affirming linguistic complication and difference.

The Poetics of Linguistic Beginnings

Huidobro's work constitutes the most overt and eloquent Latin American elaboration in the vanguard period of a quest for linguistic purity and a primeval, original language. Huidobro was also Latin America's most prolific manifesto writer and took great pains in cultivating his own theory of poetic creation, *creacionismo*. In oral presentations and written manifestos, Huidobro developed these ideas, which he reworked and sought to put into practice in *Altazor* and earlier poetry collections.

Poetry, Huidobro's manifestos affirm, is the "newborn word" developed in the "first dawn of the world." Only those who have not forgotten the "birth cries of the universal birth [or] the *accents of the world in formation*" are qualified to call themselves poets. Poetry possesses "no past and no future," and its words are to be found "before the beginning of man and after the end of man" (*OC* 1: 654–55; my emphasis). Huidobro dramatized this verbal birth poetically in *Altazor,* though he evoked similar images in numerous earlier works. In "Nouvelle Chanson" from the 1917 *Horizon Carré* collection, for example, anonymous new words spring forth spontaneously in a silent, primal scene.

In *Altazor* itself, the poetic speaker who has heard his god recount the creation of language seeks paradoxically to duplicate that singular act by playing with words, rearranging and breaking them down into particles that resist semantic association. This speaker repeatedly constructs creation scenarios for new worlds and new words. Thus the poet's words spring from the vacuum of that inaugural space and silent moment: "The cradle of my tongue rocked in the void / Prior to all time / And will guard forever the first rhythm / The rhythm that gives birth to worlds" (*OC* 1: 377).[4] As in the verses that provide an epigraph for this chapter, Altazor's probe for original words requires a return to a time before language—"We must return to silence / To the silence of the words that come from silence" (*OC* 1: 382; EW 49, 51)—and before the world itself—"I speak with a tongue moistened by unborn seas" (*OC* 1: 383; EW 53). Altazor's journey marks the death of conventional poets, the obliteration of their overused language, and a call for the revivification of words. This new activity—"the simple sport of words," the pursuit of "the pure word and nothing more"—leads back to and reemerges from a state of preverbal silence, the "spirit whisper of the wordless phrase" (*OC* 1: 394; EW 83). The untranslatable verbal fragments of *Altazor*'s final verses mark the culmination of this progressively disintegrating return to silence.

> Laribamba
> Laribambamplanerella
> Laribambamositerella
> Leiramombaririlanla
>   lirilam
> Ai i a
> Temporía
> Ai ai aia
> Ululayu
>   lulayu
>   layu yu
> Ululayu
>   ulayu
>   ayu yu (*OC* 1: 423)

And the work's closing primal sounds relinquish even the appearance of words on a page:

> Lalalí
>   io ia
> i i i o
> Ai a i ai a i i i i o ia (*OC* 1: 423)[5]

Although Huidobro's seemingly endless tale of linguistic creation is the most all-encompassing, similar imagery permeates numerous vanguardist proclamations. The "Agú" manifesto, published in Chile by contemporaries and friends of Pablo Neruda, calls for the reanimation of language through a return to verbal beginnings: "In the beginning the emotion was / Agú. The elemental. The alogical voice. / The first scream of the flesh" (*MPP* 81). Borges and other Argentine *ultraístas* defined the new metaphor they sought in "the game of linking words" as the "primordial element" (*MPP* 99). And a Puerto Rican *euforismo* manifesto conjured up a primitivist scenario for the "first word" of poetry: "I smash metrics and rhyme and pierce the future with my scream . . . of the warrior who launched the first stone" (LHA 233). Similarly, Mexico's *estridentistas* called for stripping down words to the bone, and signers of the "Somos" manifesto in Venezuela's little magazine *válvula* celebrated the language of "silence or the scream" (*MPP* 279). In a lecture during Brazil's 1922 Week of Modern Art, Menotti del Picchia urged his generation of artists to seek "the fresh flesh of the word" in a "Procrustean bed" (GMT 291), and in the "Prefácio interessantíssimo" manifesto that introduces his *Paulicéia desvairada* poetry collection (1922), Brazil's Mário de Andrade sought a new lyricism from a preverbal unconscious (GMT 299).

As in Huidobro's *Altazor*, vanguardist poetry often dramatizes this imagery of origins more forcefully. The poetic speaker in Rosamel del Valle's "Velódromo," for example, boasts that he "give[s] birth to words like the sun and the rain" (*INPA* 73). Mexican Jaime Torres Bodet's poem "Música" yearns nostalgically for the "pure language" with which the speaker has learned to create with "notes of silence" (*Obras escogidas* 39). The Peruvian poet Carlos Oquendo de Amat prefaced his *5 metros de poemas* (1927) with an epigraph that qualifies his verses as "insecure poetry like my first speaking" (n.p.). In "Poema del momento extrangero en la selva," by Nicaragua's Pablo Antonio Cuadra, the speaker pursues a moment of linguistic creation "prior to my song / Prior to myself" (*50A* 116). The Colombian poet León de Greiff, who experimented extensively with linguistic and musical forms, described the creative act *ab ovo* in one poem—"I have forged my new architecture of words . . . clear, cerebral, pure" (*OC* 1: 353)—and elaborated in another—"And in the empty world / and in the impregnated sibylline world / one hears only the nude voice / the sober voice / the mute voice / the one that says words without known meanings" (*OC* 1: 367). A similar stress between new sounds and silence marks poem xliv in *Trilce* (1922) by Peru's César Vallejo in which the poetic speaker summons up the "unseen piano" of his expressive capacity with its "muteness which deafens" (210). Guatemalan Luis Cardoza y Aragón's lengthy prose poem *Pequeña sinfonía del nuevo mundo* (1929–32) maps out repeated returns to primordial verbal newness. The poetic speaker rejects "impotent" words that do not create and have "led astray their genesic magic" (264). Instead he seeks out words that "don't dare to be born" (291) and constructs a world without names that prefigures the early days of García Márquez's Macondo when it was necessary to name by pointing: "The light was fresh, humid, the world freshly painted. . . . The night wasn't called night nor was the day called day. The mountains, the masts, the constellations, the rivers, the cows did not have names" (325).[6] Paradoxically, one of the most striking features of this verbally profuse 100-page poetic composition is its sustained homage to "transparent silence" as the source of all poetry (346). Critics often ascribe images of origins to Pablo Neruda's early work, for example, *Tentativa del hombre infinito* (1926), a poetic voyage sometimes compared to *Altazor*. Neruda himself did not spell out a primal conception of language in this work, but these tropes of verbal beginnings emerge instead in the critical discourse. Saúl Yurkievich comments, for example, that the work's language takes the reader back to the "larval" and the "germinal" (196).

These diverse imaginings of unmediated verbal worlds posit a universe with no language at all as the site for linguistic creation. Verbal activity in these mute worlds ranges from a preverbal chaos of expression without form to absolute silence. In any case, language appears to emerge from nothingness, but the closer to this original void, the greater the language's power. These images also embody connections between personal and cosmic beginnings. A child learning to speak or a poet generating a new language is an event that takes place not in specific sociolinguistic contexts or historical worlds but in a mythical time-out-of-time and in the imaginary spaces of human and univers(e)al origins. The language thus born should maintain a proximity to its formless, often silent, birthplace through a premorphological and asemantic expressiveness, as in Huidobro's "spirit whisper of the wordless phrase," de Greiff's "mute voice," Vallejo's deafening "muteness," or, in the more chaotic mode, Agú's "first scream of the flesh" or *válvula*'s language of "silence or the scream."

The international avant-gardes execute this prelinguistic ideal in Dada's sound poems and vowel concerts, the futurists' *parole in libertá*, or the Russian futurists *zaum* or transrational language. Marjorie Perloff has demonstrated the relationship between the Russian experiments and Kasimir Malevich's goal of a "zero of form."[7] In Latin American vanguardist practice, this pursuit of new languages produces a multitude of verbal experiments. These well-known verses from *Altazor* epitomize the wordplays, transpositions in morphology and sound, word chaining, and inventiveness typical of vanguardist language play:

Ya viene viene la golondrina
Ya viene viene la golonfina
Ya viene la golontrina
Ya viene la goloncima
Viene la golonchina
Viene la golonclima
Ya viene la golonrima
Ya viene la golonrisa
La golonniña
La golongira
La golonlira
La golonbrisa
La golonchilla   (*OC* 1: 398)

(Look here swoops the swooping swallow
Here swoops the whooping wallow
Here swoops the weeping wellow
Look here swoops the sweeping shrillow
Swoops the swamping shallow
Swoops the sheeping woolow
Swoops the slooping swellow
Look here swoops the sloping spillow
The scooping spellow
The souping smellow
The seeping swillow
The sleeping shellow)   (EW 97)

In the poem "Verdehalago" (1928; Green Flattery, or Flattering Word), Cuba's Mariano Brull constructed comparable sound experiments, called *jitanjáforas*, by playing with the word *verde* (green): "Por el verde, verde / verdería de verde mar / erre con erre," or, in another section, "Verdor y verdín / verdumbre y verdura. / Verde, doble verde / de col y lechuga" (83).[8] The neologisms and grammatical transgressions of poems in Vallejo's *Trilce* (1922) constitute one of Latin American vanguardism's most radical invented languages, as in lines from poem xxxii: "999 calorías. / Rumbbb. . . . Trrraprrrr rrach . . . chaz / Serpentínica u del bizcochero /enjirafada al tímpano" (163) (999 calories. / Rumbbb. . . . Trrraprrr rrach . . . ssstop / Serpentine *u* of the biscuit vendor / giraffed into the eardrum [RS 71]).[9] Other writers situated this linguistic inventiveness in explicit cultural contexts, as in the alliterations, percussive elements, and Africanist linguistic allusions of the Cuban poet Nicolás Guillén's "Canto negro" (1931), in which the black man sings, drums, and dances: "Acuememe serembó / aé; / yambó / aé. / Tamba, tamba, tamba, tamba, / tamba del negro que tumba" (*OP* 1: 122). Linguistic invention constitutes a major story line and the dominant expressive form in Mário de Andrade's Brazilian novel *Macunaíma* (1928). The work's language—a juxtaposition of regionalisms, including neologisms and Tupi derivations, that forms an original idiom that nobody actually speaks—epitomizes vanguardist verbal invention. The novel's antihero protagonist mimics the novel's linguistic resourcefulness when he makes up a language, incomprehensible to his companions, for hunting a tapir in São Paulo: "Tetápe, dzónanei pemonéite hêhê zeténe netaite" (97). Other vanguardist linguistic experiments include the tongue twisters, onomatopoeias, musical rhyme games, and echolalic effects in parts of Asturias's *Leyendas,* particularly in the play *Cuculcán* analyzed below; the radical punning in Brazilian Oswald de Andrade's poetry and manifestos; and the creation of musical languages by structuring literary compositions around musical metaphors in texts from varied genres by de Greiff, Coronel Urtecho and Pasos, Mário de Andrade, Cardoza y Aragón, and Puerto Rico's Luis Palés Matos.

Some of these experiments evolved (like the *Leyendas de Guatemala* or Guillén's poetry) in contexts of cultural specificity that contradicted, either implicitly or openly, vanguardist claims to linguistic purity. But on another level, all of them also manifested the quest for an invented, original language enacted in *Altazor*'s ill-fated odyssey. For all its eschewal of context and reference and the transgressiveness of the experiments that it generated, this imagined early verbal world embodied concrete positions on language and culture. In her brilliant analyses of the visual arts in the international avant-gardes, Rosalind Krauss has demonstrated that in vanguardist discourse, originality is equated with a literal origin, a "beginning from ground zero, a birth" (157). She has also shown how the artistic grid incarnates this goal in much of modern art. Although Krauss addresses the visual realm, her observations are useful for thinking about the vanguards' portrayal of linguistic originality. "Surfacing in pre-War cubist painting and subsequently becoming even more stringent and manifest," Krauss writes, "the grid announces, among other things, modern art's *will to silence,* its hostility to literature, to narrative, to discourse." The grid shores up the visual arts, she adds, against "the intrusion of speech" (9; my emphasis), and its "absolute stasis" embodies the posture of the avant-garde artist (158). The grid's modernity is also contained in its peculiar construction of space and time. Its flattened out, geometrical substance is "antinatural, anti-mimetic, antireal" (9). Temporally, the grid proclaims an artistic principle that has never existed before. Its apparent material quality notwithstanding, moreover, the grid provides many artists with a "staircase to the Universal" and a way to talk allegorically about "Being or Mind or Spirit" (10) and thus imbues the avant-garde concept of originality with a mythical air.

Although Krauss addresses an ideal of visual, not verbal, art that is insistently hostile to speech, her characterization of the grid points to analogous features in the avant-gardes' imagined primary language. Bakhtin's conception of poetic language provides a bridge from Krauss's visual "ground zero" to the literary vanguards' verbal void. In light of much twentieth-century poetry that deliberately exploits the heteroglossia of multiple nonartistic languages, Bakhtin's sweeping affirmation that poetic language is monologic (in contrast to the dialogic novel) seems problematic. But in constructing this dichotomy, Bakhtin is working with a circumscribed definition of poetic language in response precisely to the aestheticist impulse to empty language of history or meaning and to invent new languages. This particular view of poetic language is not universal but historically grounded, Bakhtin is quick to note.[10] Poetic language, in this view, resists the internal dialogization typical of prose and suspends any "mutual interaction with alien discourse" ("Discourse in the Novel" 285). Like the grid that shuts out history and speech (Krauss describes it as an artistic ghetto), poetic language as defined by Bakhtin is complete unto itself and manifests the individual artist's drive for absolute linguistic control.

In poetic genres, artistic consciousness—understood as a unity of all the author's semantic and expressive intentions—fully realizes itself within its own language; in them alone is such consciousness fully immanent, *expressing itself in it directly and without mediation,* without conditions and without distance. The language of the poet is *his* language, he is utterly immersed in it, inseparable from it, he makes use of each form, each word, each expression according to its unmediated power to assign meaning (as it were *"without quotation marks"*) that is, as a pure and direct expression of his own intention. (285; my emphasis; *his* emphasized in original)

Like Krauss's grid, this poetic language seeks its own kind of universality, unmediated by the contingencies of history and culture embodied in "alien speech," and harbors yearnings for metaphysical completeness through an imagined "'language of the gods'" or a "'priestly language of poetry'" ("Discourse in the Novel" 287). In imagining this kind of unified expression, poetic language struggles to elide language's historical responsiveness to the "day" or the epoch. "At any given moment," Bakhtin observes, "languages of various epochs and periods of socio-ideological life cohabit with one another. Even languages of the day exist" (291). Poetry, in his view, "depersonalizes 'days' in language," that is, the markers of time and culture.

Bakhtin's characterization of this specific kind of poetic language is particularly pertinent to the vanguards' dream of a linguistically pure, original space. Like Krauss's grid, this imagined early world is hostile to the intrusion of historically inflected language, that is, language that anybody might have used. This model for verbal creation—hostility to known languages and the preference for fabricating new ones—is also analogous to the grid in its special relationships to space and time. The grid's flattened geometrical substance parallels the architectural impulse that underlies the vanguardist reconstruction of language "from scratch," replacing the syntactical and lexical building blocks (containing historical markers) with primal screams, sounds, disconnected syllables, rhythms, whispers, and sighs. Latin American vanguardists often construed their language work with spatial metaphors, as de Greiff's forging of a "new architecture of words." Bernardo Ortiz de Montellano, a participant in Mexico's Contemporáneos group, observed that the new poetry's play of words had been born from an "architectonic intervention" in language (HV 92), and *ultraísta* manifestos called for manipulating words like playing cards (*MPP* 98). Alberto Hidalgo, Peru's poet of *simplismo,* described in his manifesto "Pequeña retórica personal" the architectural strategy in his "many-sided" poetry: "I make a poem the same way that I would build a house; I place brick by brick" (*MPP* 221).

The peculiar relationship to time established by the vanguards' verbally pure creative space is even more comparable to Krauss's grid. This creative expression from the void announces its own first-time substance as language that aspires retroactively never to have been used before. Altazor's hyperbolic claim to being "the only singer of the century" epitomizes this stance (*OC* 1: 415; *EW* 143). But the imagined linguistic purity supposes its own time-out-of-time through the resistance, in Bakhtinian terms, to the "days" inscribed in the languages of narrative and speech. This ahistorical quality is implicit in *ultraísmo*'s conception of words "as ends in themselves" (HV 267), in the very

notion of a newborn word, and in the effort to make new poetic languages mean whatever poets intended them to mean or, more important, not to mean at all. There is also overt antipathy to notions of
historical time, as in Huidobro's search for a poetry that had "no past
and no future" (*OC* 1: 654), or Altazor's search for "a ritual of *shadow-
less* words" that emerge prior to all time (*OC* 1: 393; EW 83; my emphasis). This image reverberates in numerous manifestos, as in the
Puerto Rican *noísmo* search for an art that refuses to recognize "the
limits of time and space" (LHA 244).

The analogy with Krauss's grid of modern art extends further to
aspirations for the infinite and the universal. Metaphysical quests for a
unity of expression and experience unmediated by rational discourse
often frame the vanguardist searches for newborn language. This desire
for primal links with the universe so clearly evident in *Altazor* echoes
throughout vanguardist poetry and manifestos in repeated allusions to
cosmic chaos and the human anguish it generates. But the search for a
language prior to all time intimates a universality of human experience
and emotion somehow divested of the historical and cultural accretions
that shape actual languages in real-life worlds. It also elides the compli-
cations and density of differences in experience and worldview (of the
"alien," in Bakhtin's terms) inscribed in mutually unintelligible languages. This idealized pre-Babelic language behind history—the primal
scream, the "spirit whisper of the wordless phrase," the "fresh scream
of the flesh"—would somehow obliterate the differences among languages. This aim at linguistic universality was often spelled out. We
should recall, for example, that Huidobro described the creation of new
poetic language as a "universal" birth, and in the *creacionismo* manifesto he explained that the new poetry "becomes translatable and universal, for new events remain identical in all languages" (*OC* 1: 677).
"A language," the "Granizada" proclamation of Venezuela affirms, "is
the universe translated into that language" (*MPP* 161). Puerto Rico's
euforistas proclaimed the unity of races and "the uselessness of frontiers
and languages" (*MPP* 128). In Ecuador, José Antonio Falconí Villagómez (a collaborator with the vanguardist poet Hugo Mayo) produced
a manifesto-style "Arte poética (No. 2)," directing artists toward a poetics of linguistic universality, "to speak the universal language / with
all the sirens of the World" (*MPP* 117).

But this purist image of linguistic unity was simultaneously contested
from within the vanguardist ranks. Amid the pursuit of a universal idiom behind and before all languages, groups and individual writers un-

dertook ambitious projects for recuperating what were portrayed as nationally or ethnically inflected expressive forms, for incorporating them into literary works, and for affirming their aesthetic worth and experiential validity. Some of these endeavors were expressed in precisely the same allegories of linguistic origins that framed the search for a universal language, but recast in vernacular modes, as writers claimed the imagined sites of early words as features of their own cultural formation. Because of its dialogue with Huidobro's work, the story of linguistic creation in the *Leyendas de Guatemala* with which I began this chapter presents a fitting example of this vernacular turn. Constructed from sources portrayed as Guatemala's cultural legacy, that story also embodies vanguardist inquiries into the problematic relationships between language and cultural identity formations.

Language Identities in a Vanguardist Idiom

Certainly the insertion of language into national or ethnic identity projects is not in itself a product of the literary avant-gardes. In the Western world, language's pivotal function in defining inclusive and exclusive identities is inscribed in the etymological roots of the word *barbarian:* "somebody who does not speak Greek."[11] In the modern era of nation-states, language, ethnicity, and nation interact through the development of administrative vernacular print languages, a phenomenon carefully traced by Benedict Anderson in *Imagined Communities: Reflections on the Origin and Spread of Nationalism.* Language and nation or ethnicity are also insistently juxtaposed in modern intellectual history, through romantic nationalist ideologies and the nineteenth-century consolidation of philology as a scientific discipline that sought evolutionary parallels between linguistic, literary, and national development. Because of what Anderson has identified as the "primordialness of languages" and the illusion of language as "rooted beyond almost anything else in contemporary societies" (145), attention to language in cultural contexts always generates tensions between essentialism and historicity. Language may be considered an actor in material culture but also a protagonist in the history of powerful ideas, the embodiment and raw material of myth.

As early as 1882, Ernest Renan cautioned in his address "What Is a Nation?" against forgetting that languages are historical formations and the temptation to ground national identities on idealized notions of racial, religious, or linguistic purity. From a historical perspective, Renan observed, language is, like race, merely something which is made and unmade (15–16). And yet, as Anderson points out (significantly, in his chapter "Patriotism and Racism"), a national language is also a potent and captivating idea that "looms up imperceptibly out of a horizonless past" and simultaneously the idealized embodiment, especially in poetry or song, of "a special kind of contemporaneous community" that projects an image of "unisonance" (145). But, as Mary Louise Pratt suggests in a critique of Anderson's work, investigations of links between language and identity formations may also address the dynamics of inclusion and exclusion at work in conceptualizing linguistic uniformities through these national or ethnic "linguistic utopias."

These tensions between language as a national myth and language as historically formed, between inclusive and exclusive languages, shape vanguardist discourse on linguistic identities in Latin America. As I have noted in the chapter on Americanist projects, Latin America's vanguard movements coincided historically with a renewed intensity in the discourse of cultural autonomy that had engaged Latin American writers since the post-Independence years. Language issues had played a key role in the nineteenth-century projects seeking national and continental identity, most notably in the polemic between Andrés Bello, in favor of maintaining continental linguistic uniformity, and Domingo Faustino Sarmiento, a qualified advocate of incorporating into literature the linguistic forms actually spoken in the new republics.[12] The centripetal impulse toward standardization within national boundaries and the linkage of language with state culminated in the century's last three decades with the foundation of national language academies on the French and peninsular models. The centrifugal affirmation of unofficial languages was manifested in the work of writers who sought to textualize orality as a palpable sign of desired cultural authenticities.

But the appearance of culturally patterned linguistic issues in Latin American vanguardist practice represents not merely unresolved autonomy questions that reemerged with the New World spirit surrounding centennial celebrations of independence. The singularity of this renewed inquiry lies in the modern alertness to language itself, to the stories of social and cultural struggle that its own constitution enacts, and to the critical potential inscribed in its own mercurial inconstancy. On one level, these linguistic projects do indeed affirm the creative and critical worth of culturally "authentic" languages; they struggle to bring into the linguistic and literary marketplace idioms formerly excluded. But in a more radical vein, many of these activities also reflect on the cultural processes and relationships implicit in the pursuit of linguistic uniformity or difference. Although they seek on one level the image of "unisonance" with which Benedict Anderson characterizes the concept of a national language, these projects often also foreground linguistic dissonance and complication.

NATION AND ETHNICITY IN LANGUAGE ACTIVITIES

Emerging in the context of activist cultural nationalism that I have described in the introduction, the interest in culturally specific languages constituted a significant aspect of vanguardist activity in several Latin American countries. Brazilian *modernismo* was marked by a polemically antiacademic spirit, a rejection of prescriptive expressive forms, and the explicit goal to employ the idiosyncrasies of spoken Brazilian Portuguese as the material of art. Even though from the time of its establishment in 1896 the Academia Brasileira de Letras had directed more attention to New World Portuguese than its Spanish American counterparts had done with Spanish, the academy provided a frequent target for innovators' polemics. Graça Aranha, who had given a keynote lecture in the historic Semana de Arte Moderna in São Paulo, articulated the antiacademic position in a 1924 lecture, "O espíritu moderno," before the academy itself. After criticizing the establishment of the academy on the French model as the institutionalization of a nonexistent tradition that was yet to be created, Graça Aranha suggested that creating a specifically Brazilian literature was a project at odds with the whole concept of a language academy. He proposed that the academy incorporate in its dictionary colloquial Brazilian words and expressions and deliberately exclude from its lists language used only in Portugal. In keeping with this philosophy, he suggested that all works published by the academy, all papers prepared by its members, and all works cited with awards be written in "ordinary, common language, expurgated of all archaisms or of . . . Portuguese verbal classicism" (GMT 325).

This commitment to spoken language extended to regional, indigenous, and African influences and permeated the work of avant-garde literary artists. In the "Prefácio interessantíssimo" manifesto that introduces the *Paulicéia desvairada* poetry collection, Mário de Andrade praised the Brazilian language as "one of the richest and most sonorous" and affirmed his commitment to Brazilian Portuguese (*PC* 22).

Mário imagined, but never realized, a *Gramatiquinha da fala brasileira* (a "little grammar" of Brazilian Portuguese). Mário did incorporate vernacular inflections into his poetry, in particular, the 1924 *Clã do Jaboti* collection (1927). But his major linguistic achievement is the novel *Macunaíma* (1928) that incorporates elements of regional language, idioms, and proverbs into a hybridized amalgam that has been called a "Discourse for the Defense and Illustration of the Brazilian Language" (Martins 194) and contains, as Haroldo de Campos points out, numerous "metalinguistic elaborations" on language themes (*Morfologia* 187–92). The linguistic education of the novel's eponymous antihero underscores the point, as he is forced to learn two languages: spoken Brazilian and written Portuguese.[13]

In the same vein, Oswald de Andrade's "Pau-Brasil" manifesto, a document suggestively titled a "falação" (or chat) in some versions, urges the use of language "without archaisms, without erudition. . . . The way we speak. The way we are" (GMT 327; SMSR 185). Poems in the *Pau-Brasil* collection (1924) enact linguistic encounters between "proper" language and language as spoken in Brazil. The concern with language persists in the collection activities of the Antropofagia group described by participant Raul Bopp. The group's projected verbal collections included the creation of a "subgrammar" to recapture "the simplicity of the language, in order to free it from its complex pedagogical gearings" (Bopp, *Vida e morte* 47). This endeavor was to include dropping cumbersome orthographic elements from written Portuguese and preparing a list of one hundred key words with a "Brazilian flavor." This proclivity for collecting verbal artifacts was manifested more widely in the publication of linguistic studies of regional dialects or indigenous languages, such as *O dialeto caipira* in the *Revista do Brasil* or articles on "A lingua tupy" published by the *Revista de Antropofagia* (Martins 8). A colloquial tone and antiacademic spirit also characterized the poetry of Manuel Bandeira in the *modernismo* period, for example, in his "Poética" manifesto poem: "I am sick of a lyricism that stops and goes to look up in the dictionary the pure stamp of a word" (*BMP* 66). His "Evocação do Recife" denigrates those who can only "ape Lusiad syntax" and celebrates the "correct language of the people" because they "speak the delicious Portuguese of Brazil" (*BMP* 71).

In Peru, the vanguards' antiacademic tone first emerged in the recuperation of Manuel González Prada as a cultural hero. In the prewar decades, González Prada had been the first to recommend that Peruvian art break with Spain and the linguistically conservative Lima spirit, explore Peru's indigenous traditions, seek linguistic renewal through popular sources, and search for new forms in other literatures.[14] José Carlos Mariátegui, editor of the vanguardist *Amauta,* lauded González Prada's revolutionary spirit in *El proceso de la literatura,* his essay on Peruvian literature from the *Siete ensayos de interpretación de la realidad peruana* (1928), and also in the special issue of *Amauta* dedicated to his predecessor.[15] Mariátegui and most of Peru's self-designated vanguardist writers claimed González Prada as a mentor for their attack on the attempt to reinstate colonialist cultural ideals represented by Lima's "futurist" generation. A key member in this group had been José de la Riva Agüero, whose *Carácter de la literatura del Perú independiente* (1905) had prompted Mariátegui's essay on literature. According to Mariátegui, Riva Agüero and his contemporaries had helped to institutionalize Peruvian culture and literature by establishing the Instituto Histórico del Perú, the *Revista Histórica,* and the Peruvian language academy.

Against this institutionalization of colonialist models and in keeping with his preference for "natural" language over verbal artifice, Mariátegui proposed that Latin American writers could bridge their distance from everyday experience by using vernacular language. He argued that all classical national literatures had originated from the languages of the street. Thus the Peruvian writers who had contributed most to the creation of a national literature were those who had maintained contact with popular linguistic sources. Mariátegui affirmed that popular language provided a perpetual source of literary innovation and that the innovative potential of popular language was being exploited by even the most cosmopolitan of Spanish America's vanguardist poets, including Borges, whose work frequently adopted the "prosody of the people" (*OC* 2: 242–44).[16]

This advocacy of linguistic colloquialism extended to indigenous languages and was played out in *Amauta* in the vanguardist *indigenista* poetry of Alejandro Peralta sprinkled with Quechua and Aymara words and in articles on indigenous language.[17] Linguistic *indigenismo* also shaped the work of Peru's longest-lasting regional vanguardist magazine, Puno's *Boletín Titikaka.* This magazine promoted indigenist orthography with the goal of making written Spanish appear visually more like a phonetic transcription of Quechua and labeled such experiments with alternative spellings such as "nwestra ortografía bangwardista" (for "nuestra ortografía vanguardista") and "indoameriqana" (for "indoamericana").[18] The *Boletín*'s editor Gamaliel Churata (the pseu-

donym of Arturo Peralta) devoted extensive attention to linguistic investigations in essays, bilingual poetry employing vernacular verse conventions, and the experimental novel *El pez de oro* that contains countless
digressions on the topic and defines the problem of Latin American
identity in linguistic terms. The novel comprises a vast experiment in
linguistic pluralism as exemplified in the five categories of word entries
in its glossary: Quechua, Aymara, hybridizations of the two or of each
with Spanish, "plebeianisms" of the Lake Titikaka region (the novel's
setting), and neologisms constructed by the author. As in Brazil, these
projects evolved in a general cultural environment of linguistic investigations, including, for example, José Gabriel Cosío's *Fonetismo de la
lengua quechua o runasimi* (1924) and the *Alfabeto quechua* (1925).

In Argentina, national linguistic inquiries by vanguardist writers,
though more limited than in Brazil or Peru, reflected continuing debates over popular language in literature dating back to Sarmiento and
the post-Independence era. As Francine Masiello documents, the years
immediately before the vanguards emerged witnessed rapid developments in cultural, academic, and literary institutionalization in Argentina.[19] Vanguardist writers addressed the question of whether the spoken language of Buenos Aires and its environs constituted a proper
language for literature. The *Martín Fierro* manifesto includes linguistic
independence in its affirmation of cultural autonomy—"faith in our
phonetics"—but qualified by a celebration of the country's eclectic cultural inheritance—"a Swedish dentifrice, towels from France, and . . .
English soap" (*MPP* 135). Although he later rejected such experiments
to the extreme of altering his earlier work, Borges expressed this faith
in Argentine phonetics through the lexical and phonological colloquialisms employed in the original versions of his early poetry collections,
Fervor de Buenos Aires (1923) and *Luna de enfrente* (1925). Soon,
however, Borges rejected the cultivation of deliberate linguistic ethnicity, although he also discouraged the proclivity of some writers
toward (peninsular) "Hispanophilic" purism. His 1927 lecture "El
idioma de los argentinos" expressed a common vanguardist aversion to
academic purism in an attack on the pretentious "pseudo-words" and
"purest indecisive style" ascribed to the grammar of the academy ("El
idioma" 20–21). Although as an *ultraísta*, Borges had signed manifestos that opposed using everyday language in literature (*MPP* 113), in
the lecture, he suggested that the language of writers should derive
from their everyday experience: "the unwritten Argentine language" of
"our passion, of our home, of trust, and of conversed friendship" ("El

idioma" 25). Still, he opposed the studied cultivation of popular forms. These included the common language of working-class neighborhoods and *lunfardo* (colloquial underworld language). He also denied the capacity of such unofficial language, or any kind of slang, to effect significant change in the dominant idiom.

Roberto Arlt's work stands in direct contradiction to this view. Writing from his own life experience with a very different "unwritten Argentine language" from what had been lived by Borges, Arlt combined in his novels, particularly in *Los siete locos* (1929) and *Los lanzallamas* (1931), radical innovations in narrative voice and focalization with a creative hodgepodge of spoken and, until then, nonliterary languages. These include *lunfardo*, Argentine regionalisms, foreign words, and metaphors and imagery derived from modern scientific and technological jargon.[20] In a 1930 journalistic sketch, entitled, like Borges's lecture, "El idioma de los argentinos," Arlt employed a pugilistic metaphor to take a more radical, Bakhtinian-style stand on the influence of unofficial languages on the norm. The human groups with no new ideas to express, he argued, need no new words or "strange turns of the phrase." By contrast, peoples in continuous evolution (as in Argentina) strike out, like boxers, with words "from all angles," words that "anger professors" (*OC* 2: 486). Groups impose their language through "prepotency," Arlt affirmed here, adding that it would be absurd to confine new ideas in a canonical grammar. He further supported this position that popular language has transformative power in a series of articles that highlighted individual samples from a colloquial Argentine lexicon to show their creative potential and their etymological development.[21]

The antiacademic tone of their language activities is inscribed in the Nicaraguan vanguardists' group name, the Anti-Academy. The first manifesto proposed bringing to light past linguistic and literary forms belonging to a national tradition (*50A* 24). The manifesto "Cartelón de vanguardia" polemicized against "the copy, rhetoric, the rules, academism, linguistic purity" (*50A* 173), and the manifesto "Dos perspectivas" set forth the goal to "conserve our tradition, . . . our customs, . . . our language" (*50A* 27). Following these self-directives, the Nicaraguan vanguardists gathered popular sayings, colloquialisms, children's rhyming games, songs, tongue twisters, lullabies, and popular verse forms from the Hispanic tradition. Pablo Antonio Cuadra, Joaquín Pasos, and José Coronel Urtecho, among others, incorporated many of these into their poetry and into the experimental performance piece *Chinfonía burguesa* (1931–36).[22]

In his retrospective on the group, "Los poetas en la torre," Cuadra later recalled this activity: "And we went to the people to interrogate their voices, their expressions, their living language, their forms, their namings" (188). In addition, Cuadra explained, they adjusted their literary language syntactically to approximate the language of conversation. Cuadra's own "Ars poética" of this period declares the need to "find the poetry of ordinary things," to "sing for anybody / with the ordinary tone" (*OPC* 1: 88–89). With more overtly vernacular metaphors, Pasos's brief poetic manifesto of linguistic specificity, "Por, en, sin sobre, tras . . . las palabras," celebrates "Mombacho words" and urges other poets to clothe their poetic expression in *bombacho* trousers (*50A* 139). Moreover, the performance piece *Chinfonía burguesa* by Pasos and Coronel Urtecho constitutes a manifesto of linguistic nationalism in its language theme and colloquial expressions and verse forms.

Cuban vanguardist activity developed during a period of intense cultural self-definition in Cuban arts and public life. Members of the Grupo Minorista, many of whom founded the *Revista de Avance,* committed themselves both to "vernacular art" and to "new art" (*MPP* 249). The magazine's concern with Cuban and American identities was epitomized in its consecration of José Martí as its cultural mentor, comparable to the Peruvian *Amauta*'s attention to the work of Manuel González Prada.[23] As in Brazil and Peru, Cuban intellectuals of this period dedicated themselves to retrieving and collecting *cubanismos,* as in Fernando Ortiz's *Un catauro de cubanismos* (1923) and his *Glosario de afronegrismos* (1924). Works such as these made no claims to a vanguardist character, and Ortiz, a consummate investigator, was neither a vanguardist nor a member of the Grupo Minorista. Still, it is interesting that, as Gustavo Pérez Firmat has carefully documented, the *Catauro de cubanismos* flaunted the conventions of its genre in the same anti-academic spirit so pervasive in new art ventures.[24]

The self-conscious cultivation of autochthonous language within a context of aesthetic innovation appeared primarily in the early poetry of Nicolás Guillén and, to some degree, in Alejo Carpentier's dramatic experiment *Manita en el suelo* (1931) and his novel *¡Écue-Yamba-Ó!* (1933). Guillén constructed an image of linguistic *cubanismo* through lexical and phonological colloquialisms, intonations, and stylized percussive elements associated with popular speech and Afro-Cuban culture, as well as through rhythms, acoustical elements, and responsive conventions derived from popular music. The verses from "Si tu su-

piera" in the *Sóngoro cosongo* collection (1931) are typical: "Aé / bengan a be; / aé, / bamo pa be; / bengan, sóngoro cosongo / sóngoro
cosongo de mamey" (*OP* 1: 105). Here the colloquial "bengan a be"
and "bamo pa be" ("come and see" and "let's go see") replace the
more normative "vengan a ver" or "vamos a ver." In the manifesto
poem "Llegada" that opens the collection, the poetic speaker allegorizes the "arrival" of non-European elements into Cuban cultural and
linguistic life: "Here we are! / The word comes to us moist from the
forests / and an energetic sun rises in our veins" (*OP* 1: 115).[25] Guillén's poetry of this period focuses on oral expression, not only by incorporating song and colloquial elements but also by employing forms that
evoke verbal situations and encounters. These include the *piropo*, the
verbal engagement of a woman by a man on the street in "Sóngoro
cosongo," the street vendor's cry in "Pregón," and the riddle in "Adivi-
nanzas." In the collection mode that permeated vanguardist activity,
Guillén actively gathered *pregones* from different parts of Cuba and
carefully studied their musical, improvisational, and structural features.
He even suggested, parodying conventional academic undertakings, establishing a "Municipal Academy of *Pregones*" in Camagüey, to educate
new voices that would replace the ones being lost (*Prosa de prisa* 1:
25).

Although there was some disagreement among Puerto Rico's vanguardist groups about cultivating deliberately vernacular art, Luis Palés
Matos, Puerto Rico's principal creator of *afronegrista* poetry, suggested
the Puerto Rican and Antillean poets should draw on the linguistic richness of the region's African cultures (cited in *LHA* 48).[26] In addition to
Palés Matos's *negrista* poetry, poetic compositions such as the "Fugas
diepálicas" by J. I. de Diego Padró or the "Orquestación diepálica" by
Palés Matos and de Diego Padró enacted oral situations of poematic
exchange and response, even when the participating voices were not
always human. Thus concluding verses in the latter orchestrate bird,
animal, and insect "voices" attributed to an Antillean world.

> Pit . . . pit . . . pit . . . co-quí-co-co-quí . . . quí
> Pitirr-pitirr, chi-chichichuí, chi-chichichuí . . .
> Chocla, chocla, cho cla, mmmeee . . . . . .
> Caaacaracaca, pío, pío, caaaracacaaa . . .
> Juá, juá, juá, juá; uishe-ó, uishe-ó, uishe-ó
> Cucurucú! qui qui ri quí ¡Cocorocó!   (LHA 166)

In other countries, such as Mexico and Chile, the cultivation of linguistic specificity did not constitute a major component of vanguardist

groups' agenda, although it did surface in memorable ways in the work of individual writers. Xavier Icaza's generically unstable, satirical novel *Panchito Chapopote*, for example, combines a telegraphic, synthetic vanguardist style with an eponymous antihero, Panchito, who in character and language is intended to embody the "Mexican people" of the postrevolutionary era. Pablo de Rokha's surrealist novel *Escritura de Raimundo Contreras* (1929) inserts stream-of-consciousness narration into the linguistic reality of a Chilean *huaso*. And although there was no significant vanguardist activity in Guatemala itself, Asturias's *Leyendas de Guatemala* (written in Paris), which combined the language of the *Popol Vuh* with elements from Guatemala's popular tradition, presents one of the outstanding results of vanguardist linguistic ethnicity in Latin America. Its final piece, the play *Cuculcán* (which I examine below) constitutes a discourse on language.

ANCESTRAL VOICES AND NATIONAL ESSENCE

These multiple linguistic projects cultivate the spoken word or unofficial language as repositories of national or ethnic identity and insist on the singularity and cultural worth of each vernacular idiom. All of these endeavors seek to insert the languages of concrete cultural experience into a specific literary world, "bringing [them] into writing," a phrase James Clifford uses to describe what ethnographers do when they salvage oral traditions (*Writing Culture* 113). Because of their focus on cultural difference, on the surface these undertakings appear antithetical to the vanguardist pursuit of a pristine and primal verbal world, that linguistic utopia in which poets can speak in the newborn language of a time before time. But the figures in which these cultural linguistic goals are often embedded deflect the vanguardist discourse of origins toward a specific cultural experience in which Huidobro's "cries of the universal birth" become instead the birth cries of a culturally concrete linguistic identity.

Vanguardist writers build this image by drawing on the mythical aura surrounding the idea of language itself, those qualities noted by Anderson in *Imagined Communities,* including "primordialness," an air of "rootedness," and the sensation of looming up from a "horizonless past" (144). What looms up from that imagined past is the image of a rooted ancestral voice through which the artist in tune with his or her culture might speak. In Huidobro's *creacionismo*, we should recall, only those who have not forgotten "the accents of the world in formation" are prepared to call themselves poets (*OC* 1: 654–55). By virtue of the vernacular turn, those in tune with a primordial or ancestral voice become particularly qualified to speak for their specific contemporary human community. This portrayal of language partakes of the same primitivist discourse of origins that I have explored in the vanguardist stories of America. But here the emphasis falls specifically on language, through the search for culturally inflected primal voices and originary words. Thus the unisonance of a universal language becomes the unisonance of a specific national or ethnic experience. In Latin American vanguardist discourse, this link is forged through orality, the concept of a living voice engaged in speech or song.

In this vein, Mário explained in the "Prefácio interessantíssimo" manifesto introducing the urban poetry of *Pauliceia desvairada* that he had set forth through the city's jungle with his "variegated lute" (*PC* 30). In that collection's poem "Trovador," the speaker celebrates sentiments of "the men of the first eras" and announces "I am a Tupi strumming a lute" (*PC* 32–33). Similarly Raul Bopp (of the Antropofagia group), in his lengthy primitivist poem *Cobra norato* (1928–31), portrayed a speaker whose source is "voices that come from far away" (27), and in "Negro," he invoked "the voice of ignored origins" that weighs in the black man's blood (*Cobra norato* 127). Similarly, in Guillén's "Llegada" announcing the arrival of black language into Cuban literary culture, the speaker's words derive from a prehistoric source. In the opening scene of the *Leyendas de Guatemala,* the narrator returns to his homeland to seek out the voices that lie buried under its palimpsest of "sonorous cities." Later, the storyteller proves his creative prowess by returning to the primeval forest where he hears the echoes of the earliest tribes, "where their song began" (18). Similarly, the Nicaraguan vanguardist Luis Alberto Cabrales imagined in "Canto a los sombríos ancestros" a timeless poetic voice, "filled with the ancestral soil and burning" an "ancient voice . . . impetuous and agile, like you, ancestors" (*50A* 127–28).

Not surprisingly, fashioning a linguistic identity through ancestral orality often relied on nature. The organic metaphor, so prevalent in nineteenth-century Latin American literature, is critically reexamined in the 1920s *novela de la tierra,* as Carlos Alonso has demonstrated in *The Spanish American Regional Novel,* and also reemerges to be challenged, as I have shown, by the vanguardist portrayals of America. But vanguardist dialogues specifically addressing language are also sustained by a kind of verbal tellurism through which the ancestral word of cultural identity becomes firmly rooted. The poetic speaker in Asturias's *Leyendas* provides the most literal example. His song emerges in the jungle's delirious night, as, borrowing from sacred Mayan tales, he begins to grow roots and feels himself a part of the land. Brazilian Plínio Salgado, in his article "A língua tupy" in the *Revista de Antropofagia,* analyzed phonetic and semantic elements in order to maintain that this "nascent" language provided unmediated contact between humanity and nature, a "true eucharist of man in intimate cosmic union" (Salgado 6). Luis Cardoza y Aragón's *Pequeña sinfonía del nuevo mundo* presents a disoriented poet in New York out of touch with nature: "Words were impotent, they did not create, they had lost their genesic magic" (263). In Guillén's "Llegada," we recall, the speakers' ancestral voices arise "moist from the forests." Similarly, as Cuadra urged his fellow poets in "Ars poética" to return to the sources of song, his own "Canción del momento extranjero en la selva" discovers ancestral voices in a primeval Nicaraguan setting: "Prior to my song / prior to myself, / in the heart of our mountains" (*OPC* 147). In the Andean world, the speaker in Oquendo de Amat's "madre campo" from *5 metros de poemas* draws initial words from nature with a voice "primitive like the rain and the hymns" (n.p.). And in Ecuador, Hugo Mayo employed a comparable verbal tellurism with a cumbersome image verging on parody: "men fastened like ticks / on the terrestrial pachyderm / unsheathe your orations" ("Bujía polar" 62).

Beyond the imagined ancestral voice, orality gave way to a second essentialist notion. The vanguardist utopian quest for a verbal void as a creative ground zero was marked, as I have shown, by a preference for the most basic units of expression, those that with a gridlike hostility to the "intrusion of speech" barely approximate language at all: Huidobro's "spirit whisper of the wordless phrase," de Greiff's "mute voice," or the "Agú" manifesto's "fresh scream of the flesh." The vanguards' linguistic identity projects redirect this taste for the minimal elements of language toward the search for essential units of cultural definition. Thus the spoken word, or the written version approximating oral models, is portrayed not only with the aura of presence ascribed to an ancestral voice but also as the repository of a deeply structured authenticity. Writers search for a singular sound, word, or phrase that might express the essence of a particular human community. Through this linguistic unit and often with wording that today would be regarded as racialist, biology and history, nature and culture converge, and linguistic artifacts personify national character.

In this vein, the Venezuelan "Granizada" proclamation declares that one can classify human groups in accordance with the interjections on which they rely. While this manifesto seems to speak more than slightly tongue-in-cheek, others sound more serious, as when the *Martín Fierro* manifesto pledges faith in "our phonetics" or in Luis Palés Matos's identification of an Antillean "accent" and "homogeneous cultural rhythm" (*LHA* 48). In Nicaragua, Cuadra wrote of "vernacular unity" and "vibrations" forming the soul of a people and borne out through race, blood, environment, beliefs, and language (*50A* 47–48). In Brazil, Menotti del Picchia explained that *modernistas* wanted to "write with blood" (GMT 291), and in his lecture "O espíritu moderno," Graça Aranha identified occult forces endowing the Brazilian language with its "marvelous enchantment of alluvium and solar splendor" and the capacity to express a "collective spirituality" (GMT 322). Mário celebrated the wonders of the "very admirable ão" of Brazilian Portuguese (*PC* 22), and Brazil's Antropofagia group, as I have noted, collected words with a "Brazilian flavor," selecting the word *mussangulá* to incarnate national character: "a variety of philosophical laziness, of a Brazilian cast" and "against everything that is coherent, syllogistic, geometric, Cartesian" (Bopp, *Vida e morte* 48). In "Pequeña oda a un negro boxeador cubano," Guillén's Cuban boxer on Broadway holds the power to "speak in black for real" (*OP* 120), and, addressing the idiosyncrasies of Buenos Aires language, Arlt singled out certain special words (*furbo, fraca, squenun*) as representative of a singular cultural experience.

In its customary fashion, Mário's *Macunaíma* carries the idea of cultural essence through language to the edge of parody. The eponymous Brazilian hero is born in the depth of a virgin forest in a primeval moment of silence. As if aware of his duty and destiny as a national hero to provide an ancestral voice, Macunaíma prolongs this silent moment for six years and, when forced to talk, only exclaims, "Ai! que preguiça!" (Oh! What laziness!) (5). Its parodic tone notwithstanding, Macunaíma's highly colloquial first sentence has, from the time the novel was first published, been interpreted as a verbal icon of essential Brazilianness.[27] More important, perhaps, *Macunaíma*'s parodic gesture toward its own creation of an ancestral voice and a verbal essence points to contradictions shaping the vanguards' cultural linguistic ventures and to their potential for a more critical impact.

Linguistic Estrangement as Cultural Critique

The idea that a national or ethnic essence can be summed up in a privileged verbal artifact is consonant with ideologies of cultural nationalism. As Anderson suggests, the imagined community of a nation becomes the imagined community constituted by the speakers of a given language. But Pratt addresses in "Linguistic Utopias" limitations inherent in these imaginings. It is not uncommon, Pratt notes, for the notion of "speech community" sustaining utopian visions of linguistic nationalism to be appropriated by subgroups within a given national entity to affirm the intrinsic value of those groups, as in concepts such as "black English" or "women's language." Such projects, she observes, can be "extraordinarily empowering," as they challenge "the normative forces of standard grammar" and insist on "heterogeneity, on the existence and legitimacy of lifeways other than those of dominant groups" (56). But Pratt compares the limitations of such ventures to nineteenth-century dialect studies that addressed language as a "nexus of social identity" but failed to see it as the "site of social struggle" in which dominant and dominated participate (56).

In *Myth and Archive,* Roberto González Echevarría has posited a somewhat related idea in expounding a theory of Latin American narrative. Bringing together Bakhtin and Foucault, he develops the idea that Latin American writers construct a position from which to legitimize their own stories by mimicking the rhetorical strategies of hegemonic, nonliterary discourses dominant in certain historical epochs. In this model, a Bakhtinian notion of a dialogic resistance to official discourse is tempered by a Foucaultian insistence on the power of that dominant discourse to shape individual stories. González Echevarría seeks, in part, to show the interaction of the two in Latin American development as a discursive struggle between the hegemonic practice and the individual writer staking out a legitimate position from which to speak. Pratt's work suggests a comparable approach to the problem of language identities by addressing language as the site of interaction between languages of power and languages of resistance, a struggle in which both participate.

Anderson's inquiry into the role of language in nationalist ideologies points to an additional problem in the concept of a language community, empowered or not. The idea of a national language, Anderson observes, especially in poetry or song, can project a feeling of unisonance. Considering Pratt's points about subcommunities, this could be true whether the speech community in question is official and empowered or a more marginal group through which a broader-based national identity is sought, such as blacks in a predominantly white Western society or Indians in Peru. The unisonance of the resisting speech community would be substituted for the unisonance of the dominant language, as one essentialist model of authenticity would seek to displace another. In constructing linguistic identities in Latin America, vanguardist artists used the discourse of origins, specifically, through images of the ancestral voice and cultural essence, to affirm cultural autonomy in art. The mythical return to the beginnings of an imagined ancestral language and the elevation of primary linguistic forms (sounds, interjections, phrases) to the status of cultural entities sustain the same ideal of self-present linguistic unity we saw in Huidobro's poetics. Thus the quest for linguistic difference paradoxically leads back to another "universal" language, different only because of its specific cultural context.

On one level, then, vanguardists worked to bring idioms formerly excluded into the literary marketplace, a project of cultural resistance grounded in affirming new models of authenticity. But in a more radical vein, many of these activities also reflect on the cultural relationships implicit in notions of linguistic uniformity and difference. At times these writers focused on orality not as a privileged site of linguistic presence but so as to reenact specific historical situations and to reveal language as a locus of cultural disputes and interactions. Against the unisonance implicit in a linguistically pure poetic space—or in its vernacular version, the primordial ancestral voice—many vanguardist language activities also foreground linguistic plurality, dissonance, and complication.

GRAMMAR THROUGH HISTORY AND ON THE STREETS

The antiacademic stance—against grammar, the dictionary, the genre, the book—constitutes, as I have noted, a cliché of the vanguardist enterprise. In Latin America, attacks on grammar as the nexus of normative forces and cultural institutions and, above all, as the incarnation of the written word permeate vanguardist activities with or without an autochthonous agenda. Huidobro's Altazor himself calls for "circuit breakers in the sentences" and "cataclysms in the grammar" (*OC* 1: 393; EW 81). Few vanguardist manifestos, in fact, fail to attack normative language, and, in most cases, these norms are romantically portrayed as stiflers of freedom, emotion, and creativity, as the antithesis to a desired heightened consciousness or transrational language. The affirmation in Venezuela's aphoristic "Granizada" proclamation is typical: grammar serves only to justify the injustices of language (*MPP* 161). Oliverio Girondo developed this position more fully in his aphoristic exercise *Membretes* (*Veinte poemas*, 1932). Life, Girondo observed here, is a long process of "brutalization" in which syntax and the dictionary handicap our natural ability to transform a chair into an ocean liner (96). In Ecuador, José Antonio Falconí Villagómez's "Arte poética" manifesto rejects rhetoric and the academy "because there are no longer any grammarians in the orb" (*MPP* 117). Also typical is Mário de Andrade's deflection of the antigrammar assault to the vernacular mode. In his manifesto, "A escrava que não é Isaura," the pursuit of "pure lyricism" liberates words from the "syntactic patrol" (GMT 306).

But the attack on grammar, and the orality-writing dichotomy that sustains it, represents more than a romantic rebellion against rules and responds to specific historical circumstances. Certainly these activities reconsider the interaction between oral and literate cultures inscribed in the original European-indigenous encounter. They also address the long-standing struggle between centripetal and centrifugal linguistic forces, or what Angel Rama described in *La ciudad letrada* as a struggle for literate control of cultural information embodied in the "lettered city" of Latin American life and the democratizing elements within it. As Haroldo de Campos suggests in addressing Brazilian *modernismo*, a literary focus on oral culture resonates in special ways for societies with large illiterate populations in which to write and speak well are signifiers of privilege and keys to social mobility ("Uma poética" 30). Thus the vanguards' recuperative linguistic undertakings constitute a pragmatic rapprochement between the language of literature and the language of everyday life and underscore language's complicity in social conflict.

This feature becomes most evident in works that allegorize and invert colonialist exercises in linguistic control. If we look one more time, for example, at Guillén's poem "Llegada," which announces the arrival of black language and experience into contemporary Cuban culture, we can see the inversion of a prior encounter. In their first arrival into this Western literate society, blacks controlled neither language nor cultural information. "Llegada" announces, however, the poems (in *Sóngoro cosongo* and in *Motivos de son* before it) that will seek to empower the surviving oral tradition by "bringing it into writing" (Clifford) and to underscore the role that language played in that first encounter. Thus the power to tell that story belongs to those who take possession of the word. Similarly, the Brazilian "Antropófago" manifesto, which inverts European primitivism through a "bad savage" who ingests that culture for his own ends, portrays a historic encounter in linguistic terms. Here Father Vieira, a Portuguese Jesuit colonizer and master of the spoken and written word, takes control of illiterate native inhabitants as Brazilian sugar is "signed away" (GMT 355; LB 39). But the manifesto, like the illiterate king with whom he dealt, appropriates Father Vieira's *lábia* ("lip" or "gift of gab") and retells the story with the inelegant Brazilian Portuguese supported by Antropofagia members, imbuing it with the power of the written word.

In an Andean context, vanguardist *indigenista* writers sought to invert the linguistic terms of the colonial encounter by using Quechua and Aymara words and concepts in their poetry and by writing Spanish to conform to indigenous phonology, just as the Spanish colonizers had transliterated indigenous languages through written Spanish. Gamaliel Churata's surrealist novel *El pez de oro* presents the most striking inversion story, as an autodiegetic narrative voice assumes the form of the totemic Golden Puma to retell Columbus's landing. The account interweaves words from Columbus's written diary with a variety of oral indigenous verse forms constituting the Andean world's oral account of the event as a natural catastrophe. Mário's *Macunaíma*, as I have noted, enacts an even more intricate reversal, as the eponymous hero, whose spoken language brings into writing an amalgam of Brazilian colloquialisms, parodies the language of the Portuguese explorers to describe for those at home in the virgin forest his adventures in modern São Paulo. The variety of linguistic registers in Macunaíma's letter gives testimony to the complicity of language in cross-cultural encounters. His patronizing description of the *paulistas'* language inverts the discovering culture's written account of the oral language spoken by a group it considers inferior, a situation that calls to mind defining as barbarians those who do not speak the conqueror's language. The description also lays out the hierarchy between orality and writing circumscribing such engagements.

Nas conversas, utilizam-se os paulistanos dum linguajar bárbaro e multifário, crasso de feição e impuro na vernaculidade, mas que não deixa de ter o seu sabor e força nas apóstrofes, e também nas vozes do brincar. . . . Mas si de tal desprezível língua se utilizam na conversação os naturais desta terra, logo que

tomam da pena, se despojam de tanta asperidade, e surge o Homem Latino, de
Lineu, exprimindo-se numa outra linguagem, mui próxima da vergiliana, no
dizer dum panegirista, meigo idioma, que, com imperescível galhardia, se inti-
tula: língua de Camões! (84)

(In their conversations the Paulistas use a barbarous and multifarious dialect,
uncouth and polluted with colloquialisms, but which does not lack gusto and
forcefulness in figures of speech and coital idioms. . . . But although such vulgar
and ignoble language is used in conversation, as soon as the natives of these
parts pick up a pen, they divest themselves of such crudities and emerge every
whit as Homo latinus (Linnaeus), expressing themselves in another language,
closer to that of Virgil, to speak as a eulogist in a mellow tongue which, full as
it is of everlasting grace, could be called—the language of that immortal bard—
Camões!) (EAG 78)

But vanguardist linguistic undertakings also characterize language as
the instrument of confrontation in more contemporary social situations. In the manifesto "Dos perspectivas," for example, Cuadra spelled
out the historical setting for the Nicaraguan vanguardists' linguistic nationalism: the need to create and preserve national language because of
the invasion by "a different race" and an "interventionist civilization"
(50A 27). Thus Cuadra's "Poema del momento extranjero en la selva"
establishes its telluric link with ancestral voices not only to construct a
fiction of linguistic identity but also to offer a form of resistance to U.S.
involvement in Nicaraguan affairs in the 1920s and 1930s. Guillén's
"Pequeña oda a un negro boxeador cubano" allegorizes the confrontation of culture and class between a black Cuban and Yankee urban modernity through the tale of a boxer on Broadway in which linguistic
punches mingle with the more palpable kind. In these lines, the match
is posed through language: "Your English / only a bit more shaky than
your feeble Spanish / is good enough inside the ring / for you to un-
derstand that filthy slang / spit from the jaws of those you waste / jab
by jab" (OP 119; RM 55). The poem concludes that while Europe
seeks black culture through music, the Cuban may vaunt his heritage
pugilistically by speaking "in black for real" (OP 120).[28]
    Several of Oswald's Pau Brasil poems portray sociolinguistic stand-
offs. The poem "o gramático" ironically contrasts how blacks using
colloquialisms and a learned grammarian would tell the same story.
Similarly, "pronominais" contrasts two ways of requesting a cigarette:
in the grammatical speech of a professor, a student, and a "knowing"
mulatto or in the everyday language of the "Brazilian nation" as spoken
by the "good black" and the "good white" (Poesias reunidas 114).
Other vanguardist works take these grammatical confrontations to the

street on a grand scale, situating them within social and artistic hierarchies of the epoch. Thus Huidobro's satirical play *En la luna* dramatizes the relationship between language and power in an endless sequence of political coups marked by each group's seizure of linguistic control and display of verbal virtuosity. Mário's "As enfibraturas do Ipiranga," the poetic performance manifesto concluding the *Paulicéia desvairada* collection, presents an oratorio in verse that characterizes its São Paulo participants by verbal style, social class, and aesthetic position. The oratorio, set initially on the esplanade of São Paulo's Municipal Theater, is also to be performed from diverse sections of the city designating the class of its participants. As a multivocal linguistic event, this piece represents language as the contentious site of cultural change. In a more humorous vein, similar lines are drawn by the Nicaraguan performance piece *Chinfonía burguesa* by Pasos and Coronel Urtecho. Here, too, characters' varied styles embody social positions or attitudes, of the bourgeoisie, the outmoded *modernista* artist, and a popular tradition epitomized in the irreverent language of the maid that dominates in the piece.

Oswald took the fight against grammar to the streets in the three-scene radically experimental play *A morta* (1937), dramatizing the struggle of a lyric poet to break with aestheticism and reengage his art with the world. As I have described in the chapter on theater, in scene 2, "The Land of Grammar," an urban battle between "moribund" linguistic norms and the "living" language of speech unfolds in the context of Western bourgeois values and traditions. Protagonists in this scene are linguistic forms engaged in a clamorous battle for control: the "dead," including fixed phrases, grave interjections, lustrous adjectives, and seignorial archaisms, and their "living" opponents, including gallicisms, solecisms, and barbarisms. Cremators support these living "characters," advocates of linguistic and social renewal, while a policeman maintains order and shores up the dead who are also backed by conventional politics, the press, industry, and literature. Here the pursuit of oral language reveals the social interactions intertwined with linguistic processes, in a scene that equates aesthetic renewal through language with the impulse for social change.

Roberto Arlt and Mário de Andrade both characterized language as the locus of contentious change through irreverent approaches to etymology. The etymological enterprise harbors both normative and dissident potential. Traditional etymological activity carries with it the normative and metaphysical impulses of comparative philology. The underlying myth sustaining the etymological enterprise was often the dream of a common original language also prevalent in vanguardist poetic quests but discredited by modern historical linguistics. In addition, the search for older versions and meanings of words betrays a prejudice that the oldest form is somehow the truest and the most correct, an attitude also inherent in traditional approaches to teaching grammar. Moreover, etymology's filiation with comparative philology and the latter's textual tradition align etymology with the power of the written word despite the changes brought about in language by speech. Arlt and Mário both debunked etymology's normative features and redirected etymological inquiry toward complex social and historical developments implicit in language change. They also pointed etymology toward contemporary usage and away from linguistic preservation in written texts.

In his *aguafuertes* articles on Buenos Aires language, Arlt attacked grammarians ("the dusty and bad-tempered gang of library rats") and characterized everyday speech as the inventive source of creative and changing ideas (*OC* 2: 487). His etymological analyses of Buenos Aires colloquialisms do briefly compare Spanish and Italian sources, but his language stories move from past to present in a direction contrary to that of classical etymology. Primarily he examined these words as they are used in contemporary life and provided rich material on sociolinguistic contexts through anecdotes about specific situations and speakers. These stories and their transpositions into Arlt's novels suggest a language constantly in flux and resistant to grammatical or lexical norms. Most important, in Arlt's view, language develops through human exchange and through contentious interaction for control of word and context. Arlt's pugilistic metaphor echoes Guillén's: the grammarian is well trained in the grammatical scholasticism of boxing, whereas the inventive Buenos Aires speaker throws punches "from all angles" (*OC* 2: 486).

As one comes to expect from this work, Mário's *Macunaíma* parodies etymology's penchant for fixing definitive moments of linguistic change. In the course of his São Paulo ventures, Macunaíma, still struggling to learn spoken Brazilian and written Portuguese, racks his brain to remember the word for buttonhole when a young woman places a flower in his lapel. He improvises with an obscenity, and, to the consternation of philologists, his linguistic innovation, the shift from *botoeira* to *puíto* (roughly, "buttonhole" to "arsehole" in Goodland's translation) catches on and spreads rapidly through São Paulo. Learned articles explain the change through the laws of "catalepsy, ellipsis, syncope, metonymy, metaphony, metathesis, proclesis, prothesis, aphaeresis, apocope, haplology and popular etymology." Thus etymologists trace a change that actually results from Macunaíma's proclivity for the obscene back to its "classical" (and legitimizing) sources: "the word 'buttonhole' had become transmuted into the word 'arsehole' via an intermediate Greek word, 'bumphole.' . . . But although the word 'bumphole' had never been found in any medieval documents, the highbrows swore it had existed and had been current in vulgar speech" (89; EAG 82–83).

Though diverse in tone and style, these contestations of normative forces in language all focus on the intricacies of language usage, the contingencies of history and society entangled with language change, and the power issues at work in tensions between norms and innovation. These language stories also call attention to the multiple and unstable ways in which language can mean, an enterprise that fundamentally undercuts the vanguards' own ideal of linguistic unity, whether this ideal is motivated by vernacular concerns or informed by more universalist claims.

POLYPHONY, DISSONANCE, IMPURITY

I showed earlier that vanguardist discourse on primal, original language often projects an ideal of linguistic unity that will somehow eradicate the differences among mutually unintelligible languages. Any language, in this view, is translatable into any other language, because, as Huidobro put it, "new events remain identical in all languages" (OC 1: 677), or, in the words of Venezuelan José Antonio Ramos Sucre, "a language is the universe translated into that language" (MPP 161). In Bakhtinian terms, this language (of poetry, he would say) is sufficient unto itself and assigns meaning "without quotation marks" that might bear witness to alien presences. But, at the same time, the vanguardist dialogue on language undermines its own ideal by persistently tracking down whatever in language remains inaccessible or difficult to comprehend. In fact, vanguardist works and language activities, even some with no explicit autochthonous agenda, work to incorporate the linguistically alien, not to make it completely intelligible but rather to keep it always slightly out of reach.

In his essay "The Task of the Translator," Walter Benjamin addressed contradictory qualities in language relationships that are revealed by translation. Languages, Benjamin argued, are "a priori and apart from all historical relationships, interrelated in what they want to express" (72). This "kinship" is not the equivalent to "likeness" but is based on the similarities of intention brought out by the project of translation. According to Benjamin, translation thus reveals ideals of a "pure language" and a longing for "linguistic complementation" in "the great motif of integrating many tongues into one true language," into a tensionless "language of truth" (73–78). This yearning for one true language that Benjamin described certainly recalls the vanguardist quest for a unified linguistic purity. But he also argued that the act of translation is a provisional way of "coming to terms with the foreignness of languages" (75) and that the necessity of translation itself rests on language's historical and actual plurality (75).

Vanguardist language activities in Latin America underscore the alien in language through deliberate exercises in Bakhtinian heteroglossia that foreground linguistic plurality. Antônio Alcântara Machado, editor of the Brazilian *Revista de Antropofagia*, invoked this principle in the context of linguistic identity: "The Portuguese Language is not the common patrimony of the race. First because there is not race but races. Second because there is not language but languages" ("Vaca" 1). But plurality also develops in more concretely aesthetic terms. Countering the imagined linguistically pristine space, hostile like Krauss's visual grid to the intrusion of actual speech, vanguardist manifestos and creative texts fashion polyphonic images in the Bakhtinian sense, that is, through the orchestration of multiple voices, often not harmonious. This concept of polyphony appears frequently in vanguardist manifestos and challenges the also common vanguardist goal, particularly in *ultraísmo*, of distilling language into a single synthetic image or metaphor. These writers conceived multivoicing as the polyphonous orchestration not only of actual voices but also of discrete linguistic elements, such as words, sounds, or rhythms. Thus Alberto Hidalgo's early poetic manifesto "La nueva poesía" spells out the polyphony metaphor, already with dissonant notes: "may our verses be sonorous and polyphonous / but not make the sound of crystal flutes" (*MPP* 48). Early Puerto Rican manifestos posit the concept of "polyrhythm" embracing a diversity of ideas and images (*MPP* 30). Mário explained in the "Prefácio interessantíssimo" manifesto the concept of poetic polyphony using a simultaneous overlay of disconnected phrases (*PC* 23; *JT* 12). In the "La poesía" manifesto, Huidobro described a comparable weaving together of voices through the words that have been "enemies since the beginning of the world" (*OC* 1: 655). And the Mexican *estridentistas* described "pure poetry" as a succession of "orchestrally systematized" images suggestive of varied ideological phenomena and emotional states (*MPP* 158).

Creative texts organized through multiple voicing strengthen this image of linguistic plurality. Many are organized around specific musical metaphors or principles. Musical features certainly abound in Spanish American *modernismo* and Brazilian symbolism and Parnassianism, which preceded the vanguardist movements. Although there are similarities in this musical interest, the emphasis shifts in the vanguardist works. In the earlier periods, the emphasis on musical elements derived from a driving interest in poetic form and sensory effects. In general, writers in the vanguards draw on musical motifs and structures more for their multiple voicing potential. These voices are to engage in a dialogue that maintains their discreteness rather than merges them into one. Thus the words (or voices) that have been hostile since the beginning of time, to extend Huidobro's metaphor, remain distinct or even antagonistic. This is certainly true in Mário's "As enfibraturas do Ipiranga," the oratorio in verse I have described, which brings together with distinct styles, tones, and aesthetic attitudes voices from diverse social classes in São Paulo, and in the Nicaraguan *Chinfonía burguesa* with its counterposition of bourgeois, aestheticist, and popular voices with distinct approaches to art and life.[29] Colombia's de Greiff consistently organized poems in *Tergiversaciones* (1925) and *Libro de signos* (1930) around musical motifs. Sections of these often lengthy compositions, for example, "Esquicio No. 2 Suite en Do Mayor," mark changes in tone or style ascribed to poetic speakers or shifting musical voices. The numbered sections of this composition include "Praeludium," "Scherzo," "Nenia," "Baladetta," "Giga," "Chacona," "Canción," "Serena," "Zarabanda," and "Final: Erumna." Reinforcing the polyphonous image, these musical forms are drawn from a variety of classical and autochthonous registers. Guillén's *Motivos de son* collection draws on a specific musical form, the Cuban *son*, that by definition requires multiple voicings, a principal (and sometimes secondary) voice that emits the main part of the composition (the *motivo* or the *letra*) and the multiple voices (*coro* or *estribillo*) that reply to the principal voice. These voicings correspond also to the varied musical instruments playing the *son*.[30] In Puerto Rico, musical metaphors and multiple voicings also characterize poetic experiments by Palés Matos and de Diego Padró. These include the combination of animal sounds in "Orquestación

diepálica" by both writers and the juxtaposition of these with sounds
of nature, the city, and musical instruments in "Fugas diepálicas" by
de Diego Padró alone. Also in the musical mode, Mário designated
Macunaíma a rhapsody, alluding in part to the novel's piecing together
of countless forms of Brazilian Portuguese and popular speech.

But vanguardist texts do not always organize their multiple voicings
under an all-encompassing musical metaphor, and music itself might
constitute simply one language of many. Alejo Carpentier's experimental theatrical piece *Manita en el suelo* (1931), for example, a one-act
opera buffa from the Cuban popular tradition, pieces together fragments from a variety of oral and musical spheres: prayers, common poetry, popular refrains and sayings, songs, *sones,* and *décimas.* In a different mode and cultural context, Argentine Oliverio Girondo's six-part
poematic prose piece "Semana Santa" from the collection *Calcomanías*
(1925) interweaves bells, prayers, dialogues, and vendors' refrains
heard by the poetic speaker during Holy Week in Seville. In Mexico,
Xavier Icaza's experimental novel *Panchito Chapopote* tells Panchito's
story through a variety of voices bombarding the contemporary Mexican scene: languages of Mexican *corridos,* of political and revolutionary
rhetoric, of the petroleum industry, of the media, of popular refrains
and local gossip, and even of two parrots who overhear key character
conversations. Individual entries in Oquendo de Amat's *5 metros de
poemas* display multiple linguistic registers through a typographically
diverse visual panorama reminiscent of Apollinaire's *Calligrammes,*
Huidobro's "cubist" poems, and futurist typographical experiments.
Several pieces of this kind present urban panoramas. Although the most
striking visual element in these poems is their distribution of words to
form the "picture" of a city, cityscapes are constructed from verbal artifacts synthesizing lyricism with media idioms and imagery and impinging on contemporary urban life, as in the lines from "new york" shown
in the figure on the following page.

The effect of these compendiums of multiple languages, verbal
styles, or musical rhythms is rarely harmonic. Rather these works record
the proliferation of separate languages that are not always mutually intelligible even when they are in direct dialogue. Certain works address
this problem thematically, for example, through bilingualism. Guillén's
"Tú no sabe inglé" ("You Don't Know English") recounts a linguistic
and sexual misunderstanding (portrayed through a bilingual pun) between a Cuban man and a North American woman. Cuadra's bilingual
and ironically entitled "Intervención" enacts a comparable scene of lan-

Los árboles pronto romperán sus amarras
y son ramos de flores todos los policías

CONEY ISLAND	WALL STREET
La lluvia es una moneda de afeitar	La brisa dobla los tallos
	de las artistas de la
	Paramount

El tráfico
escribe
una carta de novia

<pre>
                          T
                          I
                          M
                          E
Los teléfonos   I   Diez corredores
son depósitos de licor   S   desnudos en la Underwood
                          M
                          O
                          N
                          E
                          Y
</pre>

Top center: Soon the trees will break their ties / And all the policemen are flower bouquets; *top left:* CONEY ISLAND / The rain is a coin for shaving; *top right:* WALL STREET / The breeze bends the stems / Of the Paramount stars; *center: The traffic / writes / a bride's letter; bottom left:* Telephones / are liquor depots; *bottom right:* Ten runners / naked on the Underwood

guage encounter with a big-footed gringo and a gringa with honey hair: "Tell the yankee: / *go jón* / And the gringuita: / *veri güel*" (*50A* 115). Also in Nicaragua, José Román's bilingual "Preludio a Managua en B Flat," subtitled "with accompaniments in English," deploys the musical metaphor in a bilingual mode to document the alien presences in that city and including even a "Dios English Speaking" (an "English Speaking God") (*50A* 120; English in original). These works address the confusion and conflict provoked by linguistic interventions rather than the desirability or accuracy of given forms. Similarly, Oswald de Andrade's "vício na fala" ("vice in speech") from the *Pau Brasil* collection carries out an ironic exercise in translation between "correct" and "incorrect" speech: "To say *milho* they say *mio* / For *melhor* they say mió / For *pior pió*" (*Poesias reunidas* 80). In the long poetic composition "Noturno de Belo Horizonte," Mário portrays Brazil's multiple verbal modes, including the propensity of some to speak "lackadaisical, untroubled," of the *cariocas* to "scratch the r's in the throat," and of the *capixabas* to "widen the vowels" (*PC* 136).

These texts build a heterogeneous and alien image of language resistant to the dreams of universality or purity so evident in much avantgarde discourse on language. Not surprisingly, then, the Tower of Babel, a provocative alternative to the aestheticist ivory towers of autonomous art, appears as a repeated motif. Framers of the second *euforista* manifesto, for example, call on poets to "raise the Tower of Babel" of their thinking in order to "unite the races" through language from the Yukon to the pampas (*MPP* 127). On a more critical note, however, the calligraphic poem "Babel" by Chile's Próspero Rivas is visually arranged in the form of a pyramid-style tower. As Klaus Müller-Bergh points out, this poem employs the Babel metaphor to challenge modern Faustian dreams of aesthetic control ("El hombre y la técnica" 290). Directing the metaphor to the linguistic difference inscribed in the biblical source, Mário's "Jorobabel" protests with greater anguish against modern human misunderstanding and disconnection: "Clamor! Nobody understands one another! A God does not come! . . . Babel!" (*PC* 90). A more aesthetic emphasis and ironic tone permeate the Babel motif in "Charcos," a short poem by Salvador Novo of Mexico's Contemporáneos group, although this poem's vision of modernity is not unlike Rivas's. Here the poetic speaker contrasts the totalizing quests of a subjectivist Western aesthetic tradition with the relativism of a Babelic modern life. In the former milieu, poets reaching for the heavens show signs of a decadent tradition with "heavy tongues." In contrast, the modern poet faces a more fragmented scene of relativity in both the natural and human worlds: "But a stone / (Oh Einstein) / Made a thousand bats fly / from the Tower of Babel" (*INPA* 205). Both Mário and Novo employ the allusion to Babel to intimate a human fall through language and a relativistic view of language itself. But vanguardist discourse also often portrays linguistic disunity, manifested in the dissonance of "impure" words, as the very goal that writers pursue.

Cultivating linguistic impurities derives in part from the vanguards' studied avoidance of the banal, an orientation revealed in stands against the language of everyday life taken by Huidobro and the *ultraístas* as well. The value of poetic language, according to Huidobro, is directly proportional to its distance from the language that people speak (*OC* 1: 654–55). Borges wrote in the *ultraísmo* manifesto that to "displace everyday language toward literature is a mistake" (*MPP* 113). On the surface, then, the numerous efforts to bring spoken language and oral forms into writing would appear antithetical in spirit and intent to *creacionismo* and *ultraísmo* ideals. But these apparently antagonistic projects are akin in pursuing what is alien or not ordinary. Although vanguardists with autochthonous goals sought through oral traditions an image of unisonant national identity, they were simultaneously drawn to the spoken word's strident chords for communicating in a critical mode the radical dissonance of specific experience, contemporary and/or vernacular. Thus these writers engaged in a form of cultural or social translation, bringing specific linguistic forms, designated on one level as familiar and collectively "ours," into profoundly unfamiliar literary contexts and to readers for whom they would be strange. In the process, they called attention to language's alien substance and, in the Bakhtinian sense, deliberately spoke "with quotation marks."

Images of dissonance or impurity abound in vanguardist language tales. Thus, in the "Prefácio interessantíssimo" manifesto that lays out the project of poetic polyphony, Mário lauded "the great enchantment of dissonance" (*PC* 24), and, within their "decalogue," Puerto Rico's *atalayistas* constructed a small manifesto of disharmony: "The screeching of a crank door opening is as melodious as the sighing of a flute. The ripping of a sensual dress is more hypnotizing than a Beethoven symphony" (*MPP* 356). In a more musical but still discordant vein, Mexico's Jaime Torres Bodet, in an ars poetica composition "Música," contrasted the purity of creation in the abstract—a "music" learned in the "pure language" and "notes of silence" on the keys of a "mute instrument"—with the dissonant notes of creation executed in greater contact with life—"between irascible zithers and flutes, what I dreamed of as sonnet wounds me as symphony" (*Obras escogidas* 38–39).[31]

Not infrequently, vanguardists actively sought out the discordant, the impure, and the deliberately incorrect. The Dominican Republic *postumista* manifesto rejects the notion of "poetic words" (*MPP* 110), and Puerto Rico's *euforistas* extended this idea to proclaim a verse "full of defects, harsh and coarse" (*MPP* 124). Writers with vernacular goals were especially drawn to defects and saw linguistic impurities and mistakes as the raw material of invention. Thus Oswald's "Pau-Brasil" manifesto, in pursuing "language without archaisms, without erudition," and "natural and neologic," also praises "the millionaire-contribution of all the errors" (GMT 327; SMSR 185). Oswald's language poems that I have cited, in particular, "vício na fala" (vice in speech), defiantly bring "incorrect" language into the literary field. In the same spirit, Manuel Bandeira's poematic manifesto "Poética" assaults "the purists" of linguistic correction and praises "universal barbarisms," "the exceptional syntactical construction," and the "difficult and pungent lyricism of drunks" (*BMP* 66). In "Evocação de Recife," his poetic speaker equates the "erroneous idiom of the people" with the "correct idiom" (*BMP* 71). Guillén is particularly drawn to those elements in the language of Cuban *pregoneros* (street vendors) that evolve from the deliberate creative mistake, for example, the cry promoting "mantecao de aguacate" (avocado ice cream) because it rhymes with his refrain for "crema e' chocolate" (cream and chocolate) (*Prosa de prisa* 1: 26). Similarly, the Nicaraguan "Cartelón de vanguardia" counterpoises the "linguistic purism" it rejects with "linguistic invention" and "the dirty word" (*50A* 173). Mário's Macunaíma counters his adversary's massive collection of precious stones with an international array of dirty words, and the narrator retelling Macunaíma's story employs the "impure speech" of the Brazilian people (168).[32]

In the context of vanguardist poetry, critics normally associate the idea of "impurity," as opposed early on by Huidobro, with Pablo Neruda's memorable manifesto "Sobre una poesía sin pureza" (Toward an Impure Poetry), published in 1935 toward the end of Latin America's vanguardist period.[33] Here Neruda describes a poetry of contact by "man with the earth" and with the material objects of experience. From these, he explains, poets have much to learn. "Used surfaces," their "wearing away," the "prints of the foot and the finger" can express the "confused impurity" of human beings (*HV* 259). For some this manifesto marks a gradual shift in Neruda's work, particularly from the second stage of the *Residencia de la tierra* cycle (1933–35), to a more down-to-earth style.[34] Others associate the concept of impurity with his poetry's hermetic qualities, characterized early on by Amado Alonso as the "poetics of disintegration" in the *Residencia* collection.[35] In either case, some *Residencia* poems express the manifesto's concept of impurity by speaking directly about language. The poem "Sabor," for example, anticipates the manifesto's idea of an experiential "wearing away" in the image of "conversations worn out like used wood" (*OC* 1: 178).[36] There is certainly some similarity between this impurity as defined by Neruda and its manifestations in more broadly based vanguardist discourse, particularly in Neruda's thoughts about a poetry contaminated by the messiness of human experience. But there is also a difference in emphasis. Neruda's "impure poetry" as outlined in his manifesto focuses less on a specific image of language itself and more on how poetic language might express in more accessible ways the impurities of the human condition.

While the activities I have been describing manifest a profound interest in "disarticulated" experience, the images of dissonance and impurity they construct point to the alien and the nonorganic qualities of language itself and its potential to speak with quotation marks. There is a deliberate favoring of "bad language," not simply of dirty words like the ones Macunaíma or the Nicaraguan vanguardists collect but of the kind of *fala impura* (impure speech) used to sing Macunaíma's tale. Vanguardist discourse on language often emphasizes the critical potential of the impurities themselves, the markers of alterity that, like pauses, puns, slips of the tongue, murmurs, echoes, and creative mistakes, interrupt the smooth flow of discourse and make comprehension for listeners or readers a deliberately discontinuous and arduous experience.

Although he did not explicitly theorize in these terms, the major Latin American poet whose work of the vanguard period probably most completely embodies the approach I have just described is Peru's César Vallejo. Particularly in his most hermetic collection, *Trilce,* Vallejo transformed language drawn from the quotidian realm into the radically inaccessible. Here linguistic difficulty, played out in the poetry's fragmented syntax, morphological distortions, neologisms with colloquial roots, and vocabulary from multiple nonliterary contexts, traces a tortuous course that links poetic speaker and reader. The speaker's verbal virtuosity and the language's deceptive proximity to words from everyday life notwithstanding, language in *Trilce* remains irrevocably alien and hard to assimilate, as in these lines from the work's first poem: "Un poco más de consideración / y el mantillo líquido, seis de la tarde / DE LOS MAS SOBERBIOS BEMOLES" (43) (A little more consideration, / and the humus liquidates, six in the afternoon / OF THE MOST ARROGANT B FLATS [RS 5]).[37] As Jean Franco points out, this poetry provides "involuntary revelations offered by language itself which is never completely controlled by the speaker" (121). Christiane von Buelow's brilliant reading of poem number xxxvi in *Trilce* presents this piece as a vanguardist "nonorganic" work (in Bürger's terms) and (in Benjamin's) an allegory of linguistic fragmentation enacted through the critical "dismemberment" of the Venus de Milo as the symbol of romantic, symbolist, and Spanish American *modernista* aesthetic perfection. Most pertinent to my points about the vanguardist focus on linguistic dissonance and impurity are von Buelow's observations about Vallejo's practices of "grammatical mutation" and "verbal decomposition," his deliberate obstruction of musicality through "stammering fragments," and the fact that his use of metaphor is limited almost always to catachresis, that is, to the deliberate misuse of language (44, 47–48).[38] Von Buelow also suggests that this work's "grammatical and semantic ruins" (the linguistic equivalent of the visual ruins of the Venus de Milo) manifest a dialectical process of reconstruction. On the one hand, these evoke the artwork's (and, I would add, language's) imperfection and, on the other hand, they manifest a will to knowledge, to a "linguistic truth always about to emerge" (50). The discourse on language I have been describing throughout this chapter manifests a comparable continuing tension between images of a transcendent linguistic unity and purity and the unending attraction to language's foreign substance and the critical power released by its deliberate misuse against the norms of its historical moment.

Although critics have often ascribed a deeply structured autochthony to Vallejo's poetry, his was not a deliberately vernacular project, and, in fact, Vallejo himself rejected the idea of self-consciously vernacular art.[39] In contrast, Asturias almost always wrote in a studied vernacular mode. But Asturias also addressed the language issues we see dramatized in Vallejo's poetry, and his decontextualized autochthonous work may also be read allegorically. Regardless of the genre he undertakes, Asturias's writing is highly lyrical, and he tells his most important story about language not in poetry but in a difficult and highly experimental play drawn from pre-Columbian sources. That story, with which I now conclude, dramatizes in visually memorable scenes the language problems that preoccupied Asturias and his vanguardist contemporaries.

A Play of Linguistic Confusion: Asturias's *Cuculcán*

Asturias's *Cuculcán,* a dramatic collage of color, sound, motion, and words, is his most overtly ethnographic play and, as a product of his vanguardist years, the most radically experimental. *Cuculcán* did not appear in print until 1948,[40] but Asturias described the work in progress in a 1932 essay, "Las posibilidades de un teatro americano."[41] Like the *Leyendas de Guatemala* collection to which it was eventually added, *Cuculcán* draws on the *Popol Vuh* and the books of

Chilam Balam. James Clifford, who has documented the interaction between ethnography and art in the European avant-gardes, argues that because of its decontextualized quality, deliberately ethnographic writing undertaken either by artists or anthropologists is always allegorical *(Writing Culture).* Certainly in Latin America this situation was somewhat different because writers with ethnographic interests were responding to the non-Western cultures that, on some level, constituted part of their own milieu. Latin American artists, as I have documented, drew on ethnographic material in part to affirm the intrinsic worth of these cultures and their unofficial languages. But they also used this material allegorically to speak more broadly about culture, art, and language. In this vein, Asturias's *Cuculcán,* through its linguistic theme, brings together the dialogue between Huidobro's *Altazor* and Asturias's own *Leyendas*—the dialogue with which I began this chapter—and dramatizes the vanguardist concerns about language encompassed in that exchange.

    Described by Richard Callan as a chromatic ballet (124), the play enacts a series of encounters between the supreme plumed serpent god Cuculcán (likened in power to the sun) and the Guacamayo, the false god Vukub Cakix and a verbal trickster embodied in a parrot of many colors.[42] The piece is organized into three sets of three alternating *cortinas* (or curtains)—yellow, red, and black. These colors correspond to stages in the sun's daily journey through the sky and are reflected in the colors of onstage curtains and the clothing and accoutrements of Cuculcán and his warriors. Other participants in the encounter between Cuculcán and the Guacamayo include Yaí and Chinchibirín. Yaí, a yellow flower sometimes linked to the moon in Mayan myth, has been destined since birth to mate with the supreme god and then be cast aside. Chinchibirín, a yellow warrior serving Cuculcán, loves Yaí from afar.

    Cuculcán incorporates these characters and others into a series of interlocking dialogues and displays of color, light, sound, and dance to enact a sustained debate on the nature of the worlds they inhabit between Cuculcán and the Guacamayo. Declaring repeatedly "I am like the sun," Cuculcán affirms the palpable permanence of the world manifested in the cyclical re-creation of each day (54). The Guacamayo, or "Gran Saliva del Espejo" (Great Saliva of the Mirror), as he is called, harasses Cuculcán and his retinue with a repetitive "Acucúac, acucúac" and by endlessly asserting the transitory and illusory nature of a reality intertwined with language, "a game of mirrors, of words" (87). "What is seen is seen and is not a fiction!" declares Cuculcán's warrior, Chinchibirín (63). "Nothing exists," the Guacamayo contradicts, "all is a dream in the immobile mirage" (57). Although the play does not resolve this debate, more often than not, the Guacamayo's version of reality prevails, as Yaí's union with the supreme god is portrayed as a fall from innocence that attests to the parrot's verbal power.[43] Yaí seeks to defend her illusion of love's permanence against her fate to be with Cuculcán for only one night, but, verbally seduced by the Guacamayo, she becomes like him, "word wrapped in words" (86). The parrot offers Yaí paradoxical counsel on love: "It is eternal, but not in the Palace of the Sun, in the Palace of the Senses, where, like all things, it passes, it changes!" (87). The final dance between Cuculcán and Yaí is performed as a fleeting encounter between the sun and the moon, a Mayan motif often favored by Asturias.

The play's title names the supreme plumed serpent god, but the piece focuses more consistently on the Guacamayo who frequently steals the scene. Either in person or through the colors and the retinue that represent him, Cuculcán is omnipresent. But the Guacamayo is far more active on stage as he disrupts the vast and orderly universe that Cuculcán embodies. Visually, kinetically, and, above all, linguistically, the contrasts between the two figures are sharply drawn. The larger-than-life Cuculcán appears on stilts, appropriate to his royal stature. The Guacamayo, according to stage directions, is "the size of a man" and appears initially "standing on the ground" (54). Cuculcán traverses the stage with "priestlike movements" (80), and his rhythmical, circular dance with Yaí emulates the periodic motion of heavenly bodies. By contrast, the Guacamayo's movements are playful, erratic, and clumsy, as he spins around, "entangled" and with "childlike joy" (55). Cuculcán's realm changes regularly with the time of day, but, at any given moment, this world is pervasively monochromatic: yellow, red, or black. The Guacamayo, in contrast, a bird of many colors with plumage like a "Rainbow of Deception" (82), is multiple.

But *Cuculcán* is primarily a play about language, a sustained debate about the power of an all-encompassing language sufficient to itself, on the one hand, and the duplicity and foreignness of language and its consequent critical power, on the other. Dorita Nouhaud has suggested that the irreverent Guacamayo incarnates the spirit of the vanguardist poet.[44] I would agree but also argue that both Cuculcán and the Guacamayo personify vanguardist artists, in that they embody the vanguards' contrasting images of language. The Guacamayo may be an incorrigible verbal trickster, but Cuculcán also invariably speaks with the words of a talented lyricist. In fact, many of Cuculcán's traits in this play, in particular, his relationship to language, recall Bakhtin's characterization of aestheticist poetic language as monologic and unified with its author's semantic and expressive intentions (Bakhtin 285). Cuculcán's language, like Krauss's gridlike ground zero of creation, is hostile to the intrusion of alien speech, that is, to Bakhtinian "quotation marks" from others. By contrast, the Guacamayo, who as a parrot by definition speaks with quotation marks, that is, with the words of others, embodies the persistent foreignness of all language. On the visual level, the work's contrapuntal play of colors between a monochromatic Cuculcán and the chromatically volatile Guacamayo renders visually this profound contrast in the two beings' relationship to language. Linked, like Huidobro's Altazor, to the original sources of creation, manifested here through the sun's cyclical re-creation of each day, Cuculcán incarnates the power of a unified and unisonant cosmos. His similarity to the sun links him with the ordering of time and space, but like the absolute power of the vanguardist grid, his sunlike power is also impervious to the temporal and the contingent: "my rays turn into brilliant wasps and I fly to the honeycombs, to then continue on clothed in the yellow of my image which rises from the water without becoming wet and from the honeycombs without burning" (55). In this spirit, Cuculcán's language affirms the scope of his own power and displays a respect for power itself as well as for the language that expresses it. Thus, although the Guacamayo repeatedly tries to trick Cuculcán into a self-exalting identification with the sun ("You are the sun," the Guacamayo proclaims), the supreme god is careful always to compare himself to and never to equate himself with the sun: "I am *like* the Sun" (54; my emphasis).[45] This caution notwithstanding, Cuculcán's unifying language, even as he speaks poetically, circumscribes the orderly natural world of creation that constitutes his domain: "In my morning habitats . . . I am joined . . . by those in charge of the Treasure, of the Gardens, of the Granaries, as they inform me as to what happens in my dominions: whether the clouds have made their beds, . . . whether that which has ripened has not spoiled" (56).

Like the artist who invents a primal language to designate a new world, Cuculcán lays claim to what he names through the frequent use of possessives and affirms the uniformity of his creation: "Yellow is my tree, yellow is my sweet potato, yellow are my turkeys" (74). Cuculcán's language confidently affirms the nature of the world that it names and, in this aspect, epitomizes what Bakhtin describes as the manifestation in aestheticist poetic language of the speaker's drive for linguistic control. We recall Bakhtin's words: "In poetic genres, artistic consciousness—understood as a unity of all the author's semantic and expressive intentions—fully realizes itself within its own language." Cuculcán's frequent use of possessives in naming his world, moreover, links him inextricably with his own language in the Bakhtinian sense: "The language of the poet is *his* language, he is utterly immersed in it, inseparable from it" ("Discourse in the Novel" 284; emphasis in original). Cuculcán's regal demeanor imbues his language with the air of the "priestly language of poetry" Bakhtin ascribes to the aestheticist tradition. Cuculcán's speech is also sometimes characterized by simple declarative pronouncements and repetitions of the verb *to be*, reaffirming the stability of things as Cuculcán defines them. Such statements often exploit the grammatical equation between subject noun and predicate noun ($a = b$), a structure that implies a self-sufficient completeness of the metaphor (solar, in this case) and an equilibrium between the word and the world it evokes, for example, "The yellow flint is the morning stone" (74).[46] Cuculcán's faithful warrior Chinchibirín employs a similar grammatical structure, in which a equals b so totally that the equation could easily be rendered as $a = a$. Thus Chinchibirín intones the creed of Cuculcán's all-encompassing worldview and affirms the unisonance of his creation: "What is *seen is seen* and is not a fiction!" (my emphasis). This linguistic structure, with the quality of a word definition, also foregrounds the desire to fix meanings manifested not only in normative linguistic forces but also in the poet's dream of inventing a language to mean exactly what he wills it to mean.

The Guacamayo's response to Chinchibirín's statement "Let's play with words!" (63) affirms the bird's playful approach to language and undermines the reliability of his own words as well as the linguistic uniformity proclaimed by Cuculcán. As a diviner, a storyteller, and a verbal gymnast, the Guacamayo emerges as the disruptive artist figure in Cuculcán's world and dramatizes the vanguardist fascination with linguistic confusion and difficulty. As the "Great Saliva of the Mirror," the Guacamayo embodies linguistic deceit and impurity. His dissonant speech is described as "*jerigonza*," gibberish that twists the facts, and, in keeping with a *Popol Vuh* story of Vukub Cakix, he suffers from a twisted mouth and a painful toothache from having "chewed so many lies" (62). But though the parrot may be an inveterate liar, the auditory, chromatic, and tactile metaphors and synesthesias that characterize his language emphasize the creative and critical power of his "incorrect" or deliberately misused words. Thus the "bird of enchantment" speaks in a "*jerigonza* of colors" with words like lies "clothed in precious stones." The "rainbow of his voice" emerges from the Guacamayo's feathers, like the "rich plumage and perfect color" of his words. Most significantly, the Guacamayo's "voice of fire" constitutes an acute and acerbic critical force that disrupts the orderly flow of discourse and, as the embodiment of alterity, needles, discomfits, and consumes from within those who hear it (50–86). "Your voice," the yellow warrior Chinchibirín tells the Guacamayo, "fills my soul with ticklings" (60). "Your fine thread of colors," Yaí tells the parrot of his language, "perforated my ears in order to contaminate me within" (92).

If the pronouncements of Cuculcán and his followers affirm the stable nature of creation ("what is seen is seen"), the Guacamayo's words assert the unstable and the discontinuous. "Nothing exists," the parrot likes to quip (57), and he patiently explains to Chinchibirín that the afternoon is an illusion and life itself a "fictitious chain of days that leads to nothing" (92). To Cuculcán's pronouncements about the time-out-of-time permanence of his own creation, the Guacamayo responds with reminders of the historical and the contingent that, like the love between Yaí and Cuculcán, changes and passes. While Cuculcán's language, in the tradition of the priestly poet, shores up his own identity as a supreme creator, the Guacamayo's words undercut in those who hear him any unified sense of being, fragmenting the simulacrum of a single self into the multiple. Such is the parrot's powerful effect on Yaí whose hands are transformed into mirrors by his saliva, or his words, "in order to multiply myself into vain others . . . that are the same as me and that are nothing but an image of myself that I am not" (91).

In keeping with his parrotlike nature, the Guacamayo mimics Cuculcán's orderly syntax, the declarative affirmations that assert a stable word-reality relationship ("The yellow flint is the morning stone"). But the parrot's mimicry is critical, as he appropriates this syntax in semantic paradoxes that assert the existence of nonexistence ("The afternoon is a fiction" [64], "Life is a deception" [60]) or in vanguardist similes that construct a different order of things from that which prevails in Cuculcán's palace: "Women are vegetables" (58). It is precisely by imitating Cuculcán's speech, moreover, that the Guacamayo underscores the heteroglossic in language; unlike Cuculcán's, his speech contains Bakhtinian quotation marks against which his own words may sound, foregrounding the interaction of "alien" speech with his own. Moreover, by parodying the normative quality in Cuculcán's proclivity for self-contained definitions, the Guacamayo appropriates and questions both the centripetal impulse in language and the vanguardist poet's own dream—like Altazor's—of inventing from the void a pure and "uninflected" idiom.

This play's contraposition through characters of contrary approaches to language is reinforced by kinetic elements, staging, and dramatic structure. Cuculcán's "priestly language" of poetry (to quote Bakhtin) is visually reinforced by his "priestlike movements," his regal stature, and his rhythmical dance with Yaí emulating the universe's heavenly bodies. The Guacamayo's erratic, clumsy, and entangling movements duplicate the disruptive and discontinuous quality of his stammering and fragmented speech. In staging, the framing device of alternating series of three sets of curtains marks an unending cyclical repetition, as uniform as Cuculcán's language and as the sun's passage through the sky. By contrast, the play's visual and verbal debates enclosed by this frame enact a volatile world (in which the "fruit run like rabbits") through the interplay of darkness, light, and color and the interweaving of voices, onomatopoetic natural and instrumental sounds, and dancelike actor movements. Thus Cuculcán's orderly journey through the days that imitates the universe's primal movements is transformed by the Guacamayo's presence into a symphonic babble orchestrated by the poetic parrot's linguistic play, as indicated in stage directions: "*dog barks, chicken cacklings, tempest thunderclaps, serpent hissings, troupial, guardabarranca, and mockingbird warblings, are heard as the Guacamayo names them, just as the cry of children, the laughter of women and to close the commotion and chatter of a multitude that passes*" (57).

This cacophonic din invoked by the Guacamayo infects other characters who engage in similar verbal antics. The *Popol Vuh* figure Huaravarix, for example, composes nocturnal songs with wordplays similar in auditory effect to the tongue twisters of vanguardist poets: "¡El Cerbatanero de la Cerbatana de Sauco ha salido del Baúl de los Gigantes que en el fondo tiene arena y sobre la arena, aguarena y sobre la aguarena, agua honda y sobre el agua honda, agua queda y sobre el agua queda, agua verde y sobre el agua verde, agua azul y sobre el agua azul, aguasol y sobre el aguasol, aguacielo!" (69).

Even the powerful Cuculcán himself, in words suggestively echoing Huidobro's Altazor on his disintegrating linguistic quest, succumbs to the game of words in the final encounter with Yaí as they twirl around in opposite directions: "¡Y otra vez girasol de sol a sol, / sol, girasol y gira, girasol!" and, as he describes Yaí, "¡Otra vez picaflor de flor en flor! / Recuerdo de la flor ¿qué fue de la flor?" (97).[47]

Notwithstanding the carefully structured nine *cortinas* that frame it, the play is shaped by an alternating but continuing chain of verbal jousting, between the Guacamayo and Cuculcán, the Guacamayo and Chinchibirín, Chinchibirín and Yaí, the Guacamayo and Yaí, and Yaí and Cuculcán. Chinchibirín remarks that he yearns to "win the meet" with the Guacamayo (63). But winning in *Cuculcán* is based not so much on converting others to one's views as on the virtuosity of the performance and the power of the critique. The idea of a verbal match is reinforced by stage directions that portray Cuculcán's warriors as traders and their confrontation as an unending dance of exchange. The directions for this scene point to the underlying structure of the play itself: "*They enter and exit in interminable formation . . .* , [and] *the battle begins to be announced with strident shouts. The red warriors, by their genuflections, look more like* traders *than warriors. It is a dance of* offers and replies" (80; my emphasis). Interestingly, this reference to the performance of a verbal exchange is repeated in a 1959 piece by Asturias on Mayan elements in a contemporary Guatemalan market, "Lo maya en los mercados guatemaltecos." Echoing the stage directions and recalling the visual display from *Cuculcán*, this bargaining ballet underscores verbal exchange—"a lengthy rosary of offers and rejected demands"—and exalts the virtuosity of the performance—"a dance to the rhythm of the soft murmur of the words that fancy the flight of scores of bees over all of those black heads and bodies of colorful dress appropriate to a ballet" (*América* 256). But the explicit comparison between the verbal jousting of the Guacamayo's world and a linguistic marketplace had already been made in *Cuculcán* by the warrior Chinchibirín: "A market is like a Great Guacamayo, everybody talks, everybody offers colored things, everybody deceives" (75). The marketplace metaphor also suggestively imagines language as a conflictive activity of exchange. Thus, like much vanguardist discourse on language, the verbal commerce between Cuculcán and the Guacamayo— the difficult dialogue itself embodied in the warriors' ballet—posits language, even in its performative lyricism, as the site of contentious social exchange and struggles for power.

We must not forget, however, that *Cuculcán* is an insistently autochthonous work, and it is therefore very tempting to see the Guacamayo's approach to language as the embodiment of the vanguards' vernacular linguistic projects. In such a reading, we can see that the Guacamayo repeatedly disrupts the priestly Cuculcán's self-present and self-sufficient language with the impure, dissonant, and confusing heteroglossic language of alien "quotations," or, to extend the image, of cultural difference. This reading is reinforced by Asturias's own subsequent references to the Guacamayo as the incarnation of Latin American literary language. With strong echoes from the polychromatic, linguistically agile parrot of his play, Asturias suggested in his 1967 Nobel Prize acceptance speech, for example, that Latin American writers had created their own language, that their work constituted a "verbal feat," and that their language itself was "chromatic," "musical," "tactile, plural, and irreverent" (*América* 156, 158). Later, in a 1969 essay, "América, la engañadora," a piece that speaks extensively about a familiar parrot, Asturias recounted the *Popol Vuh's* portrayal of the bird as a colorful verbal trickster. But here he also noted the parrot's role as America's ambassador, as Columbus returned to the Old World with a parrot, not a hawk, on his arm, "a diplomat who to his jacket of live colors adds a tangled speech typical of the dialogue that would follow between Europeans and Americans." This deceptive dialogue, he added, served as a self-protective tactic that allowed Latin America to save itself from exoticism-seeking foreigners by "counterfeiting paradises" (*América* 343).

This reading of *Cuculcán* is plausible but not complete. As I have demonstrated in this chapter, the stories of linguistic encounter in a vernacular mode drew on both kinds of language images that shape vanguardist discourse: the image of linguistic purity and universality ascribed to a "ground zero" of linguistic creation and the linguistic estrangement manifested in polyphony, dissonance, and impurity. Significantly, *Cuculcán's* own drama of linguistic creation incorporates both views into a single primeval event. Thus Cuculcán himself explains that even when the world and its language were emerging for the very first time, confusion, critique, and the Guacamayo were already on the scene.

Su voz. Habla obscuridad. De lejos es lindo su plumaje de alboroto de maíz dorado sobre el mar y la sangre. Todo estaba en las jícaras de la tiniebla revuelto, descompuesto, informe. El silencio rodeaba la vida. Era insufrible el silencio y los Creadores dejaron sus sandalias para significar que no estaban ausentes de los cielos. Sus sandalias o ecos. Pero el Guacamayo, jugando con las palabras, confundió los ecos, sandalias de los dioses. El Guacamayo con su lengua enredó los dioses por los pies, al confundirles sus sandalias, al hacerles andar con los ecos del pie derecho en el pie izquierdo. (75)

His voice. It speaks darkness. From afar his plumage of the disorder of golden corn over the sea and blood is beautiful. Everything was in the gourds of the darkness scrambled, out of order, formless. Silence enveloped life. The silence was insufferable and the Creators left their sandals to signify that they were not absent from the heavens. Their sandals or echoes. But the Guacamayo, playing with words, confused the echoes, sandals of the gods. The Guacamayo with his tongue entangled the gods by their feet, by confusing their sandals, by making them walk with the echoes from the right foot on the left foot.

In fact, this scene should remind us of another: Altazor's initial encounter with his creator who shares the story of inventing language, the scene with which I opened this chapter. Even Altazor's own pursuit of a pure, original word is marred from the outset by the creator's account of primal linguistic confusion: "'I created the tongue of the mouth which man diverted from its role to make it learn to speak'" (*OC* 1: 366; EW 5). In both stories, then, with or without an explicit vernacular inflection, the possibility of a confusing, alien language is always present from the beginning, contaminating the poetic utopia of a pristine linguistic space and its pure, original word.

Conclusion

Asturias's *Cuculcán* tells a story of conflictive interaction between two kinds of language: the autonomous and unisonant language of purity and universality and the discordant language of specific worlds, the languages of power and the languages that challenge power. If this story has a vernacular turn, if it speaks to a specifically Latin American experience, it would be the tale of the linguistic conflict itself, situated in the Mayan marketplace where aesthetic and social debates intersect. But what are we to make in this reading of the alluring figure of the Guacamayo, to which Asturias himself pointed as a cultural icon by naming him in the Nobel speech as the Latin American writer? Asturias intimated a possible answer when he later observed that the Guacamayo on Columbus's arm was America's first cultural ambassador. An ambassador by definition moves between cultural domains, and the ambassador in the linguistic realm is the translator. The translator, as

Benjamin tells us, walks that precarious fine line between what is universal in language—whatever can be said in all languages—and that which remains untranslatable. But the translator's objective is communication from one linguistic and cultural realm to another. The challenge is to work simultaneously with two languages, and so the translator invariably speaks with Bakhtinian quotation marks and, like the mimicking parrot, repeats the words of the original—the other—but inflected by the translator's own intentions and style.

In *The Cuban Condition*, appropriately subtitled *Translation and Identity in Modern Cuban Culture*, Pérez Firmat portrays the contemporary Cuban writer's dilemma (epitomized in Carpentier's *Los pasos perdidos*) as a trap of "linguistic antimony," that is, a "painful and productive indecision between the mother tongue and the other tongue." If the Cuban writer, communicating in alien lands, must "speak in other words," Pérez Firmat concludes that, even in translation, he "finds, and keeps, his word" (157). Although there is a connection between Pérez Firmat's idea and Asturias's Guacamayo as a linguistic and cultural translator, there are important differences of emphasis and kind. As a product of the vanguards, the Guacamayo's "linguistic antimony" does not harbor the painful indecisions ascribed by Pérez Firmat to more contemporary writers. Instead, Asturias's parrot is a more aggressive linguistic ambassador undertaking, in the avant-garde spirit, a specific and affirmative project: to communicate in "universal" contexts, that is, in Cuculcán's royal domain, but also to showcase the untranslatably alien and impure. Like Guillén's Cuban boxer on Broadway and Macunaíma in São Paulo, the Guacamayo speaks aggressively with a will to discomfit his listeners with the difficulty of his words. Mário maps out a similar poetics of willful intractability in his small poetic manifesto "Lundu do escritor difícil," or "Lundu [a lascivious dance] of the difficult writer," published in the *Revista de Antropofagia*. Here with a deliberate "angú de caroço" (porridge or hodgepodge) of Brazilian colloquialisms, the speaker takes his reader to task for aping European culture and language but branding as difficult the poet's "Brazilian" language. The *lundu*'s speaker aggressively assaults the reader with alien words, admonishing that what is difficult is not the words themselves but for the reader to learn what they mean ("Lundu do escritor difícil" 3). In a similar mode, the Guacamayo would force others to hear him, to be aware of his words' alien quality, and, as Yaí complains of the parrot's verbal trickery, to become "infected" or contaminated from within by the strange words.

The Guacamayo's ability to infect the discourse of others is paramount. In his article "European Pedigrees/African Contagions" based on the work of the Nigerians Amos Tutuola and Chinua Achebe and the African-American Ishmael Reed, James Snead argues that writers in the African tradition seem inclined toward a "certain linguistic or cultural eclecticism or *miscegenation*" (232; emphasis in original). The linguistic approach in this writing, Snead concludes, presents a model of contagion in which "all cultures, colors, and nationalities are subject to the ubiquity of its 'pandemic'" (245). Most important, just as the Guacamayo confronts Cuculcán's universalizing language, the intent of these writers is to redefine the idea of "universal." As opposed to Samuel Johnson's concept of language as the "pedigree of nations" that sought to "discover lost but recoverable national *differences*," Snead argues, "contagion represents the existence of recoverable *affinities* between disparate races of people" (245).

As a linguistic translator, the Guacamayo operates in a somewhat comparable fashion to embody the exercises in aggressive cultural and linguistic diplomacy undertaken by Latin America's vanguardist writers with a vernacular agenda. In recuperating an ancestral voice and linguistic essences, these writers appealed to romantic models of cultural nationalism that affirmed the unisonant differences of specific Latin American identities. But pursuing linguistic dissonance and incorrectness promoted a different kind of cultural translation. Drawing on a variety of alien languages and speaking always with quotation marks, these writers, like the Guacamayo, sought to shift the site of "universality" from Cuculcán's imperial palace of linguistic purity to the contentious and contagious Mayan marketplace of literary and linguistic exchange. Like the Guacamayo, furthermore, they sought not only to communicate among themselves but also to spread their alien words into a Cuculcán-like all-encompassing domain with its claims to a universal language and to needle and discomfit all participants in the literary marketplace. Their impure words demanded that listeners and readers take notice of the persistent foreignness of many languages and of the untamed and abiding cultural differences to and of which they speak.

Notes

Introduction

1. Dates assigned to Latin American vanguardism by recent scholarship have been approximate and flexible. Forster and Jackson provide the guidelines of 1920 to 1935 *(Vanguardism in Latin American Literature)*; Osorio suggests 1918 to 1930 *(Manifiestos, proclamas y polémicas de la vanguardia literaria hispanoamericana)*; and Verani, 1916 to 1935 *(Las vanguardias literarias en Hispanoamérica)*.

2. Although the brief historical summary I provide here recounts phenomena that are widely known, I have drawn specifically on versions by Thomas E. Skidmore and Peter H. Smith in *Modern Latin America*; Tulio Halperin Donghi in *Historia contemporánea de América Latina* (280–355); and, for connections between major historical trends and the emergence of the vanguards, Nelson Osorio's prologue to *Manifiestos, proclamas y polémicas de la vanguardia literaria hispanoamericana* (ix–xxxviii), which presents a revised version of his "Para una caracterización histórica del vanguardismo literario hispanoamericano."

3. Significantly, however, women's suffrage began to be instituted in the vanguardist period's later years: Ecuador, 1929; Brazil and Uruguay, 1932; and Cuba, 1934. See Francesca Miller's *Latin American Women and the Search for Social Justice* (96).

4. In his analysis, Calinescu disagrees with Renato Poggioli's position in *The Theory of the Avant-Garde* that an abrupt division developed toward the end of the nineteenth century between the political and the artistic avant-gardes. For Calinescu's discussion, see pages 100–116 of "The Idea of the Avant-Garde" in *Five Faces of Modernity*.

5. While not denying that standoffs between aestheticism and socially engaged art do sometimes shape vanguardist polemics, Videla takes issue with

Angel Rama's theory of two sharply separate Latin American vanguards (one more aestheticist and European, the other more autochthonous and engaged) and argues instead that "the dichotomy is rarely frontal in the reality of American authors and texts" (1: 26). For Rama's concept of two vanguards, see pages 99–202 of *La novela en América Latina: Panoramas 1920–1980.*

6. See, for example, Randal Johnson's "The Institutionalization of Brazilian Modernism."

7. Other important pieces in the same line but less comprehensive in their scope include Noé Jitrik's "Papeles de trabajo: Notas sobre vanguardismo latinoamericano" (1982) and Julio Ortega's "La escritura de la vanguardia" (1979). In a related vein, Guido Podestá employs an ethnographic approach to question the pertinence of contemporary theories of the European vanguards to the experience of modernity in Latin America (and in the Harlem Renaissance) in "An Ethnographic Reproach to the Theory of the Avant-Garde: Modernity and Modernism in Latin America and the Harlem Renaissance." Yurkievich's 1984 *A través de la trama: Sobre vanguardias literarias y otras concomitancias* goes beyond the post-World War I historical avant-gardes to encompass material chronologically outside of my own study's scope. This is also true of the collection of articles edited by Fernando Burgos, *Prosa hispánica de vanguardia* (1986), based on a chronologically broader definition of vanguardism than that shaping my own work.

8. For a more detailed country-by-country overview of Latin American vanguardism, see the introduction to Verani's manifesto anthology, the national section introductions to Schwartz's anthology of vanguardist materials, and, in the Forster-Jackson anthology, introductions to the national lists as well as country studies listed in the bibliographies themselves.

9. Excellent recent studies of the vanguards in Argentina include Christopher Towne Leland's *The Last Happy Men: The Generation of 1922, Fiction, and the Argentine Reality* and Francine Masiello's *Lenguaje e ideología: Las escuelas argentinas de vanguardia.*

10. For supportive guidance through the immense bibliography on Brazilian *modernismo,* including its vanguardist phase, see the introductory comments in the Brazil section of Forster and Jackson's *Vanguardism in Latin American Literature.*

11. On the vanguards in Chile, see Klaus Müller-Bergh's "De Agú y anarquía a la Mandrágora: Notas para la génesis, la evolución y el apogeo de la vanguardia en Chile."

12. The most recent study of the *Revista de Avance,* which addresses the journal's role in Cuba's intellectual and political life is Francine Masiello's excellent piece "Rethinking Neocolonial Esthetics: Literature, Politics, and Intellectual Community in Cuba's *Revista de Avance.*"

13. For studies of Cuban vanguardism as a whole, see Klaus Müller-Bergh's "Indagación del vanguardismo en las Antillas: Cuba, Puerto Rico, Santo Domingo, Haití" and Carlos Ripoll's early study, *La generación del 23 en Cuba y otros apuntes sobre el vanguardismo* (1968). Although Labrador Ruiz has denied that he was a vanguardist (Fernández, "Conversation"), his novels of the period share the characteristics of other Latin American vanguardist prose fiction.

14. For in-depth studies of the *estridentistas* and the Contemporáneos groups, see Luis Mario Schneider's *El estridentismo, o, Una literatura de estrategia*, Merlin Forster's early study, *Los Contemporáneos, 1920–1932: Perfil de un experimento vanguardista mexicano*, and Guillermo Sheridan's *Los Contemporáneos ayer*.

15. On the Peruvian vanguards, see Luis Monguió's landmark study *La poesía postmodernista peruana* and, more recently, Mirko Lauer's "La poesía vanguardista en el Perú" and my own doctoral dissertation on literary aesthetics and cultural nationalism.

16. For a highly useful collection of primary materials documenting Ecuadorean debates about the new artistic currents, see Robles's *La noción de vanguardia en el Ecuador*, which also presents the most complete historical study of the movement. For insights into the relationship of the vanguards to *indigenismo* in Ecuador, see also chapter 4 of Regina Harrison Macdonald's doctoral dissertation, "Andean Indigenous Expression: A Textual and Cultural Study of Hispanic-American and Quichua Poetry in Ecuador."

17. On Nicaragua's vanguards, see Jorge Arellano's "El movimiento de vanguardia de Nicaragua, 1927–1932" and *Entre la tradición y la modernidad: El movimiento nicaragüense de vanguardia*.

18. For the most comprehensive study to date on vanguardist activity in Puerto Rico, see Luis Hernández Aquino's *Nuestra aventura literaria: Los ismos en la poesía puertorriqueña, 1913–1948*.

19. See Videla's "Poesía de vanguardia en Iberoamérica através de la revista *La Pluma*, de Montevideo (1927–1931)."

20. For a comprehensive view of the vanguards in Venezuela, see Nelson Osorio's *La formación de la vanguardia literaria en Venezuela (Antecedentes y documentos)*.

21. See Francine Masiello's essay "Women, State, and Family in Latin American Literature of the 1920s." Masiello affirms an opposition to "masculine avant-garde programs" and/or to the nationalist programs of *mundonovismo* in the writings of de la Parra (particularly in *Ifigenia*), Norah Lange, and María Luisa Bombal. I would also argue that in *Las memorias de Mamá Blanca*, de la Parra appropriates and recasts specific strategies of vanguardist discourse itself.

22. Francine Masiello has undertaken groundbreaking work on the relationship of women to the vanguards in "Texto, ley, transgresión: Especulación sobre la novela (feminista) de vanguardia" and the more extensive "Women, State, and Family in Latin American Literature of the 1920s."

I. Constructing an Audience, Concrete and Illusory: Manifestos for Performing and Performance Manifestos

1. With the emergence in recent decades of performance art and theory, the actual performance texts produced by international avant-garde groups have received more attention than previously. See, for example, RoseLee Goldberg,

Performance Art: From Futurism to the Present; Michael Kirby and Victoria Ness Kirby, *Futurist Performance;* and Mel Gordon (ed.), *Dada Performance.*

2. For additional descriptions of the Grupo Orkopata's activities, see chapter three of my doctoral dissertation, "The Avant-Garde in Peru: Literary Aesthetics and Cultural Nationalism," and David Wise, "Vanguardismo a 3800 metros: El caso del *Boletín Titikaka.*"

3. For a more detailed account of futurism's impact in Spanish America, see Osorio's *El futurismo y la vanguardia literaria en América Latina* (the work does not include Brazil). See also Klaus Müller-Bergh's "El hombre y la técnica: Contribución al conocimiento de corrientes vanguardistas hispanoamericanas," in which the author affirms that futurism was perhaps the "principal catalyst" of Latin American vanguardism (286).

4. These citations are drawn (in order) from the second *euforista* manifesto (LHA 231); the *postumismo* manifesto (*MPP* 111); the "For creative spirits" manifesto of *A Revista* (GMT 338); the manifesto-statement of *Rascacielos* in the *Trampolín* series (n.p.); the third *estridentismo* manifesto (*MPP* 159); the "Gesto" manifesto of *noísmo* (LHA 243); the first manifesto of *estridentismo, Actual No. 1* (*MPP* 106); the second *estridentismo* manifesto (*MPP* 125); and the *atalayismo* manifesto (LHA 247).

5. Poggioli notes the frequency of hyperbolic imagery in international vanguardist discourse (72).

6. See, for example, *Actual No. 1,* the first *estridentismo* manifesto (*MPP* 101–8); Roberto Mariani's *"Martín Fierro y yo"* (*MPP* 136–38); the Cuban "Declaración del Grupo Minorista" (*MPP* 248–50); "Nuestro programa" from the Chilean little magazine *Nguillatún* (*MPP* 149–51); the manifesto appearing in the first issue of São Paulo's *Klaxon* (GMT 294–96); and the *Verde* manifesto from Cataguazes, Minas Gerais (GMT 349–52).

7. In keeping with the practice of Brazilian literary critics, I frequently refer to Mário de Andrade and Oswald de Andrade by their first names.

8. Subtitled both a *retablo* and a *relación,* this novel combines the clipped, synthetic narration typical of some vanguardist fiction with elements from theater, song, popular refrains, radio announcements, and illustrative woodcuts by Ramón Alva de la Canal.

9. See, for example, Icaza's theatrical piece *Trayectoria,* in which *Magnavox 1926* is listed under works by the author as theater and is subtitled "farsa."

10. Brushwood regards the man on the pyramid in the woodcut illustration to be Diego Rivera, a logical interpretation supported by the figure's location and the cane in his hand. But I would argue also that the figure's humble and quiet demeanor as, head bowed, he faces the magnavoxes appears more consonant with the written text's characterization of ordinary Mexican people (audience for the speeches) than with its representation of the dynamic and powerful Rivera. But the fact that the text closely identifies Rivera with ordinary people makes both "readings" of the woodcut plausible.

11. Such cataclysmic imagery is common in Artaud's essays on theater (collected in *The Theater and Its Double*) and, more significantly, in his performative work "The Conquest of Mexico" (appearing in the same volume), a piece closely tied to Artaud's search in Mexico's indigenous cultures (the

Tarahumara) for the type of metaphysical engagement he imagined for the theater.

12. The *Chinfonía burguesa* presents a singular challenge to the translator. Much of its verse is simply untranslatable; while some of the sense can be communicated, the verbal play, rhythm, and rhyme schemes cannot. For this reason, I present approximate literal translations of the shorter citations incorporated into my own text, but I do not translate the longer passages of the work's verse.

13. I have translated the stage directions in this section to provide a sense of the piece's interweaving of voices, but translating the dialogue itself would result in a loss of the passage's alliterative and onomatopoetic impact.

14. Similar terminology appeared in writings on theater by Latin American writers associated with the vanguards. Miguel Angel Asturias, for example, employs the term "teatro de digestión" in "Las posibilidades de un teatro americano" (*Paris 1924–1933* 479).

15. For Carpentier's comments on contemporary European theater, see the collections *Crónicas 1—Arte, literatura y política* (*OC* 8), in particular, the section "Cine y Teatro," and *Crónicas 2*, in particular, "Jean Cocteau y la estética del ambiente" (*OC* 9: 17–26) and "Medgyes, escenógrafo moderno" (*OC* 9: 234–38).

16. In his landmark study *Alejo Carpentier: The Pilgrim at Home*, Roberto González Echevarría also examines this play in the context of the author's other early writings, in particular, *¡Écue-Yamba-Ó!* (86–88).

17. Carpentier addressed the issue of modern filmmakers' portrayal of Latin American cultures in the short critical piece "México, según una película europea," published in September 1931 in *Carteles*. Expressing his concern about stereotypical representations, he noted, "If to film ourselves we count on foreigners, we can be sure of always being betrayed and deformed" (*OC* 8: 389).

18. See Schechner's *Performance Theory* (especially 10–16) for a discussion of the ways in which performances generate the creation of a physical space separate from ordinary life.

2. Outward Turns of the Vagabond Eye/I: The Vanguards' Portraits of the Artist

1. The key document in this dialogue is Torres Bodet's 1928 critical essay appropriately entitled "La deshumanización del arte" (in *Contemporáneos: Notas de crítica*), a critique of Ortega's landmark work.

2. See also Jorge Olivares's thoughtful study *La novela decadente en Venezuela*, in which he highlights features of the decadent novel—one type of *modernista* novel—that I would argue point directly toward portraits of the artist in the vanguardist novels of the 1920s: the deformation of the self, a tension between artists' ideals and quotidian realities, and the portrayal of the engaged

intellectual as a possible alternative to the suffering aesthete. Significant connections (not specifically focused on fictional artist figures) between the prose fiction of Spanish American *modernismo* and that of the vanguards are also drawn by Ivan Schulman in "Las genealogías secretas de la narrativa: Del modernismo a la vanguardia."

3. See, for example, *New Perspective in Brazilian Literary Studies: Symbolism Today*, ed. Darlene J. Sadlier, in particular the study by K. David Jackson, "Hallucinated Bahia: Prefigurations of Modernism in Pedro Kilkerry" (36–46). Although to my knowledge there is no in-depth book-length study of Brazilian symbolist prose comparable to the work of Aníbal González on Spanish American *modernismo*, the Brazilian novel *Mocidade morta* by Gonzaga Duque raises similar issues on the artist's role identified by González in *modernista* prose.

4. For a detailed analysis of vision imagery in *Altazor*, see George Yúdice, *Vicente Huidobro y la motivación del lenguaje*, 149–211.

5. Vallejo's contemporary Mariátegui observed that, even in his most radical experiments, Vallejo felt "all of humanity's pain" (*OC* 2: 313).

6. Christiane von Buelow, for example, notes in her reading of *Trilce* number xxxvi that "ruined fragmentation is represented interchangeably in the poetic ego and in the artwork" ("Vallejo's *Venus de Milo*" 49).

7. Mignolo's historical definition of the vanguards is broader than mine and includes, for example, the work of Octavio Paz.

8. I have differed from the Weinberger translation here. He renders Huidobro's "En el siglo / En que moría el cristianismo" as "In the century / When Christianity died." I prefer "was dying" to maintain the imperfect verb tense *moría*.

9. Authors of these poetic compositions include, respectively, Manuel Maples Arce (Mexico), A. Brandan Caraffa (Argentina), Luis de la Jara (Peru), Rosamel del Valle (Chile), Juan Florit (Chile), Eduardo González Lanuza (Argentina), Alberto Hidalgo (Peru/Argentina), Juan Marín (Chile), Carlos Pellicer (Mexico), and José Juan Tablada (Mexico). For a discussion of the technological focus in Latin America's vanguards, see Klaus Müller-Bergh's comprehensive piece, "El hombre y la técnica: Contribución al conocimiento de corrientes vanguardistas hispanoamericanas."

10. For an in-depth study of vanguardism's urban mode in the work of Oliverio Girondo and Oswald de Andrade, see Jorge Schwartz's *Vanguarda e cosmopolitismo na década de 20: Oliverio Girondo e Oswald de Andrade*.

11. See, respectively, Rita Gnutzmann's introductory study to the 1985 Cátedra edition of *El juguete rabioso* (30–72); Christopher Towne Leland's "Treason and Transformation: Roberto Arlt's *El juguete rabioso*," chapter seven of his *Last Happy Men: The Generation of 1922, Fiction, and the Argentine Reality* (95–117); and "El final del orden: El fracaso del yo," chapter seven of Francine Masiello's *Lenguaje e ideología: Las escuelas argentinas de vanguardia*, in particular, the sections on Arlt (210–29). Also pertinent to my own reading are Alan Pauls's "Arlt: La máquina literaria" and the section on *El juguete rabioso* in Aden W. Hayes's *Roberto Arlt: La estrategia de su ficción* (11–39). Hayes examines the novel as a product of the transformation of Silvio the protagonist into Silvio the writer, "creator and inventor of his life, of his fame, of

his own identity" (39). Other important studies less directly pertinent to my concerns here include, on the major novels, Beatriz Pastor, *Roberto Arlt y la rebelión alienada* and Noé Jitrik, "Entre el dinero y el ser (lectura de *El juguete rabioso* de Roberto Arlt)."

12. My conception of the *Bildungsroman* here is based on Marianne Hirsch's "The Novel of Formation as Genre: Between Great Expectations and Lost Illusions" and on Mikhail Bakhtin's "Discourse in the Novel" and "The *Bildungsroman* and Its Significance in the History of Realism (Toward a Historical Typology of the Novel)."

13. For a description of the new writers' ambivalent relationship with Lugones, see Leland (36–37).

14. In *Roberto Arlt: La estrategia de su ficción,* Hayes traces the relationship between Silvio's movement through Buenos Aires neighborhoods and his developing characterization (29–30).

15. See also the Real Academia Española's facsimile edition of the *Diccionario de Autoridades,* which provides the identical example.

16. There are points of contact between Bürger's concept of the nonorganic, especially as I have applied it here to character, and Gustavo Pérez Firmat's idea of "decharacterization" in the Hispanic vanguard novel, a process he examines specifically in Torres Bodet's *Margarita de niebla* (81–95).

17. In *Idle Fictions,* Pérez Firmat focuses primarily on Spanish peninsular novels and deals mainly with only one kind of Latin American vanguardist prose, the subjectivist and lyric mode characteristic of Jaime Torres Bodet and other members of the Mexican Contemporáneos group. My own analysis addresses a broader range of vanguardist prose, though I find points of contact with Pérez Firmat.

18. Torres Bodet's phrase "triumph over the human" is taken directly from *La deshumanización del arte* (65). Although he later suggested in his autobiographical *Tiempo de arena* (1955) that he had been unfair in holding Ortega responsible for a phenomenon he had simply been describing, Torres Bodet remained steadfast in the aversion to Ortega's terminology: "And he even came to coin phrases like this one, with which I will never agree: 'Aesthetic pleasure emanates from the triumph over the human' " (316). Contemporary critics, in turn, have often noted Ortega's unfortunate selection of the word *dehumanized* to characterize modern art. Robert C. Spires, for example, observes that the word was "probably one of his more infelicitous word choices," not only because it obscured Ortega's sharp perceptions about contemporary art but also because it led to the subsequent indiscriminate application of the phrase to any nonmimetic art of the period (*Transparent Simulacra* 166).

19. Pérez Firmat's study of *La educación sentimental* is the most extensive, but other critics had previously noted the work's innovative qualities and poematic prose. See Sonja Karsen, *Jaime Torres Bodet* (69–73) and Merlin H. Forster, "La obra novelística de Jaime Torres Bodet" (61–62). More recently, Susan Nagel has studied Jean Giraudoux's influence on Hispanic vanguard novels. Although she does not analyze *La educación sentimental,* she notes Torres Bodet's disagreement with Ortega on art's humanity (63) and addresses the dialogue with Ortega undertaken by *Margarita de niebla.*

20. In his study of the Spanish American novel, John S. Brushwood notes the ambiguous situation for the reader created in *La educación sentimental* by the "editor-narrator-protagonist arrangement" and by inconsistencies of narrative attitude in the body of the diary-narration (77).

21. González also notes the *modernistas'* employment of sculptural metaphors to refer to their own artistic style (26), metaphors similar in kind to the architectural ones employed by the narrator in *La educación sentimental* to describe Alejandro's voice.

22. For a detailed discussion of the vanguards' challenge to the notion of a hierarchical historical succession of styles, see chapter 4 of Bürger's *Theory of the Avant-Garde,* "The Avant-Gardiste Work of Art" (55–82).

23. My use of the metaphor-metonymy contrast here is derived in part from David Lodge's *The Modes of Modern Writing: Metaphor, Metonymy, and the Typology of Modern Literature.*

24. Pérez Firmat also identifies the "anticipatory" or "embryonic" quality as typical of vanguardist fiction (*Idle Fictions* 57).

25. In "El artista como tema," a chapter in *Lo trágico y su consuelo: Estudio de la obra de Martín Adán,* Kinsella, examining the relationship between the artist portrait in *La casa de cartón* and in Adán's poetry, concludes that the prose work portrays an artist who has opted for a life of detached contemplation. My own analysis suggests greater tension between observation and engagement.

26. On the connection between the narrator and Ramón, Mirko Lauer notes that "Ramón's diary is an undisguised prolongation of the narrator who is not Ramón simply because he has chosen not to be" (28).

27. The translation of these lines is my own. Adán's text employs the verb *ensartar,* to string or link (spools, ideas), for both the girl's and the narrator's activity. The Silverman translation inverts this process, so that the youngster "inserts a rope into naked spools of thread," a rendition that eliminates the metaphoric link with the text's narrative flow.

28. The "spectacled poetry of the windows" is my own translation, again to maintain the metaphoric links that I believe Adán's text is establishing.

29. I have slightly altered the Silver translation here. She correctly renders "taquigrafía" as shorthand, but I prefer the alternative (and, in English, more archaic) "tachygraphy" offered by Simon and Schuster's *International Dictionary* because it maintains the original's etymological connotations of a tradition of writing.

30. See Rita Gnutzmann, *Roberto Arlt o el arte del calidoscopio.*

31. I use the term "heteroglossic" in the Bakhtinian sense to refer to the interaction of normative (centripetal) and decentralizing (centrifugal) forces in language, manifested in the conflicting (social, cultural, historical) worldviews embodied in varied linguistic and literary forms. (See *The Dialogic Imagination.*)

32. See Cândido's "Estouro e libertação," de Campos's "Serafim: Um grande não-livro" (translated as "Seraphim: A Great Nonbook"); and Jackson's *A prosa vanguardista na literatura brasileira: Oswald de Andrade,* "Vanguardist Prose in Oswald de Andrade," and "Vanguardist Prose in Brazilian Modern-

ism, 1912–1929." The first of these three works by Jackson is a Portuguese version of the second. To avoid back-and-forth translation from English to Portuguese, I cite here the English version even though, as a dissertation, it remains unpublished.

33. See Jackson's "Vanguardist Prose in Oswald de Andrade" (175). Haroldo de Campos also explores parallels with Joyce in "Miramar na Mira," but, although he mentions *A Portrait of the Artist as a Young Man*, he finds many more connections with *Ulysses*.

34. For a detailed analysis of Mariátegui's views on the modern artist, see my "Mariátegui's Aesthetic Thought: A Critical Reading of the Avant-Gardes."

3. "Surely from his lips a cockatoo will fly": The Vanguards' Stories of the New World

1. *Macunaíma*'s resistance to the language and cultural coordinates of a single Brazilian or Spanish American region has been brilliantly recast by Héctor Olea into a Spanish translation that synthesizes colloquialisms from all over Spanish America into a language unlikely to be used by any individual Spanish American speaker. For a detailed analysis of *Macunaíma*'s "degeographied" language (a term coined by Mário himself), see the landmark study by M. Cavalcanti Proença, *Roteiro de Macunaíma*. For further discussion of the novel's Americanist character, see pages 151–52 of Haroldo de Campos's *Morfologia do Macunaíma*.

2. Martin Stabb's *In Quest of Identity: Patterns in the Spanish American Essay of Ideas, 1890–1960* is a landmark study of the problem of Spanish American identity examined through the eyes of major essayists. Although Stabb does not address the arts directly, chapters four and five are pertinent to the vanguard period. A fairly complete list of studies of Spanish American identity published between 1899 and 1933 concludes Paul Verdevoye's "El problema de la identidad nacional e hispanoamericana," in Miguel Angel Asturias, *Paris 1924–1933: Periodismo y creación literaria*, ed. Amos Segala (727–29).

3. On the role of Ortega y Gasset and the *Revista de Occidente* in disseminating German *Lebensphilosophie* and cultural theory, see chapter two of Roberto González Echevarría's *Alejo Carpentier: The Pilgrim at Home*, and for a brief but cogent analysis of Ortega's ideas on Spanish America, see pages 68–72 of Stabb's *In Quest of Identity*.

4. Nelson Osorio has underscored the student movement's significance for the vanguards in "Para una caracterización histórica del vanguardismo literario hispanoamericano" and in its revision in the introduction to his 1988 manifesto anthology.

5. Americanist material in the *Revista de Avance* included extensive attention to José Martí; a lengthy survey of Cuban and Spanish American writers on the question of what American art should be like; articles on Waldo Frank and

Count Keyserling; and pieces such as Félix Lizaso's "Programa de criolledad" (4.41, 1929) and Carlos Alberto Erro's "Resonancias: Lo que es común en las naciones de América" (5.48, 1930).

6. Americanist pieces of note in *Amauta* included a reprint of Franz Tamayo's "Carta americana para americanos" (1.3, 1926) and a debate between Tamayo and Marti Casanovas, "Autoctonismo y Europeísmo" (3.17, 1928); Antenor Orrego's "¿Cuál es la cultura que creará América?" (3.14, 3.17, and 3.18, 1928); Luis Valcárcel's "Hay varias Américas" (3.20, 1929); Félix del Valle's "La hora de América" (3.6 and 3.7, 1927); Gerardo Gallego's "No existen nacionalidades en nuestra América" (3.13, 1928); Ricardo Martínez de la Torre's "Por la unión de los pueblos de la América Latina" (3.11, 1928); Victor Raúl Haya de la Torre's "El problema histórico de nuestra América" (3.12, 1928); and Eugenio Garro's translations of excerpts from Waldo Frank's work (3.11, 3.12, and 3.13, 1928).

7. This position, according to Hugo Verani, was echoed in the essay *El tamaño de la esperanza,* also published in 1926, in which Borges wrote, "I want to speak to the *criollos;* to the people who feel themselves live and die in this land, and not to those who believe that the sun and the moon are in Europe" (cited in HV 41).

8. For example, Mariblanca Sabás Alomá's Americanist piece "Vanguardismo" appeared on June 16, 1928, and on July 28 of the same year, the periodical published Victor Raúl Haya de la Torre's "Proposición de ciudadanía continental latinoamericana."

9. These articles are reprinted in Raúl Antelo's *Na Ilha de Marapatá: Mário de Andrade lê os hispano-americanos,* 163–88. They include "Poesía argentina" (October 30, 1927), "Literatura modernista argentina" (Parts I, II, and III, April 22 and 29 and May 13, 1928, respectively), "Literatura moderna argentina" (May 20, 1928), and "Bustamante y Ballivián" (December 14, 1930). Mário uses the term *modernista* here in the Brazilian sense (of the vanguards) rather than in the Hispanic sense. Antelo has also reproduced in this book Mário's annotations in his personal copies of selected Spanish American works.

10. See Mariblanca Sabas Alomá's "Vanguardismo" for references to the new American man (*MPP* 275–77). The other references to the new American beings cited here appear, respectively, in Gamaliel Churata's "Indoamericanismo" (1), Evaristo Ribera Chevremont's "Llamamiento" (LHA 237), Ignacio Lasso's "Elanismo" (3); and "Llamamiento" (LHA 237).

11. Though he cites no source, in the retrospective *Vida e morte da antropofagia,* Raul Bopp attributes these words to Tarsila do Amaral whom he credits with the *antropofagia* movement's leadership (69). A similar metaphor is used and comparable ideas are developed in "A 'descida' antropófaga," a *Revista de Antropofagia* piece signed by Oswaldo Costa. Augusto de Campos observes in the introduction to the facsimile edition that this was one of several pseudonyms adopted by Oswald de Andrade.

12. Mariátegui's ideas on Americanism appear primarily in "La unidad de la América Indo-española" (*OC* 12: 13–17), "Un congreso de escritores hispanoamericanos" (*OC* 12: 17–21), and "¿Existe un pensamiento hispanoamericano?" (*OC* 12: 22–26).

13. The piece is signed by Oswaldo Costa, one of Oswald de Andrade's pseudonyms, according to Augusto de Campos. See note 11.

14. Articles with impressions of America by several of these writers appeared in the single issue of the little magazine *Imán*, edited by Carpentier in Paris in 1931. See Klaus Müller-Bergh's "Alejo Carpentier: Autor y obra en su época" for illuminating material on Carpentier's changing relationship with the Parisian surrealists and the activities surrounding this little magazine.

15. Though the *Macunaíma* bibliography is dauntingly vast, important work or work related to the concerns of this study includes M. Cavalcanti Proença, *Roteiro de Macunaíma;* Maria Suzana Camargo, *Macunaíma: Ruptura e tradição;* Haroldo de Campos, *Morfologia do Macunaíma;* Telê Porto Ancona Lopez, *Macunaíma: A margem e o texto;* Gilda de Mello e Souza, *O Tupi e o Alaúde: Uma interpretação de Macunaíma;* Severino João Albuquerque, "Construction and Destruction in *Macunaíma";* and the studies and superb supporting materials presented in the 1988 Coleção Arquivos critical edition of *Macunaíma,* coordinated by Telê Porto Ancona Lopez.

16. Churata's prefatory note is signed 1927–1957. The Peruvian poet Emilio Vásquez, Churata's contemporary and colleague in the vanguardist Grupo Orkopata, reported in a 1983 interview that Churata wrote most of *El pez de oro* between 1927 and 1932, during the Orkopata period. Peruvian critics confirm this view: José Varallanos stated that the novel should be ranked "among the best books of the years between 1924 and 1930," in "Churata, su obra y el indigenismo o peruanismo profundo" (405). On the basis of my own in-depth study of Churata's writing in chapter 5 of my doctoral dissertation on the vanguards in Peru, I have omitted from my analysis here references to those sections that appear to have been written after this period.

17. According to Roberto González Echevarría in *Alejo Carpentier: The Pilgrim at Home,* the novel is a "heterogeneous text, where a series of contradictory forces meet and remain unresolved" (67). See also chapter two of Frank Janney's *Alejo Carpentier and His Early Works* and Joseph Sommers's "*Ecue-Yamba-O:* Semillas del arte narrativo de Alejo Carpentier."

18. The original collection included "Leyenda del Volcán," "Leyenda del Cadejo," "Leyenda de la Tatuana," "Leyenda del Sombrerón," and "Leyenda del tesoro del lugar florido." To the 1948 edition, Asturias added one *leyenda,* "Los brujos de la tormenta primaveral," and the play *Cuculcán.* According to the author's own account, however, by 1932, the composition of the latter was well under way. See Asturias's 1932 article, "Las posibilidades de un teatro americano," in *Paris 1924–1933* (477–79).

19. Although critical work on Asturias's *Leyendas de Guatemala* has been quite limited in comparison to the attention given his other works, issues related to my own concerns are addressed by Eladia León Hill, *Miguel Angel Asturias: Lo ancestral en su obra literaria;* by Dorita Nouhaud, in the introduction to the 1977 critical edition of *Tres de cuatro soles* and in "Quelle belle chose qu'un soleil d'aurore"; and by René Prieto in numerous articles on Asturias, but particularly "The New American Idiom of Miguel Angel Asturias."

20. In the doctoral dissertation "El poema en prosa en Hispanoamérica: A propósito de Luis Cardoza y Aragón," Elsa Dávila poses the existence in the

Pequeña sinfonía of three separate but interwoven narrative threads that recount the journeys of the adult poet, the child poet, and Dante. I agree with the notion of (at least) three perspectives, but I see an interplay more of focalization than of voicing.

21. The connection between Macunaíma's inventiveness and vanguardist aesthetics is made explicit when, after participating in a *macumba* rite to overcome the giant, the hero is joined by his "fellow celebrants," other vanguardists, and Brazilian modernist figures, including Blaise Cendrars, Manuel Bandeira, and Raul Bopp, among others (64).

22. See, for example, Octavio Paz's telluric characterization of Pablo Neruda's *Residencia en la tierra* (1925–31) in Paz's *Convergences* (208).

23. González Echevarría, in particular, notes in *Alejo Carpentier: The Pilgrim at Home* the use of a "pseudo-scientific" discourse, a language that I would characterize as ethnographic, and also notes that Marinello suggested in his 1937 piece that Carpentier attempted to describe Menegildo's world from the outside and from within simultaneously (84–85). In "El criollismo 'de esencias' en *Don Goyo* y *Ecue-Yamba-O*," John S. Brushwood notes an "anthropological tendency" on the part of the author (222), and Sommers comments on vacillations in narrative perspective (232–33).

24. For an analysis of the ways in which anthropological discourse shapes the development of twentieth-century Latin American narrative, see chapter four, "The novel as myth and archive," in González Echevarría's *Myth and Archive: A Theory of Latin American Narrative* (142–86).

25. González Echevarría notes that in his 1937 piece, Juan Marinello perceived a "crack" in the novel. González Echevarría concurs with this assessment but attributes the "crack" to "a complex narrative problem created by the crisis in the novel and the desire of the avant-garde to produce art from a consciousness that would not be supported by the *idées reçues* of the West" (*Alejo Carpentier* 85).

26. For a recent illuminating survey of Columbus's reincarnations in Western literature and observations on the problematic nature of the "discovery" concept, see Ilan Stavans's *Imagining Columbus: The Literary Voyage.*

27. My source for this translation is James L. Taylor's *Portuguese-English Dictionary.*

28. For a meticulous examination of this term's etymology, see R. Magalhães Junior, *Dicionário brasileiro de provérbios, locuções e ditos curiosos.*

29. Although I have not adhered to it completely, in translating the citations from *Macunaíma* in this paragraph, I have consulted E. A. Goodland's English translation.

30. For discussions of *antropofagia* and the "ignoble savage" and their implications, see Benedito Nunes, *Oswald, canibal* and "Antropofagia ao alcance de todos," and K. David Jackson, "Primitivismo e vanguarda: O 'Mau Selvagem' do modernismo brasileiro," or the English version, "Primitivism and the Avant-Garde: The Ignoble Savage of Brazilian Modernism."

31. Hauser notes that his source for this phrase is the work of Julien Benda.

32. This sense of being always on the move also characterizes the vanguards' portraits of the artist, as I explore in the chapter on this topic.

33. See chapter 1, on performance manifestos, for a discussion of list making as a rhetorical strategy in the vanguardist manifesto.

34. I am indebted for this term to Rosalind Krauss who used it to draw a distinction between a "utopia of vision" of high modernism and a "fleamarket of images" characterizing the postmodern, in a lecture on the postmodern for the Center for Twentieth Century Studies series "Rewriting Modernism," University of Wisconsin—Milwaukee, November 5, 1985.

35. For a detailed analysis of images of disintegration and integration in *Macunaíma,* see Severino João Albuquerque's "Construction and Destruction in *Macunaíma.*"

36. For a provocative discussion of how de Campos's work and the *antropofagia* tradition from which it emerges undermine the organicist, genealogical imagery of American culture (of "trunks, branches, and twigs"), see chapter two of Richard Morse's *New World Soundings: Culture and Ideology in the Americas,* in particular, 88–91.

4. On the Interstices of Art and Life: Theatrical Workouts in Critical Perception

1. Leon Lyday and George Woodyard, for example, affirm the following in their introduction to the landmark collection of critical essays on the new Latin American theater, *Dramatists in Revolt:* "The period between 1928 and 1943 is extremely important to Latin American drama, for it was during those years that a new consciousness of and concern for theater developed in almost all the countries with a significant literary tradition" (xii).

2. For an in-depth study of Leónidas Barletta and the development of the Teatro del Pueblo, see Raúl Larra's *Leónidas Barletta: El hombre de la campana.*

3. For information on the *estridentistas'* dramatic endeavors, see Luis Mario Schneider, *El estridentismo, o, Una literatura de la estrategia.* For a survey of the Contemporáneos' theatrical activity, see Edward J. Mullen, "The *Revista Contemporáneos* and the Development of the Mexican Theater."

4. Additional historical information on the Nicaraguan vanguardists' theatrical activity is available in Jorge Eduardo Arellano's work.

5. See, respectively, James Troiano, "Pirandellism in the Theatre of Roberto Arlt"; Alberto Gutiérrez de la Solana, "Huellas surrealistas en el teatro de Roberto Arlt"; and David William Foster, "Popular Culture as Mediating Sign between Fantasy and Reality in Arlt's *Trescientos millones.*" For a comprehensive survey of Arlt's theater, see, also, Raúl H. Castagnino's *El teatro de Roberto Arlt.*

6. My terminology here is derived from Michael Issacharoff's "Space and Reference in Drama," in which he draws a distinction between mimetic space (the space the audience sees before it) and diegetic space (the spaces imagined and constructed verbally by the characters). In this case, the Sirvienta's diegetic

dream-play space becomes concrete, mimetic space that the audience of *Trescientos millones* can actually see.

7. I am referring, of course, to Benjamin's observations on art's loss of aura in the modern age in "The Work of Art in the Age of Mechanical Reproduction."

8. A passage in *Los siete locos* maps out the blueprint for *Trescientos millones:* a woman character who has been a prostitute and a servant imagines a scenario for a better life identical in many ways to the Sirvienta's dream world in the play (*OC* 1: 271–74).

9. In his study of Villaurrutia's work, Frank Dauster uses *Incredible* as a translation for the title *Parece mentira;* I suggest the expanded title *That's Incredible* because I believe that this captures the colloquial quality of the Spanish original.

10. See Vera F. Beck, "Xavier Villaurrutia, dramaturgo moderno"; Sandra Messinger Cypess, "The Influence of French Theatre in the Plays of Xavier Villaurrutia"; Alyce de Kuehne, "Xavier Villaurrutia: Un alto exponente de Pirandello" (316–17); Donald Shaw, "Pasión y verdad en el teatro de Villaurrutia" (337–41); and Adolfo Snaidas, *El teatro de Xavier Villaurrutia* (9–19). Snaidas identifies in greater detail than the others some of the aesthetic issues addressed here.

11. Interestingly, a contemporary witness to the experimental productions by the Teatro Orientación (the group that performed *Parece mentira* for the first time) notes among the innovative procedures the elimination of the traditional three bell strokes at the beginning of Orientación performances (Mendoza-López 31).

12. Compare, for example, the aestheticist posture of "La creación pura" (1921), calling for an art "superior to the surroundings" (*OC* 1: 656), to the mellowing of tone in the humbler "Contacto externo" (1932), a poem with imagery that contrasts the ambitious, personalized, internal quests of Huidobro's earlier work with a lower-key, though still visionary, rapprochement with poetic tradition and the world: "One must leap from the heart to the world / One must construct a bit of the infinite for mankind" (*OC* 1: 477).

13. For an analysis of the astronomical-terrestrial imagery in Huidobro's poetry, see Jaime Concha, *Vicente Huidobro* (18–27).

14. In the *En la tierra* play-within-the-play, the monarch Nortesur III, whose repetitive "Tarántulas" and deformed expletive "Miedra" echo Ubu's language, proudly proclaims his lineage: "I am the grandson of my grandfather, my grandfather Ubu Magno, the unforgettable King Ubu" (*OC* 2: 1632).

15. Language was a fundamental concern in European vanguardist experimental theater. Works such as Tristan Tzara's *Le Coeur à Gaz* (1922) and *S'il vous plâit* (1919) by André Breton and Philippe Soupault constituted linguistic experiments addressing the performative over the semantic aspects of communication. See the chapters on Tzara and Breton in J. H. Matthews, *Theatre in Dada and Surrealism.*

16. The hybrid words and wordplays render this passage virtually untranslatable.

17. For a meticulous analysis of the specular relationships in *En la luna,* as

well as the linguistic strategies that manifest them, see Sergio Saldes Báez, "El juego de los espejos en *En la luna* de Vicente Huidobro: Función ideológica y función poética." Other studies take note of Huidobro's skillful use of innovative dramatic techniques, the play's debt to the avant-gardes, and its status as a precursor of Latin America's experimental theater of the 1960s and 1970s, particularly the work of the Chilean dramatist Jorge Díaz. See "Politics (and Theatre)," chapter six of René de Costa's *Vicente Huidobro: The Careers of a Poet;* Lidia Neghme Echeverría, "El creacionismo poético de Huidobro en *En la luna";* and Erminio Neglia, "El vanguardismo teatral de Huidobro en una de sus incursiones escénicas."

18. In Huidobro's manifesto "Yo encuentro . . . ," for example, the bad poet is equated with "charlatanes de feria" (marketplace charlatans) who, like Maese López and his troupe, call out to passersby to display their wares (*OC* 1: 681).

19. For a detailed analysis of the imagery of vision in *Altazor,* see George Yúdice's *Vicente Huidobro y la motivación del lenguaje* (149–211).

20. Although I have frequently not followed it, in the English citations from *A morta,* I have periodically consulted an unpublished translation by the late Luis Roberto Galizia made available to me by Kenneth David Jackson.

21. For lucid critical interpretations of *A morta,* see the work of Fred M. Clark and Ana Lúcia Gazolla de García; Elizabeth A. Jackson, "Paródia e mito em *A morta";* and Ronald D. Burgess, "Birth. Life. *A morta*. de Andrade."

5. From Early Words to the Vernacular Inflection: Vanguard Tales of Linguistic Encounter

1. For critical studies of *Altazor* that address the vanguards and/or their linguistic issues, see the insightful work of René de Costa, especially the chapter on *Altazor* in *Vicente Huidobro: The Careers of a Poet* and, for much of the same analysis in Spanish, his introduction to the Cátedra critical edition of *Altazor* and *Temblor del cielo.* Also pertinent are Enrique Caracciolo Trejo, *La poesía de Vicente Huidobro y la vanguardia;* Jaime Concha, "*Altazor* de Vicente Huidobro"; Merlin Forster, "Vicente Huidobro's *Altazor:* A Re-evaluation"; Nancy B. Mandlove, "At the Outer Limits of Language: Mallarmé's *Un Coup de Dés* and Huidobro's *Altazor*"; and George Yúdice, *Vicente Huidobro y la motivación del lenguaje.*

2. See, for example, Inez Hedges's *Languages of Revolt: Dada and Surrealist Literature and Film* and Marjorie Perloff's *The Futurist Moment: Avant-Garde, Avant Guerre, and the Language of Rupture.* Perloff specifically addresses this process in her chapter "The Word Set Free: Text and Image in the Russian Futurist Book" (116–60).

3. The term "aura" is Walter Benjamin's from "The Work of Art in the Age of Mechanical Reproduction."

4. Although I usually rely on Eliot Weinberger's English translation of *Altazor*, to sustain key images from the Spanish here I translated this segment more literally.

5. Although Weinberger's masterful English translation of *Altazor* includes these verses from the final Canto, I have cited only the Spanish here because the translation process not only inevitably teases out semantic associations that in the original remain latent but also, in this case, adds semantic possibilities not present in the Spanish, for example, in rendering "Ululayu / ulayu / ayu yu" as "Ululayou / lullayou / ahyou you" (EW 165).

6. The third sentence of *Cien años de soledad* describes the earliest days in mythical Macondo: "The world was so recent that many things lacked names, and in order to indicate them it was necessary to point" (71; trans. Rabassa 1).

7. Perloff cites this opening declaration from Malevich's manifesto *From Cubism and Futurism to Suprematism:* "I have transformed myself in *the zero of form* and have fished myself out of the *rubbishy slough of academic art*" (Perloff 118; emphasis in original).

8. To my knowledge, there is no poetic translation of these verses into English; a literal translation would eliminate the onomatopoetic play and playful semantic suggestiveness of verses whose impact is primarily auditory.

9. David Smith provides a somewhat different translation of these verses, a variation that underscores the hermetic quality of Vallejo's work: "999 CALORIES. / Rumbbb. . . . . Trraprrrr track. . . . . chaz / Serpentinic 'u' engiraffed / to the drums of the biscuitmaker" (97).

10. In a footnote to his comments on poetic language, Bakhtin explains the following: "It goes without saying that we continually advance as typical the extreme to which poetic genres aspire; in concrete examples of poetic works it is possible to find features fundamental to prose, and numerous hybrids of various generic types exist. These are especially widespread in periods of shift in literary poetic languages" ("Discourse in the Novel" 287).

11. I am indebted for this observation to Anthony Pagden in *The Fall of Natural Man: The American Indian and the Origins of Comparative Ethnology* (15–16). It has also been applied to a Latin American context by Regina Harrison in *Signs, Songs, and Memory in the Andes: Translating Quechua Language and Culture* (35).

12. For a fresh and insightful analysis of Sarmiento's ambivalent relationship with oral culture and of the points of contact and divergence between Sarmiento and Bello, see Julio Ramos, *Desencuentros de la modernidad en América Latina: Literatura y política en el siglo XIX,* in particular, chapter one, "Saber del *otro:* Escritura y oralidad en *Facundo* de D. F. Sarmiento" (19–34), and chapter two, "*Saber decir:* Lengua y política en Andrés Bello" (35–49).

13. On Mário de Andrade's work in the Brazilian language, see Leonor Scliar Cabral, *As idéias linguísticas de Mário de Andrade;* João Roberto Gomes de Faria, "Mário de Andrade e a questão da língua brasileira"; and José M. Barbosa Gomes, *Mário de Andrade e a revolução da linguagem: A gramatiquinha da fala brasileira.* On Brazilian modernism and Brazilian Portuguese, see Luiz Carlos Lessa, *O modernismo brasileiro e a língua portuguesa.*

14. For González Prada's ideas on language and literature, see "Discurso

en el Teatro Olimpo," "Conferencia en el Ateneo de Lima," and "Notas acerca del idioma," in *Páginas libres / Horas de Lucha*.

15. Issue number 16, July 1928, of *Amauta* was dedicated to González Prada and included essays on his poetic work and ideas written by Eugenio Garro, Antenor Orrego, and Mariátegui himself.

16. For a more detailed discussion of Mariátegui's response to Riva Agüero and of his views on language, see my study, "Mariátegui's Aesthetic Thought: A Critical Reading of the Avant-Gardes."

17. See, for example, Eugenio Garro's "Los 'Amautas' en la historia peruana: Capítulo de una interpretación filológica de la cultura inkaika" and Abelardo Solis's "La cuestión del Quechua."

18. In Latin America, orthographic debates over the approximation of written language to speech date back to Sarmiento and Bello. In Peru, these receive their initial impulse from the vanguardists' cultural mentor, González Prada. For a look at González Prada's attention to orthographic reform and its connections with the ideas of Sarmiento and Bello, see Julio Díaz Falconi, "La reforma ortográfica de González Prada."

19. See, in particular, chapter 1, "La condición del escritor," in Masiello's *Lenguaje e ideología: Las escuelas argentinas de vanguardia* (27–49).

20. For a detailed and discerning accounting of the varied elements making up Arlt's peculiar idiom, see Rita Gnutzmann's work, including her introduction to the Cátedra edition of Arlt's *El juguete rabioso* and her *Roberto Arlt o el arte del calidoscopio*.

21. See the *Aguafuertes porteñas* section in volume 2 of the *Obra completa* for the following sketches on language: "El furbo" (399–401), "El origen de algunas palabras de nuestro léxico popular" (401–3), "Divertido origen de la palabra 'squenun' " (403–5), and "El idioma de los argentinos" (485–87). For a brief discussion of Arlt's attention to popular language in the *aguafuertes*, see Daniel L. Scroggins, *Las aguafuertes porteñas de Roberto Arlt* (68–71). Scroggins also provides in a footnote on page 69 a more complete listing of Arlt's *aguafuertes* on popular speech, not all of which have been anthologized.

22. For specific examples of the language play in the *Chinfonía burguesa*, see my analysis of this piece in chapter 1, on performance manifestos.

23. For a comprehensive review of Martí's importance for Cuba's vanguardists of the 1920s, see Carlos Ripoll's work, including "La *Revista de Avance* (1927–1930): Vocero de vanguardismo y pórtico de revolución" and *La generación del 23 en Cuba y otros apuntes sobre el vanguardismo*, especially chapter 3, "La nueva literatura" (69–108). For a listing of pieces on Martí appearing in the *Revista de Avance*, see the supplementary subject matter index in Ripoll's *Indice de la Revista de Avance: Cuba 1927–1930*.

24. See Pérez Firmat's "The Devil's Dictionary" in *Literature and Liminality: Festive Readings in the Hispanic Tradition* (93–108) and pages 18–19 of *The Cuban Condition: Translation and Identity in Modern Cuban Literature*.

25. Speaking of himself in the third person, Guillén identified this poem's linguistic agenda in a 1932 lecture before a Havana literary group: "In 'Llegada,' Guillén appears to salute the arrival of his race to culture and its contribution of young blood to the ancient veins of the world" (*Prosa de prisa* 1: 46).

26. Palés Matos expressed these ideas in an interview with Angela Negrón Muñoz that originally appeared in *El Mundo,* November 13, 1932, p. 1, under the title "Entrevista con Palés Matos."

27. Antônio Alcântara Machado's review of *Macunaíma* in the *Revista de Antropofagia* epitomizes this view. Macunaíma's refrain, the reviewer observed, was "worth more as Brazilianism" than countless literary works filled with neighborhood streets, black beans, and dark women ("Vaca" 1).

28. Although I have used the Robert Márquez and David Arthur McMurray translation for this poem's earlier verses, I have provided my own more literal translation of the final line because it sustains the linguistic metaphor essential for the point I am making.

29. For concrete examples of the interplay of voices in "As enfibraturas do Ipiranga" and the *Chinfonía burguesa,* see chapter 1, on performance manifestos.

30. See Keith Ellis's *Cuba's Nicolás Guillén: Poetry and Ideology* (71–81) for a more detailed description of the musical models for Guillén's early work.

31. I have translated these verses literally, but in rendering "me hiere" as "wounds me," I have lost an additional nuance present in the Spanish. *Herir* can mean to wound or offend (figuratively, as with sensibilities, as well as literally), but it can also mean to play (or pluck) a stringed instrument. This metaphoric identification of the poetic speaker with his instrument, the means of his art (the symphony "wounds" or "plays" him), is lost in the translation.

32. To maintain the original text's image of "a fala impura" (impure speech), I have rendered my own translation here.

33. In his introduction to *Las vanguardias literarias en Hispanoamérica,* for example, Hugo Verani writes that "while Huidobro aspires to be the leader of a movement, to liberate art from all sentimentalism and all impurity, . . . Neruda desires neither to create a school nor to be the spokesman for any movement; he rarely formulates the principles of his own aesthetics, and when he does so, he defends 'impure poetry' " (32–33).

34. In addition to René de Costa's chapter on the *Residencia* cycle (*Pablo Neruda* 58–104), in which he discusses the relationship between the manifesto on impurity and a change in Neruda's poetic language and style, see Manuel Durán, "Sobre la poesía de Neruda, la tradición simbolista y la desintegración del yo" (on the tensions between the *Residencia* poems and the concept of pure poetry); Luis F. González-Cruz, *Neruda: De Tentativa a la totalidad* (on language in *Tentativa del hombre infinito*); Merlin H. Forster, "Pablo Neruda and the Avant-Garde," on his relationship to the vanguards; and Saúl Yurkievich, "La imaginación mitológica de Pablo Neruda" in *Fundadores de la nueva poesía latinoamericana* (171–230).

35. Verani, for example, cites the syntactical disruptions and disconnected imagery of the *Residencia* as symptomatic of the "Nerudian vision of a disarticulated reality in which everything disintegrates" (34).

36. One of Neruda's principal translators, Ben Belitt, renders "De conversaciones gastadas como usadas maderas" as "From table-talk flimsy as scrapwood" (*Five Decades* 7). I have used my own more literal (and less poetic)

translation to make clear the connection with the manifesto's image of "wearing away."

37. David Smith's translation of these verses, whose differences with the Seiferle version once again underscore *Trilce*'s inaccessibility, is "A bit more consideration, / and the runny humus, six in the afternoon / WITH THE MOST POMPOUS FLATS" (19).

38. Although the readings by von Buelow and Franco are the most pertinent to my own points here about the vanguards' images of language, Julio Ortega's meticulously annotated critical edition of *Trilce* provides an invaluable guide through the daunting Vallejo bibliography. See, in particular, his detailed summaries of critical studies (including his own) on each poem in the collection. On poem xxxvi, see pages 178–83. On *Trilce*, see also Yurkievich's chapter, "En torno de *Trilce*," in *Fundadores de la nueva poesía latinoamericana* (17–30) and Ortega's own *La teoría poética de César Vallejo*.

39. In the polemical piece "Contra el secreto profesional" (1927), Vallejo attacked his generation for its "false and epidermic Latin Americanism" that resulted from aping Europe and argued instead that vernacular art resulted from being autochthonous without saying it (*MPP* 241–44).

40. Asturias included *Cuculcán* and the prose piece "Los brujos de la tormenta primaveral" in the 1948 edition of the *Leyendas de Guatemala*, a work written in the 1920s and first published in 1930. The 1930 edition of the *Leyendas*, published by Madrid's Editorial Oriente, included "Guatemala," "Ahora que me acuerdo," "Leyenda del Volcán," "Leyenda del Cadejo," "Leyenda de la Tatuana," "Leyenda del Sombrerón," and "Leyenda del tesoro del lugar florido." The 1948 expanded Spanish edition that included *Cuculcán* was published in Buenos Aires by Pleamar. Four more *leyendas* were published in the 1967 prose piece collection *El espejo de Lida Sal* (Mexico: Siglo XXI), and some recent editions of the expanded *Leyendas* have also incorporated these: "Leyendas de las tablillas que cantan," "Leyenda de la máscara de cristal," "Leyenda de la campana difunta," and "Leyenda de Matachines." Since I am interested in *Cuculcán* as a product of the vanguard period, my own references to the *Leyendas* as an integral work do not take into account these last four pieces.

41. Between 1924 and 1932, Asturias served as a Parisian correspondent for Guatemala's *El Imparcial* and wrote 440 articles, including the theater piece. These have recently become accessible through Amos Segala's critical edition, *Paris 1924–1933: Periodismo y creación literaria*.

42. In the notes to *Cuculcán*, Asturias observes that there is a strong connection here between the Kukulkán of the Mayas, the Gucumatz of the Quichés, and the Quetzalcouatl of the Nahuas (115). The Guacamayo, "Gran Saliva del Espejo," is a recurring figure in Asturias's work. In the *Leyendas de Guatemala*, he appears in "Leyenda del tesoro del lugar florido" and "Los brujos de la tormenta primaveral."

43. Eladia León Hill, in her study of "the ancestral" in Asturias's work, suggests that Yaí ultimately embraces both points of view: the Guacamayo's affirmation of life's transitory quality and Cuculcán's embodiment of the eternal

creation and re-creation of the world (68–69). Although the dramatic world of *Cuculcán* does indeed incorporate the two views, if one focuses on the play's linguistic themes and qualities, the Guacamayo's views seem to prevail. For recent attention to Asturias's use of Mayan sources, particularly in *Hombres de maíz*, see René Prieto's outstanding work, such as "The New American Idiom of Miguel Angel Asturias."

44. Nouhaud suggests this in "Quelle belle chose qu'un soleil d'aurore" (252). A more extensive analysis of *Cuculcán* appears in her introduction to the critical edition of *Tres de cuatro soles*, in which she relates the questions of orality, writing, and textuality in *Cuculcán* to the treatment of these issues in the other work.

45. As Asturias explains in the notes to *Cuculcán*, in the *Popol Vuh*, the Guacamayo's pride is his downfall, as he declares immodestly, "I the sun, I the light, I the moon" (115).

46. Asturias observes in the notes to *Cuculcán* that these references, to the "yellow flint," the "red flint," the "black flint," etc., re-create the descriptions in the books of *Chilam Balam* of Mayan conceptions of the world's four cardinal points (115).

47. I have not translated the last two passages cited because a literal rendering would eliminate the alliterative word plays that constitute the substance of these scenes and illustrate my point.

Works Cited

Adán, Martín [Rafael de la Fuente Benavides]. *The Cardboard House.* Trans. Katherine Silver. St. Paul: Graywolf, 1990.
———. *La casa de cartón.* In *Obras en prosa.* Ed. Ricardo Silva-Santisteban. Lima: Edubanco, 1982. 1–87.
Albuquerque, Severino João. "Construction and Destruction in *Macunaíma.*" *Hispania* 70.1 (Mar. 1987): 67–72.
Alcântara Machado, Antônio de. "Vaca." *Revista de Antropofagia* 1.6 (Oct. 1928): 1.
Alonso, Carlos. *The Spanish American Regional Novel: Modernity and Autochthony.* Cambridge: Cambridge UP, 1990.
Anderson, Benedict. *Imagined Communities: Reflections on the Origin and Spread of Nationalism.* Rev. ed. London: Verso, 1991.
Andrade, Mário de. "As enfibraturas do Ipiranga." In *Poesias Completas.* 6th ed. Vol. 2 of *Obras completas de Mário de Andrade.* São Paulo: Livraria Martins, 1980. 52–64.
———. *Hallucinated City.* Trans. Jack E. Tomlins. Nashville: Vanderbilt UP, 1968.
———. "Lundu do escritor difícil." *Revista de Antropofagia* 1.7 (Nov. 1928): 3.
———. *Macunaíma.* Trans. E. A. Goodland. New York: Random House, 1984.
———. *Macunaíma: El héroe sin ningún carácter.* Trans. Héctor Olea. Barcelona: Seix Barral, 1977.
———. *Macunaíma: O herói sem nenhum caráter.* Ed. Telê Porto Ancona Lopez. Colección Archivos Series 6. Florianópolis, S.C., Braz.: Editora da UFSC, 1988.
———. *Poesias completas.* 6th ed. Vol. 2 of *Obras completas de Mário de Andrade.* São Paulo: Livraria Martins, 1980.

Andrade, Oswald de. "Cannibalist Manifesto." Trans. Leslie Bary. *Latin American Literary Review* 19.38 (July-Dec. 1991): 38–47.

———. "The Dead Woman." Trans. Luiz Roberto Galizia. Unpublished translation. 1981.

———. "Manifesto of Pau-Brasil Poetry." Trans. Stella M. de Sá Rego. *Latin American Literary Review* 14.27 (Jan.-June 1986): 184–87.

———. *Memórias sentimentais de João Miramar. Serafim Ponte Grande.* Vol. 2 of *Obras completas de Oswald de Andrade.* Rio de Janeiro: Civilização Brasileira, 1972.

———. *A morta.* In *Teatro.* Vol. 8 of *Obras completas de Oswald de Andrade.* Rio de Janeiro: Civilização Brasileira, 1976.

———. *Poesias reunidas Oswald de Andrade.* Ed. Haroldo de Campos. São Paulo: Difusão Européia do Livro, 1966.

———. *Sentimental Memoirs of John Seaborne.* Trans. Ralph Niebuhr and Albert Bork. *Texas Quarterly* 15.4 (Winter 1972): 112–60.

———. *Seraphim Grosse Pointe.* Trans. Kenneth D. Jackson and Albert G. Bork. Austin: New Latin Quarter, 1979.

Antelo, Raul. *Na Ilha de Marapatá: Mário de Andrade lê os hispano-americanos.* São Paulo: HUCITEC, 1986.

Apollinaire, Guillaume. *Selected Writings of Guillaume Apollinaire.* Trans. and ed. Roger Shattuck. New York: New Directions, 1971.

"Apresentação." *Terra Roxa e Outras Terras.* In *Vanguarda européia e modernismo brasileiro.* By Gilberto Mendonça Teles. 7th ed. Petrópolis, Braz.: Vozes, 1976. 341–42.

Arellano, Jorge. *Entre la tradición y la modernidad: El movimiento nicaragüense de vanguardia.* San José, Costa Rica: Libro Libre, 1992.

———. "El movimiento de vanguardia de Nicaragua, 1927–1932 (gérmenes, desarrollo, significado)." *Revista Conservadora del Pensamiento Centroamericano* 22.106 (July 1969): 1–76.

Arlt, Roberto. *El juguete rabioso.* Ed. Rita Gnutzmann. Madrid: Cátedra, 1985.

———. *Obra completa.* 3 vols. Buenos Aires: Biblioteca del Sur, 1981 and 1991.

Armaza, Emilio. "Confesiones de izquierda." *Boletín Titikaka* (Puno, Peru) 25 (Dec. 1928): 1.

Artaud, Antonin. *The Theater and Its Double.* Trans. Mary Caroline Richards. New York: Grove, 1958.

Asturias, Miguel Angel. *América, fábula de fábulas y otros ensayos.* Ed. Richard Callan. Caracas: Monte Avila, 1972.

———. *Paris 1924–1933: Periodismo y creación literaria.* Ed. Amos Segala. Paris: Colección Archivos, 1988.

———. "Las posibilidades de un teatro americano." In *Paris 1924–1933: Periodismo y creación literaria.* Ed. Amos Segala. Paris: Colección Archivos, 1988. 476–79.

———. *Tres obras: Leyendas de Guatemala. El Alhajadito. El Señor Presidente.* Caracas: Ayacucho, 1977.

Bakhtin, M. M. "The *Bildungsroman* and Its Significance in the History of Realism (Toward a Historical Typology of the Novel)." In *Speech Genres and Other Late Essays.* By M. M. Bakhtin. Trans. Vern W. McGee. Ed. Caryl Emerson and Michael Holquist. Austin: U of Texas P, 1986. 10–59.

———. "Discourse in the Novel." In *The Dialogic Imagination: Four Essays.* By M. M. Bakhtin. Ed. Michael Holquist. Trans. Caryl Emerson and Michael Holquist. Austin: U of Texas P, 1981. 259–422.

Balakian, Anna. *Surrealism: The Road to the Absolute.* Rev. ed. New York: E. P. Dutton, 1957.

Beck, Vera F. "Xavier Villaurrutia, dramaturgo moderno." *Revista Iberoamericana* 18.35 (Dec. 1952): 27–39.

Benjamin, Walter. "The Task of the Translator." In *Illuminations.* By Walter Benjamin. Ed. Hannah Arendt. Trans. Harry Zohn. New York: Schocken, 1969. 69–82.

———. "Unpacking My Library: A Talk about Book Collecting." In *Illuminations.* By Walter Benjamin. Ed. Hannah Arendt. Trans. Harry Zohn. New York: Schocken, 1969. 59–67.

———. "The Work of Art in the Age of Mechanical Reproduction." In *Illuminations.* By Walter Benjamin. Ed. Hannah Arendt. Trans. Harry Zohn. New York: Schocken, 1969. 217–51.

Blau, Herbert. *Blooded Thought: Occasions of Theatre.* New York: PAJ, 1982.

———. *The Eye of Prey: Subversions of the Postmodern.* Theories of Contemporary Culture 9 (Center for Twentieth Century Studies, U of Wisconsin–Milwaukee). Bloomington: Indiana UP, 1987.

Bloom, Harold E., ed. *Dante's Divine Comedy.* Modern Critical Interpretations Series. New York: Chelsea House, 1987.

Bopp, Raul. *Cobra norato e outros poemas.* Rio de Janeiro: Civilização Brasileira, 1973.

———. *Vida e morte da antropofagia.* Rio de Janeiro: Civilização Brasileira, 1977.

Borges, Jorge Luis. *El idioma de los argentinos.* Buenos Aires: Peña Del Giudice, 1953.

Brecht, Bertolt. *Brecht on Theatre: The Development of an Aesthetic.* Ed. and trans. John Willett. New York: Hill and Wang, 1964.

Breton, André. *Manifestoes of Surrealism.* Trans. Richard Seavar and Helen R. Lane. Ann Arbor: U of Michigan P, 1972.

———. *Surrealism and Painting.* Trans. Simon Watson Taylor. New York: Harper, 1972.

———. *What Is Surrealism? Works of Andre Breton and Other Documents of Surrealism.* Ed. Franklin Rosemont. New York: Pathfinder, 1978.

Bruenig, LeRoy C. *Guillaume Apollinaire.* New York: Columbia UP, 1969.

Brull, Mariano. *La casa del silencio (Antología de su obra: 1916–1954).* Madrid: Ediciones Cultura Hispánica, 1976.

Brushwood, John S. "Las bases del vanguardismo en Xavier Icaza." In *Panchito Chapopote.* By Xavier Icaza. Facsimile ed. Xalapa, Mex.: Universidad Veracruzana, n.d. 7–16.

————. "El criollismo 'de esencias' en *Don Goyo* y *Ecue-Yamba-O.*" In *Estudios de literatura hispanoamericana en honor a José Juan Arrom.* Ed. Andrew P. Debicki and Enrique Pupo-Walker. North Carolina Studies in the Romance Languages and Literatures Symposia 2. Chapel Hill: UNC Dept. of Romance Languages, 1974. 215–25.

————. *The Spanish American Novel: A Twentieth-Century Survey.* Austin: U of Texas P, 1975.

Burgess, Ronald D. "Birth. Life. *A morta.* de Andrade." *Luso-Brazilian Review* 22.2 (Winter 1985): 103–10.

Bürger, Peter. *Theory of the Avant-Garde.* Trans. Michael Shaw. Theory and History of Literature Series 4. Minneapolis: U of Minnesota P, 1984.

Burgos, Fernando, ed. *Prosa hispánica de vanguardia.* Madrid: Orígenes, 1986.

Cabral, Leonor Scliar. *As idéias linguísticas de Mário de Andrade.* Florianópolis, Braz.: UFSC, 1986.

Calinescu, Matei. *Five Faces of Modernity: Modernism, Avant-Garde, Decadence, Kitsch, Postmodernism.* Durham: Duke UP, 1987.

Callan, Richard. *Miguel Angel Asturias.* New York: Twayne, 1970.

Camargo, Maria Suzana. *Macunaíma: Ruptura e tradição.* São Paulo: Massao Ohno, João Farkas, 1977.

Campos, Augusto de. "Revistas re-vistas: Os antropófagos." In *Revista de Antropofagia.* Facsimile ed. São Paulo: Abril/Metal Leve, 1975.

Campos, Haroldo de. "Da razão antropofágica: A Europa sob o signo da devoração." *Colóquio: Letras* 62 (July 1981): 10–25.

————. "Miramar na Mira." In *Memórias sentimentais de João Miramar. Serafim Ponte Grande.* Vol. 2 of *Obras completas de Oswald de Andrade.* Rio de Janeiro: Civilização Brasileira, 1972. xi–xlv.

————. *Morfologia do Macunaíma.* São Paulo: Perspectiva, 1973.

————. "The Rule of Anthropophagy: Europe Under the Sign of Devoration." Trans. María Tai Wolff. *Latin American Literary Review* 14.27 (Jan.-June 1986): 42–60.

————. "Serafim: Um grande não-livro." In *Memórias sentimentais de João Miramar. Serafim Ponte Grande.* Vol. 2 of *Obras completas de Oswald de Andrade.* Rio de Janeiro: Civilização Brasileira, 1972. 99–127.

————. "Seraphim: A Great Nonbook." In *Seraphim Grosse Pointe.* Trans. Kenneth D. Jackson and Albert G. Bork. Austin: New Latin Quarter, 1979. 113–31.

————. "Uma poética da radicalidade." In *Poesias reunidas Oswald de Andrade.* Ed. Haroldo de Campos. São Paulo: Difusão Européia do Livro, 1966. 7–54.

Cândido, Antônio. "Estouro e libertação." In *Brigada ligeira.* By Antôonio Cândido. São Paulo: Martins, 1945. 11–39.

————. *Literatura e sociedade: Estudios de teoria e história literária.* 6th ed. São Paulo: Nacional, 1980.

Caracciolo Trejo, Enrique. *La poesía de Vicente Huidobro y la vanguardia.* Madrid: Gredos, 1974.

Cardoza y Aragón, Luis. *Pequeña sinfonía del nuevo mundo.* In *Poesías com-*

pletas y algunas prosas. By Luis Cardoza y Aragón. México, D.F.: Fondo de Cultura Económica, 1977. 244–349.

Carpentier, Alejo. Vols. 1, 8, and 9 of *Obras completas de Alejo Carpentier.* 15 vols. México, D.F.: Siglo Veintiuno, 1983, 1985, and 1986.

"Cartel." *Guerrilla* 1.4 (1927): n.p.

Carvalho, Ronald de. *Toda a América.* São Paulo: Editora Hispano-Brasileña, 1935.

Casanovas, Martí [Martín Casanovas]. "Arte nuevo." In *Revista de Avance.* Prologue and selection by Martín Casanovas. 2d ed. Havana: Colección Orbita, 1972. 115–21.

Castagnino, Raúl. *El teatro de Roberto Arlt.* 2d ed. Buenos Aires: Nova, 1970.

Churata, Gamaliel [Arturo Peralta]. *El pez de oro: Retablos del Laykhakuy.* La Paz: Editorial Canata, 1957.

———. "Indoamericanismo." *Boletín Titikaka* 22 (May 1928): 1.

Clark, Fred M., and Ana Lúcia Gazolla de García. "*A morta:* Theatre of Synthesis." In *Twentieth-Century Brazilian Theatre: Essays.* Ed. Fred M. Clark and Ana Lúcia Gazolla de García. Hispanófila Series 50. Chapel Hill: U of NC. 35–50.

———. "The Revolutionary Theatre of Oswald de Andrade." In *Twentieth-Century Brazilian Theatre: Essays.* Ed. Fred M. Clark and Ana Lúcia Gazolla de García. 15–33.

Clifford, James. *The Predicament of Culture: Twentieth-Century Ethnography, Literature, and Art.* Cambridge: Harvard UP, 1988.

Clifford, James, and George Marcus, eds. *Writing Culture: The Poetics and Politics of Ethnography.* Berkeley: U of California P, 1986.

Concha, Jaime. "*Altazor,* de Vicente Huidobro." In *Vicente Huidobro y el creacionismo.* Ed. René de Costa. Madrid: Taurus, 1975. 283–302.

———. *Vicente Huidobro.* Madrid: Jucar, 1980.

Costa, Oswaldo [Oswald de Andrade]. "A 'Descida' Antropóphaga." *Revista de Antropofagia* 1.1 (May 1928): 8.

———. "Revisão necessária." *Revista de Antropofagia—2da dentição. Diário de São Paulo* (Mar. 1929): 6.

Costa, René de. Introducción. *Altazor. Temblor de cielo.* By Vicente Huidobro. Ed. René de Costa. 3d ed. Madrid: Cátedra, 1986. 9–45.

———. *The Poetry of Pablo Neruda.* Cambridge: Harvard UP, 1979.

———. *Vicente Huidobro: The Careers of a Poet.* Oxford: Clarendon, 1984.

Cuadra, Pablo Antonio. *The Birth of the Sun: Selected Poems, 1935–1985.* Ed. and trans. Steven F. White. Greensboro, N.C.: Unicorn, 1988.

———. *Canciones de Pájaro y Señora y Poemas nicaragüenses.* Vol. 1 of *Obra poética completa.* 8 vols. San José, Costa Rica: Libro Libre, 1983.

———, ed. *50 años del movimiento de vanguardia de Nicaragua.* Special issue of *El Pez y la Serpiente* (Managua) 22/23 (Winter 1978–Summer 1979).

———. "Los poetas en la torre (Memorias del movimiento de 'vanguardia')." In *Torres de Dios: Ensayos sobre poetas.* By Pablo Antonio Cuadra. Managua: Academia Nicaragüense de la Lengua, 1958. 143–208.

Cypess, Sandra Messinger. "The Influence of French Theatre in the Plays of Xavier Villaurrutia." *Latin American Theatre Review* 3.1 (Fall 1969): 9–15.

Dauster, Frank. *Xavier Villaurrutia.* New York: Twayne, 1971.

Dávila, Elsa. "El poema en prosa en Hispanoamérica: A propósito de Luis Cardoza y Aragón." Diss. U of California, Santa Barbara, 1982.

Derrida, Jacques. "The Theater of Cruelty and the Closure of Representation." *Writing and Difference.* By Jacques Derrida. Trans. Alan Bass. Chicago: U of Chicago P, 1978. 232–50.

Díaz Falconi, Julio. "La reforma ortográfica de González Prada." *SPHINX* (Anuario del Instituto de Filología) 13 (1960): 170–98.

Durán, Manuel. "Sobre la poesía de Neruda, la tradición simbolista y la desintegración del yo." In *Simposio Pablo Neruda: Actas.* Ed. Isaac Jack Lévy and Juan Loveluck. Columbia: U of South Carolina P, 1975. 123–44.

Echeverría, Lidia Neghme. "El creacionismo poético de Huidobro en *En la luna.*" *Latin American Theatre Review* 18.1 (Fall 1984): 78–82.

"Editorial." *Elán* (Ecuador) 3 (n.d.): 59.

Ellis, Keith. *Cuba's Nicolás Guillén: Poetry and Ideology.* Toronto: U of Toronto P, 1983.

Faria, João Roberto Gomes de. "Mário de Andrade e a questão da língua brasileira." *Estudos Brasileiros* 3.6 (Nov. 1978): 135–56.

Fernández, José B. "Conversation with Enrique Labrador Ruiz." *Latin American Literary Review* 8.16 (Spring-Summer 1980): 266–72.

Forster, Merlin H. *Los Contemporáneos, 1920–1932: Perfil de un experimento vanguardista mexicano.* México, D.F.: Andrea, 1964.

———. "Latin American *Vanguardismo:* Chronology and Terminology." In *Tradition and Renewal: Essays on Twentieth-Century Latin American Literature and Culture.* Ed. Merlin H. Forster. Urbana: U of Illinois P, 1975. 12–50.

———. "La obra novelística de Jaime Torres Bodet." *Ensayos contemporáneos sobre Jaime Torres Bodet.* Ed. Beth Miller. México, D.F.: UNAM, 1976. 61–72.

———. "Pablo Neruda and the Avant-Garde." *Symposium* 32.3 (Fall 1978): 208–20.

———. "Toward a Synthesis of Latin American Vanguardism." In *Vanguardism in Latin American Literature: An Annotated Bibliographical Guide.* Comp. Merlin H. Forster and K. David Jackson. New York: Greenwood, 1990. 1–11.

———. "Vicente Huidobro's *Altazor:* A Re-evaluation." *Kentucky Romance Quarterly* 17 (1970): 297–307.

Forster, Merlin H., and K. David Jackson, comps. *Vanguardism in Latin American Literature: An Annotated Bibliographical Guide.* New York: Greenwood, 1990.

Foster, David William. "Popular Culture as Mediating Sign between Fantasy and Reality in Arlt's *Trescientos millones.*" In *The Argentine* Teatro Independiente, *1930–1955.* By David William Foster. York, S.C.: Spanish Literature Publishing, 1986. 1–18.

Franco, Jean. *César Vallejo: The Dialectics of Poetry and Silence.* Cambridge: Cambridge UP, 1976.

Frank, Waldo. "El redescubrimiento de América." Excerpts trans. by Eugenio Garro. *Amauta* 3.11 (1928): 1–3; 3.12 (1928): 16–18; and 3.13 (1928): 5–6.

———. *The Re-discovery of America.* New York: Scribner's, 1929.

García Márquez, Gabriel. *Cien años de soledad.* Ed. Jacques Joset. 3d ed. Madrid: Cátedra, 1984.

———. *One Hundred Years of Solitude.* Trans. Gregory Rabassa. New York: Harper, 1970.

Garro, Eugenio J. "Los 'Amautas' en la historia peruana: Capítulo de una interpretación filológica de la cultura inkaika." *Amauta* 1.3 (November 1926): 38–39.

Girondo, Oliverio. *Veinte poemas para ser leídos en el tranvía; Calcomanías y otros poemas.* Ed. Trinidad Barrera. Madrid: Visor, 1989.

Goldberg, RoseLee. *Performance Art: From Futurism to the Present.* Rev. ed. New York: Harry N. Abrams, 1988.

Gomes, José M. Barbosa. *Mário de Andrade e a revolução da linguagem: A gramatiquinha da fala brasileira.* João Pessoa, Braz.: Ed. Univ./UFPB, 1979.

González-Cruz, Luis F. *Neruda: De Tentativa a la totalidad.* New York: ABRA-Las Américas, 1979.

González Echevarría, Roberto. *Alejo Carpentier: The Pilgrim at Home.* Rev. ed. Austin: U of Texas P, 1990.

———. *Myth and Archive: A Theory of Latin American Narrative.* Cambridge: Cambridge UP, 1990.

———. *The Voice of the Masters: Writing and Authority in Modern Latin American Literature.* Austin: U of Texas P, 1985.

González, Aníbal. *La novela modernista hispanoamericana.* Madrid: Gredos, 1987.

González Prada, Manuel. *Páginas libres/Horas de lucha.* Ed. Luis Alberto Sánchez. Caracas: Ayacucho, 1976.

Gordon, Mel, ed. *Dada Performance.* New York: PAJ, 1987.

Gnutzmann, Rita. Introducción. *El juguete rabioso.* By Roberto Arlt. Ed. Rita Gnutzmann. Madrid: Cátedra, 1985. 9–72.

———. *Roberto Arlt o el arte del calidoscopio.* Bilbao: U del País Vasco, 1984.

Greiff, León de. *Tergiversaciones (1925) y Libro de signos.* Vol. 1 of *Obra completa.* 3 vols. Ed. Hjalmar de Greiff. Bogotá: Procultura, 1985.

Guillén, Nicolás. *Man-Making Words: Selected Poems of Nicolás Guillén.* Trans. Robert Márquez and David Arthur McMurray. Amherst: U of Mass. P, 1972.

———. *Obra poética, 1920–1972.* 2 vols. Havana: Arte y Literatura, 1974.

———. *Prosa de prisa, 1929–1972.* 3 vols. Havana: Arte y Literatura, 1975–76.

Gutiérrez de la Solana, Alberto. "Huellas surrealistas en el teatro de Roberto Arlt." *Surrealismo/surrealismos: Latinoamérica y España.* Ed. Peter G. Earle and Germán Gullón. Philadelphia: U of Pennsylvania, 1977. 99–107.

Halperin Donghi, Tulio. *Historia contemporánea de América Latina*. 4th ed. Madrid: Alianza, 1975.

Harrison, Regina. *Signs, Songs, and Memory in the Andes: Translating Quechua Language and Culture*. Austin: U of Texas P, 1989.

Harrison Macdonald, Regina. "Andean Indigenous Expression: A Textual and Cultural Study of Hispanic-American and Quichua Poetry in Ecuador." Diss. U of Illinois, 1979.

Hauser, Arnold. *Naturalism, Impressionism, the Film Age*. Vol. 4 of *The Social History of Art*. 4 vols. New York: Vintage, 1951.

Hayes, Aden W. *Roberto Arlt: La estrategia de su ficción*. London: Tamesis, 1981.

Hedges, Inez. *Languages of Revolt: Dada and Surrealist Literature and Film*. Durham: Duke UP, 1983.

Hernández Aquino, Luis. *Nuestra aventura literaria: Los ismos en la poesía puertorriqueña, 1913–1948*. 2d ed. San Juan: Ediciones de la Torre, U of Puerto Rico, 1966.

Hidalgo, Alberto, Vicente Huidobro, and Jorge Luis Borges. *Indice de la nueva poesía americana*. Buenos Aires: Sociedad de Publicaciones El Inca, 1926.

Hirsch, Marianne. "The Novel of Formation as Genre: Between Great Expectations and Lost Illusions." *Genre* 12.3 (Fall 1979): 293–311.

Huidobro, Vicente. *Altazor or A Voyage in a Parachute*. Trans. Eliot Weinberger. St. Paul: Graywolf, 1988.

———. *Obras completas de Vicente Huidobro*. Ed. Braulio Arenas. 2 vols. Santiago, Chile: Zig-Zag, 1964.

Huyssen, Andreas. *After the Great Divide: Modernism, Mass Culture, Postmodernism*. Bloomington: Indiana UP, 1986.

Icaza, Xavier. *Magnavox 1926*. Xalapa, Mex.: Gobierno de Veracruz, 1926.

———. *Panchito Chapopote*. Facsimile ed. Xalapa, Mex.: Universidad Veracruzana, n.d.

———. *Trayectoria*. México, D.F.: Universidad Obrera de México, 1936.

Issacharoff, Michael. "Space and Reference in Drama." *Drama, Theater, Performance: A Semiotic Perspective*. Ed. Ruth Amossy. Special issue of *Poetics Today* 2.3 (Spring 1981): 211–24.

Jackson, Elizabeth A. "Paródia e mito em *A morta*." *Travessia* 5.8/9 (Jan.-June 1984): 20–31.

Jackson, K. David. "Hallucinated Bahia: Prefigurations of Modernism in Pedro Kilkerry." In *New Perspectives in Brazilian Literary Studies: Symbolism Today*. Ed. Darlene Sadlier. Bloomington: Indiana UP, 1984. 36–46.

———. "Primitivism and the Avant-Garde: The Ignoble Savage of Brazilian Modernism." *Dactylus* (Austin, Texas) 7 (Spring 1987): 4–7.

———. "Primitivismo e vanguarda: O 'mau selvagem' do modernismo brasileiro." *Arquivos do Centro Gulbenkian: Homenagem a Paul Teyssier* (Lisbon/Paris) 23 (1987): 975–87.

———. *A prosa vanguardista na literatura brasileira: Oswald de Andrade*. São Paulo: Perspectiva, 1978.

——. "Vanguardist Prose in Brazilian Modernism, 1912–1929." *Aufsätze zur Portugiesieschen Kulturgeschichte* 13 (1974–75): 142–49.

——. "Vanguardist Prose in Oswald de Andrade." Diss. U of Wisconsin, 1973.

Janney, Frank. *Alejo Carpentier and His Early Works*. London: Tamesis, 1981.

Jitrik, Noé. "Entre el dinero y el ser (lectura de *El juguete rabioso* de Roberto Arlt)." *Dispositio* 1.2 (1976): 100–33.

——. "Papeles de trabajo: Notas sobre vanguardismo latinoamericano." *Revista de Crítica Literaria Latinoamericana* 8.15 (1st Semester 1982) 13–24.

Johnson, Randal. "The Institutionalization of Brazilian Modernism." *Brasil/Brazil* 3.4 (1990): 5–23.

Joyce, James. *A Portrait of the Artist as a Young Man*. New York: Viking, 1966.

Kadir, Djelal. *Questing Fictions: Latin America's Family Romance*. Theory and History of Literature Series 32. Minneapolis: U of Minnesota P, 1986.

Karsen, Sonja. *Jaime Torres Bodet*. New York: Twayne, 1971.

Kinsella, John. "La creación de Barranco: Un estudio de *La casa de cartón* de Martín Adán." *Revista de Crítica Literaria Latinoamericana* 8.26 (2d Semester 1987): 87–96.

——. *Lo trágico y su consuelo: Estudio de la obra de Martín Adán*. Lima: Mosca Azul, 1989.

Kirby, Michael, and Victoria Ness Kirby. *Futurist Performance*. New York: PAJ, 1988.

Kirkpatrick, Gwen. *The Dissonant Legacy of Modernismo: Lugones, Herrera y Reissig, and the Voices of Modern Spanish American Poetry*. Berkeley: U of California P, 1989.

Krauss, Rosalind E. *The Originality of the Avant-Garde and Other Modernist Myths*. Cambridge: MIT P, 1985.

Kuehne, Alyce de. "Xavier Villaurrutia: Un alto exponente de Pirandello." *Revista Iberoamericana* 34.66 (July-Dec. 1968): 313–22.

Larra, Raúl. *Leónidas Barletta: El hombre de la campana*. Buenos Aires: Conducta, 1978.

Lasso, Ignacio. "Elanismo." *Elán* 6 (Oct. 1932): 1–3.

Lauer, Mirko. *Los exilios interiores: Una introducción a Martín Adán*. Lima: Mosca Azul, 1983.

——. "La poesía vanguardista en el Perú." *Revista de Crítica Literaria Latinoamericana* 8.15 (1st Semester 1982): 77–86.

Leland, Christopher Towne. *The Last Happy Men: The Generation of 1922, Fiction, and the Argentine Reality*. Syracuse: Syracuse UP, 1986.

León Hill, Eladia. *Miguel Angel Asturias: Lo ancestral en su obra literaria*. Eastchester, N.Y.: Eliseo Torres, 1972.

Lessa, Luiz Carlos. *O modernismo brasileiro e a língua portuguesa*. 2d ed. Rio de Janeiro: Grifo, 1976.

"Ligera exposición y proclama de la Anti-Academia Nicaragüense." In *Mani-*

fiestos, proclamas y polémicas de la vanguardia literaria hispanoamericana. By Nelson Osorio. Caracas: Ayacucho, 1988. 377–79.

Lippard, Lucy, ed. *Dadas on Art.* Englewood Cliffs, N.J.: Prentice-Hall, 1971.

Loayza, Luis. "Martín Adán en *La casa de cartón.*" *El sol de lima.* Lima: Mosca Azul, 1974. 294–95.

Lodge, David. *The Modes of Modern Writing: Metaphor, Metonymy, and the Typology of Modern Literature.* 2d ed. Chicago: U of Chicago P, 1988.

Lopez, Telê Porto Ancona. *Macunaíma: A margem e o texto.* São Paulo: HUCITEC, 1974.

Lyday, Leon F., and George Woodyard, eds., *Dramatists in Revolt: The New Latin American Theater.* Austin: U of Texas P, 1976.

McHale, Brian. *Postmodernist Fiction.* New York: Methuen, 1987.

Magalhães Junior, R. *Dicionário brasileiro de provérbios, locuções e ditos curiosos, bem como de curiosidades verbais, frases feitas, ditos históricos e citações literárias, de curso corrente na língua falada e escrita.* 3d ed. Rio de Janeiro: Documentário, 1974.

Mandlove, Nancy B. "At the Outer Limits of Language: Mallarmé's *Un Coup de Dés* and Huidobro's *Altazor.*" *Studies in Twentieth Century Literature* 8.2 (Spring 1984): 163–83.

Maples Arce, Manuel. *Actual—No. 1—Hoja de Vanguardia.* In *Las vanguardias literarias en Hispanoamérica: Manifiestos, proclamas y otros escritos.* By Hugo Verani. Rome: Bulzoni, 1986. 71–78.

Mariátegui, José Carlos. Vols. 2, 3, 6, 12, and 15 of *Obras completas de José Carlos Mariátegui.* 20 vols. Lima: Amauta, 1982, 1983, 1983, 1980, and 1980.

———. "Waldo Frank." In *El alma matinal.* Vol. 3 of *Obras completas de José Carlos Mariátegui.* Lima: Amauta, 1983. 181–95.

Marinello, Juan. "Una novela cubana." In *Literatura hispanoamericana: Hombres-meditaciones.* By Juan Marinello. México, D.F.: Ediciones de la Universidad de México, 1937. 167–78.

Marinetti, Filippo Tommaso. *Selected Writings.* Trans. R. W. Flint and Arthur A. Cappotelli. Ed. R. W. Flint. New York: Farrar, Strauss and Giroux, 1972.

Martins, Wilson. *The Modernist Idea: A Critical Survey of Brazilian Writing in the Twentieth Century.* Trans. Jack E. Tomlins. New York: NYU P, 1970.

Masiello, Francine. *Lenguaje e ideología: Las escuelas argentinas de vanguardia.* Buenos Aires: Librería Hachette, 1986.

———. "Rethinking Neocolonial Esthetics: Literature, Politics, and Intellectual Community in Cuba's *Revista de Avance.*" *Latin American Research Review* 28.2 (1993): 3–31.

———. "Texto, ley, transgresión: Especulación sobre la novela (feminista) de vanguardia." *Revista Iberoamericana* 51.132–133 (July-December 1985): 807–22.

———. "Women, State, and Family in Latin American Literature of the 1920s." In *Women, Culture, and Politics in Latin America.* Seminar on

Feminism and Culture in Latin America. Berkeley: U of California P, 1990. 27–47.

Matthews, J. H. *Theatre in Dada and Surrealism.* Syracuse: Syracuse UP, 1974.

Mayo, Hugo. "Bujía Polar." *Síngulus* 1.1 (1921): 47–65.

Mendoza-López, Margarita. *Primeros renovadores del teatro en México, 1928–1941.* México, D.F.: Instituto Mexicano de Seguro Social, 1985.

Mignolo, Walter D. "La figura del poeta en la lírica de vanguardia." *Revista Iberoamericana* 48.118–119 (Jan.-June 1982): 131–48.

Miller, Francesca. *Latin American Women and the Search for Social Justice.* Hanover, N.H.: U Press of New England, 1991.

Moliner, María. *Diccionario de uso del español.* 2 vols. Madrid: Gredos, 1970.

Monguió, Luis. *La poesía postmodernista peruana.* México, D.F.: Fondo de Cultura Económica, 1954.

Morse, Richard M. *New World Soundings: Culture and Ideology in the Americas.* Baltimore: Johns Hopkins UP, 1989.

Motherwell, Robert, ed. *The Dada Painters and Poets: An Anthology.* New York: Wittenborn, Schulz, 1951.

Mullen, Edward J. "The *Revista Contemporáneos* and the Development of the Mexican Theater." *Comparative Drama* 4.4 (Winter 1970–71): 272–82.

Müller-Bergh, Klaus. "Alejo Carpentier: Autor y obra en su época." *La Torre* (NE) 4.15 (1990): 263–316.

———. "De Agú y anarquía a la Mandrágora: Notas para la génesis, la evolución y el apogeo de la vanguardia en Chile." *Revista Chilena de Literatura* 31 (April 1988): 33–61.

———. "El hombre y la técnica: Contribución al conocimiento de corrientes vanguardistas hispanoamericanas." In Vol. 4 of *Philologica Hispaniensia in Honorem Manuel Alvar.* 4 vols. Madrid: Gredos, 1983. 279–302.

———. "Indagación del vanguardismo en las Antillas: Cuba, Puerto Rico, Santo Domingo, Haití." In *Prosa hispánica de vanguardia.* Ed. Fernando Burgos. Madrid: Orígenes, 1986. 55–76.

Nagel, Susan. *The Influence of the Novels of Jean Giraudoux on the Hispanic Vanguard Novels of the 1920s–1930s.* Lewisburg, Pa.: Bucknell UP, 1991.

Neglia, Erminio. "El vanguardismo teatral de Huidobro en una de sus incursiones escénicas." *Revista Iberoamericana* 45.106–107 (Jan.-June 1979): 277–83.

Neruda, Pablo. *Five Decades: A Selection (Poems: 1925–1970).* Trans. and ed. Ben Bellitt. New York: Grove, 1974.

———. Vol. 1 of *Obras completas.* 3d ed. 2 vols. Buenos Aires: Losada, 1967.

Nouhaud, Dorita. Introducción. *Tres de cuatro soles.* By Miguel Angel Asturias. Ed. Dorita Nouhaud. México, D.F.: Fondo de Cultura Económica, 1977. xv–xcv.

———. "Quelle belle chose qu'un soleil d'aurore." In *Le personnage en question: Actes du IVe Colloque du S.E.L.* Ed. J. Alsina. Tolouse: Université de Tolouse-Le Mirail, 1984. 251–59.

Nunes, Benedito. "Antropofagia ao alcance de todos." In *Do Pau-Brasil à Antropofagia e às Utopias*. By Oswald de Andrade. Vol. 6 of *Obras completas de Oswald de Andrade*. Rio de Janeiro: Civilização Brasileira, 1972. xiii–liii.

———. *Oswald, canibal*. São Paulo: Perspectiva, 1979.

———. "Mário de Andrade: As enfibraturas do modernismo." *Revista Iberoamericana* 50.126 (Jan.–Mar. 1984): 63–75.

Olivares, Jorge. *La novela decadente en Venezuela*. Caracas: Armitano, 1984.

Oquendo de Amat, Carlos. *5 metros de poemas*. Facsimile ed. Lima: Decantar, 1962.

Ortega, Julio. "La escritura de la vanguardia." *Revista Iberoamericana* 45.106–107 (Jan.–June 1979): 187–98.

———. Introducción. *Trilce*. By César Vallejo. Ed. Julio Ortega. Madrid: Cátedra, 1991. 7–23.

———. *La teoría poética de César Vallejo*. Providence, R.I.: Del Sol, 1986.

Ortega y Gasset, José. *The Dehumanization of Art and Other Essays on Art, Culture, and Literature*. Trans. Helene Weyl. Princeton: Princeton UP, 1968.

———. *La deshumanización del arte y otros ensayos de estética*. Madrid: Espasa-Calpe, 1987.

Osorio T., Nelson. *La formación de la vanguardia literaria en Venezuela (Antecedentes y documentos)*. Caracas: Academia Nacional de la Historia, 1985.

———. *El futurismo y la vanguardia literaria en América Latina*. Caracas: CELARG, 1982.

———. *Manifiestos, proclamas y polémicas de la vanguardia literaria hispanoamericana*. Caracas: Ayacucho, 1988.

———. "Para una caracterización histórica del vanguardismo literario hispanoamericano." *Revista Iberoamericana* 47.114–115 (Jan.–June 1981): 227–54.

Pacheco, José Emilio. Prólogo. *Poesías completas y algunas prosas*. By Luis Cardoza y Aragón. México, D.F.: Fondo de Cultura Económica, 1977. 7–26.

Pagden, Anthony. *The Fall of Natural Man: The American Indian and the Origins of Comparative Ethnology*. Cambridge: Cambridge UP, 1982.

Pasos, Joaquín, and José Coronel Urtecho. "Chinfonía burguesa." (Poetic version.) *50 años del movimiento de vanguardia de Nicaragua*. Ed. Pablo Antonio Cuadra. Special issue of *El pez y la serpiente* (Managua) 22/23 (Winter 1978–Summer 1979). 97–102.

———. *Chinfonía burguesa*. (Dramatic version.) In *Tres obras de teatro de vanguardia nicaragüense*. Managua: El Pez y la Serpiente, 1975. 9–45.

Pastor, Beatriz. *Roberto Arlt y la rebelión alienada*. Gaithersburg, Md.: Hispamérica, 1980.

Pauls, Alan. "Arlt: La máquina literaria." In *Yrigoyen entre Borges y Arlt (1916–1930)*. Ed. Graciela Montaldo. Vol. 7 of *Historia social de la literatura argentina*. Ed. David Viñas. Buenos Aires: Contrapunto, 1989. 307–20.

Paz, Octavio. *Convergences: Essays on Art and Literature.* Trans. Helen Lane. New York: Harcourt, Brace, Jovanovich, 1987.

Peralta Vásquez, Antero. "Indoamericanismo estético." *Boletín Titikaka* (Puno, Peru) 14 (1927): 2.

———. "El uno y vario del arte vanguardista." *Chirapu* (Arequipa, Perú) 1.1 (Jan. 1928): 2.

Pérez Firmat, Gustavo. *The Cuban Condition: Translation and Identity in Modern Cuban Literature.* Cambridge: Cambridge UP, 1989.

———. *Idle Fictions: The Hispanic Vanguard Novel, 1926–1934.* Durham: Duke UP, 1982.

———. *Literature and Liminality: Festive Readings in the Hispanic Tradition.* Durham: Duke UP, 1986.

Perloff, Marjorie. *The Futurist Moment: Avant-Garde, Avant Guerre, and the Language of Rupture.* Chicago: U of Chicago P, 1986.

Podestá, Guido A. "An Ethnographic Reproach to the Theory of the Avant-Garde: Modernity and Modernism in Latin America and the Harlem Renaissance." *Modern Language Notes* 106.2 (Mar. 1991): 395–422.

Poggioli, Renato. *The Theory of the Avant-Garde.* Trans. Gerald Fitzgerald. Cambridge: Harvard UP, 1968.

Pontiero, Giovanni, ed. *An Anthology of Brazilian Modernist Poetry.* Oxford: Pergamon, 1969.

Pratt, Mary Louise. "Linguistic Utopias." In *The Linguistics of Writing: Arguments between Language and Literature.* Ed. Nigel Fabb, Derek Attridge, Alan Durant, and Colin MacCabe. New York: Methuen, 1988. 48–66.

Preminger, Alex, ed. *Princeton Encyclopedia of Poetry and Poetics.* 2d ed. Princeton: Princeton UP, 1974.

Prieto, René. "The New American Idiom of Miguel Angel Asturias." *Hispanic Review* 56.2 (Spring 1988): 191–208.

Proença, M. Cavalcanti. *Roteiro de Macunaíma.* 3d ed. Rio de Janeiro: Civilização Brasileira, 1974.

"Prólogo-Manifiesto." *Flechas* (Lima) 1.1 (Oct. 1924): 1–2.

Quigley, Austin. *The Modern Stage and Other Worlds.* New York: Methuen, 1985.

Quinones, Ricardo J. *Dante Alighieri.* Boston: Twayne, 1979.

Rama, Angel. *La ciudad letrada.* Hanover, N.H.: Ediciones del Norte, 1984.

———. *La novela en América Latina: Panoramas 1920–1980.* Xalapa, Mex.: Universidad Veracruzana, 1986.

Ramos, Julio. *Desencuentros de la modernidad en América Latina: Literatura y política en el siglo XIX.* México, D.F.: Fondo de Cultura Económica, 1989.

Real Academia Española. *Diccionario de autoridades.* 3 vols. Facsimile ed. Madrid: Gredos, 1964.

———. *Diccionario de la lengua española.* 20th ed. 2 vols. Madrid: Espasa-Calpe, 1984.

Renan, Ernest. "What is a nation?" In *Nation and Narration.* Ed. Homi K. Bhabha. London: Routledge, 1990. 8–22.

Ribera Chevremont, Evaristo. "Trazos." *Vórtice* 1.1 (Apr. 1927): 1–2.

Ribemont-Dessaignes, Georges. *History of Dada.* Trans. Ralph Manheim. In *Dada Painters and Poets.* Ed. Robert Motherwell. New York: Wittenborn, Schulz, 1951. 99–120.

Ripoll, Carlos. *La generación del 23 en Cuba y otros apuntes sobre el vanguardismo.* New York: Las Américas, 1968.

———. *Indice de la Revista de Avance: Cuba 1927–1930.* New York: Las Américas, 1969.

———. "La *Revista de Avance* (1927–1930): Vocero de vanguardismo y pórtico de revolución." *Revista Iberoamericana* 30.57 (July-Dec. 1964): 261–82.

Robles, Humberto. *La noción de vanguardia en el Ecuador: Recepción—Trayectoria—Documentos (1918–1934).* Guayaquil, Ecuador: Casa de la Cultura Ecuatoriana, 1989.

Sadlier, Darlene, ed. *New Perspectives in Brazilian Literary Studies: Symbolism Today.* Bloomington: Indiana UP, 1984.

Said, Edward. *Beginnings: Intention and Method.* New York: Columbia UP, 1985.

Saldes Báez, Sergio. "El juego de los espejos en *En la luna* de Vicente Huidobro: Función ideológica y función poética." *Revista Chilena de Literatura* 29 (Apr. 1987): 97–117.

Salgado, Plínio. "A língua Tupy." *Revista de Antropofagia* 1.1 (May 1928): 5–6.

Scarry, Elaine. *The Body in Pain: The Making and Unmaking of the World.* Oxford: Oxford UP, 1985.

Schechner, Richard. *Performance Theory.* Rev. ed. New York: Routledge, 1988.

Schneider, Luis Mario, ed. *El estridentismo: México, 1921–1927.* México, D.F.: UNAM, 1985.

———. *El estridentismo, o, Una literatura de estrategia.* México, D.F.: Bellas Artes, 1970.

Schulman, Ivan A. "Las genealogías secretas de la narrativa: Del modernismo a la vanguardia." In *Prosa hispánica de vanguardia.* Ed. Fernando Burgos. Madrid: Orígenes, 1986. 29–41.

Schwartz, Jorge. "Estética comparada entre los movimientos de vanguardia en América Latina." In vol. 3 of *Proceedings of the 10th Congress of the International Comparative Literature Association.* 3 vols. New York: Garland, 1985. 51–58.

———. *Vanguarda e cosmopolitismo na década de 20: Oliverio Girondo e Oswald de Andrade.* São Paulo: Perspectiva, 1983.

———. *Las vanguardias latinoamericanas: Textos programáticos y críticos.* Madrid: Cátedra, 1991.

Scroggins, Daniel C., ed. *Las aguafuertes porteñas de Roberto Arlt.* Buenos Aires: Ediciones Culturales Argentinas, 1981.

Shaw, Donald. "Pasión y verdad en el teatro de Villaurrutia." *Revista Iberoamericana* 28.54 (July-Dec. 1962): 337–46.

Sheridan, Guillermo. *Los Contemporáneos ayer.* México, D.F.: Fondo de Cultura Económica, 1985.

Shklovsky, Victor. "Art as Technique." In *Russian Formalist Criticism: Four Essays.* Trans. and ed. Lee T. Lemon and Marion J. Reis. Lincoln: U of Nebraska P, 1965. 5–22.

Skidmore, Thomas E., and Peter H. Smith. *Modern Latin America.* 2d ed. New York: Oxford UP, 1989.

Snaidas, Adolfo. *El teatro de Xavier Villaurrutia.* México, D.F.: Sep/Setentas, 1973.

Snead, James. "European Pedigrees/African Contagions: Nationality, Narrative, and Communality in Tutuola, Achebe, and Reed." In *Nation and Narration.* Ed. Homi K. Bhabha. London: Routledge, 1990. 231–49.

Solis, Abelardo. "La cuestión del Quechua." *Amauta* 4.29 (Feb.–Mar. 1930): 31–36.

Sommers, Joseph. "*Ecue-Yamba-O:* Semillas del arte narrativo de Alejo Carpentier." In *Estudios de literatura hispanoamericana en honor a José Juan Arrom.* Ed. Andrew P. Debicki and Enrique Pupo-Walker. North Carolina Studies in the Romance Languages and Literatures Symposia 2. Chapel Hill: UNC Dept. of Romance Languages, 1974. 227–38.

Souza, Gilda de Mello e. *O Tupi e o Alaúde: Uma interpretação de Macunaíma.* São Paulo: Duas Cidades, 1979.

Spires, Robert C. *Transparent Simulacra: Spanish Fiction, 1902–1926.* Columbia: U of Missouri P, 1988.

Stabb, Martin. *In Quest of Identity: Patterns in the Spanish American Essay of Ideas, 1890–1960.* Chapel Hill: U of NC P, 1967.

Stavans, Ilan. *Imagining Columbus: The Literary Voyage.* New York: Twayne, 1993.

Tamayo Herrera, José. *Historia social e indigenismo en el altiplano.* Lima: Treintaitrés, 1982.

Taylor, James L. *A Portuguese-English Dictionary.* Rev. ed. Stanford: Stanford UP, 1975.

Teles, Gilberto Mendonça. *Vanguarda européia e modernismo brasileiro.* 7th ed. Petrópolis, Braz.: Vozes, 1976.

Terán, Enrique. "El arte de vanguardia." *Elán* (Ecuador) 4–5 (Mar.–Apr. 1932): 122–28.

Torgovnick, Marianna. *Gone Primitive: Savage Intellects, Modern Lives.* Chicago: U of Chicago P, 1990.

Torres Bodet, Jaime. *Contemporáneos: Notas de crítica.* México, D.F.: Herrero, 1928.

———. *La educación sentimental.* In vol. 1 of *Narrativa completa.* By Jaime Torres Bodet. 2 vols. México, D.F.: Colección Biblioteca, 1985. 99–153.

———. *Margarita de niebla.* In vol. 1 of *Narrativa completa.* By Jaime Torres Bodet. 2 vols. México, D.F.: Colección Biblioteca, 1985. 23–97.

———. *Obras escogidas.* México, D.F.: Fondo de Cultura Económica, 1961.

———. *Tiempo de arena.* In *Obras escogidas.* By Jaime Torres Bodet. México, D.F.: Fondo de Cultura Económica, 1961. 189–384.

Trampolín: revista supra-cosmopolita; *Hangar:* ex-trampolín-arte supra-cosmopolita; *Rascacielos:* ex-hangar-revista de arte internacional; *Timonel:* ex-rascacielos (Lima 1926–27). Facsimile ed. *Hueso Húmero 7* (Oct.-Dec. 1980).

Troiano, James. "Pirandellism in the Theatre of Roberto Arlt." *Latin American Theatre Review* 8.1 (Fall 1974): 37–44.

Turner, Victor. "Frame, Flow and Reflection: Ritual Drama as Public Liminality." In *Performance in Postmodern Culture.* Ed. Michel Benamou and Charles Caramello. Theories of Contemporary Culture 1. Milwaukee: Center for Twentieth Century Studies, University of Wisconsin–Milwaukee, 1977. 33–55.

Tzara, Tristan. *Approximate Man and Other Writings.* Trans. Mary Ann Caws. Detroit: Wayne State UP, 1973.

Unruh, Katherine Vickers [Vicky Unruh]. "The Avant-Garde in Peru: Literary Aesthetics and Cultural Nationalism." Diss. U of Texas, 1984.

Unruh, Vicky. "Mariátegui's Aesthetic Thought: A Critical Reading of the Avant-Gardes." *Latin American Research Review* 24.3 (1989): 45–69.

Valcárcel, Luis. "Hay varias Américas." *Amauta* 3.20 (1929): 38–40.

Vallejo, César. *Trilce.* Ed. Julio Ortega. Madrid: Cátedra, 1991.

———. *Trilce.* Trans. Rebecca Seiferle. Riverdale-on-Hudson, N.Y.: Sheep Meadow, 1992.

———. *Trilce.* Trans. David Smith. New York: Grossman, 1973.

Varallanos, José. "Churata, su obra y el indigenismo o peruanismo profundo." In *Gamaliel Churata: Antología y valoración.* Lima: Instituto Puneño de Cultura, 1971. 400–14.

Vargas Llosa, Mario. *"La casa de cartón."* *Cultura Peruana* (Lima) 19.135–136 (1959): 9 and 62; 19.137 (1959): 7 and 46.

Vásquez, Emilio. Personal interview (Lima, Peru). 24 and 26 July, 1983.

Verani, Hugo J. *Las vanguardias literarias en Hispanoamérica: Manifiestos, proclamas y otros escritos.* Rome: Bulzoni, 1986.

Videla de Rivero, Gloria. *Direcciones del vanguardismo hispanoamericano.* 2 vols. Mendoza, Arg.: Universidad Nacional de Cuyo, Facultad de Filosofía y Letras, 1990.

———. "Poesía de vanguardia en Iberoamérica através de la revista *La Pluma,* de Montevideo (1927–1931)." *Revista Iberoamericana* 48.118–119 (Jan.–June 1982): 331–49.

Villaurrutia, Xavier. *Parece mentira.* In *Autos profanos.* By Xavier Villaurrutia. México, D.F.: Letras de México, 1943. 11–44.

von Buelow, Christiane. "Vallejo's *Venus de Milo* and the Ruins of Language." *PMLA* 104.1 (Jan. 1989): 41–52.

Williams, Raymond. "Language and the Avant-Garde." In *The Linguistics of Writing: Arguments between Language and Literature.* Ed. Nigel Fabb, Derek Attridge, Alan Durant, and Colin MacCabe. New York: Methuen, 1988. 33–47.

Wise, David. "Vanguardismo a 3800 metros: El caso del *Boletín Titikaka* (Puno, 1926–30). *Revista de Crítica Literaria Latinoamericana* 10.20 (2d Semester 1984): 89–100.

Yúdice, George. *Vicente Huidobro y la motivación del lenguaje.* Buenos Aires: Galerna, 1978.

Yurkievich, Saúl. *A través de la trama: Sobre vanguardias literarias y otras concomitancias.* Barcelona: Muchnik, 1984.

———. "Los avatares de la vanguardia." *Revista Iberoamericana* 48.118–119 (Jan.–June 1982): 351–66.

———. *Fundadores de la nueva poesía latinoamericana.* Barcelona: Ariel, 1984.

Index

Academia Brasileira de Letras, 224
Acción (periodical), 13
Achebe, Chinua, 262
Activism: aesthetic, 8, 14; of artists, 80,
81, 82; political vs. cultural, 7
Actual (periodical), 15
Adán, Martín: *La casa de cartón*, 2, 17,
72, 83, 103–15, 270nn25–28
Aestheticism: Bürger on, 212; in depiction of artists, 76, 106, 268n2; and intellectual engagement, 75, 240; of
Latin American vanguards, 264n5; literary, 265n15; of Oswald de Andrade,
197, 200; poetic language of, 254; role
of language in, 210; and socially engaged art, 7, 263n5
Aesthetics: Afro-Cuban, 66; avant-garde
critiques of, 38; in *La casa de cartón*,
105; and fascism, 35; of Huidobro,
195, 197; manifestos concerning, 26,
27; in *modernista* novels, 100, 101; of
Nicaraguan Anti-Academy, 61; of Oswald de Andrade, 197, 200; Pérez Firmat on, 105; as performance, 70; of
Spanish American *modernismo*, 101,
250; in vanguard theatrical projects,
173–74
"Agú" manifesto (Chile), 214–15, 216,
233
Albizu Campos, Pedro, 7
Albuquerque, Severino João, 273n15,
275n35

Alcântara Machado, Antônio, 243,
280n27
Almeida, Guilherme de, 33
Alonso, Carlos, 143, 232
Alva de la Canal, Ramón, 15, 51, 266n8
Alvear, Marcelo T., 11
Amaral, Tarsila do, 13, 131, 272n11
Amauta (periodical), 6, 24, 79, 122; aes-
thetic goals of, 82; Americanist con-
cerns of, 129, 272n6; and González
Prada, 226, 279n15; and indigenous
culture, 16; linguistic concerns of, 226;
on modernity, 128; on theater, 172
America: as collection of images, 164–65;
inaugural impulse in, 153; in manifestos, 127–34; originary discourse concerning, 141–50, 168; totality of, 160,
161; in vanguardist discourse, 134–41.
See also New World; United States
Ande (poetry collection), 128
Anderson, Benedict, 222, 223, 224, 231,
235–36
Andes: cosmology of, 158, 166; indigenous underworld of, 140; poetry of,
162; vanguard movements of, 17, 34,
136
Andrade, Carlos Drummond de, 13, 24,
76–77
Andrade, Mário de, 13, 27, 33, 155; on
Americanism, 133; on Brazilian Portuguese, 224–25, 234, 246–47, 261;
278n13; concept of totality, 160–61;

vanguardists' conceptualization of, 3–4, 21–26, 70, 79, 93, 159–61, 167

Artaud, Antonin: Derrida on, 28, 174; journey to New World, 133; on theater, 180, 204, 266n11

Artist, depiction of, 71–124, 274n32; as aesthete, 76, 106, 268n2; as fabricator, 91; as hero, 75–76, 92, 116, 123; in manifestos, 75–83, 120; as reader, 104; in Spanish American *modernismo*, 100; as vagabond, 89, 97, 102, 105, 109–10; in vanguardist expression, 71–74, 77; in works of Adán, 105–13; in works of Arlt, 84–94; in works of Oswald de Andrade, 114–22; in works of Torres Bodet, 94–105

Artists: concept of self among, 75–83; role in modern life, 122–23

Asturias, Miguel Angel, 20–21, 134, 160, 273n18; on cultural identity, 271n2; discovery in works of, 154–55; human body in works of, 167; linguistic concerns of, 209, 231; on Mayan culture, 258, 260, 282n43; New World in works of, 27, 135; Nobel Prize acceptance speech, 259, 260; as Parisian correspondent, 281n41; political activities of, 6; and *Popul Vuh*, 136–37, 231, 251, 255, 257, 259, 282n45; studies of folklore, 138; symphonic motifs of, 162; theatrical writings of, 173, 267n14

—*Cuculcán*, 209, 218, 251–68, 273n18; 281nn40,42,43, 282n44

— *Leyendas de Guatemala*, 2, 128, 135, 165, 273n18; creation myths in, 143–44; criticism of, 273n19; discovery in, 154–55; human body in, 167; indigenous culture in, 140; and language, 138, 145, 208–9, 231, 252; linguistic invention in, 218, 222; lists in, 163, 166; narrative structure of, 147–48; narrator of, 160, 208; originary discourse in, 232, 233; pre-Columbian folklore in, 136–37; publication of, 208, 281n40; symphonic motifs in, 162

Atalayismo (Puerto Rico), 7, 19; on Columbus, 151; on dissonance, 248; manifestos of, 37, 42; performance manifestos of, 34; view of technology, 81

Autochthonism, cultural, 129–34, 264n5; agenda of, 142, 242, 248; in *Cuculcán*, 258–59; Vallejo on, 132, 251, 281n39. *See also* Culture

Autonomy: of art, 123, 183; cultural, 223, 227

Avant-gardes, 150, 219; divergences among, 6, 263n4, 264n5; historical, 2–3, 22, 264n7; linguistic experiments of, 209, 210; Mariátegui's studies of, 38–39; theatrical experiments of, 170–71. *See also* Vanguard movements

Avant-gardes, European, 6, 7, 38; ethnographic studies of, 252; influence of, 3, 9; and Latin American culture, 131; linguistic concerns of, 210–13, 216; performance phase of, 32, 265n1; theatrical experiments of, 276n14; use of primitivism, 139–40, 159, 169

Avelino, Andrés, 20

Aymara language, 226, 227, 238

Bakhtin, Mikhail, 85–86, 93, 115, 235, 269n12; on language, 219–21, 242, 243, 248, 254, 255, 257, 270n31, 278n10

Bandeira, Manuel, 13, 33, 225, 249, 274n21

Barbusse, Henri, 12

Barletta, Leónidas, 171, 175, 275n2

Baroja, Pío, 92

Barrios Cruz, Luis, 20, 128

Bary, Leslie, 238

Bataille, Georges, 134

Batlle y Ordóñez, José, 19

Baudelaire, Charles, 87, 88, 92, 93, 182

Beck, Vera F., 276n10

Belitt, Ben, 280n36

Bello, Andrés, 223, 278n12

Benavente, Jacinto, 107

Benjamin, Walter, 35, 66, 98, 163; on aura of art, 182, 276n7, 277n3; on translation, 242–43

Bildungsroman, 269n12; *La casa de cartón* as, 106, 108; characteristics of, 117; *¡Écue-Yamba-Ó!* as, 136, 138; *La educación sentimental* as, 95–96, 104; influence on Latin American fiction, 83; *El juguete rabioso* as, 85, 91, 92, 94; *Memórias sentimentais de João Miramar* as, 115–17, 120; *Serafim Ponte Grande* as, 115–17, 120

Bilingualism, 245–46

314   INDEX

Printed in the United States
16169LVS00001B/242